Windows MFC Programming III

Vic Broquard

Windows MFC Programming III
2nd Edition
Vic Broquard
Copyright 2008, 2014 by Vic Broquard

ISBN: 978-1-941415-59-7

Broquard eBooks
103 Timberlane
East Peoria, IL 61611
author@Broquard-eBooks.com

Table of Contents

To all of my dedicated, persevering students,
and to L. Ron Hubbard, who taught me to "Simplify"

Preface

This is the sequel to <u>Windows MFC Programming I</u> and an extension of the old out of print <u>Intermediate MFC</u>. Unfortunately, this intermediate text ended up being nearly a thousand pages long. Rather than dealing with a overly thick book, I've opted to divide it in half. The first book, <u>Windows MFC Programming II</u>, covers the first nine chapters, while this book, <u>Windows MFC Programming III</u> covers chapters ten onward. Thus, any references to samples of Chapter 9 or earlier are found in <u>Windows MFC Programming II</u>.

A word about the copyright of the sample programs. If you have purchased this book, you are free to use the sample programs and any included coding in any of your applications. No permission is required. However, if you do not substantially alter my coding, it would be nice of you to acknowledge my contribution. Of course, I assume no responsibility for any adverse effects of the sample programs—the old use at your own risk.

If you have any questions, problems, comments, want to report bugs, or just to chat, I can be reached at <u>author@Broquard-eBooks.com</u>.

The samples can be downloaded from <u>http://www.broquard-ebooks.com/pb/winmfciii</u>, take the appropriate link.

Please note right here at the start that this book is not intended to be a "reference manual" rather it is a learner's manual. For further details, consult the hard copy documentation or the on-line documentation that comes with your software.

What software do you need? For this book, I have used Microsoft's Visual Studio .NET 2008. However, you can use older versions as far back as Version 4.0 with only some slight changes.

If you find any errors or have any suggestions or comments, please email me.

Chapter 10 An In-depth Look At Control, Dialog and Tool Bars

It is time that we take a closer look at the construction and use of control bars, tool bars and dialog bars—the decorations that users desire in their applications. In this chapter, we examine how to hide and show the bars, float and dock the bars or not, and how to save and restore the state of dockable tool bars including their last position. The sample program has control bar overkill so that different aspects can be illustrated.

Control bars can be used for many purposes. The most common, naturally, is to provide button short cuts to menu commands, such as File|Open or Print. Sometimes, the tool bars contain other controls such as a combo box or list box to enable user selections. Floating palettes are common to paint programs and usually provide radio button style push buttons. In yet other circumstances, the tool bar may house what may be termed a user control panel of buttons. Others my be simple panels that reflect the current status of application specific data.

Figure 10.1 shows Pgm10a in operation with its overabundance of controls. Assume that this application is some form of world geographical mapping program. Beginning at the top, the main application tool bar is docked just below the menu bar and contains the expected file menu buttons and those for editing and printing. Notice also that I have docked another Edit type bar just to the main tool bar's left edge. It repeats the familiar editing buttons and also provides a choose font combo box. The status bar is across the very bottom; a test status message appears on it. Floating at the left edge of the main scroll view window , which contains a map of England, France and Germany, is a floating palette with line width and color selection buttons.

On the right side are three controls illustrating other uses for control bars. The topmost of the trio is the Map Local Stats bar whose total purpose is to reflect application control information; it is basically a status panel for there are no buttons or controls for user interaction. Below it is the Map Controls box which provides a combination of special bitmapped buttons (the arrow cluster), some normal text buttons and four status controls reflecting the current state of the application data the buttons alter. Finally, hanging vertically below these two is the Options control; it's purpose presumably would be to apply grid or map overlay options to the map being viewed.

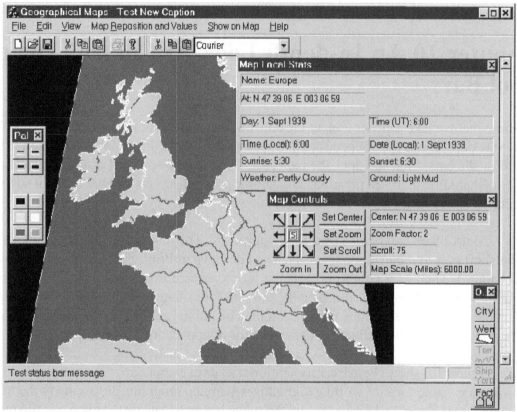

Figure 10.1 The Many Controls of Pgm10a

Of course, with this many active tool bars, the application should **remember** the user's last arrangement. That is, which are hidden and which are visible, which are docked where and which are floating and where. Since this information is relative to the position and dimensions of the main application window, the corresponding main window information should also be saved. Thus, when the user relaunches the application, the main window should appear with the same dimensions as it last was and his or her arrangement of the tool bars restored.

The Basic Tool Bar—Using the CToolBar Class

Frequently, when constructing a new application, the programmer lets the App Wizard generate the basic framework, including an initial tool bar which one then modifies as needed. Commonly, the main frame window class owns the instances of the tool bars and status bar. Let's review those actions required to simply construct and use an instance of the **CToolBar** class.

As we have seen in chapters 5 and 6, there are two approaches that can be used to create tool bar instances in the frame window. The approach used in chapter 6 is used of defining the tool bar in the resource file is used here. In the file MainFrame.h, the **CToolBar** instance, generated by the frame work is called

```
CToolBar            m_wndToolBar;            // main tool bar
```

It is defined in the resource file, Pgm10a.rc as follows

```
IDR_MAINFRAME TOOLBAR DISCARDABLE  16, 15
BEGIN
     BUTTON        ID_FILE_NEW
     BUTTON        ID_FILE_OPEN
     BUTTON        ID_FILE_SAVE
     SEPARATOR
     BUTTON        ID_EDIT_CUT
     BUTTON        ID_EDIT_COPY
     BUTTON        ID_EDIT_PASTE
     SEPARATOR
     BUTTON        ID_FILE_PRINT
     BUTTON        ID_APP_ABOUT
END
```

along with the actual bitmap resource itself

```
IDR_MAINFRAME    BITMAP   MOVEABLE PURE    "res\\Toolbar.bmp"
```

Then in MainFrame's **OnCreate** function, it is first created and then loaded using **LoadToolBar**

```
if (m_wndToolBar.Create(this) &&
    m_wndToolBar.LoadToolBar(IDR_MAINFRAME))
else {
 TRACE0("Failed to create toolbar\n");
 return -1;
}
```

Next, the frame window must be notified to expect docking to occur on any side or all sides. Often, any side is allowed for maximum user flexibility

```
EnableDocking (CBRS_ALIGN_ANY);
```

Tool tips are usually wanted as are flyby hints. These options are then installed in the **CToolBar** instance by using **SetBarStyle** after the current style is retrieved using **GetBarStyle**

```
m_wndToolBar.SetBarStyle (m_wndToolBar.GetBarStyle() |
                CBRS_TOOLTIPS | CBRS_FLYBY | CBRS_SIZE_DYNAMIC);
```

The dynamic size option is used should the tool bar be undocked and float. In such an eventuality, we should provide a caption for the tool bar to use when floating. Additionally, we need to tell our instance where it is acceptable for it to be docked, and then to dock our tool bar instance in its initial position

```
m_wndToolBar.SetWindowText (_T("Main Tool Bar"));
m_wndToolBar.EnableDocking (CBRS_ALIGN_ANY);
DockControlBar (&m_wndToolBar);
```

Should this main tool bar be undocked and closed by the user, it is not actually destroyed, rather the framework merely hides it. Thus, we can implement the Hide/Show tool box menu item rather easily. In the resource file, the framework provided the menu item, ID, and string table entries

```
MENUITEM "&Toolbar", ID_VIEW_TOOLBAR
ID_VIEW_TOOLBAR         "Show or hide the toolbar\nViewToolBar"
```

Then, in MainFrame.h, we define the command function and the command enabler function as

```
afx_msg void OnViewToolbar();
afx_msg void OnUpdateViewToolbar(CCmdUI* pCmdUI);
```

And add the following to out response table

```
ON_COMMAND(ID_VIEW_TOOLBAR, OnViewToolbar)
ON_UPDATE_COMMAND_UI(ID_VIEW_TOOLBAR, OnUpdateViewToolbar)
```

To detect whether to the tool box is currently hidden or visible, use the **CToolBar** member function **GetBarStyle** which returns the window's current style flags. The convenient function **ShowControlBar** can then be called to either hide or reshow the tool bar. In addition to the control bar pointer, **ShowControlBar** is passed two BOOLs. The first, if TRUE causes the tool bar to be shown and if FALSE, to be hidden. The second is for synchronization purposes; if TRUE, the framework delays showing the tool bar immediately, if FALSE, it is shown at once. Here is the common coding to hide or show the tool bar

```
void     MainFrame::OnViewToolbar () {
 if ((m_wndToolBar.GetStyle () & WS_VISIBLE) != 0)
  ShowControlBar (&m_wndToolBar, FALSE, FALSE);
 else ShowControlBar (&m_wndToolBar, TRUE, FALSE);
 m_wndToolBar.Invalidate ();
}
```

Finally, based upon the tool bar's visibility, the command enabler is used to place a check mark beside the menu item or remove it when the View pop-up menu is pulled down

```
void     MainFrame::OnUpdateViewToolbar (CCmdUI* pCmdUI) {
 pCmdUI->SetCheck (m_wndToolBar.GetStyle () & WS_VISIBLE);
}
```

Constructing a Floating Palette Box—Deriving from CToolBar

Typically, floating palette type of tool bars are often derived from the **CToolBar** class. A derived class is necessary in order to fully control the number of columns and to set up which buttons are in which radio button style groups. That is, in this example we must identify that the four line width buttons act as if they are a set of radio buttons and the six color buttons are another group. It is the **SetColumns** function that must be overridden to provide this extra functionality and to ensure correct placement of the button. The Palette.h file defines member **m_nColumns** to contain the current number of columns in the tool bar.

Listing for Palette.h

```
...
class PaletteBox : public CToolBar {
protected:
 UINT    m_nColumns;                    // number of columns

public:
        PaletteBox();
void    SetColumns (UINT nColumns); // set the number of columns
UINT    GetColumns ();                 // get the number of columns
virtual ~PaletteBox();

    DECLARE_MESSAGE_MAP()
};
```

The constructor initially sets the number of columns to 2. In this example, no provision is made for changing the number of columns, for with groups of 4 and 6 buttons, any other number yields a strange look and feel. Additionally, the derived class inherits four members that determine the number of border pixels around the buttons. Here I have set these to only one pixel. Experiment with these values and see the effect of an increasing border. Member function **GetColumns** simply returns the current contents of **m_nColumns**.

All the real work is done in **SetColumns** as shown in the excerpt of PaletteBox.cpp. The underlying **CToolBarCtrl** class provides access to the number of buttons via **GetButtonCount**. Our task is to simply iterate through the buttons and append the **TBBS_WRAPPED** style to those buttons that must be wrapped into the next row. For each button, obtain the current style flags using **GetButtonStyle**. Next either add or remove the wrapped style based on the current column and the number of columns in the control. Add in the **TBBS_CHECKBOX** style which applies to both check boxes and radio button actions of the buttons. In the command enablers we shall determine which is in which group. Finally, install the modified style using **SetButtonStyle**.

Listing for File: PaletteBox.cpp

```
...
PaletteBox::PaletteBox () {
```

```
m_nColumns        = 2; // set for two columns
m_cxLeftBorder    = 1; // set 5 pels as a margin

// these fields belong to the base CtoolBar class
m_cxRightBorder   = 1;
m_cyTopBorder     = 1;
m_cyBottomBorder  = 1;
}

UINT       PaletteBox::GetColumns () {
 return m_nColumns;
}

void       PaletteBox::SetColumns (UINT numcols) {
 m_nColumns = numcols;

 // get total number btns
 int numbtns = GetToolBarCtrl ().GetButtonCount ();

 // for each button, install checkbox style
 // for each button that begins a new row, install wrapped style
 for (int i=0; i<numbtns; i++) {
  UINT style = GetButtonStyle (i);         // get current button style
  BOOL wrap = (((i + 1) % numcols) == 0);// set wrap mod num columns
  if (wrap) style |= TBBS_WRAPPED;         // enable wrapped on this one
  else style &= ~TBBS_WRAPPED;             // or disable wrapped
  style |= TBBS_CHECKBOX;                  // add in the check box style
  SetButtonStyle (i, style);               // and save as it's new style
 }

 Invalidate ();
 GetParentFrame ()->RecalcLayout ();// force toolbar to use new layout
}
...
```

Now to implement our palette box, the resource.h file has defines for each of the buttons and an additional on for hiding and showing the palette box

```
#define CM_LINE1                    1054
#define CM_LINE2                    1055
#define CM_LINE3                    1056
#define CM_LINE4                    1057
#define CM_COLOR_BLACK              1058
#define CM_COLOR_RED                1059
#define CM_COLOR_GREEN              1060
#define CM_COLOR_YELLOW             1061
#define CM_COLOR_BLUE               1062
#define CM_COLOR_PURPLE             1063

#define ID_VIEW_PALETTEBOX          32774
```

Similarly, the Pgm10a.rc file contains appropriate strings for flyby hints and tool tips along with the actual bitmap, for example

```
CM_LINE1              "Select 1 pixel line width\nLinewidth 1"
CM_COLOR_BLACK        "Select Black as the drawing color\nBlack"
ID_VIEW_PALETTEBOX "Hide or Show the Palette Box\nView Palette Box"

IDB_PALETTEBOX       BITMAP  DISCARDABLE     "res\\PaletteBox.bmp"
```

In the MainFrame header file, the instance of the Palette Box is defined as
```
PaletteBox       palettebox;
```

However, in the MainFrame.cpp file, the implementation uses the alternative method in which the button IDs are defined as a static UINT array
```
static UINT BASED_CODE PaletteBox[] = {
 CM_LINE1,
 CM_LINE2,
 CM_LINE3,
 CM_LINE4,
 ID_SEPARATOR,
 ID_SEPARATOR,
 CM_COLOR_BLACK,
 CM_COLOR_RED,
 CM_COLOR_GREEN,
 CM_COLOR_YELLOW,
 CM_COLOR_BLUE,
 CM_COLOR_PURPLE,
};
```

Using the alternative method, after invoking the **Create** function, the **LoadBitmap** is called followed by manually invoking **SetButtons**
```
if (palettebox.Create (this, WS_CHILD | WS_VISIBLE |
        CBRS_SIZE_FIXED | CBRS_TOP | CBRS_TOOLTIPS | CBRS_FLYBY,
        IDB_PALETTEBOX)
   && palettebox.LoadBitmap (IDB_PALETTEBOX)
   && palettebox.SetButtons (PaletteBox,
                             sizeof(PaletteBox)/sizeof(UINT)));
else {
 TRACE0("Failed to create palette box\n");
 return -1;
}
```

Then the number of columns are set to 2 and the normal docking sequence is done adding flyby hints, tool tips, a caption, permitting docking and finally docking it on the left
```
palettebox.SetColumns (2);
palettebox.SetBarStyle (palettebox.GetBarStyle() |CBRS_TOOLTIPS |
                        CBRS_FLYBY);
palettebox.SetWindowText (_T("Pal"));
palettebox.EnableDocking (CBRS_ALIGN_ANY);
DockControlBar (&palettebox, AFX_IDW_DOCKBAR_LEFT);
```
Handling the hide and show operation uses exactly the same coding as the main tool bar. The view class actually responds to the button presses. There is no need for the MainFrame class to do so.

Handling the Status Bar

The application framework creates the status bar as an instance of **CStatusBar**. The resource file contains the identifier uses to hide and show the status bar

```
ID_VIEW_STATUS_BAR        "Show or hide the status bar\nView StatusBar"
```

In the MainFrame class, **m_wndStatusBar** represents our instance

```
        CStatusBar          m_wndStatusBar;
```

In the implementation, the static UINT array is used to install the commonly used indicator panes on the right side. If you wished to install your own indicators, replace these with your own identifiers

```
        static UINT indicators[] = {
         ID_SEPARATOR,               // status line indicator
         ID_INDICATOR_CAPS,
         ID_INDICATOR_NUM,
         ID_INDICATOR_SCRL,
        };
```

In MainFrame's **OnCreate**, our instance is created and the indicators installed as usual

```
        if (m_wndStatusBar.Create (this) &&
            m_wndStatusBar.SetIndicators (indicators,
                                    sizeof (indicators) / sizeof (UINT)))
        else {
         TRACE0("Failed to create status bar\n");
         return -1;
        }
```

The framework then handles the flyby hints. Hiding and showing the status bar is done with same coding sequences as the main tool bar.

However, sometimes the application would like to display messages on the status bar as well. One can gain access to the status bar dynamically or by a member function. Here I illustrate using a member function which becomes perhaps a better approach if the application would be displaying information from many different areas.

```
        void        MainFrame::DisplayOnStatusBar (char *s) {
         m_wndStatusBar.SetPaneText (0, s);
        }
```

Note that to display information in user panes to the right of the main pane, pass the index of the pane as the first parameter and the text as the second. The not shown third parameter defaults to TRUE, that is to invalidate the pane after the text is painted, which is the normal action required.

Dynamically Obtaining a Pointer to the Status Bar or the Main Tool Bar

Often when an application occasionally desires to display some information on the status bar, a pointer to the status bar can be retrieved dynamically. This also applies to tool bars as well.

Dynamically obtaining a pointer to the status bar can be done is several ways. The ID for the status bar is **AFX_IDW_STATUS_BAR**. Since it is owned by the main frame window, one could call the main frame's **CWnd**'s **GetDescendantWindow** function. It is best to pass TRUE as the second parameter which is requests the function only return pointers to permanent windows, not to any temporary ones.

```
CStatusBar *ptrbar = (CStatusBar*) AfxGetMainWnd ()->
                 GetDescendantWindow (AFX_IDW_STATUS_BAR, TRUE);
```

or use a **static_cast**

```
CStatusBar *ptrbar = static_cast<CStatusBar*> AfxGetMainWnd ()->
                 GetDescendantWindow (AFX_IDW_STATUS_BAR, TRUE);
```

Alternatively, one can use the **GetMessageBar** function of **CFrameWnd**

```
CStatusBar *ptrbar = static_cast<CStatusBar*> AfxGetMainWnd ()->
                 GetMessageBar ();
```

The **static_cast** converts the pointer (likely a **CWnd*** from **GetDescendentWindow**) into the derived class **CStatusBar**; no runtime type checking is done. One could use a **dynamic_cast** if one wanted more stringent verifications done at runtime. In the case here of the status bar class, no confusions are likely. The article "Casting Operators" in the Visual C++ Online Documentation has a complete discussion of the various casting operators. However, a simple example can illustrate the fundamental difference between a **static_cast** and a **dynamic_cast**. Consider the following class DerivedClass and the potential problem in its function Fun

```
class BaseClass {
...
}

class DerivedClass : public BaseClass {
...
}

void Fun (BaseClass *ptrbase, DerivedClass *ptrderived) {

  // the following static_cast is totally safe because BaseClass
  // is part of the DerivedClass
  BaseClass *ptrb = static_cast<BaseClass*> (ptrderived);

  // the following static_cast could be disastrous because ptrbase
  // may only be an instance of BaseClass and not part of an
  // instance of DerivedClass
  DerivedClass *ptrd = static_cast<DerivedClass*> (ptrbase);

  // here dynamic_cast would be a better choice
  DerivedClass *ptrd = dyamic_cast<DerivedClass*> (ptrbase);
  if (!ptrd) ..... // here it's NULL
}
```

These same principles can be used to acquire a pointer to the main tool bar, whose ID is AFX_IDW_TOOLBAR

```
CToolBar *ptrbar = (CToolBar*) AfxGetMainWnd ()->
                       GetDescendantWindow (AFX_IDW_TOOLBAR, TRUE);
```

The EditBar—Placing a Combo Box in a Tool Bar

Now, let's get even fancier and place a combo box within a **CToolBar** object. The EditBar class is derived from **CToolBar** so that the added functionality can be incorporated. I have chosen to convert the earlier font enumeration set that was in a **CListCtrl** into our combo box, making the font in use therefore visible in the tool bar and allowing for less keystrokes to change fonts. To better illustrate how this is done, I have chosen to replicate other edit buttons that are also on the main tool bar. The actual bitmap for the edit bar contains only the normal edit bitmaps, for cut, copy and paste. When the EditBar is created, the dimensions and location of the combo box are installed dynamically.

Some of the construction actions are totally parallel to those of the normal tool bar. So let's examine the EditBar from the top level view on down into the details. In the Pgm10a.rc resource file, the bitmap is defined and the various buttons of the tool bar are laid out. Notice in particular that SEPARATOR is used as a temporary placeholder for the location of the dynamically constructed combo box. Specifically, I will replace the second SEPARATOR with the combo box

```
IDR_EDITBAR    BITMAP   DISCARDABLE     "res\\Editbar.bmp"
IDR_EDITBAR    TOOLBAR  DISCARDABLE     16, 15
BEGIN
    BUTTON        ID_EDIT_CUT
    BUTTON        ID_EDIT_COPY
    BUTTON        ID_EDIT_PASTE
    SEPARATOR
    SEPARATOR
END
```

Listing for File: EditBar.h
```
#include "FontEnumCBox.h"

/**************************************************************************/
/*                                                                        */
/* EditBar Class: provide Edit buttons and ChooseFont ComboBox            */
/*                                                                        */
/**************************************************************************/

class EditBar : public CToolBar {
// Construction
public:
    FontEnumComboBox m_SearchBox;   // the font enumeration Combobox
    BOOL             m_bVertical;

        EditBar();
    BOOL Create(CWnd* pParentWnd);
```

```
BOOL SetHorizontal();
BOOL SetVertical();
virtual ~EditBar();
virtual CSize CalcDynamicLayout(int nLength, DWORD dwMode);
protected:
afx_msg LRESULT FontChange (WPARAM, LPARAM);
    DECLARE_MESSAGE_MAP()
};
```

Next, in the main frame class definition, our instance of the EditBar is defined along with a FontChange message response handler. Why? The combo box has no way of knowing what actual view class or window wants the font change message. Thus, the combo box and EditBar class simply posts the user's request for a font change to the main frame window. It is the responsibility of the main frame window to then pass along that change request to the active view. Note that the **LPARAM** shall contain a pointer to the requested **LOGFONT** structure.

```
afx_msg LRESULT FontChange (WPARAM, LPARAM);
```

The main frame uses **GetActiveView** to obtain a pointer to the currently active view which should be given this font change request message. The response table therefore contains

```
ON_MESSAGE(CM_FONT_CHANGE, FontChange)
```
and the FontChange function handles the passing of the message to the view as follows

```
LRESULT  MainFrame::FontChange (WPARAM, LPARAM lf) {
 CView *ptrview = GetActiveView ();
 if (ptrview) ptrview->PostMessage (CM_FONT_CHANGE, 0, lf);
 return 0;
}
```

In the main frame **OnCreate** function, the EditBar is constructed similar to the other tool bars. However, there is one twist. I chose to dock the EditBar just to the left of the main tool bar. I have adapted the **DockControlBarLeftOf** function from the VC samples for our use here

```
if (editbar.Create (this))
else {
 TRACE0("Failed to create edit bar\n");
 return -1;
}

editbar.SetWindowText (_T("Edit Bar"));
editbar.EnableDocking (CBRS_ALIGN_TOP | CBRS_ALIGN_BOTTOM);
DockControlBarLeftOf (&editbar,&m_wndToolBar);
...
```

```
/********************************************************************/
/*                                                                  */
/* DockControlBarLeftOf: dock a control bar to the left of another bar   */
/*                                                                  */
/********************************************************************/

void      MainFrame::DockControlBarLeftOf (CToolBar* Bar,CToolBar* LeftOf) {
 CRect rect;
 DWORD dw;
```

```
UINT n;
RecalcLayout (); // force MFC to adjust the dimensions of all docked ToolBars
LeftOf->GetWindowRect (&rect);// get correct rectangle
rect.OffsetRect (1,0);          // get first pixel position beyond for this bar
dw=LeftOf->GetBarStyle ();      // determine how main bar is docked
n = 0;
n = (dw&CBRS_ALIGN_TOP) ? AFX_IDW_DOCKBAR_TOP : n;
n = (dw&CBRS_ALIGN_BOTTOM && n==0) ? AFX_IDW_DOCKBAR_BOTTOM : n;
n = (dw&CBRS_ALIGN_LEFT && n==0) ? AFX_IDW_DOCKBAR_LEFT : n;
n = (dw&CBRS_ALIGN_RIGHT && n==0) ? AFX_IDW_DOCKBAR_RIGHT : n;

// if the default parms are used,
// DockControlBar will dock each Toolbar on a seperate line
// By calculating a rectangle, we simulate a Toolbar being dragged to
// that location and docked
DockControlBar (Bar, n, &rect);
}
```

In the GeoView class header, I then define the FontChange function that will respond to the frame window's message

```
LRESULT  FontChange (WPARAM, LPARAM);
```

In the GeoView implementation, GeoView.cpp, the message response table includes

```
ON_MESSAGE (CM_FONT_CHANGE, FontChange)
```

The FontChange function must allocate a **LOGFONT** structure if none yet exists and copy the new **LOGFONT** choice pointed to by the LPARAM into the view's local **LOGFONT** member. Here I just assume that a 12 point font is to be built. By invalidating the window, I let **OnDraw** handle the actual displaying of the text in that new font

```
LRESULT   GeoView::FontChange (WPARAM, LPARAM lf) {
  // if no LOGFONT is allocated, get one; otherwise reuse it
  if (!ptrlf) ptrlf = new LOGFONT ();
  // copy in the user's choice
  memcpy (ptrlf, (LOGFONT*) lf, sizeof(LOGFONT));
  // install a 12 point version
  ptrlf->lfHeight = -12;
  ptrlf->lfWidth = 0;
  // paint the text window in this font
  Invalidate ();
  return 0;
}
```

OnDraw then displays a bit of text in this font

```
  if (ptrlf) {
   CFont font;
   font.CreateFontIndirect (ptrlf);
        CFont *ptroldfont = pDC->SelectObject (&font);
   pDC->TextOut (10, 10, "Hello");
   pDC->SelectObject (ptroldfont);
  }
```

The EditBar class contains the instance of FontEnumComboBox, the derived combo box class. This class receives the actual notifications of combo box selection changes and must therefore pass these messages on up to the main frame class; it should not be the responsibility, in my view, for the tool bar to determine what view actually gets the font change message. However, there is one complication. What do you do when the user makes the EditBar layout vertically? That is, if the combo box is 100 units wide, when laid out vertically, the tool bar would then be enormously wide. Here, I leave it actually be very wide so that you can see the effect. In the VC sample programs, another approach is used, replacing the combo box with another button; perhaps it could launch the original **CListCtrl** font enumeration used in the earlier samples. Member **m_bVertical** tracks whether the layout is vertical or horizontal. In this sample, there is no real difference.

In the EditBar implementation, I define the combo box index within the tool bar bitmap layout given in the resource file, replacing one of the SEPARATORs. Also I define the initial width as 150. **Create** must be overridden to actually construct the combo box, once the basic tool bar is loaded. The combo box construction consists first of defining a rectangle with the desired initial dimensions; the width is the major factor. Then the combo box **Create** function is called, passing the desired style which includes **CBS_HAASSTRINGS** and the rectangle with its dimensions. I used a default stock font for the strings within the combo box, but you can use any desired font. Note that some provisions should be made for failure to find your desired font. Here if the default GUI font is not available, I revert back to the main ANSI variable pitch font that must always be present. To install a font in the combo box, send the box the **WM_SETFONT** message with the handle to the font passed as the **WPARAM**. The last step in the creation process is to set the box to a horizontal position, for I am initially placing it to the left of the main tool bar.

Listing for File: EditBar.cpp

```
...
/****************************************************************************/
/*                                                                          */
/* ComboBox: special Defines                                                */
/*                                                                          */
/****************************************************************************/

#define COMBOBOX_INDEX 3
#define COMBOBOX_WIDTH 150
#define COMBOBOX_HEIGHT 150
#define COMBOBOX_BITMAP 3

/****************************************************************************/
/*                                                                          */
/* EditBar Buttons: But leave space for the ComboBox which replaces one     */
/*                  of the separators                                       */
/*                                                                          */
/****************************************************************************/

static UINT BASED_CODE EditButtons[] = {
 // same order as in the bitmap 'EditBar.bmp'
 ID_EDIT_CUT,
 ID_EDIT_COPY,
```

```
  ID_EDIT_PASTE,
  ID_SEPARATOR,
  ID_SEPARATOR,
};

BEGIN_MESSAGE_MAP(EditBar, CToolBar)
  ON_MESSAGE(CM_FONT_CHANGE, FontChange)
END_MESSAGE_MAP()

EditBar::EditBar() { }
EditBar::~EditBar() { }

/**********************************************************************/
/*                                                                    */
/* Create: create the edit bar and add in the Combobox                */
/*                                                                    */
/**********************************************************************/

BOOL      EditBar::Create (CWnd* pParentWnd) {
  m_bVertical = FALSE;

  // set the main editbar style
  DWORD dwStyle = WS_CHILD | WS_VISIBLE | CBRS_TOP | CBRS_SIZE_DYNAMIC |
                  CBRS_TOOLTIPS | CBRS_FLYBY;

  // create and load the bitmap buttoms
  if (!(CToolBar::Create (pParentWnd, dwStyle, IDR_EDITBAR) &&
      LoadToolBar (IDR_EDITBAR)))
    return FALSE;

  // setup a default size for the Combobox
  CRect rect(-COMBOBOX_WIDTH, -COMBOBOX_HEIGHT, 0, 0);
  // create the Combobox
  if (!m_SearchBox.Create  (WS_CHILD | CBS_DROPDOWN | CBS_AUTOHSCROLL |
                            WS_VSCROLL | CBS_HASSTRINGS, rect, this,
                            IDC_FONTENUM_CBOX))
        return FALSE;

  // create and install a Combobox font
  HFONT hFont = (HFONT)GetStockObject(DEFAULT_GUI_FONT);
  if (hFont == NULL) hFont = (HFONT)GetStockObject(ANSI_VAR_FONT);
  m_SearchBox.SendMessage(WM_SETFONT, (WPARAM)hFont);
  DeleteObject (hFont);

  // setup the location of the Combobox
  if(!SetHorizontal()) return FALSE;

  return TRUE;
}

/**********************************************************************/
/*                                                                    */
/* SetHorizontal: setup window positon of Combobox                    */
/*                                                                    */
/**********************************************************************/

BOOL      EditBar::SetHorizontal () {
  CRect rect;
```

```
 m_bVertical = FALSE;
 SetBarStyle (GetBarStyle () | CBRS_ALIGN_BOTTOM);
 // replace the separator with the combobox control id
 SetButtonInfo (COMBOBOX_INDEX, IDC_FONTENUM_CBOX, TBBS_SEPARATOR,
                COMBOBOX_WIDTH);
 // if box exists, reposition it by getting the current position of the
 // replaced button and placing the Combobox there
 if (m_SearchBox.m_hWnd != NULL)      {
  GetItemRect (COMBOBOX_INDEX, rect);
  m_SearchBox.SetWindowPos (NULL, rect.left, rect.top, 0, 0, SWP_NOZORDER |
                                 SWP_NOACTIVATE | SWP_NOSIZE | SWP_NOCOPYBITS);
  m_SearchBox.ShowWindow (SW_SHOW);
 }
 return TRUE;
}

/************************************************************************/
/*                                                                      */
/* SetVertical: reset for a vertical toolbar - combobox will look strange */
/*                                                                      */
/************************************************************************/

BOOL      EditBar::SetVertical() {
 CRect rect;
 m_bVertical = TRUE;
 // perform the same sequence as when horizontal
 SetBarStyle (GetBarStyle () | CBRS_ALIGN_BOTTOM);
 SetButtonInfo (COMBOBOX_INDEX, IDC_FONTENUM_CBOX, TBBS_SEPARATOR,
                COMBOBOX_WIDTH);
 if (m_SearchBox.m_hWnd != NULL)      {
  GetItemRect(COMBOBOX_INDEX, rect);
  m_SearchBox.SetWindowPos (NULL, rect.left, rect.top, 0, 0, SWP_NOZORDER |
                                 SWP_NOACTIVATE | SWP_NOSIZE | SWP_NOCOPYBITS);
  m_SearchBox.ShowWindow (SW_SHOW);
 }
 return TRUE;
}

/************************************************************************/
/*                                                                      */
/* CalcDynamicLayout: dynamically switch between laying out horz or vert */
/*                                                                      */
/************************************************************************/

CSize     EditBar::CalcDynamicLayout (int nLength, DWORD dwMode) {
 // if we're committing, then set the buttons appropriately
 if (dwMode & LM_COMMIT)        {
  if (dwMode & LM_VERTDOCK)     {
   if (!m_bVertical) SetVertical ();
  }
  else {
   if (m_bVertical) SetHorizontal ();
  }
  return CToolBar::CalcDynamicLayout (nLength, dwMode);
 }
 // here we are not yet changing them, so get the proposed new size
 else {
  BOOL bOld = m_bVertical;
```

```
 BOOL bSwitch = (dwMode & LM_HORZ) ? bOld : !bOld;
 if (bSwitch) {
  if (bOld) SetHorizontal ();
  else SetVertical ();
 }
 CSize sizeResult = CToolBar::CalcDynamicLayout (nLength, dwMode);
 if (bSwitch) {
  if (bOld) SetHorizontal ();
  else SetVertical ();
 }
 return sizeResult;
 }
}


/*************************************************************************/
/*                                                                     */
/* FontChange: pass on user chosen font change request from Combobox    */
/*                                                                     */
/*************************************************************************/

LRESULT   EditBar::FontChange (WPARAM, LPARAM lf) {
 AfxGetApp()->m_pMainWnd->PostMessage (CM_FONT_CHANGE, 0, lf);
 return 0;
}
...
```

The **SetHorizontal** function begins by setting **m_bVertical** to FALSE and setting the current bar style to one of the positions that would have a horizontal layout, **CBRS_ALIGN_BOTTOM**. Next, the separator at index 3 here is replaced with the ID for the combo box and it's flyby/tool tips string using **SetButtonInfo** whose syntax is

```
     SetButtonInfo (int index, UINT id, UINT style, int image);
```
where **index** represents the button or separator (in this case) whose information is to be changed, **id** is the new value to be used for the button's command ID, **style** is the new button style to be used, and **image** is the new index for the button within the bitmap. The style can be **TBBS_BUTTON**, **TBBS_SEPARATOR**, **TBBS_CHECKBOX**, **TBBS_GROUP**, **TBBS_CHECKGROUP**. Here I used

```
     SetButtonInfo (COMBOBOX_INDEX, IDC_FONTENUM_CBOX, TBBS_SEPARATOR,
                     COMBOBOX_WIDTH);
```
There is a special case with this function, if the style is **TBBS_SEPARATOR**, as it is here, then the image parameter becomes the width of the separator or the combo box in this case.

Finally, assuming that the combo box construction succeeded, then the window position of the box is set and made visible

```
     if (m_SearchBox.m_hWnd != NULL) {
      GetItemRect (COMBOBOX_INDEX, rect);
      m_SearchBox.SetWindowPos (NULL, rect.left, rect.top, 0,
       0,SWP_NOZORDER| SWP_NOACTIVATE | SWP_NOSIZE | SWP_NOCOPYBITS);
      m_SearchBox.ShowWindow (SW_SHOW);
     }
```

CalcDynamicLayout is overridden to assist the calculation of the total size of the tool bar, depending upon the horizontal or vertical layout. Sometimes, the framework calls this function to get an estimate of the size before it really wants to commit to that layout. Thus, the function first separates out these two cases, for if the estimate only case occurs, we may have to temporarily relay out in another order (ie is horizontal and not is vertical) and when done, put it back the way it was. In all cases, just let the framework do the actual work. Our **SetVertical** and **SetHorizontal** functions handle the relaying out of the combo box. Here, there is little difference. Should you decide to replace the combo box when the EditBar is vertical, then **SetVertical** would install a different button and ID.

The FontEnumCBox class is basically just a modification from the earlier **CListCtrl** class. It is now derived from the **CComboBox** class instead. **OnSelChange** responds to a user selection within the combo box.

Listing for File: FontEnumCBox.h

```
...
/*************************************************************************/
/*                                                                       */
/* FONTITEM structure                                                    */
/*                                                                       */
/*************************************************************************/

struct FONTITEM {
 LOGFONT  lf;
 BOOL     ttFont;
};

/*************************************************************************/
/*                                                                       */
/* FontEnumComboBox: User Font Selection Via ComboBox in a toolbar       */
/*                                                                       */
/*************************************************************************/

class FontEnumComboBox : public CComboBox {
// Construction
public:
 FontEnumComboBox();

protected:
LOGFONT     *ptrlf;        // the transfer LOGFONT buffer
CPtrArray   fonts_array;   // the array of font items
int         curfontid;     // the combo box id of current font

protected:
        void  BuildFontList (CDC*); // enum fonts and build array
        void  AddFontsToList ();     // add array of fonts to list view
afx_msg void  OnSelChange();
public:
// call back font enumeration function
static  BOOL CALLBACK AFX_EXPORT  EnumPrinterFonts (ENUMLOGFONT*,
                                   NEWTEXTMETRICEX*, int, LPVOID);
virtual BOOL PreTranslateMessage(MSG* pMsg);
virtual BOOL Create (DWORD dwStyle, const RECT& rect, CWnd* pParentWnd,
```

```
                              UINT nID);
virtual      ~FontEnumComboBox();
     DECLARE_MESSAGE_MAP()
};
```

The constructor does no actions while the destructor deletes the array of fonts as before. The message response table has a new entry

```
     ON_CONTROL_REFLECT(CBN_SELCHANGE, OnSelChange)
```

The idea is to have the selection changes within the combo box be reflected up to this class, the combo box's direct parent. **OnSelChange** in turn retrieves the corresponding **LOGFONT** for this font and builds the initial FontChange message and sends it on up to it's parent, the main frame window, which in turn then posts it to the currently active view.

PreTranslateMessage does not need to be overridden for this sample. However, sometimes you might wish to take other actions when the user presses say the enter key within the combo box. So I have included this function so indicate where you could trap these kinds of events.

The **Create** function first invokes the **Create** function of the combo box and then proceeds as it did in the earlier version to get the default printer and enumerate the available fonts, storing them in the array and adding the font names into the combo box using **AddString**

```
     AddString (ptrf->lf.lfFaceName);
```

Listing for File: FontEnumCBox.cpp

```
...
FontEnumComboBox::FontEnumComboBox() {
}


/******************************************************************************/
/*                                                                          */
/* ~FontEnumComboBox: remove the fonts in the array and delete the items    */
/*                                                                          */
/******************************************************************************/

FontEnumComboBox::~FontEnumComboBox() {
 int num, i;
 num = fonts_array.GetSize ();
 for (i=0; i<num; i++) delete (FONTITEM*) fonts_array.GetAt (i);
 fonts_array.RemoveAll ();
}


/******************************************************************************/
/*                                                                          */
/* FontEnumComboBox Message Response Table: trap Selection Changed          */
/*                                                                          */
/******************************************************************************/

BEGIN_MESSAGE_MAP(FontEnumComboBox, CComboBox)
 ON_CONTROL_REFLECT(CBN_SELCHANGE, OnSelChange)
END_MESSAGE_MAP()


/******************************************************************************/
/*                                                                          */
```

```
/* PreTraslateMessage: check on key strokes in the ComboBox if desired     */
/*                                                                         */
/***************************************************************************/

BOOL FontEnumComboBox::PreTranslateMessage(MSG* pMsg) {
 // for example, looking for the enter key
 //if ((pMsg->message != WM_KEYDOWN) || (pMsg->wParam != VK_RETURN))
   return CComboBox::PreTranslateMessage(pMsg);
}


/***************************************************************************/
/*                                                                         */
/* Create: get Printer dc and enum fonts and load ComboBox                 */
/*                                                                         */
/***************************************************************************/

BOOL FontEnumComboBox::Create (DWORD dwStyle, const RECT& rect,
                               CWnd* pParentWnd, UINT nID) {
 // create the ComboBox first
 if (CComboBox::Create(dwStyle, rect, pParentWnd, nID)) {
  static char    printer[80];
  char           *device, *driver, *output, *next;
  CDC            *ptrprinterDC = new CDC;

  // get access to a printer DC from the ini file installed printer
  GetProfileString ("windows", "device", "...", printer, 80);
  if ((device = strtok_s (printer, ",", &next)) != NULL &&
      (driver = strtok_s (NULL,    ",", &next)) != NULL &&
      (output = strtok_s (NULL,    ",", &next)) != NULL) {

   // a default printer exists, so get a DC for it
   ptrprinterDC->CreateDC (driver, device, output, NULL);
   // build font list by enumerating fonts, adding to CPtrArray & to list view
   BuildFontList (ptrprinterDC);
   delete ptrprinterDC;
  }
 }
 else return FALSE;
 return TRUE;
}


/***************************************************************************/
/*                                                                         */
/* OnSelChange: respond when the user selection has changed                */
/*                                                                         */
/***************************************************************************/

void      FontEnumComboBox::OnSelChange () {
 int i;
 FONTITEM *ptrf;
 i = GetCurSel ();                        // get the current selection
 if (i <= fonts_array.GetSize ()) {  // if within range,
  curfontid = i;
  ptrf = (FONTITEM*) fonts_array.GetAt (i); //retrieve the font
  // and post the font has changed user message on up the line
  GetParent ()-> PostMessage (CM_FONT_CHANGE, 0, (LPARAM) (&(ptrf->lf)));
 }
}
```

```
/************************************************************************/
/*                                                                      */
/* BuildFontList: enumerates fonts and adds to the list view and array  */
/*                                                                      */
/************************************************************************/

void       FontEnumComboBox::BuildFontList (CDC *ptrprinterDC) {
 // determine whether running under Windows 95 or NT
 DWORD version = ::GetVersion ();
 BOOL  win95   = (BYTE) version >= 4; // TRUE for Win 95; FALSE for Win NT

 // construct the model LOGFONT to enumerate - use only DEFAULT_CHARSET
 LOGFONT lf;
 memset (&lf, 0, sizeof (LOGFONT));
 lf.lfCharSet = DEFAULT_CHARSET;

 // enumerate all fonts on either Win 95 or Win NT system
 if (win95) ::EnumFontFamiliesEx (ptrprinterDC->GetSafeHdc (), &lf,
                      (FONTENUMPROC) EnumPrinterFonts, (LPARAM) this, NULL);
 else ::EnumFontFamilies (ptrprinterDC->GetSafeHdc (), NULL,
                      (FONTENUMPROC) EnumPrinterFonts, (LPARAM) this);
 // now add the array of fonts to the list view
 AddFontsToList ();
}


/************************************************************************/
/*                                                                      */
/* EnumPrinterFonts: call back function to handle each font             */
/*                                                                      */
/************************************************************************/

BOOL CALLBACK AFX_EXPORT  FontEnumComboBox::EnumPrinterFonts (
              ENUMLOGFONT *ptrelf, NEWTEXTMETRICEX* /* ptrntm*/,
              int fonttype, LPVOID pthis) {
 // eliminate unwanted fonts, such as Turkish and MAC fonts
 if (ptrelf->elfLogFont.lfCharSet == DEFAULT_CHARSET ||
     ptrelf->elfLogFont.lfCharSet == ANSI_CHARSET ||
     ptrelf->elfLogFont.lfCharSet == SYMBOL_CHARSET ||
     ptrelf->elfLogFont.lfCharSet == OEM_CHARSET) {
  // if TrueType, construct our copy of the enumerated font and add to array
  if (fonttype & TRUETYPE_FONTTYPE) {
   FONTITEM *ptrf = new FONTITEM;
   memcpy (&ptrf->lf, &ptrelf->elfLogFont, sizeof (LOGFONT));
   ptrf->ttFont = TRUE;
   ((FontEnumComboBox*) pthis)->fonts_array.Add (ptrf);
  }
  // if printer font, construct our copy of the enumerated font & add to array
  else if (fonttype & DEVICE_FONTTYPE) {
   FONTITEM *ptrf = new FONTITEM;
   memcpy (&ptrf->lf, &ptrelf->elfLogFont, sizeof (LOGFONT));
   ptrf->ttFont = FALSE;
   ((FontEnumComboBox*) pthis)->fonts_array.Add (ptrf);
  }
 }
 return 1;
}


/************************************************************************/
```

```
/*                                                                    */
/* AddFontsToList: adds all of the fonts to the list view control     */
/*                                                                    */
/********************************************************************/

void       FontEnumComboBox::AddFontsToList () {
 int num, i;
 FONTITEM *ptrf;

 num = fonts_array.GetSize (); // get total number of fonts to add
 for (i=0; i<num; i++) {
  // access the current font
  ptrf = (FONTITEM*) fonts_array.GetAt (i);
  // use the face name in the list view
  AddString (ptrf->lf.lfFaceName);
 }
 SetCurSel (0);
 curfontid = 0;
}
```

Using CDialogBars

CDialogBars permit a greater flexibility of controls in an easier implementation. In most ways, the dialog bars appear just like tool bars.

One use of a **CDialogBar** is to easily use fancier bitmapped buttons without resorting to owner drawing. This is illustrated in the simple OptionsBar which has a series of potential map overlay options, such as showing factories or cities. Another use is to present status information in convenient 3d text windows. This is shown in the MapLocalStatsBar. And finally, I combined all these into one fancy control panel, MapControlBar. Again, let's begin with the simplest case and work toward the fancier one.

The OptionsBar

The OptionsBar potentially would create map overlays of cities, terrain features, factories and so on. The control only has **CBitmapButton**s in it. The **CBitmapButton** class creates push-button controls from bitmapped images instead displaying text on the button's surface. **CBitmapButton** objects house up to four bitmaps, which contain the images for the four different states a button can assume: up, down, focused, and disabled. Only the first bitmap is required; the others are optional.

Here I use both up and down versions. Thus I have made two bitmap images for each button, one for each state. Each image includes the border area as well as the main image. I used an edge line of black and white pixels which reverse sides between the images. Additionally, I chose to offset the images proper in the down or selected image. Thus the black and white reversal gives the image the illusion of a button press and the offset to the lower right adds to the illusion of downward motion when the button is pressed.

Thus, the first step to use a **CBitmapButton** is the construction of the images. The Pgm10a.rc file then contains the following bitmaps

```
CM_OPTIONS_SHOW_CITYU      BITMAP MOVEABLE PURE  "res\\cityu.bmp"
CM_OPTIONS_SHOW_CITYD      BITMAP DISCARDABLE    "res\\cityd.bmp"
CM_OPTIONS_SHOW_TERRAINU   BITMAP MOVEABLE PURE  "res\\terrainu.bmp"
CM_OPTIONS_SHOW_TERRAIND   BITMAP DISCARDABLE    "res\\terraind.bmp"
CM_OPTIONS_SHOW_FACTORYU   BITMAP MOVEABLE PURE  "res\\factoryu.bmp"
CM_OPTIONS_SHOW_FACTORYD   BITMAP DISCARDABLE    "res\\factoryd.bmp"
CM_OPTIONS_SHOW_WEATHERU   BITMAP MOVEABLE PURE  "res\\weatheru.bmp"
CM_OPTIONS_SHOW_WEATHERD   BITMAP DISCARDABLE    "res\\weatherd.bmp"
CM_OPTIONS_SHOW_SHIPYARDU  BITMAP MOVEABLE PURE  "res\\shipyardu.bmp"
CM_OPTIONS_SHOW_SHIPYARDD  BITMAP DISCARDABLE    "res\\shipyardd.bmp"
```

One **important** note. The identifiers must end in **U** for up or **D** for down so that the framework can tell which version to load as needed. Also **F** for focused and **X** for disabled are allowed.

Next one constructs the actual resource dialog model for the **CDialogBar** to follow. In Pgm10a.rc, the IDD_OPTIONS_DLG is defined as

```
IDD_OPTIONS_DLG DIALOGEX 0, 0, 20, 78
STYLE WS_CHILD
FONT 8, "MS Sans Serif", 0, 0, 0x1
BEGIN
    CONTROL         "CM_OPTIONS_SHOW_CITY",CM_OPTIONS_SHOW_CITY,"Button",
                    BS_OWNERDRAW | WS_TABSTOP,2,2,15,12
    CONTROL         "CM_OPTIONS_SHOW_TERRAIN",CM_OPTIONS_SHOW_TERRAIN,
                    "Button",BS_OWNERDRAW | WS_TABSTOP,2,32,16,12
    CONTROL         "CM_OPTIONS_SHOW_FACTORY",CM_OPTIONS_SHOW_FACTORY,
                    "Button",BS_OWNERDRAW | WS_TABSTOP,2,62,14,12
    CONTROL         "CM_OPTIONS_SHOW_WEATHER",CM_OPTIONS_SHOW_WEATHER,
                    "Button",BS_OWNERDRAW | WS_TABSTOP,2,17,15,12
    CONTROL         "CM_OPTIONS_SHOW_SHIPYARD",CM_OPTIONS_SHOW_SHIPYARD,
                    "Button",BS_OWNERDRAW | WS_TABSTOP,2,47,15,12,
                    WS_EX_TRANSPARENT
END
```

Notice that the dialog is of style **DIALOGEX** and only **WS_CHILD** is specified. **Remove** all other style options. Place a button control at the desired locations. Note that the actual size of the button in immaterial, the dialog resource is used to determine button placement only, not size, for the size comes from the actual button bitmaps. Notice also that the buttons have only the **BS_OWNERDRAW** and tab stop styles. Additionally, notice that the button identifiers lack the appended U or D characters.

Additionally, add in string to be used for flyby and tool tips

```
CM_OPTIONS_SHOW_CITY "Toggle Displaying Cities on the Map\nToggle Show Cities"
CM_OPTIONS_SHOW_TERRAIN
        "Toggle Displaying the Terrain Overlay on the Map\nToggle Show Terrain"
CM_OPTIONS_SHOW_FACTORY
            "Toggle Displaying Factories on the Map\nToggle Show Factories"
```

```
CM_OPTIONS_SHOW_WEATHER
                "Toggle Displaying the Weather Map Overlay\nToggle Show Weather"
CM_OPTIONS_SHOW_SHIPYARD
            "Toggle Displaying Naval Shipyards on the Map\nToggle Show Shipyards"
```

The actual construction of the OptionsBar in the main frame class totally parallels the tool boxes. The header contains the instance of the derived class

```
        OptionsBar          optionsbar;
```

and also I provide an access function to retrieve a pointer to the control. In this case, the access function is not needed at all, but similar ones are required for the other **CDialogBar** controls

```
        OptionsBar* GetOptionsBar ()
```

In the man frame's **OnCreate**, the OptionsBar's **Create** function is invoked, all that must be passed is the pointer to this parent window

```
        if (optionsbar.Create (this))
        else {
         TRACE0("Failed to create options bar\n");
         return -1;
        }
```

Likewise, the control is given a text string to show when it becomes a floating control bar and docking is enabled as desired

```
        optionsbar.SetWindowText(_T("Opt"));
        optionsbar.EnableDocking (0);
```

For now, we are ignoring the initial positioning because I am going to tie all three dialog control's position to each other; their location is dependent upon one another.

Next, derive the OptionsBar from the **CDialogBar** class, including members for each of the **CBitmapButton** controls as shown in the listing for OptionsBar.h. Only the **Create** function must be overridden.

Listing for File: OptionsBar.h

```
...
class OptionsBar : public CDialogBar {
public:
 CBitmapButton cities;
 CBitmapButton factories;
 CBitmapButton terrain;
 CBitmapButton weather;
 CBitmapButton shipyards;

public:
        OptionsBar ();          // construct the dialog bar
 BOOL    Create (CWnd*);       // create the dialog bar
};
```

The class constructor enables tool tips if desired. Most all of the work is done in the **Create** function.

Listing for File: OptionsBar.cpp

```
...
/**********************************************************************/
/*                                                                    */
/* OptionsBar: Houses options button controls for cities, factories etc */
/*                                                                    */
/**********************************************************************/

OptionsBar::OptionsBar () : CDialogBar () {
 EnableToolTips (TRUE);
}


/**********************************************************************/
/*                                                                    */
/* Create: setup the Options Dialog Bar                               */
/*                                                                    */
/**********************************************************************/

BOOL      OptionsBar::Create (CWnd *ptrparent) {
 if (CDialogBar::Create (ptrparent, IDD_OPTIONS_DLG,
                         CBRS_FLOATING | CBRS_TOOLTIPS | CBRS_FLYBY,
                         AFX_IDW_CONTROLBAR_FIRST + 3)) {
  cities.AutoLoad (CM_OPTIONS_SHOW_CITY, this);
  factories.AutoLoad (CM_OPTIONS_SHOW_FACTORY, this);
  weather.AutoLoad (CM_OPTIONS_SHOW_WEATHER, this);
  terrain.AutoLoad (CM_OPTIONS_SHOW_TERRAIN, this);
  shipyards.AutoLoad (CM_OPTIONS_SHOW_SHIPYARD, this);
  return TRUE;
 }
 else return FALSE;
}
```

The base class is invoked as you would expect, passing the parent pointer, the style flags, the dialog ID in the resource file, plus one more vital piece of information, the control's ID. In order to have the framework automatically handle and find the control bars dynamically, use an identifier in the range of **AFX_IDW_CONTROLBAR_FIRST** through **AFX_IDW_CONTROLBAR_LAST**. Since this application has three of these, I used here **AFX_IDW_CONTROLBAR_FIRST** + 3. Now one can dynamically get access from the main frame class by asking for this control ID.

Next, invoke the **AutoLoad** function of the **CBitmapButton** class, providing the button ID without the U or D suffixes. And the framework takes care of all the remaining details as needed. Simply put in command handlers for the button IDs (without the D or U suffixes).

The MapLocalStatsBar—Displaying Information in CDialogBar Text Controls

The MapLocalStatsBar has no buttons, rather it has numerous text controls in which the application can display information about the current processes. It's construction is far simpler. The Pgm10a.rc file contains the dialog model

```
IDD_MAP_LOCAL_STATS DIALOG DISCARDABLE  0, 0, 202, 84
STYLE WS_CHILD
FONT 8, "MS Sans Serif"
BEGIN
    LTEXT    "Name:",IDC_MLS_CON_AT,3,2,196,10,SS_SUNKEN
    LTEXT    "At:",IDC_MLS_LATLON_AT,3,15,96,10,SS_SUNKEN
    LTEXT    "Day: ",IDC_MLS_GAMEDAY,3,31,96,10,SS_SUNKEN
    LTEXT    "Time (UT):",IDC_MLS_GAMETIMEUT,102,31,96,10,SS_SUNKEN
    LTEXT    "Time (Local):",IDC_MLS_TIME_LCL,3,47,96,10,SS_SUNKEN
    LTEXT    "Date (Local):",IDC_MLS_DATE_LCL,102,47,96,10,SS_SUNKEN
    LTEXT    "Sunrise:",IDC_MLS_SUNRISE,3,59,96,10,SS_SUNKEN
    LTEXT    "Sunset:",IDC_MLS_SUNSET,102,59,96,10,SS_SUNKEN
    LTEXT    "Weather: Light Snow",IDC_MLS_WEATHER,3,71,96,10, SS_SUNKEN
    LTEXT    "Ground: Heavy Mud",IDC_MLS_GROUND,102,71,96,10, SS_SUNKEN
END
```

The method I used to display the information is to concatenate the constant portion of the strings and the user supplied right portions. To avoid numerous dynamic loading of strings, I have chosen to maintain the constant left portion of the strings as members. Alternatively, one could use constant character strings that are not stored in the resource file. As you examine the class header file, notice that there are several public access functions for the application to invoke to update the information in the controls.

Listing for File: MapLocalStatsBar.h

```
...
/********************************************************************/
/*                                                                  */
/* MapLocalStatsBar: Allocate and provides access to the Map Local StatsBar*/
/*                                                                  */
/********************************************************************/

class MapLocalStatsBar : public CDialogBar {
protected:
 char   sname[20];
 char   snowat[20];
 char   sgday[20];
 char   sgtime[20];
 char   stlcl[20];
 char   sdlcl[20];
 char   swea[20];
 char   sgrnd[20];
 char   srise[20];
 char   sset[20];

public:
        MapLocalStatsBar ();                 // construct the dialog bar
 BOOL   Create (CWnd*);                      // create the dialog bar
 void   DisplayDay (char*);                  // display the game day
 void   DisplayTimeUT (char*);               // display the UT game time
 void   DisplayDayTime (char*, char*);       // display both day and time
 void   DisplayMapNowAtValues (             // display all local stats
           char *mnam, char *mpos, char *mtl, char *mdl,  char *mrise,
           char *mset, char *mwea, char *mgrnd);
};
...
```

SetDlgItemText is used to actually insert the new text strings in the controls. This function requires first the text control's ID and then the string to be inserted. Other creation details are similar to the OptionsBar.

Listing for File: MapLocalStatsBar.cpp

```
...
/********************************************************************/
/*                                                                  */
/* MapLocalStatsBar: displays local map statistics in a dialog bar  */
/*                                                                  */
/********************************************************************/

/********************************************************************/
/*                                                                  */
/* MapLocalStatsBar: constructor                                    */
/*                                                                  */
/********************************************************************/

MapLocalStatsBar::MapLocalStatsBar () : CDialogBar () {
 EnableToolTips (TRUE);
 HINSTANCE hs = AfxGetApp()->m_hInstance;
 LoadString (hs, IDS_MLS_NAME,      sname,  sizeof(sname));
 LoadString (hs, IDS_MLS_NOW_AT,    snowat, sizeof(snowat));
```

```
LoadString (hs, IDS_MLS_GAMEDAYM,   sgday,  sizeof(sgday));
LoadString (hs, IDS_MLS_GAMETIMEUTM,sgtime, sizeof(sgtime));
LoadString (hs, IDS_MLS_TIME_LCL,   stlcl,  sizeof(stlcl));
LoadString (hs, IDS_MLS_DATE_LCL,   sdlcl,  sizeof(sdlcl));
LoadString (hs, IDS_MLS_WEATHER,    swea,   sizeof(swea));
LoadString (hs, IDS_MLS_GROUND,     sgrnd,  sizeof(sgrnd));
LoadString (hs, IDS_MLS_SUNRISE,    srise,  sizeof(srise));
LoadString (hs, IDS_MLS_SUNSET,     sset,   sizeof(sset));
}

/************************************************************************/
/*                                                                    */
/* Create: setup the Map Local Status Bar                             */
/*                                                                    */
/************************************************************************/

BOOL      MapLocalStatsBar::Create (CWnd *ptrparent) {
 if (CDialogBar::Create (ptrparent, IDD_MAP_LOCAL_STATS,
                         CBRS_FLOATING | CBRS_TOOLTIPS | CBRS_FLYBY,
                         AFX_IDW_CONTROLBAR_FIRST + 2)) {
  return TRUE;
 }
 else return FALSE;
}

/************************************************************************/
/*                                                                    */
/* DisplayDay: displays the game date in the control                  */
/*                                                                    */
/************************************************************************/

void      MapLocalStatsBar::DisplayDay (char *msg) {
 char m[80];
 strcpy_s (m, sizeof(m), sgday);
 strcat_s (m, sizeof(m), msg);
 SetDlgItemText (IDC_MLS_GAMEDAY, m);
}

/************************************************************************/
/*                                                                    */
/* DisplayTimeUT: displays game time UT in the control                */
/*                                                                    */
/************************************************************************/

void      MapLocalStatsBar::DisplayTimeUT (char *msg) {
 char m[80];
 strcpy_s (m, sizeof(m), sgtime);
 strcat_s (m, sizeof(m), msg);
 SetDlgItemText (IDC_MLS_GAMETIMEUT, m);
}

/************************************************************************/
/*                                                                    */
/* DisplayDayTime: displays game day and time UT in the control       */
/*                                                                    */
/************************************************************************/

void      MapLocalStatsBar::DisplayDayTime (char *mday, char *mtime) {
```

```
DisplayDay (mday);
DisplayTimeUT (mtime);
}


/****************************************************************************/
/*                                                                          */
/* DisplayMapNowAtValues: show the where, location, date, time local etc    */
/*                                                                          */
/****************************************************************************/

void       MapLocalStatsBar::DisplayMapNowAtValues (char *mnam, char *mpos,
                           char *mtl, char *mdl,  char *mrise, char *mset,
                           char *mw, char *mg) {
char m[80];
strcpy_s (m, sizeof(m), sname);
strcat_s (m, sizeof(m), mnam);
SetDlgItemText (IDC_MLS_CON_AT, m);
strcpy_s (m, sizeof(m), snowat);
strcat_s (m, sizeof(m), mpos);
SetDlgItemText (IDC_MLS_LATLON_AT, m);
strcpy_s (m, sizeof(m), stlcl);
strcat_s (m, sizeof(m), mtl);
SetDlgItemText (IDC_MLS_TIME_LCL, m);
strcpy_s (m, sizeof(m), sdlcl);
strcat_s (m, sizeof(m), mdl);
SetDlgItemText (IDC_MLS_DATE_LCL, m);
strcpy_s (m, sizeof(m), srise);
strcat_s (m, sizeof(m), mrise);
SetDlgItemText (IDC_MLS_SUNRISE, m);
strcpy_s (m, sizeof(m), sset);
strcat_s (m, sizeof(m), mset);
SetDlgItemText (IDC_MLS_SUNSET, m);
strcpy_s (m, sizeof(m), swea);
strcat_s (m, sizeof(m), mw);
SetDlgItemText (IDC_MLS_WEATHER, m);
strcpy_s (m, sizeof(m), sgrnd);
strcat_s (m, sizeof(m), mg);
SetDlgItemText (IDC_MLS_GROUND, m);
}
```

In the main frame window class, the instance and it's public access function is

```
MapLocalStatsBar maplocalstatsbar;
MapLocalStatsBar*  GetMapLocalStatsBar ();
```

In the main frame's **OnCreate**, the construction sequence follows the same pattern as before. Again, ignore the repositioning code for now

```
if (maplocalstatsbar.Create (this))
else {
 TRACE0("Failed to create map local stats bar\n");
 return -1;
}
...
maplocalstatsbar.SetWindowText(_T("Map Local Stats"));
maplocalstatsbar.EnableDocking (0);
```

The hiding and showing of the MapLocalStatsBar is identical to that of the main tool bar.

The GeoView class actually invokes the display functions to insert information into these text controls. Often, the application ought to save and restore the previous map settings for the user. Three choices are at hand. Place the information in the main ini file located in the Windows folder (which is now frowned upon), place the information in a private ini file located in the application's folder, or place the information in the System Registry. Because at this time there are not good tools for cleaning up obsolete registration entries, I have initially opted to place this view specific information in a private ini file.

Working With Private Ini Files

GeoView stores and retrieves the current map information from a private ini file located in the folder of the application, here Pgm10a. The ini file is called Pgm10a.ini. Its contents represent the current map situation

```
[Demo Map]
Date=1 Sept 1939
Time=6:00
Lat=171546
Lon=11219
Zoom=2
Scroll=75
Scale=6000.00
```

Notice that there is a section header and each of the values are preceded by a keyword.

In GeoView, data members are defined to hold these parameters. However, with latitude and longitude, I created a Position class to encapsulate a geographic position. Various member functions permit construction of a Position object in various ways, allow for manipulation of a Position object, and to nicely format a position as shown in the MapLocalStatsBar. There is insufficient space in this chapter to reproduce this fairly simple class, so if you are interested in how I encapsulated a latitude-longitude pair, please see the full coding on the CD. In the GeoView class definition are the following members and two key helper functions to read and write the private ini file

```
Position  center;
double    scale;
int       zoom;
int       scroll;
char      date[20];
char      time[20];

protected:
void ReadSetUpProfileData ();
void WriteSetUpProfileData ();
```

The private ini file is input during the **OnInitialUpdate** invocation. The ReadSetupProfileData function is called to do the actual input operations. Then a pointer to the main frame window is obtained and via its public access function, a pointer to the MapLocalStatsBar is obtained. That pointer is then used to invoke the display public functions of the MapLocalStatsBar

class.
```
void        GeoView::OnInitialUpdate () {
// load user profile data
MainFrame *ptrfrm = (MainFrame*) (AfxGetApp()->m_pMainWnd);
if (!ptrfrm) return;
ReadSetUpProfileData ();
// display initial settings on the Map Control Bar
ptrfrm->GetMapControlBar ()->DisplayAll (&center, zoom, scroll,
                                         scale);
// display some data on the Map Local Stats Bar
char pos[30];
center.FormatPosition (pos);
ptrfrm->GetMapLocalStatsBar ()->DisplayDayTime (date, time);
ptrfrm->GetMapLocalStatsBar ()->DisplayMapNowAtValues (
 "Europe", pos, time, date, "5:30", "6:30", "Partly Cloudy",
 "Light Mud");

// display a new caption and a test message on the statusbar
ptrfrm->DisplayNewCaption ("Geographical Maps - Test New Caption");
ptrfrm->DisplayOnStatusBar ("Test status bar message");
...
```

The actual access of the ini file is done using **GetPrivateProfileString** which requires first the string that identifies the section to read from, the identifier of the string keyword to input, the default string to return if the desired string is not present, the maximum size of the string buffer, and the filename string.
```
void        GeoView::ReadSetUpProfileData () {
char section[40];
char entry[40];
char latstr[10], lonstr[10];
long lat, lon;
char file[80];

HINSTANCE hs = AfxGetApp()->m_hInstance;
LoadString (hs, IDS_GEO_INI, file, sizeof(file));

LoadString (hs, IDS_GEO_PROFILE_DEMOMAP, section, sizeof(section));
LoadString (hs, IDS_GEO_PROFILE_DATE, entry, sizeof (entry));
GetPrivateProfileString (section, entry, "0", date, sizeof(date),
                         file);
LoadString (hs, IDS_GEO_PROFILE_TIME, entry, sizeof (entry));
GetPrivateProfileString (section, entry, "0", time, sizeof(time),
                         file);

LoadString (hs, IDS_GEO_PROFILE_LAT, entry, sizeof (entry));
GetPrivateProfileString (section, entry, "0", latstr,
                         sizeof (latstr), file);
LoadString (hs, IDS_GEO_PROFILE_LON, entry, sizeof (entry));
GetPrivateProfileString (section, entry, "0", lonstr,
                         sizeof (lonstr), file);
lat = atol (latstr);
```

```
lon = atol (lonstr);
center.SetLatLon (lat, lon);

LoadString (hs, IDS_GEO_PROFILE_ZOOM, entry, sizeof (entry));
zoom = GetPrivateProfileInt (section, entry, INITZOOM, file);
LoadString (hs, IDS_GEO_PROFILE_SCROL, entry, sizeof (entry));
scroll = GetPrivateProfileInt (section, entry, INITSCROLL, file);
LoadString (hs, IDS_GEO_PROFILE_SCALE, entry, sizeof (entry));
GetPrivateProfileString (section, entry, "INITSCALE", lonstr,
                          sizeof (lonstr), file);
scale = atof (lonstr);
}
```

The **WritePrivateProfileString** requires the same parameters except the maximum length of the string is not coded.

```
void        GeoView::WriteSetUpProfileData () {
char section[40];
char entry[40];
char latstr[10], lonstr[10];
char file[80];

HINSTANCE hs = AfxGetApp()->m_hInstance;
LoadString (hs, IDS_GEO_INI, file, sizeof(file));

LoadString (hs, IDS_GEO_PROFILE_DEMOMAP, section, sizeof(section));
LoadString (hs, IDS_GEO_PROFILE_DATE, entry, sizeof (entry));
WritePrivateProfileString (section, entry, date, file);
LoadString (hs, IDS_GEO_PROFILE_TIME, entry, sizeof (entry));
WritePrivateProfileString (section, entry, time, file);

wsprintf (latstr, "%ld", center.Latitude);
wsprintf (lonstr, "%ld", center.Longitude);
LoadString (hs, IDS_GEO_PROFILE_LAT, entry, sizeof (entry));
WritePrivateProfileString (section, entry, latstr, file);
LoadString (hs, IDS_GEO_PROFILE_LON, entry, sizeof (entry));
WritePrivateProfileString (section, entry, lonstr, file);

LoadString (hs, IDS_GEO_PROFILE_ZOOM, entry, sizeof (entry));
wsprintf (latstr, "%d",  zoom);
WritePrivateProfileString (section, entry, latstr, file);
LoadString (hs, IDS_GEO_PROFILE_SCROL, entry, sizeof (entry));
wsprintf (latstr, "%d",  scroll);
WritePrivateProfileString (section, entry, latstr, file);
LoadString (hs, IDS_GEO_PROFILE_SCALE, entry, sizeof (entry));
sprintf_s (latstr, sizeof(latstr), "%7.2f", scale);
WritePrivateProfileString (section, entry, latstr, file);
}
```

Finally, when the view is being destroyed, in **OnDestroy**, the current map settings are then written to the private ini file

```
void GeoView::OnDestroy () {
 WriteSetUpProfileData ();
 CScrollView::OnDestroy ();
}
```

The MapControlBar—Combining Text and CBitmapButtons

The last control bar is the most complex, for it has an arrow button cluster of **CBitmapButton**s, regular text buttons and text information controls. It is derived from **CDialogBar** as well and the model dialog in the Pgm10a.rc file is as follows

```
IDD_MAP_CONTROLS DIALOGEX 0, 0, 179, 54
STYLE WS_CHILD
FONT 8, "MS Sans Serif", 0, 0, 0x1
BEGIN
    CONTROL "CM_MAPCB_UPLEFT",CM_MAPCB_UPLEFT,"Button",BS_OWNERDRAW |
            WS_TABSTOP,5,5,22,12
    CONTROL "CM_MAPCB_UP",CM_MAPCB_UP,"Button",BS_OWNERDRAW |
            WS_TABSTOP,16,5,22,12
    CONTROL "CM_MAPCB_UPRIGHT",CM_MAPCB_UPRIGHT,"Button",
            BS_OWNERDRAW | WS_TABSTOP,27,5,22,12
    CONTROL "CM_MAPCB_LEFT",CM_MAPCB_LEFT,"Button",BS_OWNERDRAW |
            WS_TABSTOP,5,16,22,12
    CONTROL "CM_MAPCB_SETSCALE",CM_MAPCB_SETSCALE,"Button",
            BS_OWNERDRAW | WS_TABSTOP,16,16,22,12,WS_EX_TRANSPARENT
    CONTROL "CM_MAPCB_RIGHT",CM_MAPCB_RIGHT,"Button",BS_OWNERDRAW |
            WS_TABSTOP,27,16,22,12
    CONTROL "CM_MAPCB_DOWNLEFT",CM_MAPCB_DOWNLEFT,"Button",
            BS_OWNERDRAW | WS_TABSTOP,5,27,22,12
    CONTROL "CM_MAPCB_DOWN",CM_MAPCB_DOWN,"Button",BS_OWNERDRAW |
            WS_TABSTOP,16,27,22,12
    CONTROL "CM_MAPCB_DOWNRIGHT",CM_MAPCB_DOWNRIGHT,"Button",
            BS_OWNERDRAW | WS_TABSTOP,27,27,22,12
    PUSHBUTTON      "Zoom In",CM_MAPCB_ZOOM_IN,5,40,35,11
    PUSHBUTTON      "Zoom Out",CM_MAPCB_ZOOM_OUT,41,40,35,11
    PUSHBUTTON      "Set Center",CM_MAPCB_SETCENTER,41,3,35,11
    PUSHBUTTON      "Set Zoom",CM_MAPCB_SETZOOM,41,15,35,11
    PUSHBUTTON      "Set Scroll",CM_MAPCB_SETSCROLL,41,27,35,11
    LTEXT   "Center: S 08 20 27  E 118 45 53", IDC_MAPCB_CENTERPOS,
            80, 3,92,10,SS_SUNKEN
    LTEXT   "Zoom Factor: 99",IDC_MAPCB_ZOOM,80,15,52,10,SS_SUNKEN
    LTEXT   "Scroll : 125%",IDC_MAPCB_SCROLL,80,27,52,10,SS_SUNKEN
    LTEXT   "Map Scale (Miles): 6000.00",IDC_MAPCB_SCALE,80,40,94,10,
            SS_SUNKEN
END
```

Notice that the actual upper left point determines the real location of the **CBitmapButton**. When you look at the dialog in the resource editor, it appears that the buttons of the arrow cluster overlap. Yet when the dialog bar is created, the positions yield a nice compact arrow cluster. Also the resource file contains the bitmaps. Note the arrow cluster have a D and U appended to the identifiers

```
CM_MAPCB_SETCENTER     BITMAP  MOVEABLE PURE    "res\\setcentr.bmp"
CM_MAPCB_SETZOOM       BITMAP  MOVEABLE PURE    "res\\setzoom.bmp"
CM_MAPCB_SETSCROLL     BITMAP  MOVEABLE PURE    "res\\setscrol.bmp"
CM_MAPCB_ZOOM_IN       BITMAP  MOVEABLE PURE    "res\\zoomin.bmp"
CM_MAPCB_ZOOM_OUT      BITMAP  MOVEABLE PURE    "res\\zoomout.bmp"
CM_MAPCB_UPU           BITMAP  MOVEABLE PURE    "res\\supu.bmp"
CM_MAPCB_UPD           BITMAP  MOVEABLE PURE    "res\\supd.bmp"
CM_MAPCB_DOWNU         BITMAP  MOVEABLE PURE    "res\\sdownu.bmp"
CM_MAPCB_DOWND         BITMAP  MOVEABLE PURE    "res\\sdownd.bmp"
CM_MAPCB_LEFTU         BITMAP  MOVEABLE PURE    "res\\sleftu.bmp"
CM_MAPCB_LEFTD         BITMAP  MOVEABLE PURE    "res\\sleftd.bmp"
... and so on
```

In the main frame window class, the MapControlBar instance is defined along with a public access function that returns a pointer to this MapControlBar instance so that its display functions can easily be invoked. In MainFrame's **OnCreate** it is created similar to the others

```
MapControlBar     mapcontrolbar;            // map control bar
MapControlBar*    GetMapControlBar ();

if (mapcontrolbar.Create (this))
else {
 TRACE0("Failed to create map control bar\n");
 return -1;
}

mapcontrolbar.SetWindowText(_T("Map Controls"));
mapcontrolbar.EnableDocking (0);
```

In GeoView, the button clicks are processed. GeoView's message response table appears as

```
ON_BN_CLICKED (CM_MAPCB_UPLEFT, CmDummy)
...
ON_BN_CLICKED (CM_MAPCB_DOWNRIGHT, CmDummy)
ON_BN_CLICKED (CM_MAPCB_SETCENTER, CmDummy)
ON_BN_CLICKED (CM_MAPCB_SETZOOM, CmDummy)
ON_BN_CLICKED (CM_MAPCB_SETSCROLL, CmDummy)
ON_BN_CLICKED (CM_MAPCB_ZOOM_IN, CmDummy)
ON_BN_CLICKED (CM_MAPCB_ZOOM_OUT, CmDummy)
```

The MapControlBar definition includes the cluster of **CBitmapButton**s and a number of public display functions to enable the application to easily adjust the text information that corresponds to several of the buttons.

Listing for File: MapControlBar.h

```
...
/****************************************************************************/
/*                                                                      */
```

```
/* MapControlBar: Allocate and provides access to the Map Control Dlg bar  */
/*                                                                          */
/****************************************************************************/

class MapControlBar : public CDialogBar {
public:
 CBitmapButton upleft;
 CBitmapButton up;
 CBitmapButton upright;
 CBitmapButton left;
 CBitmapButton scale;
 CBitmapButton right;
 CBitmapButton downleft;
 CBitmapButton down;
 CBitmapButton downright;

protected:
 char   scen[20];      // map center message
 char   szoom[20];     // map zoom value message
 char   sscroll[20];   // map scroll percentage message
 char   sscale[20];    // map scale message

public:
         MapControlBar ();              // construct the dialog bar
 BOOL    Create (CWnd*);                // create the dialog bar
 void    DisplayCenter (Position*);
 void    DisplayZoom (int);
 void    DisplayScroll (int);
 void    DisplayScale (double);
 void    DisplayAll (Position*, int, int, double);
};
```

Similar to the other dialog bar, the constructor enables tool tips and loads the constant portions of the text messages. After first constructing the **CDialogBar**, **Create** then autoloads the bitmap buttons. The various display functions are quite similar to those in the MapLocalStatsBar; only a few are shown here.

Listing for File: MapControlBar.cpp

```
...
/****************************************************************************/
/*                                                                          */
/* MapControlBar: Houses map button controls, arrow cluster, dlg launchers */
/*                                                                          */
/****************************************************************************/

/****************************************************************************/
/*                                                                          */
/* MapControlBar: constructor                                               */
/*                                                                          */
/****************************************************************************/

MapControlBar::MapControlBar () : CDialogBar () {
 EnableToolTips (TRUE);
 HINSTANCE hs = AfxGetApp()->m_hInstance;
```

```
    LoadString (hs, IDS_MAPCB_CENTERPOS, scen,    sizeof(scen));
    LoadString (hs, IDS_MAPCB_ZOOM,      szoom,   sizeof(szoom));
    LoadString (hs, IDS_MAPCB_SCROLL,    sscroll, sizeof(sscroll));
    LoadString (hs, IDS_MAPCB_SCALE,     sscale,  sizeof(sscale));
}

/**************************************************************************/
/*                                                                        */
/* Create: setup the Map control dialog bar                               */
/*                                                                        */
/**************************************************************************/

BOOL     MapControlBar::Create (CWnd *ptrparent) {
  if (CDialogBar::Create (ptrparent, IDD_MAP_CONTROLS,
                          //CBRS_BOTTOM
                          CBRS_FLOATING
                          | CBRS_TOOLTIPS | CBRS_FLYBY,
                          AFX_IDW_CONTROLBAR_FIRST+1)) {
    upleft.AutoLoad (CM_MAPCB_UPLEFT, this);
    up.AutoLoad (CM_MAPCB_UP, this);
    upright.AutoLoad (CM_MAPCB_UPRIGHT, this);
    left.AutoLoad (CM_MAPCB_LEFT, this);
    scale.AutoLoad (CM_MAPCB_SETSCALE, this);
    right.AutoLoad (CM_MAPCB_RIGHT, this);
    downleft.AutoLoad (CM_MAPCB_DOWNLEFT, this);
    down.AutoLoad (CM_MAPCB_DOWN, this);
    downright.AutoLoad (CM_MAPCB_DOWNRIGHT, this);
    return TRUE;
  }
  else return FALSE;
}

/**************************************************************************/
/*                                                                        */
/* DisplayCenter: show the map center position in the static control      */
/*                                                                        */
/**************************************************************************/

void     MapControlBar::DisplayCenter (Position *ptrpos) {
  char pos[30];
  char msg[80];
  ptrpos->FormatPosition (pos, sizeof(pos));
  strcpy_s (msg, sizeof(msg), scen);
  strcat_s (msg, sizeof(msg), pos);
  SetDlgItemText (IDC_MAPCB_CENTERPOS, msg);
}

/**************************************************************************/
/*                                                                        */
/* DisplayZoom: show the zoom factor in the static control                */
/*                                                                        */
/**************************************************************************/

void     MapControlBar::DisplayZoom (int zoom) {
  char msg[80];
  char s[20];
  strcpy_s (msg, sizeof(msg), szoom);
  wsprintf (s, "%d", zoom);
```

```
strcat_s (msg, sizeof(msg), s);
SetDlgItemText (IDC_MAPCB_ZOOM, msg);
}

/**************************************************************************/
/*                                                                        */
/* DisplayScroll: show the scroll percentage in the static control        */
/*                                                                        */
/**************************************************************************/

void      MapControlBar::DisplayScroll (int scroll) {
char msg[80];
char s[20];
strcpy_s (msg, sizeof(msg), sscroll);
sprintf_s (s, sizeof(s), "%d", scroll);
strcat_s (msg, sizeof(msg), s);
SetDlgItemText (IDC_MAPCB_SCROLL, msg);
}

/**************************************************************************/
/*                                                                        */
/* DisplayScale: show scale value in static control                       */
/*                                                                        */
/**************************************************************************/

void      MapControlBar::DisplayScale (double scale) {
char msg[80];
char s[20];
strcpy_s (msg, sizeof(msg), sscale);
sprintf_s (s, sizeof(s), "%7.2f", scale);
strcat_s (msg, sizeof(msg), s);
SetDlgItemText (IDC_MAPCB_SCALE, msg);
}

/**************************************************************************/
/*                                                                        */
/* DisplayAll: show all four values in the static controls                */
/*                                                                        */
/**************************************************************************/

void      MapControlBar::DisplayAll (Position *ptrpos, int zoom, int scroll,
double scale) {
DisplayCenter (ptrpos);
DisplayZoom (zoom);
DisplayScroll (scroll);
DisplayScale (scale);
}
```

With the **CDialogBar**s operational, let's turn our attention to their initial placement on-screen.

Controlling the Initial Placement of the Three Dialog Bars

When the application is launched for the first time and no ini files or saved tool bar state has been done, these three control bars must be placed in a reasonable location with respect to the main window view itself, similar to Figure 10.1 above. In the main frame's **OnCreate**, the three instances have been created, but the initial view has not. If you watch the application as it is launched, you will see that the basic frame appears first, then the controls and finally the map view appears. Thus, I used a two stage approach for initial placement. I initially placed the controls at a reasonable location and then forced them to be actually positioned and shown there using

```
RepositionBars (AFX_IDW_CONTROLBAR_FIRST,
                AFX_IDW_CONTROLBAR_LAST, 0, reposQuery, r);
```

Using the **reposQuery** option permits the framework to actually place the bars in their locations and then calculate the client area and so on. Once they are actually in place, I then repeat the repositioning process to move them to their final locations, snuggled against the respective frames.

By giving each of the dialog bars an identifier within the range of **AFX_IDW_CONTROLBAR_FIRST** to **AFX_IDW_CONTROLBAR_LAST**, the framework can **automatically** handle them. Admittedly it does look a bit jerky to see the bars appear and then move to their final locations. The real solution lies in the next section below.

```
// in case this is the first time that the app is run and no state
// info is yet saved, set up an initial first position, and then
// based upon the actual setup, repeat process with the better guess
// for initial position
CRect r, q;
CPoint p;

GetClientRect (&r);               // get window area less bars
maplocalstatsbar.GetWindowRect(&q);// get dims of Map Local Stats Bar
p.x = r.right - q.Width ();    // convert into a point placement
p.y = r.top + 30;
FloatControlBar (&maplocalstatsbar, p); // and float it here

p.y += 100;                             // insert an educated guess offset
FloatControlBar (&optionsbar, p);   // float the Options Bar below it

mapcontrolbar.GetWindowRect (&q);   // get dims of Map Control Bar
p.x = r.right - q.Width ();          // install its location in point
p.y = r.bottom - q.Height ();
FloatControlBar (&mapcontrolbar, p);// now float it here

// force the layout to take effect
RepositionBars (AFX_IDW_CONTROLBAR_FIRST, AFX_IDW_CONTROLBAR_LAST,
                0, reposQuery, r);

// now construct a more optimum layout of the three floating bars
int top = r.top;
maplocalstatsbar.GetWindowRect(&q);
```

```
p.x = r.right - q.Width ();
p.y = top;
ClientToScreen (&p);
FloatControlBar (&maplocalstatsbar, p);

top += q.Height () + 22;
p.y = top;
mapcontrolbar.GetWindowRect (&q);
p.x = r.right - q.Width ();
ClientToScreen (&p);
FloatControlBar (&mapcontrolbar, p);

top += q.Height () + 22;
p.y = top;
optionsbar.GetWindowRect (&q);
p.x = r.right - q.Width ();
ClientToScreen (&p);
FloatControlBar (&optionsbar, p);
```

Additionally, when the application terminates, ideally we would like to save the locations and status of all the tool bars. Then when the application is relaunched, restore the tool bars to their previous states.

Saving and Restoring Tool Bar States— Using the System Registry

Saving and restoring the tool bar state is quite easy to do. The **CFrameWnd** has **SaveBarState** and **LoadBarState** functions to do this for us. The locations, docking status and so on are saved to the System Registry or to the main application ini file in the Windows directory and restored from there. If the application has called **SetRegistryKey**, then this information is stored in the System Registry. If not, the information is stored in the main application ini file located in the Windows folder. Since Microsoft now want applications to avoid creating ini files in the Windows folder, we should use the Registry exclusively.

The only piece of information that is not saved is the number of columns a control is currently using. Thus, we must manually obtain the current number of columns using **GetColumns** and then when reloading, call **SetColumns** for those controls where columns are important. In this sample, it it the palette box which has columns to consider.

The main frame's **OnClose** function is a good place to save the state of all of the tool bars. The **SaveBarState** requires a string section identifier, here "General."

```
void        MainFrame::OnClose () {
  // save all control bar states
  SaveBarState (_T("General"));
  AfxGetApp ()->WriteProfileInt (_T("General"), _T("Columns"),
                      palettebox.GetColumns ());
```

The **WriteProfileInt** function writes to the main application ini file in the Windows folder or to the Registry. Of course there are several variations of the write profile function, such as **WriteProfileString**. The function requires the section string, the keyword identifier, here "Columns" and the integer to write.

The reverse operation, is done in the main frame's **OnCreate** function once the various bars are created and initially placed. Thus, the last step on **OnCreate** is

```
// now load in any previously saved states, beginning with the number
// of columns which is not saved by the SaveBarState function
palettebox.SetColumns (AfxGetApp ()->GetProfileInt (_T("General"),
                                              _T("Columns"), 2));

LoadBarState(_T("General"));
```

One could also get fancier than I have. Optimally, the flickering of my tool bars is not good. Perhaps it might be tolerable for the very first time an application is launched when there is no initial main application ini file or the Registry is empty. Of course, your installation process could always copy a pre-made ini file into the Windows folder or install Registration information.

So give this a try. Run Pgm10a and reposition the tool bars to some desired locations and terminate the application, forcing the saving of the tool bars' states. Then in **OnCreate** of MainFrame.cpp, after the tool bars construction is finished, I have placed a // **cut here** through a // **end cut** pair of comments. Just comment out this whole repositioning sequence, and rebuild the application. Now what the dramatic difference as the windows appear. All flicker is gone; the tool bars just appear at their last locations.

Saving and Restoring the Main Window Position

The last effect to consider is saving and restoring the actual location and size of the main application window. The key to these actions lies in the **WINDOWPLACEMENT** structure which is defined as

```
struct WINDOWPLACEMENT {
  UINT  length;
  UINT  flags;
  UINT  showCmd;
  POINT ptMinPosition;
  POINT ptMaxPosition;
  RECT  rcNormalPosition;
};
```

The **length** member specifies the length, in bytes, of the structure. Make sure that you set this member before calling the **GetWindowPlacement** or **SetWindowPlacement** functions —use `sizeof (WINDOWPLACEMENT)`.

The **flags** member control the position of the minimized window and how the window is to be restored. It can be either or both of these **WPF_RESTORETOMAXIMIZED** or **WPF_SETMINPOSITION**. **WPF_RESTORETOMAXIMIZED** says that the restored window will be maximized. It is only valid the next time the window is restored and does not change the default restoration behavior. It is only valid when the **SW_SHOWMINIMIZED** value is specified for the **showCmd** member. **WPF_SETMINPOSITION** says that the coordinates of the minimized window are specified in the **ptMinPosition** member.

The **showCmd** member provides the current show state of the window and can be one of:

SW_HIDE	**SW_MINIMIZE**	**SW_RESTORE**
SW_SHOW	**SW_SHOWMAXIMIZED**	**SW_SHOWMINIMIZED**
SW_SHOWNA	**SW_SHOWNOACTIVATE**	**SW_SHOWMINNOACTIVE**
SW_SHOWNORMAL		

The **ptMinPosition** member provides the coordinates of the window's upper-left corner when the window is minimized. The **ptMaxPosition** member gives the coordinates of the window's upper-left corner when the window is maximized. The **rcNormalPosition** contains the window's coordinates when the window is in the restored position.

I created two helper functions to read and write the window position. Both put the information into the main application ini file in the Windows folder. Each needs a section and a key word string, hence I used

```
static TCHAR BASED_CODE szSection[] = _T("Settings");
static TCHAR BASED_CODE szWindowPos[] = _T("WindowPos");
static TCHAR szFormat[] = _T("%u,%u,%d,%d,%d,%d,%d,%d,%d,%d");
```

The ReadWindowPlacement function begins by attempting to input the complete window placement string that was stored, placing the data in a **CString** object. If the data was obtained, I use a string scanf to convert the string data into the various members of a local copy of the **WINDOWPLACEMENT** structure. If the extraction process succeeds, I also move in the length of the structure and copy the entire contents into the passed structure

```
static BOOL PASCAL NEAR ReadWindowPlacement (LPWINDOWPLACEMENT pwp) {
CString strBuffer = AfxGetApp()->GetProfileString(szSection,
                                                  szWindowPos);
if (strBuffer.IsEmpty()) return FALSE;

WINDOWPLACEMENT wp;
int nRead = _stscanf (strBuffer, szFormat,
            &wp.flags, &wp.showCmd,
            &wp.ptMinPosition.x, &wp.ptMinPosition.y,
            &wp.ptMaxPosition.x, &wp.ptMaxPosition.y,
            &wp.rcNormalPosition.left, &wp.rcNormalPosition.top,
            &wp.rcNormalPosition.right, &wp.rcNormalPosition.bottom);
if (nRead != 10) return FALSE;

wp.length = sizeof wp;
```

```
*pwp = wp;
return TRUE;
}
```

The WriteWindowPlacement function does the reverse, given a **WINDOWPLACEMENT** instance, I convert the data into a long string and use **WriteProfileString** to save it in the ini file or in the Registry

```
static void PASCAL NEAR WriteWindowPlacement (LPWINDOWPLACEMENT pwp) {
 TCHAR szBuffer[sizeof("-32767")*8 + sizeof("65535")*2];
 wsprintf(szBuffer, szFormat,
            pwp->flags, pwp->showCmd,
            pwp->ptMinPosition.x, pwp->ptMinPosition.y,
            pwp->ptMaxPosition.x, pwp->ptMaxPosition.y,
            pwp->rcNormalPosition.left, pwp->rcNormalPosition.top,
            pwp->rcNormalPosition.right, pwp->rcNormalPosition.bottom);
 AfxGetApp ()->WriteProfileString (szSection, szWindowPos, szBuffer);
}
```

In **OnCreate** of the main window, after the base class is invoked and before the tool bars are created, I attempt to input any saved window placement data using the ReadWindowPlacement helper function. If the data exists, I call the **SetWindowPlacement** function passing this instance of the **WINDOWPLACEMENT** data

```
int        MainFrame::OnCreate (LPCREATESTRUCT lpCreateStruct) {
  if (CFrameWnd::OnCreate(lpCreateStruct) == -1) return -1;
  // load in any possible saved window placement data
  WINDOWPLACEMENT wp;
  if (ReadWindowPlacement(&wp))
   SetWindowPlacement(&wp);
```

Then in **OnClose**, I call **GetWindowPlacement** to retrieve the current state information. If the **IsZoomed** function returns TRUE, then the window is maximized and I set the flags accordingly by ORing in **WPF_RESTORETOMAXIMIZED**. And the WriteWindowPlacement helper function is called to actually write the information to the ini file or the Registry

```
WINDOWPLACEMENT wp;
wp.length = sizeof wp;
// get window location
if (GetWindowPlacement (&wp)) {
 wp.flags = 0;
 if (IsZoomed ()) wp.flags |= WPF_RESTORETOMAXIMIZED;
 // and write it to the .INI file
 WriteWindowPlacement(&wp);
}
CFrameWnd::OnClose();
```

The MainFrame Class Coding

For your reference, here is the complete MainFrame definition and implementation in one location.

Listing for MainFrame.h

```
#pragma once
#include "OptionsBar.h"        // access to the options controlbar
#include "MapControlBar.h"     // access to the map control bar
#include "MapLocalStatsBar.h"  // access to the map local stats bar
#include "EditBar.h"           // access to the edit bar
#include "PaletteBox.h"        // access to the palette box

#define INITSCROLL  25      // initial scroll percentage
#define INITZOOM     2      // initial zoom factor
#define INITSCALE 6000      // initial map scale
#define INITLAT      0      // initial map position
#define INITLON      0

/**********************************************************************/
/*                                                                    */
/* MainFrame: Apps main frame controls the various tool bars          */
/*                                                                    */
/**********************************************************************/

class MainFrame : public CFrameWnd {
protected: // create from serialization only
 MainFrame();
 DECLARE_DYNCREATE(MainFrame)
                                    // control bar embedded members
 CStatusBar          m_wndStatusBar;      // main status bar
 CToolBar            m_wndToolBar;        // main tool bar
 MapLocalStatsBar    maplocalstatsbar;    // map local stat bar
 MapControlBar       mapcontrolbar;       // map control bar
 OptionsBar          optionsbar;          // options bar
 EditBar             editbar;             // edit bar
 PaletteBox          palettebox;          // floating palette

public:
                     // helper function for docking
 void                DockControlBarLeftOf (CToolBar* Bar,CToolBar* LeftOf);

                     // get access to various control bars for displaying
 OptionsBar*         GetOptionsBar ();
 MapControlBar*      GetMapControlBar ();
 MapLocalStatsBar*   GetMapLocalStatsBar ();

 void                DisplayNewCaption (char*);  // display a new title
 void                DisplayOnStatusBar (char*); // display msg on statusbar
 virtual BOOL        PreCreateWindow(CREATESTRUCT& cs);
 virtual             ~MainFrame();

#ifdef _DEBUG
     virtual void AssertValid() const;
     virtual void Dump(CDumpContext& dc) const;
```

```
#endif

protected:
      afx_msg int OnCreate(LPCREATESTRUCT lpCreateStruct);
      afx_msg void OnViewToolbar();
      afx_msg void OnUpdateViewToolbar(CCmdUI* pCmdUI);
      afx_msg void OnViewStatusBar();
      afx_msg void OnUpdateViewStatusBar(CCmdUI* pCmdUI);
      afx_msg void OnViewMapControlBar();
      afx_msg void OnUpdateViewMapControlBar(CCmdUI* pCmdUI);
      afx_msg void OnViewMapLocalStatsBar();
      afx_msg void OnUpdateViewMapLocalStatsBar(CCmdUI* pCmdUI);
      afx_msg void OnViewOptionsBar();
      afx_msg void OnUpdateViewOptionsBar(CCmdUI* pCmdUI);
      afx_msg void OnClose();
      afx_msg void OnViewEditBar();
      afx_msg void OnUpdateViewEditBar(CCmdUI* pCmdUI);
      afx_msg void OnViewPaletteBox();
      afx_msg void OnUpdateViewPaletteBox(CCmdUI* pCmdUI);
 afx_msg void CmDummy ();
 afx_msg LRESULT FontChange (WPARAM, LPARAM); // respond to font changes
      DECLARE_MESSAGE_MAP()
};
```

Listing for MainFrame.cpp

```
...
IMPLEMENT_DYNCREATE(MainFrame, CFrameWnd)

/**************************************************************************/
/*                                                                        */
/* MainFrame Message Response Table                                       */
/*                                                                        */
/**************************************************************************/

BEGIN_MESSAGE_MAP(MainFrame, CFrameWnd)
 ON_WM_CREATE()
 ON_COMMAND(ID_VIEW_TOOLBAR, OnViewToolbar)
 ON_UPDATE_COMMAND_UI(ID_VIEW_TOOLBAR, OnUpdateViewToolbar)
 ON_COMMAND(ID_VIEW_STATUS_BAR, OnViewStatusBar)
 ON_UPDATE_COMMAND_UI(ID_VIEW_STATUS_BAR, OnUpdateViewStatusBar)
 ON_COMMAND(ID_VIEW_MAPCONTROLBAR, OnViewMapControlBar)
 ON_UPDATE_COMMAND_UI(ID_VIEW_MAPCONTROLBAR, OnUpdateViewMapControlBar)
 ON_COMMAND(ID_VIEW_MAPLOCALSTATSBAR, OnViewMapLocalStatsBar)
 ON_UPDATE_COMMAND_UI(ID_VIEW_MAPLOCALSTATSBAR, OnUpdateViewMapLocalStatsBar)
 ON_COMMAND(ID_VIEW_OPTIONSBAR, OnViewOptionsBar)
 ON_UPDATE_COMMAND_UI(ID_VIEW_OPTIONSBAR, OnUpdateViewOptionsBar)
 ON_WM_CLOSE()
 ON_COMMAND(ID_VIEW_EDITBAR, OnViewEditBar)
 ON_UPDATE_COMMAND_UI(ID_VIEW_EDITBAR, OnUpdateViewEditBar)
 ON_COMMAND(ID_VIEW_PALETTEBOX, OnViewPaletteBox)
 ON_MESSAGE(CM_FONT_CHANGE, FontChange)
 ON_UPDATE_COMMAND_UI(ID_VIEW_PALETTEBOX, OnUpdateViewPaletteBox)
END_MESSAGE_MAP()

static UINT indicators[] = {
      ID_SEPARATOR,              // status line indicator
```

```
        ID_INDICATOR_CAPS,
        ID_INDICATOR_NUM,
        ID_INDICATOR_SCRL,
};

static UINT BASED_CODE PaletteBox[] = {
  CM_LINE1,
  CM_LINE2,
  CM_LINE3,
  CM_LINE4,
  ID_SEPARATOR,
  ID_SEPARATOR,
  CM_COLOR_BLACK,
  CM_COLOR_RED,
  CM_COLOR_GREEN,
  CM_COLOR_YELLOW,
  CM_COLOR_BLUE,
  CM_COLOR_PURPLE,
};

/******************************************************************************/
/*                                                                          */
/* App's ini file section identifiers to be used to read/write placement    */
/*                                                                          */
/******************************************************************************/

static TCHAR BASED_CODE szSection[] = _T("Settings");
static TCHAR BASED_CODE szWindowPos[] = _T("WindowPos");
static TCHAR szFormat[] = _T("%u,%u,%d,%d,%d,%d,%d,%d,%d,%d");

/******************************************************************************/
/*                                                                          */
/* ReadWindowPlacement: read a window placement from the settings section   */
/*                      of an app's ini file                                */
/*                                                                          */
/******************************************************************************/

static BOOL PASCAL NEAR ReadWindowPlacement (LPWINDOWPLACEMENT pwp) {
 CString strBuffer = AfxGetApp()->GetProfileString(szSection, szWindowPos);
 if (strBuffer.IsEmpty())
  return FALSE;

 WINDOWPLACEMENT wp;
 int nRead = sscanf_s (strBuffer, szFormat,
                        &wp.flags, &wp.showCmd,
                        &wp.ptMinPosition.x, &wp.ptMinPosition.y,
                        &wp.ptMaxPosition.x, &wp.ptMaxPosition.y,
                        &wp.rcNormalPosition.left, &wp.rcNormalPosition.top,
                        &wp.rcNormalPosition.right,
                        &wp.rcNormalPosition.bottom);
 if (nRead != 10) return FALSE;

 wp.length = sizeof wp;
 *pwp = wp;
 return TRUE;
}

/******************************************************************************/
```

```
/*                                                                          */
/* WriteWindowPlacement: write window placement to settings section of      */
/*                       app's ini file                                     */
/*                                                                          */
/***************************************************************************/

static void PASCAL NEAR WriteWindowPlacement (LPWINDOWPLACEMENT pwp) {
 TCHAR szBuffer[sizeof("-32767")*8 + sizeof("65535")*2];
 wsprintf(szBuffer, szFormat,
          pwp->flags, pwp->showCmd,
          pwp->ptMinPosition.x, pwp->ptMinPosition.y,
          pwp->ptMaxPosition.x, pwp->ptMaxPosition.y,
          pwp->rcNormalPosition.left, pwp->rcNormalPosition.top,
          pwp->rcNormalPosition.right, pwp->rcNormalPosition.bottom);
 AfxGetApp ()->WriteProfileString (szSection, szWindowPos, szBuffer);
}

/***************************************************************************/
/*                                                                          */
/* MainFrame and ~MainFrame: default constuctor and destructor              */
/*                                                                          */
/***************************************************************************/

MainFrame::MainFrame () { }
MainFrame::~MainFrame () { }

/***************************************************************************/
/*                                                                          */
/* FontChange: pass on any user font change from the ComboBox               */
/*                                                                          */
/***************************************************************************/

LRESULT   MainFrame::FontChange (WPARAM, LPARAM lf) {
 CView *ptrview = GetActiveView ();
 if (ptrview) ptrview->PostMessage (CM_FONT_CHANGE, 0, lf);
 return 0;
}

/***************************************************************************/
/*                                                                          */
/* CmDummy: dummy command handler                                           */
/*                                                                          */
/***************************************************************************/

void      MainFrame::CmDummy () {
 MessageBox ("Not Implemented Yet", MB_OK);
}

/***************************************************************************/
/*                                                                          */
/* GetOptionsBar: retrieve the Options bar                                  */
/*                                                                          */
/***************************************************************************/

OptionsBar*        MainFrame::GetOptionsBar () {
 return &optionsbar;
}
```

```
/******************************************************************************/
/*                                                                            */
/* GetMapControlBar: retrieve the Map Control bar                             */
/*                                                                            */
/******************************************************************************/

MapControlBar*    MainFrame::GetMapControlBar () {
 return &mapcontrolbar;
}

/******************************************************************************/
/*                                                                            */
/* GetMapLocalStatsBar: retrieve the Map Local Stats Bar                      */
/*                                                                            */
/******************************************************************************/

MapLocalStatsBar* MainFrame::GetMapLocalStatsBar () {
 return &maplocalstatsbar;
}

/******************************************************************************/
/*                                                                            */
/* OnCreate: load tool bars and handle docking and any saved locations    */
/*                                                                            */
/******************************************************************************/

int       MainFrame::OnCreate (LPCREATESTRUCT lpCreateStruct) {
 if (CFrameWnd::OnCreate(lpCreateStruct) == -1)
  return -1;

 // load in any possible saved window placement data
 WINDOWPLACEMENT wp;
 if (ReadWindowPlacement(&wp))
  SetWindowPlacement(&wp);  // data exists so set up the window as it last was

 // create all bars
 if (m_wndToolBar.Create(this) &&    m_wndToolBar.LoadToolBar(IDR_MAINFRAME))
  if (maplocalstatsbar.Create (this))
   if (mapcontrolbar.Create (this))
    if (optionsbar.Create (this))
     if (editbar.Create (this))
      if (m_wndStatusBar.Create (this) &&
          m_wndStatusBar.SetIndicators (indicators,
          sizeof (indicators) / sizeof (UINT)))
       if (palettebox.Create (this, WS_CHILD | WS_VISIBLE | CBRS_SIZE_FIXED |
                      CBRS_TOP | CBRS_TOOLTIPS | CBRS_FLYBY, IDB_PALETTEBOX)
          && palettebox.LoadBitmap (IDB_PALETTEBOX)
          && palettebox.SetButtons (PaletteBox,
                                    sizeof(PaletteBox)/sizeof(UINT)));
       else {
        TRACE0 ("Failed to create palette box\n");
        return -1;
       }
      else {
       TRACE0 ("Failed to create status bar\n");
       return -1;
      }
     else {
```

```
      TRACE0("Failed to create edit bar\n");
      return -1;
     }
    else {
     TRACE0("Failed to create options bar\n");
     return -1;
    }
  else {
   TRACE0("Failed to create map control bar\n");
   return -1;
  }
 else {
  TRACE0("Failed to create map local stats bar\n");
  return -1;
 }
else {
 TRACE0("Failed to create toolbar\n");
 return -1;
}

// notify the framewindow of docking requirements
EnableDocking (CBRS_ALIGN_ANY);

m_wndToolBar.SetBarStyle (m_wndToolBar.GetBarStyle() |
                             CBRS_TOOLTIPS | CBRS_FLYBY | CBRS_SIZE_DYNAMIC);
m_wndToolBar.SetWindowText (_T("Main Tool Bar"));
m_wndToolBar.EnableDocking (CBRS_ALIGN_ANY);
DockControlBar (&m_wndToolBar);

editbar.SetWindowText (_T("Edit Bar"));
editbar.EnableDocking (CBRS_ALIGN_TOP | CBRS_ALIGN_BOTTOM);
DockControlBarLeftOf (&editbar,&m_wndToolBar);

palettebox.SetColumns (2); // set the palette box to 2 columns
palettebox.SetBarStyle (palettebox.GetBarStyle() |CBRS_TOOLTIPS |
                           CBRS_FLYBY);
palettebox.SetWindowText (_T("Pal"));
palettebox.EnableDocking (CBRS_ALIGN_ANY);
DockControlBar (&palettebox, AFX_IDW_DOCKBAR_LEFT);

mapcontrolbar.SetWindowText(_T("Map Controls"));
mapcontrolbar.EnableDocking (0);

maplocalstatsbar.SetWindowText(_T("Map Local Stats"));
maplocalstatsbar.EnableDocking (0);

optionsbar.SetWindowText(_T("Opt"));
optionsbar.EnableDocking (0);

// begin cut section - once you have the tool bars positioned to your
// desired location and have terminated the app, try commenting out
// this cut section from this point through the end cut comment below
// and just reload the tool bars - notice the very different actions

// in case this is the first time that the app is run and no state info
// is yet saved, set up an initial first position, and then based upon
// the actual setup, repeat process with the better guess for initial
// position
```

```
CRect r, q;
CPoint p;

GetClientRect (&r);                    // get window area less bars
maplocalstatsbar.GetWindowRect(&q); // get dims of Map Local Stats Bar
p.x = r.right - q.Width ();            // convert into a point placement
p.y = r.top + 30;
FloatControlBar (&maplocalstatsbar, p); // and float it here

p.y += 100;                            // insert an educated guess offset
FloatControlBar (&optionsbar, p);     // and float the Options Bar below it

mapcontrolbar.GetWindowRect (&q);     // get dims of Map Control Bar
p.x = r.right - q.Width ();            // install its location in point
p.y = r.bottom - q.Height ();
FloatControlBar (&mapcontrolbar, p);// now float it here

// force the layout to take effect
RepositionBars (AFX_IDW_CONTROLBAR_FIRST, AFX_IDW_CONTROLBAR_LAST,
                0, reposQuery, r);

// now construct a more optimum layout of the three floating bars
int top = r.top;
maplocalstatsbar.GetWindowRect(&q);
p.x = r.right - q.Width();
p.y = top;
ClientToScreen (&p);
FloatControlBar (&maplocalstatsbar, p);

top += q.Height () + 22;
p.y = top;
mapcontrolbar.GetWindowRect (&q);
p.x = r.right - q.Width ();
ClientToScreen (&p);
FloatControlBar (&mapcontrolbar, p);

top += q.Height () + 22;
p.y = top;
optionsbar.GetWindowRect (&q);
p.x = r.right - q.Width ();
ClientToScreen (&p);
FloatControlBar (&optionsbar, p);
// end of cut section

// now load in any previously saved states, beginning with the number of
// columns which is not saved by the SaveBarState function
palettebox.SetColumns (AfxGetApp ()->GetProfileInt (_T("General"),
                                        _T("Columns"), 2));
LoadBarState(_T("General"));
return 0;
}

/******************************************************************************/
/*                                                                          */
/* DockControlBarLeftOf: dock a control bar to the left of another bar      */
/*                                                                          */
/******************************************************************************/
```

```
void        MainFrame::DockControlBarLeftOf (CToolBar* Bar,CToolBar* LeftOf) {
 CRect rect;
 DWORD dw;
 UINT n;

 RecalcLayout (); // force MFC to adjust the dimensions of all docked ToolBars
 LeftOf->GetWindowRect (&rect);// get correct rectangle
 rect.OffsetRect (1,0);        // get first pixel position beyond for this bar
 dw=LeftOf->GetBarStyle ();    // determine how main bar is docked
 n = 0;
 n = (dw&CBRS_ALIGN_TOP) ? AFX_IDW_DOCKBAR_TOP : n;
 n = (dw&CBRS_ALIGN_BOTTOM && n==0) ? AFX_IDW_DOCKBAR_BOTTOM : n;
 n = (dw&CBRS_ALIGN_LEFT && n==0) ? AFX_IDW_DOCKBAR_LEFT : n;
 n = (dw&CBRS_ALIGN_RIGHT && n==0) ? AFX_IDW_DOCKBAR_RIGHT : n;

 // if the default parms are used,
 // DockControlBar will dock each Toolbar on a seperate line
 // By calculating a rectangle, we simulate a Toolbar being dragged to
 // that location and docked
 DockControlBar (Bar, n, &rect);
}

/******************************************************************************/
/*                                                                          */
/* DisplayNewCaption: install a new caption on the title bar                */
/*                                                                          */
/******************************************************************************/

void        MainFrame::DisplayNewCaption (char *msg) {
 SetWindowText (msg);
}

/******************************************************************************/
/*                                                                          */
/* DisplayOnStatusBar: show a message on the main status bar                */
/*                                                                          */
/******************************************************************************/

void        MainFrame::DisplayOnStatusBar (char *s) {
 m_wndStatusBar.SetPaneText (0, s);
}

/******************************************************************************/
/*                                                                          */
/* OnClose: store number of columns & store window placement with barstates*/
/*                                                                          */
/******************************************************************************/

void        MainFrame::OnClose () {
 // save all control bar states
 SaveBarState (_T("General"));
 AfxGetApp ()->WriteProfileInt (_T("General"), _T("Columns"),
                                palettebox.GetColumns ());
 WINDOWPLACEMENT wp;
 wp.length = sizeof wp;
 // get window location
 if (GetWindowPlacement (&wp)) {
  wp.flags = 0;
```

```
  if (IsZoomed ())          wp.flags |= WPF_RESTORETOMAXIMIZED;
  // and write it to the .INI file
  WriteWindowPlacement (&wp);
 }
 CFrameWnd::OnClose ();
}


/*************************************************************************/
/*                                                                     */
/* PreCreateWindow: setup window style options                         */
/*                                                                     */
/*************************************************************************/

BOOL      MainFrame::PreCreateWindow (CREATESTRUCT& cs) {
 cs.style = WS_OVERLAPPED | WS_CAPTION | FWS_ADDTOTITLE | WS_THICKFRAME |
            WS_SYSMENU | WS_MINIMIZEBOX | WS_MAXIMIZEBOX | WS_MAXIMIZE;
 return CFrameWnd::PreCreateWindow (cs);
}


/*************************************************************************/
/*                                                                     */
/* OnViewToolbar: hide/show main tool bar                              */
/*                                                                     */
/*************************************************************************/

void      MainFrame::OnViewToolbar () {
 if ((m_wndToolBar.GetStyle () & WS_VISIBLE) != 0)
  ShowControlBar (&m_wndToolBar, FALSE, FALSE);
 else
  ShowControlBar (&m_wndToolBar, TRUE, FALSE);
 m_wndToolBar.Invalidate ();
}


/*************************************************************************/
/*                                                                     */
/* OnUpdateViewToolbar: enable hide/show main tool bar                 */
/*                                                                     */
/*************************************************************************/

void      MainFrame::OnUpdateViewToolbar (CCmdUI* pCmdUI) {
 pCmdUI->SetCheck (m_wndToolBar.GetStyle () & WS_VISIBLE);
}


/*************************************************************************/
/*                                                                     */
/* OnViewStatusBar: hide/show the main status bar                      */
/*                                                                     */
/*************************************************************************/

void      MainFrame::OnViewStatusBar () {
 if ((m_wndStatusBar.GetStyle () & WS_VISIBLE) != 0)
  ShowControlBar (&m_wndStatusBar, FALSE, FALSE);
 else
  ShowControlBar (&m_wndStatusBar, TRUE, FALSE);
 m_wndStatusBar.Invalidate ();
}


/*************************************************************************/
```

```
/*                                                                          */
/* OnUpdateViewStatusBar: enable hide/show the main status bar              */
/*                                                                          */
/****************************************************************************/

void      MainFrame::OnUpdateViewStatusBar (CCmdUI* pCmdUI) {
 pCmdUI->SetCheck (m_wndStatusBar.GetStyle () & WS_VISIBLE);
}

/****************************************************************************/
/*                                                                          */
/* OnViewMapControlBar: hide/show Map Control Bar                           */
/*                                                                          */
/****************************************************************************/

void      MainFrame::OnViewMapControlBar () {
 if ((mapcontrolbar.GetStyle () & WS_VISIBLE) != 0)
  ShowControlBar (&mapcontrolbar, FALSE, FALSE);
 else
  ShowControlBar (&mapcontrolbar, TRUE, FALSE);
 mapcontrolbar.Invalidate ();
}

/****************************************************************************/
/*                                                                          */
/* OnUpdateViewMapControlBar: enable hide/show Map Control Bar              */
/*                                                                          */
/****************************************************************************/

void      MainFrame::OnUpdateViewMapControlBar (CCmdUI* pCmdUI) {
 pCmdUI->SetCheck (mapcontrolbar.GetStyle () & WS_VISIBLE);
}

/****************************************************************************/
/*                                                                          */
/* OnViewMapLocalStatsBar: hide/show Map Local Stats Bar                    */
/*                                                                          */
/****************************************************************************/

void      MainFrame::OnViewMapLocalStatsBar () {
 if ((maplocalstatsbar.GetStyle () & WS_VISIBLE) != 0)
  ShowControlBar (&maplocalstatsbar, FALSE, FALSE);
 else
  ShowControlBar (&maplocalstatsbar, TRUE, FALSE);
 maplocalstatsbar.Invalidate ();
}

/****************************************************************************/
/*                                                                          */
/* OnUpdateViewMapLocalStatsBar: enable hide/show Map Local Stats Bar       */
/*                                                                          */
/****************************************************************************/

void      MainFrame::OnUpdateViewMapLocalStatsBar (CCmdUI* pCmdUI) {
 pCmdUI->SetCheck (maplocalstatsbar.GetStyle () & WS_VISIBLE);
}

/****************************************************************************/
```

```
/*                                                                      */
/* OnViewOptionsBar: hide/show the Options Bar                          */
/*                                                                      */
/**********************************************************************/

void      MainFrame::OnViewOptionsBar () {
 if ((optionsbar.GetStyle () & WS_VISIBLE) != 0)
  ShowControlBar (&optionsbar, FALSE, FALSE);
 else
  ShowControlBar (&optionsbar, TRUE, FALSE);
 optionsbar.Invalidate ();
}


/**********************************************************************/
/*                                                                      */
/* OnUpdateViewOptionsBar: enable hide/show Options bar                 */
/*                                                                      */
/**********************************************************************/

void      MainFrame::OnUpdateViewOptionsBar (CCmdUI* pCmdUI) {
 pCmdUI->SetCheck (optionsbar.GetStyle () & WS_VISIBLE);
}


/**********************************************************************/
/*                                                                      */
/* OnViewEditBar: hide/show the Edit Bar                                */
/*                                                                      */
/**********************************************************************/

void      MainFrame::OnViewEditBar () {
 if ((editbar.GetStyle () & WS_VISIBLE) != 0)
  ShowControlBar (&editbar, FALSE, FALSE);
 else
  ShowControlBar (&editbar, TRUE, FALSE);
 editbar.Invalidate ();
}


/**********************************************************************/
/*                                                                      */
/* OnUpdateViewEditBar: enable hide/show EditBar                        */
/*                                                                      */
/**********************************************************************/

void      MainFrame::OnUpdateViewEditBar (CCmdUI* pCmdUI) {
 pCmdUI->SetCheck (editbar.GetStyle () & WS_VISIBLE);
}


/**********************************************************************/
/*                                                                      */
/* OnViewPaletteBox: hide/show the Palette Box                          */
/*                                                                      */
/**********************************************************************/

void      MainFrame::OnViewPaletteBox() {
 if ((palettebox.GetStyle () & WS_VISIBLE) != 0)
  ShowControlBar (&palettebox, FALSE, FALSE);
 else
  ShowControlBar (&palettebox, TRUE, FALSE);
```

```
palettebox.Invalidate ();
}

/******************************************************************/
/*                                                                */
/* OnUpdateViewPaletteBox: enable hide/show Palette Box           */
/*                                                                */
/******************************************************************/

void      MainFrame::OnUpdateViewPaletteBox (CCmdUI *pCmdUI) {
 pCmdUI->SetCheck (palettebox.GetStyle () & WS_VISIBLE);
}
...
```

The Pgm10aApp class launches the MainFrame and the doc-view components. The RetrievePath function locates from the registry, if possible, the name of the image file to load into the document class.

Listing for Pgm10aApp.cpp

```
/******************************************************************/
/*                                                                */
/* Pgm10aApp Message Response Table                               */
/*                                                                */
/******************************************************************/

BEGIN_MESSAGE_MAP(Pgm10aApp, CWinApp)
 ON_COMMAND(ID_APP_ABOUT, OnAppAbout)
 ON_COMMAND(ID_FILE_NEW, CWinApp::OnFileNew)
 ON_COMMAND(ID_FILE_OPEN, CWinApp::OnFileOpen)
END_MESSAGE_MAP()

Pgm10aApp::Pgm10aApp() { }

/******************************************************************/
/*                                                                */
/* The actual instance of this app                               */
/*                                                                */
/******************************************************************/

Pgm10aApp theApp;

/******************************************************************/
/*                                                                */
/* InitInstance: launch the app with a default file              */
/*                                                                */
/******************************************************************/

BOOL Pgm10aApp::InitInstance () {
 SetRegistryKey ("WindowsMFCII"); // setup the higher level reg key
 LoadStdProfileSettings (); // Load standard INI file options (including MRU)

 // Register document templates
 CSingleDocTemplate* pDocTemplate;
 pDocTemplate = new CSingleDocTemplate (IDR_MAINFRAME,
                                        RUNTIME_CLASS (GeoDoc),
```

```
                                    RUNTIME_CLASS (MainFrame),
                                    RUNTIME_CLASS (GeoView));
AddDocTemplate (pDocTemplate);

// Enable DDE Execute open
EnableShellOpen ();
RegisterShellFileTypes (TRUE);

// Parse command line for standard shell commands, DDE, file open
CCommandLineInfo cmdInfo;
ParseCommandLine (cmdInfo);
// can set a default filename if there are none on the command line
if (cmdInfo.m_nShellCommand == CCommandLineInfo::FileNew) {
 cmdInfo.m_nShellCommand = CCommandLineInfo::FileOpen;
 cmdInfo.m_strFileName = RetrievePath ();
 if (cmdInfo.m_strFileName.IsEmpty())
   cmdInfo.m_strFileName = "res\\Europe.bmp";
}

// Dispatch commands specified on the command line
if (!ProcessShellCommand (cmdInfo))
 return FALSE;

// Enable drag/drop open
m_pMainWnd->DragAcceptFiles ();

return TRUE;
}

/******************************************************************************/
/*                                                                            */
/* RetrievePath: obtain the installed path from the system registry           */
/*                                                                            */
/******************************************************************************/

CString   Pgm10aApp::RetrievePath () {
 CString subkey = "SOFTWARE\\WindowsMFCII\\Pgm10a\\Recent File List";
 CString entry = "File1";
 CString filename = "";

 HKEY hkey;
 // attempt to open the current user main key with our value
 LONG ok = RegOpenKeyEx (HKEY_CURRENT_USER, subkey, 0, KEY_READ, &hkey);
 if (ok == ERROR_SUCCESS) {
  DWORD dwType, dwCount;
  // key exists, now verify config path entry is a string
  ok = RegQueryValueEx (hkey, entry, NULL, &dwType, NULL, &dwCount);
  if (ok == ERROR_SUCCESS && dwType == REG_SZ) {
   // now retrieve the actual path string
   ok = RegQueryValueEx (hkey, entry, NULL, &dwType,
                        (LPBYTE) filename.GetBuffer (dwCount/sizeof(TCHAR)),
                        &dwCount);
   filename.ReleaseBuffer(); // release the CString buffer locked by GetBuffer
  }
  RegCloseKey (hkey);
 }
 return filename;
}
```

The GeoDoc and GeoView Classes

The GeoDoc class simply inputs a bitmap image using our CDib class discussed in chapter 7. The CDib class is not shown here.

Listing for File: GeoDoc.h

```
#pragma once
#include "CDib.h"

class GeoDoc : public CDocument {
protected: // create from serialization only
     GeoDoc();
     DECLARE_DYNCREATE(GeoDoc)

 CDib    *ptrdocdib;    // the CDib object
public:
       CDib* GetDib ();
     virtual BOOL OnNewDocument();
     virtual void Serialize(CArchive& ar);
     virtual void DeleteContents();
     virtual      ~GeoDoc();

#ifdef _DEBUG
     virtual void AssertValid() const;
     virtual void Dump(CDumpContext& dc) const;
#endif
     DECLARE_MESSAGE_MAP()
};
```

Listing for File: GeoDoc.cpp

```
...
/*********************************************************************/
/*                                                                   */
/* GeoDoc: container for the CDib Object                             */
/*                                                                   */
/*********************************************************************/

IMPLEMENT_DYNCREATE(GeoDoc, CDocument)

BEGIN_MESSAGE_MAP(GeoDoc, CDocument)
END_MESSAGE_MAP()

GeoDoc::GeoDoc() {
 ptrdocdib  = NULL;
}

GeoDoc::~GeoDoc() {
 if (ptrdocdib)  delete ptrdocdib;
}

BOOL GeoDoc::OnNewDocument() {
 if (!CDocument::OnNewDocument())
  return FALSE;
```

```
 return TRUE;
}

/*****************************************************************/
/*                                                               */
/* Serialization: construct the CDib object                      */
/*                                                               */
/*****************************************************************/

void GeoDoc::Serialize(CArchive& ar) {
 if (ar.IsStoring()) { }
 else {
  CFile *ptrfile = ar.GetFile ();      // get the CFile in use
  ptrdocdib = new CDib (ptrfile);      // construct the DIB using the CFile
  if (!ptrdocdib || !ptrdocdib->IsValid ()) {
   AfxMessageBox ("Bmp Viewer Error: Unable to Load the .BMP file", MB_OK);
   delete ptrdocdib;
  }
 }
}

/*****************************************************************/
/*                                                               */
/* GetDib: returns ptr to the CDib object                        */
/*                                                               */
/*****************************************************************/

CDib*      GeoDoc::GetDib () {
 if (ptrdocdib && ptrdocdib->IsValid ()) return ptrdocdib;
 else return NULL;
}

void GeoDoc::DeleteContents() {
 if (ptrdocdib) delete ptrdocdib;
 ptrdocdib  = NULL;
     CDocument::DeleteContents();
}
...
```

The GeoView class is derived from **CScrollView** and pretty much parallels the view discussed in chapter 7 also.

Listing for File: GeoView.h

```
#pragma once
#include "Position.h"
#include "CDib.h"

class GeoView : public CScrollView {
protected: // create from serialization only
 GeoView();
 DECLARE_DYNCREATE(GeoView)

 Position center;
 double   scale;
 int      zoom;
```

```
int       scroll;
char      date[20];
char      time[20];
CDib      *ptrdib;          // the CDib itself
CPalette *ptrpalette;       // the palette for the memory dc
CSize     bmp_size;         // the size of the DIB
CSize     t_size;           // CScrollView scrolling total size
LOGFONT  *ptrlf;

public:
          GeoDoc* GetDocument ();
     virtual void OnDraw(CDC* pDC);  // overridden to draw this view
     virtual void OnInitialUpdate();
     virtual     ~GeoView();
          void  OnUpdate (CView*, LPARAM, CObject*);
protected:
 void ReadSetUpProfileData ();
 void WriteSetUpProfileData ();

 afx_msg void  CmDummy ();
 afx_msg void  OnDestroy();
 afx_msg void  OnKeyDown (UINT key, UINT, UINT); // provide keybd scroll help
 afx_msg void  OnPaletteChanged (CWnd*);         // make best of another palette
 afx_msg BOOL  OnQueryNewPalette ();             // reset palette when gain focus

 LRESULT   FontChange (WPARAM, LPARAM);          // respond to font changes
 LRESULT   OnDisplayChange (WPARAM, LPARAM);     // changed display settings
 void      AdjustBmpLoading ();                  // handle new load options
 void      AdjustDisplayOptions ();              // handle new display options
 void      RemoveObjects ();                     // deletes all memory DC obj
 DECLARE_MESSAGE_MAP()

#ifndef _DEBUG  // debug version in Pgm10aView.cpp
inline GeoDoc* GeoView::GetDocument() { return (GeoDoc*)m_pDocument; }
#endif
...
```

Listing for File: GeoView.h

```
...
/**********************************************************************************/
/*                                                                              */
/* defines for the default settings                                             */
/*                                                                              */
/**********************************************************************************/

#define INITSCROLL  25      // initial scroll percentage
#define INITZOOM     2      // initial zoom factor
#define INITSCALE 6000      // initial map scale

IMPLEMENT_DYNCREATE(GeoView, CScrollView)

/**********************************************************************************/
/*                                                                              */
/* GeoView Message Response Table                                               */
/*                                                                              */
/**********************************************************************************/
```

```
BEGIN_MESSAGE_MAP(GeoView, CScrollView)
 ON_WM_DESTROY()
 ON_WM_PALETTECHANGED ()
 ON_WM_QUERYNEWPALETTE ()
 ON_MESSAGE (CM_FONT_CHANGE, FontChange)
 ON_MESSAGE(WM_DISPLAYCHANGE,        OnDisplayChange)
 ON_BN_CLICKED (CM_MAPCB_UPLEFT, CmDummy)
 ON_BN_CLICKED (CM_MAPCB_UP, CmDummy)
 ON_BN_CLICKED (CM_MAPCB_UPRIGHT, CmDummy)
 ON_BN_CLICKED (CM_MAPCB_LEFT, CmDummy)
 ON_BN_CLICKED (CM_MAPCB_RIGHT, CmDummy)
 ON_BN_CLICKED (CM_MAPCB_SETSCALE, CmDummy)
 ON_BN_CLICKED (CM_MAPCB_DOWNLEFT, CmDummy)
 ON_BN_CLICKED (CM_MAPCB_DOWN, CmDummy)
 ON_BN_CLICKED (CM_MAPCB_DOWNRIGHT, CmDummy)
 ON_BN_CLICKED (CM_MAPCB_SETCENTER, CmDummy)
 ON_BN_CLICKED (CM_MAPCB_SETZOOM, CmDummy)
 ON_BN_CLICKED (CM_MAPCB_SETSCROLL, CmDummy)
 ON_BN_CLICKED (CM_MAPCB_ZOOM_IN, CmDummy)
 ON_BN_CLICKED (CM_MAPCB_ZOOM_OUT, CmDummy)
 ON_BN_CLICKED (CM_OPTIONS_SHOW_CITY, CmDummy)
 ON_BN_CLICKED (CM_OPTIONS_SHOW_TERRAIN, CmDummy)
 ON_BN_CLICKED (CM_OPTIONS_SHOW_FACTORY, CmDummy)
 ON_BN_CLICKED (CM_OPTIONS_SHOW_WEATHER, CmDummy)
 ON_BN_CLICKED (CM_OPTIONS_SHOW_SHIPYARD, CmDummy)
 ON_BN_CLICKED (ID_EDIT_CUT, CmDummy)
 ON_BN_CLICKED (ID_EDIT_COPY, CmDummy)
 ON_BN_CLICKED (ID_EDIT_PASTE, CmDummy)
 ON_BN_CLICKED (CM_LINE1, CmDummy)
 ON_BN_CLICKED (CM_LINE2, CmDummy)
 ON_BN_CLICKED (CM_LINE3, CmDummy)
 ON_BN_CLICKED (CM_LINE4, CmDummy)
 ON_BN_CLICKED (CM_COLOR_BLACK, CmDummy)
 ON_BN_CLICKED (CM_COLOR_RED, CmDummy)
 ON_BN_CLICKED (CM_COLOR_BLUE, CmDummy)
 ON_BN_CLICKED (CM_COLOR_GREEN, CmDummy)
 ON_BN_CLICKED (CM_COLOR_YELLOW, CmDummy)
 ON_BN_CLICKED (CM_COLOR_PURPLE, CmDummy)
END_MESSAGE_MAP()

/*******************************************************************************/
/*                                                                            */
/* GeoView: constructor sets object pointers to NULL                          */
/*                                                                            */
/*******************************************************************************/

GeoView::GeoView () {
 ptrpalette = NULL;
 ptrdib     = NULL;
 ptrlf      = NULL;
}


/*******************************************************************************/
/*                                                                            */
/* ~GeoView: remove objects                                                   */
/*                                                                            */
/*******************************************************************************/
```

```
GeoView::~GeoView () {
 RemoveObjects ();
 if (ptrlf) delete ptrlf;
}

/****************************************************************************/
/*                                                                        */
/* FontChange: respond to font change messages from ComboBox              */
/*                                                                        */
/****************************************************************************/

LRESULT   GeoView::FontChange (WPARAM, LPARAM lf) {
 // if no LOGFONT is allocated, get one; otherwise reuse it
 if (!ptrlf) ptrlf = new LOGFONT;
 // copy in the user's choice
 memcpy (ptrlf, (LOGFONT*) lf, sizeof(LOGFONT));
 // install a 12 point version
 ptrlf->lfHeight = -12;
 ptrlf->lfWidth = 0;
 // paint the text window in this font
 Invalidate ();
 return 0;
}

/****************************************************************************/
/*                                                                        */
/* CmDummy: dummy function for command handlers                           */
/*                                                                        */
/****************************************************************************/

void      GeoView::CmDummy () {
 MessageBox ("Not Implemented Yet", MB_OK);
}

/****************************************************************************/
/*                                                                        */
/* OnDraw: paint the CDib and if there is a font, show the text           */
/*                                                                        */
/****************************************************************************/

void      GeoView::OnDraw (CDC* pDC) {
 GeoDoc* pDoc = GetDocument ();
 ASSERT_VALID(pDoc);
 MainFrame *ptrfrm = (MainFrame*) (AfxGetApp()->m_pMainWnd);
 if (!ptrfrm) return;

 // display a new caption and display a test statusbar message
 ptrfrm->DisplayNewCaption ("Geographical Maps - Test New Caption");
 ptrfrm->DisplayOnStatusBar ("Test status bar message");

 // first step is to install a color palette if doing screen or preview
 if (ptrdib) {
  if (!ptrpalette) {                    // case LOADDIB has no palette yet
   ptrpalette = new CPalette ();        // so make the basic palette
   ptrdib->MakePalette (ptrpalette);
  }
  if (ptrpalette) {                     // use existing palette
   pDC->SelectPalette (ptrpalette, FALSE);
```

```
    pDC->RealizePalette ();
  }
  pDC->SetStretchBltMode (COLORONCOLOR); // set for optimum color convert
 }

 // screen display - use the Dib
 if (ptrdib)
  // dib origin is backwards in height - copy dib bits to screen
  // fairly slow operation, if much copying is needed, use memory DC
  SetDIBitsToDevice (pDC->m_hDC, 0, 0, bmp_size.cx, bmp_size.cy,
                     0, 0, 0, bmp_size.cy, ptrdib-> GetDibBitsAddr (),
                     ptrdib->GetBitmapInfo (), DIB_RGB_COLORS);

 // if there is a user font chosen, display a bit of text in that font
 if (ptrlf) {
  CFont font;
  font.CreateFontIndirect (ptrlf);
  CFont *ptroldfont = pDC->SelectObject (&font);
  pDC->TextOut (10, 10, "Hello");
  pDC->SelectObject (ptroldfont);
 }
}

/**********************************************************************/
/*                                                                    */
/* OnInitialUpdate: Load user profile data, display on MapControlBar  */
/*                                                                    */
/**********************************************************************/

void      GeoView::OnInitialUpdate () {
 // load user profile data
 MainFrame *ptrfrm = (MainFrame*) (AfxGetApp ()->m_pMainWnd);
 if (!ptrfrm) return;
 ReadSetUpProfileData ();
 // display initial settings on the Map Control Bar
  ptrfrm->GetMapControlBar ()->DisplayAll (&center,  zoom,  scroll,  scale);


 // display some data on the Map Local Stats Bar
 char pos[30];
 center.FormatPosition (pos, sizeof (pos));
 ptrfrm->GetMapLocalStatsBar ()->DisplayDayTime (date, time);
 ptrfrm->GetMapLocalStatsBar ()->DisplayMapNowAtValues (
  "Europe", pos, time, date, "5:30", "6:30", "Partly Cloudy", "Light Mud");

 // display a new caption and a test message on the statusbar
 ptrfrm->DisplayNewCaption ("Geographical Maps - Test New Caption");
 ptrfrm->DisplayOnStatusBar ("Test status bar message");

 AdjustBmpLoading ();      // handle load options
 AdjustDisplayOptions (); // handle display options
 CScrollView::OnInitialUpdate();
}

/**********************************************************************/
/*                                                                    */
/* ReadSetUpProfileData - input any position, map values, and date/time */
/*                                                                    */
```

```
/**************************************************************************/

void       GeoView::ReadSetUpProfileData () {
 char section[40];
 char entry[40];
 char latstr[10], lonstr[10];
 long lat, lon;
 char file[80];

 HINSTANCE hs = AfxGetApp()->m_hInstance;
 LoadString (hs, IDS_GEO_INI, file, sizeof(file));

 LoadString (hs, IDS_GEO_PROFILE_DEMOMAP, section, sizeof(section));
 LoadString (hs, IDS_GEO_PROFILE_DATE, entry, sizeof (entry));
 GetPrivateProfileString (section, entry, "0", date, sizeof(date), file);
 LoadString (hs, IDS_GEO_PROFILE_TIME, entry, sizeof (entry));
 GetPrivateProfileString (section, entry, "0", time, sizeof(time), file);

 LoadString (hs, IDS_GEO_PROFILE_LAT, entry, sizeof (entry));
 GetPrivateProfileString (section, entry, "0", latstr, sizeof (latstr),
                          file);
 LoadString (hs, IDS_GEO_PROFILE_LON, entry, sizeof (entry));
 GetPrivateProfileString (section, entry, "0", lonstr, sizeof (lonstr),
                          file);
 lat = atol (latstr);
 lon = atol (lonstr);
 center.SetLatLon (lat, lon);

 LoadString (hs, IDS_GEO_PROFILE_ZOOM, entry, sizeof (entry));
 zoom = GetPrivateProfileInt (section, entry, INITZOOM, file);
 LoadString (hs, IDS_GEO_PROFILE_SCROL, entry, sizeof (entry));
 scroll = GetPrivateProfileInt (section, entry, INITSCROLL, file);
 LoadString (hs, IDS_GEO_PROFILE_SCALE, entry, sizeof (entry));
 GetPrivateProfileString (section, entry, "INITSCALE", lonstr,
                          sizeof (lonstr), file);
 scale = atof (lonstr);
}

/**************************************************************************/
/*                                                                        */
/* WriteSetUpProfileData - output any position, map values, and date/time */
/*                                                                        */
/**************************************************************************/

void       GeoView::WriteSetUpProfileData () {
 char section[40];
 char entry[40];
 char latstr[10], lonstr[10];
 char file[80];

 HINSTANCE hs = AfxGetApp()->m_hInstance;
 LoadString (hs, IDS_GEO_INI, file, sizeof(file));

 LoadString (hs, IDS_GEO_PROFILE_DEMOMAP, section, sizeof(section));
 LoadString (hs, IDS_GEO_PROFILE_DATE, entry, sizeof (entry));
 WritePrivateProfileString (section, entry, date, file);
 LoadString (hs, IDS_GEO_PROFILE_TIME, entry, sizeof (entry));
 WritePrivateProfileString (section, entry, time, file);
```

```
wsprintf (latstr, "%ld", center.Latitude);
wsprintf (lonstr, "%ld", center.Longitude);
LoadString (hs, IDS_GEO_PROFILE_LAT, entry, sizeof (entry));
WritePrivateProfileString (section, entry, latstr, file);
LoadString (hs, IDS_GEO_PROFILE_LON, entry, sizeof (entry));
WritePrivateProfileString (section, entry, lonstr, file);

LoadString (hs, IDS_GEO_PROFILE_ZOOM, entry, sizeof (entry));
wsprintf (latstr, "%d",  zoom);
WritePrivateProfileString (section, entry, latstr, file);
LoadString (hs, IDS_GEO_PROFILE_SCROL, entry, sizeof (entry));
wsprintf (latstr, "%d",  scroll);
WritePrivateProfileString (section, entry, latstr, file);
LoadString (hs, IDS_GEO_PROFILE_SCALE, entry, sizeof (entry));
sprintf_s (latstr, sizeof(latstr), "%7.2f", scale);
WritePrivateProfileString (section, entry, latstr, file);
}

/****************************************************************************/
/*                                                                        */
/* OnDestroy: save the user profile data                                  */
/*                                                                        */
/****************************************************************************/

void GeoView::OnDestroy () {
 WriteSetUpProfileData ();
     CScrollView::OnDestroy ();
}

/****************************************************************************/
/*                                                                        */
/* RemoveObjects: delete all items associated with a dib                  */
/*                                                                        */
/****************************************************************************/

void     GeoView::RemoveObjects () {
 if (ptrpalette) delete ptrpalette;
 ptrpalette = NULL;
}

/****************************************************************************/
/*                                                                        */
/* OnUpdate: reload bitmap, set display options, update window            */
/*                                                                        */
/****************************************************************************/

void     GeoView::OnUpdate (CView *ptrsender, LPARAM hint, CObject *ptrdata) {
 AdjustBmpLoading ();      // handle load options
 AdjustDisplayOptions (); // handle display options
 CScrollView::OnUpdate (ptrsender, hint, ptrdata); // pass on to base class
}

/****************************************************************************/
/*                                                                        */
/* AdjustBmpLoading: handle Bmp Load options                              */
/*                                                                        */
/****************************************************************************/
```

```
void        GeoView::AdjustBmpLoading () {
 RemoveObjects ();
 ptrdib = GetDocument ()->GetDib ();          // acquire the DIB from the document
 if (!ptrdib) {                               // here there is no DIB loaded
  bmp_size = CSize (0, 0);                     // set sizes to null
  t_size = bmp_size;
 }
 else {                                       // here there is a DIB
  bmp_size.cx = ptrdib->GetDibWidth ();       // save DIB's true size
  bmp_size.cy = ptrdib->GetDibHeight ();
  t_size = bmp_size;                          // use DIB size as scroll view's size
  ptrpalette = new CPalette ();               // construct a basic palette
  ptrdib->MakePalette (ptrpalette);
 }
}

/***************************************************************************/
/*                                                                       */
/* AdjustDisplayOptions: handle display options                          */
/*                                                                       */
/***************************************************************************/

void        GeoView::AdjustDisplayOptions () {
 if (ptrdib) SetScrollSizes (MM_TEXT, t_size, CSize (10, 10), CSize (1, 1));
 else SetScrollSizes (MM_TEXT, CSize (0, 0), CSize (10, 10), CSize (1, 1));
}

/***************************************************************************/
/*                                                                       */
/* OnPaletteChanged: realize our palette when system palette changes     */
/*                                                                       */
/***************************************************************************/

void        GeoView::OnPaletteChanged (CWnd *ptrwin) {
 if (ptrwin == this) return;     // ignore our own changing
 OnQueryNewPalette ();
}

/***************************************************************************/
/*                                                                       */
/* OnQueryNewPalette: upon window activation, realize our palette        */
/*                                                                       */
/***************************************************************************/

BOOL        GeoView::OnQueryNewPalette () {
 if (!ptrdib) return 0;
 BOOL delete_palette = FALSE;
 CDC *ptrdc = GetDC ();
 if (!ptrpalette) {
  ptrpalette = new CPalette ();
  ptrdib->MakePalette (ptrpalette);
  if (ptrpalette) delete_palette = TRUE;  // flag it for deletion
  else return 0;
 }
 CPalette *ptroldpal = ptrdc->SelectPalette (ptrpalette, FALSE);
 UINT num = ptrdc->RealizePalette ();
 if (num) InvalidateRect (NULL, TRUE);
 ptrdc->SelectPalette (ptroldpal, TRUE);
```

```
 ptrdc->RealizePalette ();
 ReleaseDC (ptrdc);
 if (delete_palette) delete ptrpalette;
 return (BOOL) num;
}

/****************************************************************************/
/*                                                                        */
/* OnDisplayChange: user has changed the display settings, must update    */
/*                                                                        */
/****************************************************************************/

LRESULT   GeoView::OnDisplayChange (WPARAM which, LPARAM lp) {
 LRESULT retcd = CScrollView::OnDisplayChange (which, lp);
 AdjustBmpLoading ();
 AdjustDisplayOptions ();
 return retcd;
}

/****************************************************************************/
/*                                                                        */
/* OnKeyDown: provide a keyboard scroller interface                       */
/*                                                                        */
/****************************************************************************/

void      GeoView::OnKeyDown (UINT key, UINT, UINT) {
 // check for and handle any possible keyboard scroll request
 switch (key) {

  case VK_UP:                      // requests scroll up 1 line
    SendMessage (WM_VSCROLL, SB_LINEUP, 0L);  break;

  case VK_DOWN:                     // requests scroll down 1 line
    SendMessage (WM_VSCROLL, SB_LINEDOWN, 0L); break;

  case VK_LEFT:  // requests scroll left 1 col
    SendMessage (WM_HSCROLL, SB_LINEUP, 0L); break;

  case VK_RIGHT: // requests scroll right 1 col
    SendMessage (WM_HSCROLL, SB_LINEDOWN, 0L); break;

  case VK_PRIOR: // request scroll 1 page up
    SendMessage (WM_VSCROLL, SB_PAGEUP, 0L); break;

  case VK_NEXT:  // request scroll 1 page down
    SendMessage (WM_VSCROLL, SB_PAGEDOWN, 0L); break;

  case VK_END:    // request goto the bottom
    SendMessage (WM_HSCROLL, SB_PAGEDOWN, 0L); break;

  case VK_HOME:  // request goto the top
    SendMessage (WM_HSCROLL, SB_PAGEUP, 0L);  break;
 }
}

#ifdef _DEBUG
void GeoView::AssertValid() const { CScrollView::AssertValid(); }
void GeoView::Dump(CDumpContext& dc) const { CScrollView::Dump(dc); }
```

```
GeoDoc* GeoView::GetDocument() {// non-debug version is inline
        ASSERT(m_pDocument->IsKindOf(RUNTIME_CLASS(GeoDoc)));
        return (GeoDoc*)m_pDocument;
}
#endif //_DEBUG
```

There are just a couple of minor points in **OnDraw**. In order to display information in either the caption bar or the status bar, a pointer to the main frame window is needed. Thus, the first actions of **OnDraw** are

```
GeoDoc* pDoc = GetDocument();
ASSERT_VALID(pDoc);
MainFrame *ptrfrm = (MainFrame*) (AfxGetApp()->m_pMainWnd);
if (!ptrfrm) return;
```

Next, the sample messages are shown using these new helper functions of the MainFrame class. Notice that it is more convenient to use helper functions if frequent messages are needed than to continually dynamically obtain a pointer to the status bar

```
// display a new caption and display a test statusbar message
ptrfrm->DisplayNewCaption (
                          "Geographical Maps - Test New Caption");
ptrfrm->DisplayOnStatusBar ("Test status bar message");
```

The middle section of **OnDraw** handles obtaining a palette if needed and displaying the bitmap

```
// first step is to install a color palette if doing screen or preview
    if (ptrdib) {
      if (!ptrpalette) {              // case LOADDIB has no palette yet
       ptrpalette = new CPalette ();      // so make the basic palette
       ptrdib->MakePalette (ptrpalette);
      }
      if (ptrpalette) {                        // use existing palette
       pDC->SelectPalette (ptrpalette, FALSE);
       pDC->RealizePalette ();
      }
     pDC->SetStretchBltMode (COLORONCOLOR);
     // set for optimum color convert
    }
    // screen display - use the Dib
    if (ptrdib)
     // dib origin is backwards in height - copy dib bits to screen
// fairly slow operation, if much copying is needed, use memory DC
    SetDIBitsToDevice (pDC->m_hDC, 0, 0, bmp_size.cx, bmp_size.cy,
                  0, 0, 0, bmp_size.cy, ptrdib-> GetDibBitsAddr (),
                  ptrdib->GetBitmapInfo (), DIB_RGB_COLORS);
```

Finally, if the user has chosen a font from the combo box, the text is displayed

```
    if (ptrlf) {
     CFont font;
     font.CreateFontIndirect (ptrlf);
     CFont *ptroldfont = pDC->SelectObject (&font);
```

```
    pDC->TextOut (10, 10, "Hello");
    pDC->SelectObject (ptroldfont);
}
```

The Position Class

The game deals a lot with latitude and longitude, denoting locations on the earth. The Position class encapsulates a lat, lon location, providing support for keeping the values in range.

Listing for File: Position.h

```
#pragma once

//              convert long latitude into degrees, minutes, seconds, N/S
void  cvdlat (long &deg, long &min, long &sec, char *ns, long &llat);

//              convert long longitude into degrees, minutes, seconds, E/W
void  cvdlon (long &deg, long &min, long &sec, char *ew, long &llon);

/*********************************************************************/
/*                                                                 */
/* Map Defines: Map Limits and related constants                   */
/*                                                                 */
/*********************************************************************/

#define MAXLON      1296000L                // maximum longitude = 360 degrees
#define HALFLON      648000L                // 180 degrees longitude

#define TOPLAT      80*3600L                // upper map limit = 80 degrees
#define BOTLAT     -60*3600L                // lower map limit = -60 degrees

/*********************************************************************/
/*                                                                 */
/* Position: Stores a map position Latitude and Longitude          */
/*                                                                 */
/*********************************************************************/

class Position {

    /*********************************************************************/
    /*                                                                 */
    /* Data Members                                                    */
    /*                                                                 */
    /*********************************************************************/

public:

    long Latitude;
    long Longitude;

    /*********************************************************************/
    /*                                                                 */
    /* Functions:                                                      */
    /*                                                                 */
```

```
    /*****************************************************************/

public:

    // constructors

                // null constructor - sets lat, lon to 0
        Position ();

                // long constructor - sets lat,lon to long values
        Position (long lat, long lon);

                // construct from deg, min, sec, and string dirs N,S and E,W
        Position (long& latdeg, long& latmin, long& latsec, char *latdir,
                  long& londeg, long& lonmin, long& lonsec, char *londir);

                // construct from deg, min, sec, where S and W are negative
        Position (long& latdeg, long& latmin, long& latsec,
                  long& londeg, long& lonmin, long& lonsec);

                // copy constructor
        Position (Position& pos);


    // set lat or lon functions - follow above schemes

    void    SetLat (long lat);
    void    SetLat (long& deg, long& min, long& sec, char *dir);
    void    SetLat (long& deg, long& min, long& sec);

    void    SetLon (long lon);
    void    SetLon (long& deg, long& min, long& sec, char *dir);
    void    SetLon (long& deg, long& min, long& sec);

    void    SetLatLon (long lat, long lon);

    // accessing functions

    // formats a 24 byte char far string: N 75 34 22   E 123 43 22

    void     FormatPosition (char* line, unsigned int maxlen);

    // converts lat, lon into deg, min, sec and string directions

    void     PositionToLong (long& latdeg, long& latmin, long& latsec,
                             char *latdir, long& londeg, long& lonmin,
                             long& lonsec, char *londir);

    Position&  operator= (Position& pos);
    };
```

Listing for File: Position.cpp

```
#include "stdafx.h"
#pragma hdrstop
#include <math.h>
#include "position.h"              // class definition

/******************************************************************************/
/*                                                                          */
/* Position Class Functions: Store and Manipulate a Position - Lat, Lon     */
/*                                                                          */
/******************************************************************************/

/******************************************************************************/
/*                                                                          */
/* Position (); Null Constructor - assigns 0,0                              */
/*                                                                          */
/******************************************************************************/

Position::Position () {
 Latitude  = 0;
 Longitude = 0;
}

/******************************************************************************/
/*                                                                          */
/* Position (long, long) - constructs Lat, Lon from long values             */
/*                                                                          */
/******************************************************************************/

Position::Position (long lat, long lon) {
 // verify in range
 if (lat > TOPLAT) lat = TOPLAT;
 else if (lat < BOTLAT) lat = BOTLAT;

 while (lon > MAXLON) lon -= MAXLON;
 while (lon < 0 ) lon += MAXLON;

 // assign valid position
 Latitude = lat;
 Longitude = lon;
}

/******************************************************************************/
/*                                                                          */
/* Position - constructs Lat, Lon from deg, min, sec, and string Direction */
/*                                                                          */
/******************************************************************************/

Position::Position (long& latdeg, long& latmin, long& latsec, char *latdir,
                    long& londeg, long& lonmin, long& lonsec, char *londir){
 SetLat (latdeg, latmin, latsec, latdir);
 SetLon (londeg, lonmin, lonsec, londir);
}

/******************************************************************************/
/*                                                                          */
/* Position - constructs Lat, Lon from deg, min, sec, where negatives = S/W*/
/*                                                                          */
```

```
/******************************************************************************/

Position::Position (long& latdeg, long& latmin, long& latsec,
                    long& londeg, long& lonmin, long& lonsec) {
 SetLat (latdeg, latmin, latsec);
 SetLon (londeg, lonmin, lonsec);
}

/******************************************************************************/
/*                                                                          */
/* Position (Position&) copy constructor                                    */
/*                                                                          */
/******************************************************************************/

Position::Position (Position& pos) { // copy constructor
 Latitude  = pos.Latitude;
 Longitude = pos.Longitude;
}

/******************************************************************************/
/*                                                                          */
/* SetLat (long) - sets Lat from a long latitude value                      */
/*                                                                          */
/******************************************************************************/

void Position::SetLat    (long lat) {
 if (lat > TOPLAT) lat = TOPLAT;         // force into in range
 else if (lat < BOTLAT) lat = BOTLAT;
 Latitude = lat;                         // and store latitude
}

/******************************************************************************/
/*                                                                          */
/* SetLat - sets Lat from deg, min, sec and string direction N or S         */
/*                                                                          */
/******************************************************************************/

void Position::SetLat    (long& deg, long& min, long& sec, char *dir) {
 long lat = (deg<90)? abs(deg)*3600L + abs(min)*60L + abs(sec): 90*3600L;
 if (dir[0] == 'S' || dir[0] == 's') lat = -lat;
 if (lat > TOPLAT) lat = TOPLAT;         // force into in range
 else if (lat < BOTLAT) lat = BOTLAT;
 Latitude = lat;                         // and store latitude
}

/******************************************************************************/
/*                                                                          */
/* SetLat - sets Lat from deg, min, sec where neg values = S lat            */
/*                                                                          */
/******************************************************************************/

void Position::SetLat    (long& deg, long& min, long& sec) {
 // N latitudes are positive, S latitudes are negative
 long lat = abs(deg)*3600L + abs(min)*60L + abs(sec);
 if (deg<0) lat = -lat;
 if (lat > TOPLAT) lat = TOPLAT;         // force into in range
 else if (lat < BOTLAT) lat = BOTLAT;
 Latitude = lat;                         // and store latitude
```

```
}
/**********************************************************************/
/*                                                                    */
/* SetLon (long) - sets Lon from a long value                         */
/*                                                                    */
/**********************************************************************/

void Position::SetLon    (long lon) {
 while (lon > MAXLON) lon -= MAXLON;
 while (lon < 0 ) lon += MAXLON;
 Longitude = lon;
}


/**********************************************************************/
/*                                                                    */
/* SetLon - sets Lon from deg, min, sec, and string direction W or E  */
/*                                                                    */
/**********************************************************************/

void Position::SetLon    (long& deg, long& min, long& sec, char *dir) {
 // dir W longitude is negative, E long is positive
 // if - deg => W long => 180 + (180 -(|deg.min.sec|)) => 360 + deg.min.sec
 // if + deg => E long => deg.min.sec
 long lon = abs(deg)*3600L + abs(min)*60L + abs(sec);
 if (lon>HALFLON) lon = HALFLON;
 if (lon<-HALFLON) lon = -HALFLON;
 lon = (dir[0] == 'W' || dir[0] == 'w') ? MAXLON - lon : lon;
 while (lon > MAXLON) lon -= MAXLON;
 while (lon < 0 ) lon += MAXLON;
 Longitude = lon;
}


/**********************************************************************/
/*                                                                    */
/* SetLon - sets Lon from deg, min, sec where W longs are negative    */
/*                                                                    */
/**********************************************************************/

void Position::SetLon    (long& deg, long& min, long& sec) {
 // W longitude is negative, E long is positive
 // if - deg => W long => 180 + (180 -(|deg.min.sec|)) => 360 + deg.min.sec
 // if + deg => E long => deg.min.sec
 long lon = abs(deg)*3600L + abs(min)*60L + abs(sec);
 lon = (deg<0 || min<0 || sec<0) ? MAXLON - lon : lon;
 while (lon > MAXLON) lon -= MAXLON;
 while (lon < 0 ) lon += MAXLON;
 Longitude = lon;
}


/**********************************************************************/
/*                                                                    */
/* SetLatLon - sets both Lat and Lon from pair of longs               */
/*                                                                    */
/**********************************************************************/

void    Position::SetLatLon (long lat, long lon) {
 SetLat (lat);
```

```
  SetLon (lon);
}

/*******************************************************************************/
/*                                                                           */
/* FormatPosition - fills string with displayable form of position           */
/*                                                                           */
/* requires a string of length: 24 bytes: N 73 32 13   E 123 43 12           */
/*                                                                           */
/*******************************************************************************/

void  Position::FormatPosition (char* line, unsigned int maxlen) {
 long latdeg, latmin, latsec, londeg, lonmin, lonsec;
 char latdir[2], londir[2];

 cvdlat (latdeg, latmin, latsec, latdir, Latitude);
 cvdlon (londeg, lonmin, lonsec, londir, Longitude);

 sprintf_s (line, maxlen, "%c %02ld %02ld %02ld   %c %03ld %02ld %02ld",
        latdir[0], latdeg, latmin, latsec, londir[0], londeg, lonmin, lonsec);
}

/*******************************************************************************/
/*                                                                           */
/* PositionToInt - converts a Position into long values for updating         */
/*                                                                           */
/*******************************************************************************/

void  Position::PositionToLong (
                long& latdeg, long& latmin, long& latsec, char *latdir,
                long& londeg, long& lonmin, long& lonsec, char *londir) {
 cvdlat (latdeg, latmin, latsec, latdir, Latitude);
 cvdlon (londeg, lonmin, lonsec, londir, Longitude);
}

/*******************************************************************************/
/*                                                                           */
/* Operator = assigns passed position into this position                     */
/*                                                                           */
/*******************************************************************************/

Position&  Position::operator= (Position& pos) {
 Latitude  = pos.Latitude;
 Longitude = pos.Longitude;
 return *this;
}

/*******************************************************************************/
/*                                                                           */
/* cvdlat: long latitude in sec converted to deg, min, sec and N/S letter     */
/*                                                                           */
/*******************************************************************************/

void cvdlat (long &deg, long &min, long &sec, char *ns, long &llat) {
 long x = labs(llat);

 if (x > TOPLAT) x = TOPLAT;          // force into range
 else if (x < BOTLAT) x = BOTLAT;
```

```
deg = (long) (x/3600);
x -= deg*3600L;
min = (long) (x/60);
sec = (long) (x - min*60L);
if (llat<0) {
 ns[0]='S';
 ns[1]=0;
 }
 else {
 ns[0]='N';
 ns[1]=0;
 }
}

/*****************************************************************************/
/*                                                                         */
/* cvdlon: converts long lon in sec to deg, min, sec and E/W letter        */
/*                                                                         */
/*****************************************************************************/

void cvdlon (long &deg, long &min, long &sec, char *ew, long &llon) {
 long x = llon;

 while (x > MAXLON) x -= MAXLON; // guarantee in range
 while (x < 0) x += MAXLON;

 // if - deg => W long => 180 + (180 -(|deg.min.sec|)) => 360 + deg.min.sec
 // if + deg => E long => deg.min.sec

 if (x > HALFLON) {
 ew[0]='W';
 ew[1]=0;
 x = MAXLON - x;
 }
 else {
 ew[0]='E';
 ew[1]=0;
 }
 deg = (long) (x/3600);
 x -= deg*3600L;
 min = (long) (x/60);
 sec = (long) (x - min*60L);
}
```

In summary, by saving and restoring both the window placement and the state of the tool bars, a more professional looking application can be created.

Chapter 11 Complex Document Handling

Pgm11b contains four Multi-view sample programs. The idea is to have two different document classes, each with two different view classes on them. One by one, we will improve the working model.

Multi-view Sample 1

In this first sample, I took totally wizard generated coding for all documents and views. So that we can tell them apart, document one handles .txt files, while document two handles .dat files. The files are below and Figure 11.1 shows both docs are open with both views.

MultiviewDatDoc
MultiviewDatView—a green window
MultiviewDat2View—a blue window

MultiviewTxtDoc
MultiviewTxtView—a red window
MultiviewTxt2View—a yellow

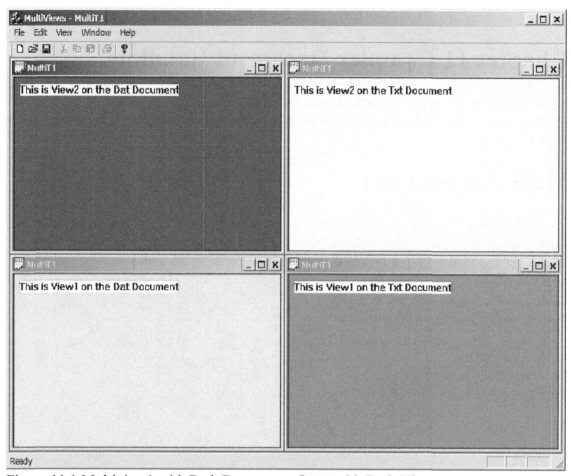

Figure 11.1 Multiview1 with Both Documents Open with Both Views

Notice several important points. On the menu, there is nothing to tell us what is what, which document is active or which view. On the View menu is the default item New View. What view gets opened? It all depends on which view is active of the four! Not much help. It's worse than that. When you choose New Document, the Document Manager does not know which one is desired and so presents you with the menu shown in Figure 11.2.

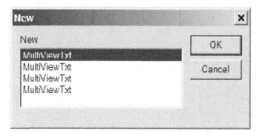

Figure 11.2 Choose Document Desired

Ugh, this does not have the dat document here at all, or so it seems. Yet, if you select either of the bottom two entries, you get view one or two of the dat document. This is totally confusing to the user.

Let's see how the coding goes. In the **CWinApp** class, the document templates are allocated, before the main window is created.

```
BOOL MultiViewsApp::InitInstance() {
 // Change the registry key under which our settings are stored.
 SetRegistryKey(_T("WindowsMFCII"));
 LoadStdProfileSettings();  // Load standard INI file options (including MRU)

 // Register document templates
 CMultiDocTemplate* pDocTemplateTxt1;
 CMultiDocTemplate* pDocTemplateTxt2;
 CMultiDocTemplate* pDocTemplateDat1;
 CMultiDocTemplate* pDocTemplateDat2;

 pDocTemplateTxt1 = new CMultiDocTemplate(
         IDR_MULTITTYPE,
         RUNTIME_CLASS(MultiViewTxtDoc),
         RUNTIME_CLASS(ChildFrame), // custom MDI child frame
         RUNTIME_CLASS(MultiViewTxtView));
 AddDocTemplate(pDocTemplateTxt1);

 pDocTemplateTxt2 = new CMultiDocTemplate(
         IDR_MULTITTYPE,
         RUNTIME_CLASS(MultiViewTxtDoc),
         RUNTIME_CLASS(ChildFrame), // custom MDI child frame
         RUNTIME_CLASS(MultiViewTxt2View));
 AddDocTemplate(pDocTemplateTxt2);

 pDocTemplateDat1 = new CMultiDocTemplate(
         IDR_MULTITTYPE,
         RUNTIME_CLASS(MultiViewDatDoc),
         RUNTIME_CLASS(ChildFrame), // custom MDI child frame
         RUNTIME_CLASS(MultiViewDatView));
 AddDocTemplate(pDocTemplateDat1);

 pDocTemplateDat2 = new CMultiDocTemplate(
         IDR_MULTITTYPE,
         RUNTIME_CLASS(MultiViewDatDoc),
         RUNTIME_CLASS(ChildFrame), // custom MDI child frame
         RUNTIME_CLASS(MultiViewDat2View));
 AddDocTemplate(pDocTemplateDat2);

 // create main MDI Frame window
 MainFrame* pMainFrame = new MainFrame;
 if (!pMainFrame->LoadFrame(IDR_MAINFRAME))
  return FALSE;
 m_pMainWnd = pMainFrame;
...
```

The key to part of the misbehavior lies in the duplicated use of the identifier IDR_MULTITYPE in all four templates. Tied to this identifier are all of the needed resources for this template, including the all important string.

```
IDR_MULTITTYPE    "\nMultiT\nMultiViewTxt\nMultiViewTxt    Files
(*.txt)\n.txt\nMultiViewTxt.Document\nMultiViewTxt Document"
```

This is why we see the identical messages in Figure 11.2 above.

Each document class should have its own string defining the types of files it can handle.

Each of these classes are just shells created by the wizard. All they do is show the colored window with the text identifier message. Open the project and examine them, if desired. Run the sample to observe the "bad" behavior. Obviously, we cannot just take basic default behavior from the framework when we have multiple documents and views in our applications. Further, what if there are different menus that must be present for each type of document? Remember that this ID also tells the framework which toolbar and menu must be loaded.

Multi-View Sample 2

In the second sample, part of the deficiencies are remedied. Figure 11.3 shows the same windows. That is, both docs are opened, each with both views. However, notice that with the dat view 2 being the active view, on the main menu, there is now a Dat Menu specific to this doc-view. In Figure 11.4, the Document Manager's menu now shows the two different documents, although we have to guess which view is which on each document.

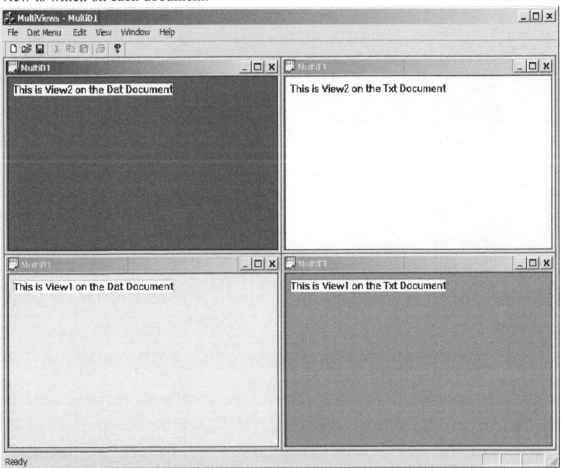

Figure 11.3 Multiview2 with Both Docs, Each with Both Views Open + Menu

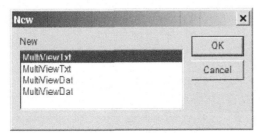

Figure 11.4 Doc Manager Menu

What changes have been made? First, in the resource file, I defined another type string and associated menu.

```
IDR_MULTITXT     "\nMultiT\nMultiViewTxt\nMultiViewTxt    Files
(*.txt)\n.txt\nMultiViewTxt.Document\nMultiViewTxt Document"
IDR_MULTIDAT     "\nMultiD\nMultiViewDat\nMultiViewDat    Files
(*.dat)\n.dat\nMultiViewDat.Document\nMultiViewDat Document"

IDR_MULTITXT MENU PRELOAD DISCARDABLE
BEGIN
    POPUP "&File"
    BEGIN
        MENUITEM "&New\tCtrl+N",                 ID_FILE_NEW
        MENUITEM "&Open...\tCtrl+O",             ID_FILE_OPEN
        MENUITEM "&Close",                       ID_FILE_CLOSE
        MENUITEM "&Save\tCtrl+S",                ID_FILE_SAVE
        MENUITEM "Save &As...",                  ID_FILE_SAVE_AS
        MENUITEM SEPARATOR
        MENUITEM "Recent File",                  ID_FILE_MRU_FILE1, GRAYED
        MENUITEM SEPARATOR
        MENUITEM "E&xit",                        ID_APP_EXIT
    END
    MENUITEM "Txt Menu",                 CM_TXTDOC
    POPUP "&Edit"
    BEGIN
        MENUITEM "&Undo\tCtrl+Z",            ID_EDIT_UNDO
        MENUITEM SEPARATOR
        MENUITEM "Cu&t\tCtrl+X",             ID_EDIT_CUT
        MENUITEM "&Copy\tCtrl+C",            ID_EDIT_COPY
        MENUITEM "&Paste\tCtrl+V",           ID_EDIT_PASTE
    END
    POPUP "&View"
    BEGIN
        MENUITEM "&Toolbar",                 ID_VIEW_TOOLBAR
        MENUITEM "&Status Bar",              ID_VIEW_STATUS_BAR
    END
    POPUP "&Window"
    BEGIN
        MENUITEM "&New Window",              ID_WINDOW_NEW
        MENUITEM "&Cascade",                 ID_WINDOW_CASCADE
        MENUITEM "&Tile",                    ID_WINDOW_TILE_HORZ
        MENUITEM "&Arrange Icons",           ID_WINDOW_ARRANGE
    END
    POPUP "&Help"
    BEGIN
        MENUITEM "&About MultiViews...",     ID_APP_ABOUT
    END
END

IDR_MULTIDAT MENU PRELOAD DISCARDABLE
BEGIN
    POPUP "&File"
    BEGIN
        MENUITEM "&New\tCtrl+N",                 ID_FILE_NEW
        MENUITEM "&Open...\tCtrl+O",             ID_FILE_OPEN
        MENUITEM "&Close",                       ID_FILE_CLOSE
        MENUITEM "&Save\tCtrl+S",                ID_FILE_SAVE
```

```
        MENUITEM "Save &As...",                         ID_FILE_SAVE_AS
        MENUITEM SEPARATOR
        MENUITEM "Recent File",                         ID_FILE_MRU_FILE1, GRAYED
        MENUITEM SEPARATOR
        MENUITEM "E&xit",                               ID_APP_EXIT
    END
    MENUITEM "&Dat Menu ",                      CM_MULTIDAT
    POPUP "&Edit"
    BEGIN
        MENUITEM "&Undo\tCtrl+Z",                       ID_EDIT_UNDO
        MENUITEM SEPARATOR
        MENUITEM "Cu&t\tCtrl+X",                        ID_EDIT_CUT
        MENUITEM "&Copy\tCtrl+C",                       ID_EDIT_COPY
        MENUITEM "&Paste\tCtrl+V",                      ID_EDIT_PASTE
    END
    POPUP "&View"
    BEGIN
        MENUITEM "&Toolbar",                            ID_VIEW_TOOLBAR
        MENUITEM "&Status Bar",                         ID_VIEW_STATUS_BAR
    END
    POPUP "&Window"
    BEGIN
        MENUITEM "&New Window",                         ID_WINDOW_NEW
        MENUITEM "&Cascade",                            ID_WINDOW_CASCADE
        MENUITEM "&Tile",                               ID_WINDOW_TILE_HORZ
        MENUITEM "&Arrange Icons",                      ID_WINDOW_ARRANGE
    END
    POPUP "&Help"
    BEGIN
        MENUITEM "&About MultiViews...",        ID_APP_ABOUT
    END
END
```

Next, in the app class, I used the two different identifiers in the template constructions. No coding in the different classes was done. Now we get a better working model, well mostly.

```
BOOL MultiViewsApp::InitInstance() {
 SetRegistryKey(_T("WindowsMFCII"));
 LoadStdProfileSettings();  // Load standard INI file options (including MRU)

 // Register document templates
 CMultiDocTemplate* pDocTemplateTxt1;
 CMultiDocTemplate* pDocTemplateTxt2;
 CMultiDocTemplate* pDocTemplateDat1;
 CMultiDocTemplate* pDocTemplateDat2;

 pDocTemplateTxt1 = new CMultiDocTemplate(
        IDR_MULTITXT,
        RUNTIME_CLASS(MultiViewTxtDoc),
        RUNTIME_CLASS(ChildFrame), // custom MDI child frame
        RUNTIME_CLASS(MultiViewTxtView));
 AddDocTemplate(pDocTemplateTxt1);

 pDocTemplateTxt2 = new CMultiDocTemplate(
        IDR_MULTITXT,
        RUNTIME_CLASS(MultiViewTxtDoc),
        RUNTIME_CLASS(ChildFrame), // custom MDI child frame
        RUNTIME_CLASS(MultiViewTxt2View));
```

```
AddDocTemplate(pDocTemplateTxt2);


pDocTemplateDat1 = new CMultiDocTemplate(
        IDR_MULTIDAT,
        RUNTIME_CLASS(MultiViewDatDoc),
        RUNTIME_CLASS(ChildFrame), // custom MDI child frame
        RUNTIME_CLASS(MultiViewDatView));
AddDocTemplate(pDocTemplateDat1);

pDocTemplateDat2 = new CMultiDocTemplate(
        IDR_MULTIDAT,
        RUNTIME_CLASS(MultiViewDatDoc),
        RUNTIME_CLASS(ChildFrame), // custom MDI child frame
        RUNTIME_CLASS(MultiViewDat2View));
AddDocTemplate(pDocTemplateDat2);

// create main MDI Frame window
MainFrame* pMainFrame = new MainFrame;
if (!pMainFrame->LoadFrame(IDR_MAINFRAME))
 return FALSE;
m_pMainWnd = pMainFrame;
```

Everything is handled except the views. The next sample handles that.

Multi-View Sample 3

In this next version, I am overriding the Document Manager to display a far better dialog for the user to pick which doc and view to launch. Figure 11.5 shows the views while Figure 11.6 shows the Document Manager menu. Notice too that the document is keeping track of the number of open views on it.

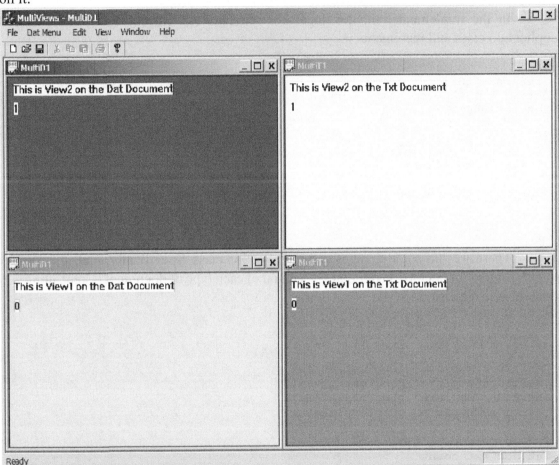

Figure 11.5 Multiview 3 with Both Documents Open with Both Views

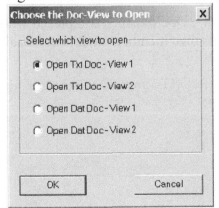

Figure 11.6 Choose Doc to Open

First, the document classes have a new data member, our_id.

```
class MultiViewTxtDoc : public CDocument {
protected: // create from serialization only
 MultiViewTxtDoc();
 DECLARE_DYNCREATE(MultiViewTxtDoc)

 int our_id;
```

In the implementation, the document retrieves the current count being stored in the application class and increments it.

```
BOOL MultiViewTxtDoc::OnNewDocument() {
 if (!CDocument::OnNewDocument())
  return FALSE;
 our_id = theApp.doc_txt_count++;
 return TRUE;
}

void MultiViewTxtDoc::Serialize(CArchive& ar) {
 if (ar.IsStoring()) { }
 else {
  our_id = theApp.doc_txt_count++;
 }
}
```

There are thus some changes to the application class. Specifically, each document template must be stored for later use in our dialog. A count of each type of document is kept along with which document is requested.

```
class MultiViewsApp : public CWinApp {
public:
 MultiViewsApp();

 CMultiDocTemplate* pDocTemplateTxt1;
 CMultiDocTemplate* pDocTemplateTxt2;
 CMultiDocTemplate* pDocTemplateDat1;
 CMultiDocTemplate* pDocTemplateDat2;

 int which_doc;
 int doc_txt_count;
 int doc_dat_count;
```

In the implementation, notice that the member m_pDocManager is replaced with a new instance of mine. Each of the four templates is stored in its own member variable as it is allocated.

```
BOOL MultiViewsApp::InitInstance() {
 SetRegistryKey(_T("WindowsMFCII"));
 LoadStdProfileSettings();  // Load standard INI file options (including MRU)

 // Register document templates
 which_doc = 0;
 m_pDocManager = new MyDocManager;
 doc_txt_count = 0;
 doc_dat_count = 0;

 pDocTemplateTxt1 = new CMultiDocTemplate(
           IDR_MULTITXT,
```

```
              RUNTIME_CLASS(MultiViewTxtDoc),
              RUNTIME_CLASS(ChildFrame), // custom MDI child frame
              RUNTIME_CLASS(MultiViewTxtView));
AddDocTemplate(pDocTemplateTxt1);

pDocTemplateTxt2 = new CMultiDocTemplate(
              IDR_MULTITXT,
              RUNTIME_CLASS(MultiViewTxtDoc),
              RUNTIME_CLASS(ChildFrame), // custom MDI child frame
              RUNTIME_CLASS(MultiViewTxt2View));
AddDocTemplate(pDocTemplateTxt2);


pDocTemplateDat1 = new CMultiDocTemplate(
              IDR_MULTIDAT,
              RUNTIME_CLASS(MultiViewDatDoc),
              RUNTIME_CLASS(ChildFrame), // custom MDI child frame
              RUNTIME_CLASS(MultiViewDatView));
AddDocTemplate(pDocTemplateDat1);

pDocTemplateDat2 = new CMultiDocTemplate(
              IDR_MULTIDAT,
              RUNTIME_CLASS(MultiViewDatDoc),
              RUNTIME_CLASS(ChildFrame), // custom MDI child frame
              RUNTIME_CLASS(MultiViewDat2View));
AddDocTemplate(pDocTemplateDat2);

// create main MDI Frame window
MainFrame* pMainFrame = new MainFrame;
if (!pMainFrame->LoadFrame(IDR_MAINFRAME))
  return FALSE;
m_pMainWnd = pMainFrame;
```

Here is the definition of MyDocManager replacement class. I want to override OnFileNew to show the proper choose dialog. I must also override DoPromptFileName and AppendFilerSuffix, the latter is a static member function of the Document Manager.

```
#pragma once

class MyDocManager : public CDocManager {

public:
      MyDocManager ();
 void  OnFileNew();
 BOOL  DoPromptFileName (CString &fileName, UINT nIDSTitle,
                         DWORD lFlags, BOOL bOpenFileDialog,
                         CDocTemplate* pTemplate);

static void  AppendFilterSuffix (CString& filter, OPENFILENAME& ofn,
                         CDocTemplate* pTemplate,
                         CString* pstrDefaultExt);
int which;
};
```

The implementation is a bit involved. Let's examine it piece by piece.

```
...
extern MultiViewsApp theApp;
```

```
MyDocManager::MyDocManager () : CDocManager () {
 which = 0;
}

void  MyDocManager::OnFileNew() {
 if (m_templateList.IsEmpty()) {
  TRACE0("Error: no document templates registered with CWinApp.\n");
  AfxMessageBox(AFX_IDP_FAILED_TO_CREATE_DOC);
  return;
 }
 bool newf = true;
```

Now grab the first template in the array and launch our fancy ChooseViewToOpen dialog. Save the user's choice in the app's member which and switch on it. Store the correct template in pTemplate. Then if once is chosen, use that template pointer to invoke **OpenDocumentFile**. Either a new file is opened or DoPromptFIleName is called to get that new filename.

```
 CDocTemplate* pTemplate = (CDocTemplate*)m_templateList.GetHead();
 which = 0;
 ChooseViewToOpen dlg (&which);
 if (dlg.DoModal() != IDOK) return;
 theApp.which_doc = which;
 switch (which) {
  case CHOOSE_TXT_VIEW_1:
   pTemplate = theApp.pDocTemplateTxt1;
   break;
  case CHOOSE_TXT_VIEW_2:
   pTemplate = theApp.pDocTemplateTxt2;
   newf = true;
// you can force an open to occur and never a new  by setting newf to false
   break;
  case CHOOSE_DAT_VIEW_1:
   pTemplate = theApp.pDocTemplateDat1;
   break;
  case CHOOSE_DAT_VIEW_2:
   pTemplate = theApp.pDocTemplateDat2;
   break;
  default:
   pTemplate = theApp.pDocTemplateTxt1;
 };

 if (newf) pTemplate->OpenDocumentFile(NULL);
 else {
  CString newName;
  if (!DoPromptFileName(newName, AFX_IDS_OPENFILE,
     OFN_HIDEREADONLY | OFN_FILEMUSTEXIST, TRUE, pTemplate))
   return; // open cancelled
  pTemplate->OpenDocumentFile(newName);
 }
}
```

When prompting the user for the file to open, we must construct the file filters that appear in the drop down combo box, files of type. In this case, *.txt and *.dat.

```
BOOL     MyDocManager::DoPromptFileName (CString& fileName, UINT nIDSTitle,
                                DWORD lFlags, BOOL bOpenFileDialog,
                                CDocTemplate* pTemplate) {
 CFileDialog dlgFile(bOpenFileDialog);
```

```
CString title;
VERIFY(title.LoadString(nIDSTitle));
dlgFile.m_ofn.Flags |= lFlags;
CString strFilter;
CString strDefault;
if (pTemplate != NULL)          {
 ASSERT_VALID(pTemplate);
 AppendFilterSuffix(strFilter, dlgFile.m_ofn, pTemplate, &strDefault);
 dlgFile.m_ofn.nFilterIndex = 1;
}
else {
 pTemplate = theApp.pDocTemplateTxt1;
 AppendFilterSuffix (strFilter, dlgFile.m_ofn, pTemplate, &strDefault);
 pTemplate = theApp.pDocTemplateTxt2;
 AppendFilterSuffix (strFilter, dlgFile.m_ofn, pTemplate, NULL);
 pTemplate = theApp.pDocTemplateDat1;
 AppendFilterSuffix (strFilter, dlgFile.m_ofn, pTemplate, NULL);
 pTemplate = theApp.pDocTemplateDat2;
 AppendFilterSuffix (strFilter, dlgFile.m_ofn, pTemplate, NULL);
 switch (which) {
   case 0: case 1: dlgFile.m_ofn.nFilterIndex = 0; break;
   case 2: case 3: dlgFile.m_ofn.nFilterIndex = 2; break;
 };
}
// append the "*.*" all files filter
CString allFilter;
VERIFY(allFilter.LoadString(AFX_IDS_ALLFILTER));
strFilter += allFilter;
strFilter += (TCHAR)'\0';   // next string please
strFilter += _T("*.*");
strFilter += (TCHAR)'\0';   // last string
dlgFile.m_ofn.nMaxCustFilter++;

dlgFile.m_ofn.lpstrFilter = strFilter;
dlgFile.m_ofn.lpstrTitle = title;
dlgFile.m_ofn.lpstrFile = fileName.GetBuffer(_MAX_PATH);

dlgFile.m_ofn.lpstrInitialDir = "";
BOOL bResult = dlgFile.DoModal() == IDOK ? TRUE : FALSE;
fileName.ReleaseBuffer();
return bResult;
}

void  MyDocManager::AppendFilterSuffix (CString& filter,
                                        OPENFILENAME& ofn,
                                        CDocTemplate* pTemplate,
                                        CString* pstrDefaultExt) {
CString strFilterExt, strFilterName;
if (pTemplate->GetDocString(strFilterExt, CDocTemplate::filterExt) &&
 !strFilterExt.IsEmpty() &&
  pTemplate->GetDocString(strFilterName, CDocTemplate::filterName) &&
 !strFilterName.IsEmpty())    {
 // a file based document template - add to filter list
 ASSERT(strFilterExt[0] == '.');
 if (pstrDefaultExt != NULL)          {
  // set the default extension
  *pstrDefaultExt = ((LPCTSTR)strFilterExt) + 1;  // skip the '.'
  ofn.lpstrDefExt = (LPTSTR)(LPCTSTR)(*pstrDefaultExt);
```

```
  ofn.nFilterIndex = ofn.nMaxCustFilter + 1;   // 1 based number
  }

  // add to filter
  filter += strFilterName;
  ASSERT(!filter.IsEmpty());   // must have a file type name
  filter += (TCHAR)'\0';   // next string please
  filter += (TCHAR)'*';
  filter += strFilterExt;
  filter += (TCHAR)'\0';   // next string please
  ofn.nMaxCustFilter++;
 }
}
```

If you examine the behavior in File Open, it still is not yet perfect, since there are two entries for each document type, one for each view. The above coding ought to be modified to also specify a view as part of the file picking prompt.

Multi-View Sample 4

In the last sample, I added a menu item to facilitate opening other views on the document. Figure 11.7 shows that menu dropped down.

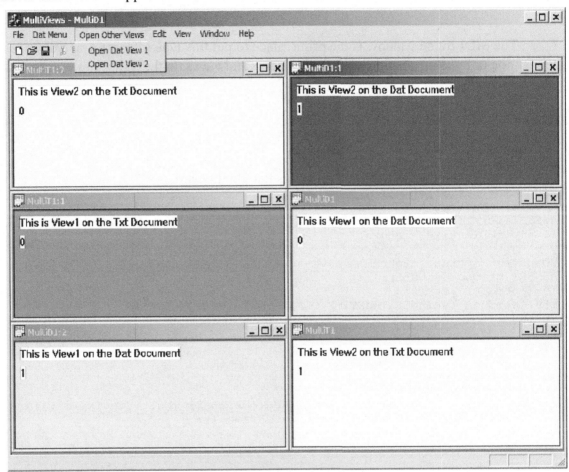

Figure 11.7 Multiview 4 Showing Menu for View Picking

In the document class, add two member functions to respond to the Open Other View menu choices. For the dat document, they are:

```
afx_msg void OnOpenDat1();
afx_msg void OnOpenDat2();
```

while for the txt document they are:

```
afx_msg void OnOpenTxt1();
afx_msg void OnOpenTxt2();
```

Their implementation is simple, call the frame window function to do the work.

```
BEGIN_MESSAGE_MAP(MultiViewDatDoc, CDocument)
 ON_COMMAND(CM_OPEN_DAT_1, OnOpenDat1)
 ON_COMMAND(CM_OPEN_DAT_2, OnOpenDat2)
END_MESSAGE_MAP()
```

```
void MultiViewDatDoc::OnOpenDat1() {
 ((MainFrame*)(theApp.m_pMainWnd))->OpenDat1 ();
}

void MultiViewDatDoc::OnOpenDat2() {
 ((MainFrame*)(theApp.m_pMainWnd))->OpenDat2 ();
}
```

The MDI frame window is the prime place to put this type of control operation, since it is maintaining or housing all of the child MDI frames and views. In the MainFrame class, I added the four functions.

```
void OpenTxt1 ();
void OpenTxt2 ();
void OpenDat1 ();
void OpenDat2 ();
```

Here are the four MainFrame functions that do the work.

```
void MainFrame::OpenTxt1 () {
 CMDIChildWnd *ptrMDIActive = MDIGetActive ();
 ASSERT(ptrMDIActive != NULL);
 if (!ptrMDIActive) return;

 CDocument *ptrdoc = ptrMDIActive->GetActiveDocument ();
 ASSERT(ptrdoc != NULL);
 if (!ptrdoc) return;
 if (!ptrdoc->IsKindOf (RUNTIME_CLASS (MultiViewTxtDoc)))
  return;

 CView *ptrview;
 POSITION pos = ptrdoc->GetFirstViewPosition ();
 while (pos != NULL) {
  ptrview = ptrdoc->GetNextView (pos);
  if (ptrview && ptrview->IsKindOf (RUNTIME_CLASS (MultiViewTxtView))) {
   ptrview->GetParentFrame ()->ActivateFrame ();
   return;
  }
 }

 MultiViewTxtDoc *ptrbdoc = (MultiViewTxtDoc*) ptrdoc;
 CMDIChildWnd *ptrNewFrame;
 ptrNewFrame =
     (CMDIChildWnd*) (theApp.pDocTemplateTxt1->CreateNewFrame (ptrdoc, NULL));
 if (!ptrNewFrame) return;      // not created
 if (ptrNewFrame->IsKindOf (RUNTIME_CLASS (CMDIChildWnd)))
  theApp.pDocTemplateTxt1->InitialUpdateFrame (ptrNewFrame, ptrdoc);
 pos = ptrdoc->GetFirstViewPosition ();
 while (pos != NULL) {
  ptrview = ptrdoc->GetNextView (pos);
  if (ptrview && ptrview->IsKindOf (RUNTIME_CLASS (MultiViewTxtView))) {
   ChildFrame *ptrw = (ChildFrame*) ptrview->GetParentFrame ();
   ptrw->ActivateFrame ();
// you can also specify precise locations as follows:
//   ptrview->GetParentFrame ()->SetWindowPos (0, 20, 20, 0, 0, SWP_NOSIZE | //
              SWP_NOZORDER);
//     ptrw->PositionWindow ();
   break;
```

```
    }
   }
  }

void MainFrame::OpenTxt2 () {
 CMDIChildWnd *ptrMDIActive = MDIGetActive ();
 ASSERT(ptrMDIActive != NULL);
 if (!ptrMDIActive) return;

 CDocument *ptrdoc = ptrMDIActive->GetActiveDocument ();
 ASSERT(ptrdoc != NULL);
 if (!ptrdoc) return;
 if (!ptrdoc->IsKindOf (RUNTIME_CLASS (MultiViewTxtDoc)))
  return;

 CView *ptrview;
 POSITION pos = ptrdoc->GetFirstViewPosition ();
 while (pos != NULL) {
  ptrview = ptrdoc->GetNextView (pos);
  if (ptrview && ptrview->IsKindOf (RUNTIME_CLASS (MultiViewTxt2View))) {
   ptrview->GetParentFrame ()->ActivateFrame ();
   return;
  }
 }

 MultiViewTxtDoc *ptrbdoc = (MultiViewTxtDoc*) ptrdoc;
 CMDIChildWnd *ptrNewFrame;
 ptrNewFrame =
     (CMDIChildWnd*) (theApp.pDocTemplateTxt2->CreateNewFrame (ptrdoc, NULL));
 if (!ptrNewFrame) return;       // not created
 if (ptrNewFrame->IsKindOf (RUNTIME_CLASS (CMDIChildWnd)))
  theApp.pDocTemplateTxt2->InitialUpdateFrame (ptrNewFrame, ptrdoc);
 pos = ptrdoc->GetFirstViewPosition ();
 while (pos != NULL) {
  ptrview = ptrdoc->GetNextView (pos);
  if (ptrview && ptrview->IsKindOf (RUNTIME_CLASS (MultiViewTxt2View))) {
   ChildFrame *ptrw = (ChildFrame*) ptrview->GetParentFrame ();
   ptrw->ActivateFrame ();
   break;
  }
 }
}

void MainFrame::OpenDat1 () {
 CMDIChildWnd *ptrMDIActive = MDIGetActive ();
 ASSERT(ptrMDIActive != NULL);
 if (!ptrMDIActive) return;

 CDocument *ptrdoc = ptrMDIActive->GetActiveDocument ();
 ASSERT(ptrdoc != NULL);
 if (!ptrdoc) return;
 if (!ptrdoc->IsKindOf (RUNTIME_CLASS (MultiViewDatDoc)))
  return;

 CView *ptrview;
 POSITION pos = ptrdoc->GetFirstViewPosition ();
 while (pos != NULL) {
  ptrview = ptrdoc->GetNextView (pos);
```

```
  if (ptrview && ptrview->IsKindOf (RUNTIME_CLASS (MultiViewDatView))) {
   ptrview->GetParentFrame ()->ActivateFrame ();
   return;
   }
 }

 MultiViewDatDoc *ptrbdoc = (MultiViewDatDoc*) ptrdoc;
 CMDIChildWnd *ptrNewFrame;
 ptrNewFrame =
     (CMDIChildWnd*) (theApp.pDocTemplateDat1->CreateNewFrame (ptrdoc, NULL));
 if (!ptrNewFrame) return;      // not created
 if (ptrNewFrame->IsKindOf (RUNTIME_CLASS (CMDIChildWnd)))
  theApp.pDocTemplateDat1->InitialUpdateFrame (ptrNewFrame, ptrdoc);
 pos = ptrdoc->GetFirstViewPosition ();
 while (pos != NULL) {
  ptrview = ptrdoc->GetNextView (pos);
  if (ptrview && ptrview->IsKindOf (RUNTIME_CLASS (MultiViewDatView))) {
   ChildFrame *ptrw = (ChildFrame*) ptrview->GetParentFrame ();
   ptrw->ActivateFrame ();
   break;
   }
 }
}

void MainFrame::OpenDat2 () {
 CMDIChildWnd *ptrMDIActive = MDIGetActive ();
 ASSERT(ptrMDIActive != NULL);
 if (!ptrMDIActive) return;

 CDocument *ptrdoc = ptrMDIActive->GetActiveDocument ();
 ASSERT(ptrdoc != NULL);
 if (!ptrdoc) return;
 if (!ptrdoc->IsKindOf (RUNTIME_CLASS (MultiViewDatDoc)))
  return;

 CView *ptrview;
 POSITION pos = ptrdoc->GetFirstViewPosition ();
 while (pos != NULL) {
  ptrview = ptrdoc->GetNextView (pos);
  if (ptrview && ptrview->IsKindOf (RUNTIME_CLASS (MultiViewDat2View))) {
   ptrview->GetParentFrame ()->ActivateFrame ();
   return;
   }
 }

 MultiViewDatDoc *ptrbdoc = (MultiViewDatDoc*) ptrdoc;
 CMDIChildWnd *ptrNewFrame;
 ptrNewFrame =
     (CMDIChildWnd*) (theApp.pDocTemplateDat2->CreateNewFrame (ptrdoc, NULL));
 if (!ptrNewFrame) return;      // not created
 if (ptrNewFrame->IsKindOf (RUNTIME_CLASS (CMDIChildWnd)))
  theApp.pDocTemplateDat2->InitialUpdateFrame (ptrNewFrame, ptrdoc);
 pos = ptrdoc->GetFirstViewPosition ();
 while (pos != NULL) {
  ptrview = ptrdoc->GetNextView (pos);
  if (ptrview && ptrview->IsKindOf (RUNTIME_CLASS (MultiViewDat2View))) {
   ChildFrame *ptrw = (ChildFrame*) ptrview->GetParentFrame ();
   ptrw->ActivateFrame ();
```

```
    break;
  }
 }
}
```

Let's examine one of these in detail. The other three are totally parallel. First, get the active MDI child frame window using **MDIGetActive**. If there is none, return, there is no documents open. Using that child frame pointer, get the active document calling **GetActiveDocument**. Now see if it is the proper document class, MultiViewtxtDoc by using the run time identification **IsKindOf**. If not, return. Next, using that document pointer, obtain its first view position by calling **GetFirstViewPosition**, which returns a **POSITION** structure.

Now move through all views on this document looking for the view type 1 which the user has requested. If it is found, then make that view now the active window. **GetNextView** returns the **CView** pointer. To activate it, remember, it is surrounded by the MDI child frame window which is what must be activated. **GetParentFrame** returns that pointer. **ActivateFrame** makes it now the active window.

```
void MainFrame::OpenTxt1 () {
CMDIChildWnd *ptrMDIActive = MDIGetActive ();
ASSERT(ptrMDIActive != NULL);
 if (!ptrMDIActive) return;

 CDocument *ptrdoc = ptrMDIActive->GetActiveDocument ();
ASSERT(ptrdoc != NULL);
 if (!ptrdoc) return;
 if (!ptrdoc->IsKindOf (RUNTIME_CLASS (MultiViewTxtDoc)))
  return;

 CView *ptrview;
POSITION pos = ptrdoc->GetFirstViewPosition ();
while (pos != NULL) {
 ptrview = ptrdoc->GetNextView (pos);
 if (ptrview && ptrview->IsKindOf (RUNTIME_CLASS (MultiViewTxtView))) {
  ptrview->GetParentFrame ()->ActivateFrame ();
  return;
 }
}
```

Here, this specific view is not opened yet, so we must now open that requested view. Obtain a pointer to the text document. The application has stored the different document templates. Here we want pDocTemplateTxt1, which uses the first text view class that the user wishes opened. Using that template, call **CreateNewFrame**, passing along the document pointer. After verifying that one was allocated and that it is a **CMDIChildWnd** as expected, invoke its **InitialUpdateFrame**, which then creates the frame window and allocated the actual view class instance.

```
MultiViewTxtDoc *ptrbdoc = (MultiViewTxtDoc*) ptrdoc;
CMDIChildWnd *ptrNewFrame;
ptrNewFrame =
    (CMDIChildWnd*) (theApp.pDocTemplateTxt1->CreateNewFrame (ptrdoc, NULL));
 if (!ptrNewFrame) return;        // not created
 if (ptrNewFrame->IsKindOf (RUNTIME_CLASS (CMDIChildWnd)))
  theApp.pDocTemplateTxt1->InitialUpdateFrame (ptrNewFrame, ptrdoc);
```

All that remains to be done is make it the active child window. GetFirstViewPosition is called and then iterate through the various views on this document, looking for the type that we just built, the first view. Once found, activate it.

```
pos = ptrdoc->GetFirstViewPosition ();
while (pos != NULL) {
 ptrview = ptrdoc->GetNextView (pos);
 if (ptrview && ptrview->IsKindOf (RUNTIME_CLASS (MultiViewTxtView))) {
  ChildFrame *ptrw = (ChildFrame*) ptrview->GetParentFrame ();
  ptrw->ActivateFrame ();
  break;
  }
 }
}
```

Another action you could do is to precisely locate and size that view. Use coding such as follows.

```
    ptrview->GetParentFrame ()->SetWindowPos (0, 20, 20, 0, 0,
                                        SWP_NOSIZE | SWP_NOZORDER);
    ptrw->PositionWindow ();
```

Handling Complex Documents

This chapter illustrates far more complex document-view handling. The base application is an App Wizard multiple document-view program. However, the main document and its view then provide a mechanism for the user to open an additional document and view. That second document then provides access to up to eight other documents and views to be opened, all are interlinked, working together. Many details of document handling and view handling are discussed. These actions simulate the log on procedure from my WWII game. Additionally, the main game document-view illustrates how to utilize an off-screen buffer class for better graphics performance.

The basic idea is to have a set of top level documents that represent complete game scenarios in progress. Each game scenario, the header documents with the bth extension, such as say the Assault on France, can be composed of one or more battles. A battle control document with the btl extension contains the detailed information required to run the battle, including which players are needed and so on. The control document permits only the required sides to log on to the battle. Finally, each player in a battle has their own battle document view object in which they play out their side of the battle. A battle may have up to eight players or sides in the conflict, although two is the norm, so up to 8 separate battle documents can be active at one time for one battle attack.

When a player wishes to log on to the game system, the first action is to connect to the game scenario header document which effectively provides a pick list of the different battle control documents representing the attacks in progress. This header view is shown in Figure 11.8.

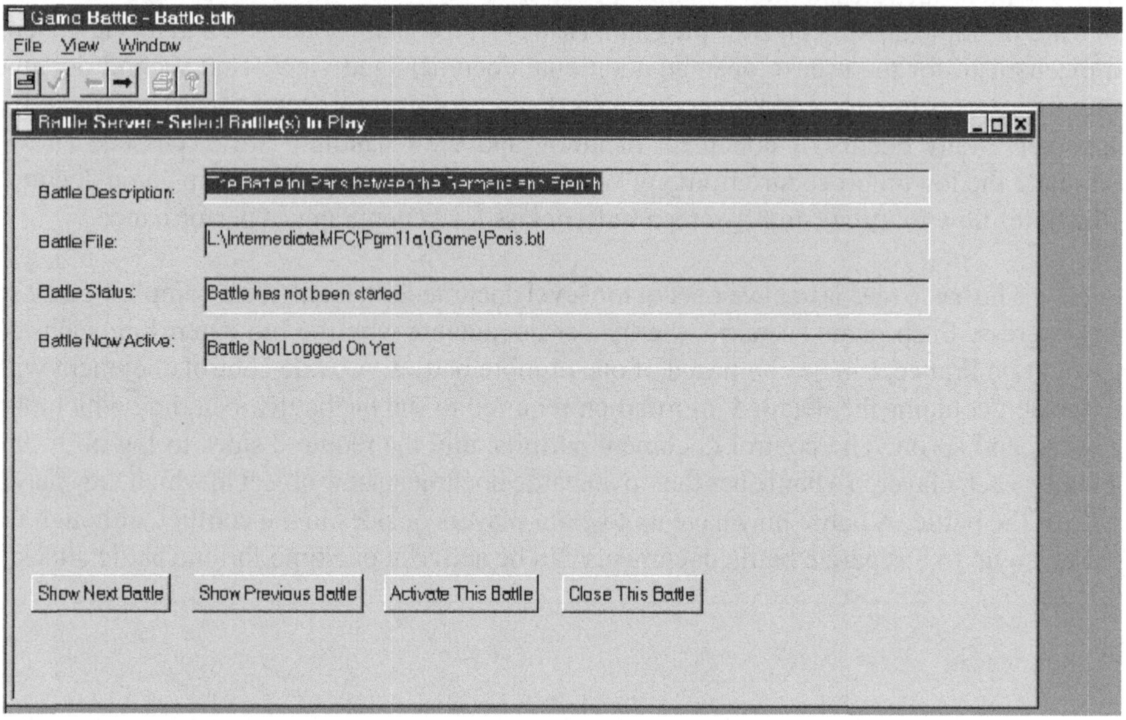

Figure 11.8 The Battle Header View Showing the Pick List

When the player picks which battle he wishes to join, the corresponding battle control document is opened, as shown in Figure 11.9. Notice that when the control document is opened and its view appears, the header view has been minimized in the lower left corner of the screen.

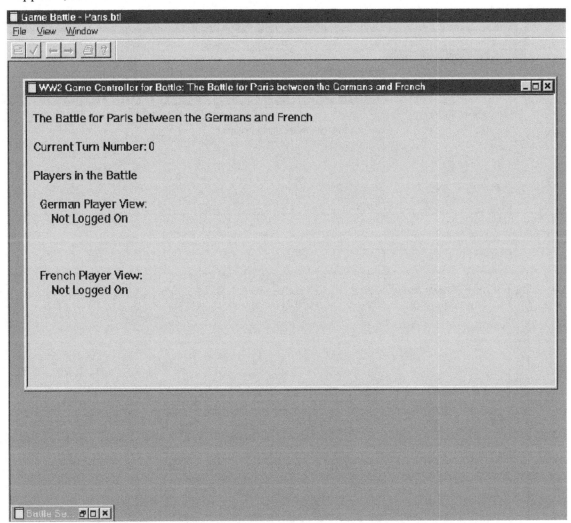

Figure 11.9 The Battle Control View Which Monitors the Game In Progress

The battle control view permits the correct players to log on to the game. Figure 11.10 shows the File|Logon menu for the Battle for Paris. As indicated both the German and French players may log on. Only when all parties have logged on does the control document begin the turn sequences of the game.

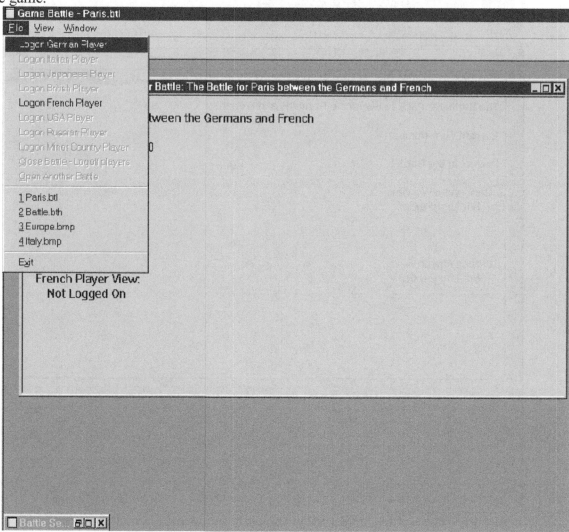

Figure 11.10 The Log on Menu of the Battle Control View

Figure 11.11 shows what the actual battle document for the German player looks like. Notice that the control view is still partially visible behind the German player's battle view. It is waiting for the French player to log on.

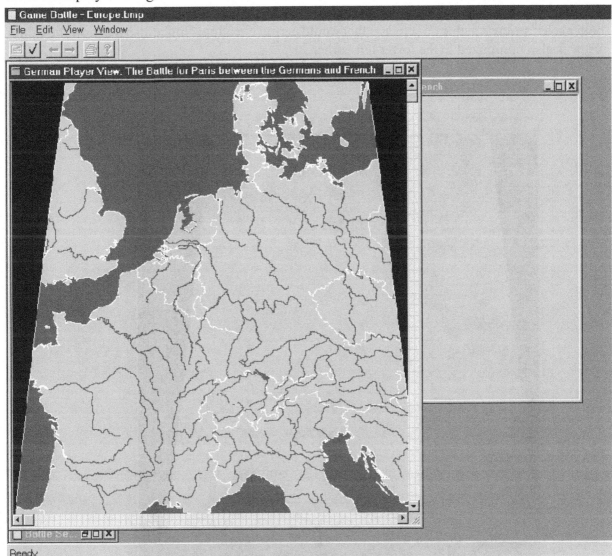

Figure 11.11 The German Player's Battle View After Logging On

Figure 11.12 shows what the French player's view looks like once logged on. Since all sides required for the battle are now on line, the control view has begun the game sequencing. When a player has finished his moves, the Do It! menu item is selected or the large Check Mark Button is pressed. Then that player's view is hidden and the other player's view is re-shown. At no time are both player's views visible on screen—that would permit cheating! Notice also that now the Control View is also minimized in the lower left corner.

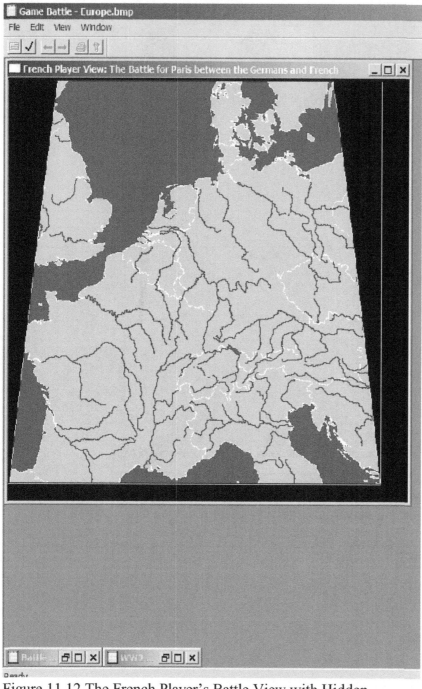

Figure 11.12 The French Player's Battle View with Hidden
German View and Minimized Control View

Should a player log off, the turn sequencing halts for all players. Only available memory limits how many header documents, control documents, and player battle documents can be active at one time.

Also, what's a game without "god-mode?" Thus each player can open another view, the OtherView which displays what he knows about the opposition. It would show what the opposing player might know of his armies. Figure 11.13 shows the player and other player views.

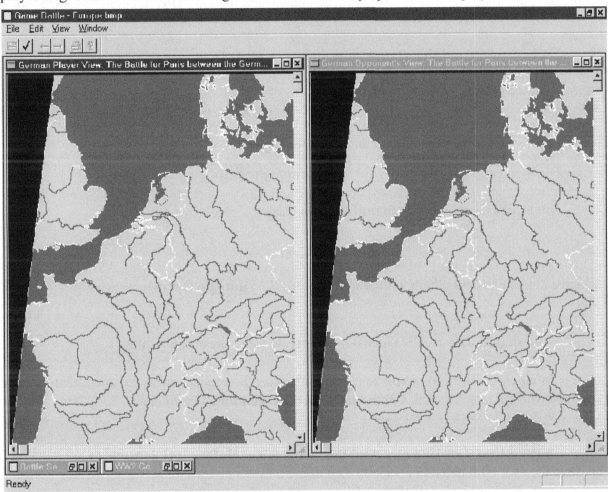

Figure 11.13 The Player and Other Views Tiled

Thus, we have documents dynamically launching other documents, and quite a bit of communication between documents to explore.

The Framework Actions to Open a Document File

In **CWinApp::InitApplication**, the **CWinApp** member, **m_pDocManager**, is initialized to the **CDocManager** instance so that the framework is then ready to respond to document creation.

Typically, to open a document, several approaches are possible. The Message Response Table can respond to **ID_FILE_OPEN** menu choices by invoking **OnFileOpen** of **CWinApp**

```
ON_COMMAND(ID_FILE_OPEN, CWinApp::OnFileOpen)
```

Alternatively, in **InitInstance**, directly invoke **OpenDocumentFile** passing the command line or a specific file

```
OpenDocumentFile (m_lpCmdLine);
OpenDocumentFile ("c:\\IntermediateMFC\\Pgm11a\\Game\\Battle.bth");
```

From some other location not in the **CWinApp** class, use

```
AfxGetApp()->OpenDocumentFile (
                  "c:\\IntermediateMFC\\Pgm11a\\Game\\Battle.bth");
```

Or utilize the new **CCommandLineInfo** class

```
CCommandLineInfo cmdInfo;
ParseCommandLine(cmdInfo);
// Dispatch commands specified on the command line
if (!ProcessShellCommand(cmdInfo)) return FALSE;
```

where within the **ProcessShellCommand** function of **CWinnApp OpenDocumentFile** is called for you.

Also drag and drop calls **OpenDocumentFile** using the dropped files.

In all cases, the **CWinApp** functions only pass the request on to the document manager instance where it gets handled. **CWinApp**'s **OnFileOpen** function invokes

```
m_pDocManager->OnFileOpen();
```

So now the **CDocManager::OnFileOpen** invokes **DoPromptFileName** to use a dialog to retrieve the user's filename to open and then does

```
AfxGetApp()->OpenDocumentFile(newName);
```

CWinApp's **OpenDocumentFile** function invokes the document manager to open the file and additionally returns a pointer to the opened document

```
return m_pDocManager->OpenDocumentFile(lpszFileName);
```

Thus, we must look into the document manager to see what actions are done to open the file.

Basically, the document manager's **OpenDocumentFile** function iterates through the list of document templates looking for the best matching template, stripped down to basics as follows. Notice that if the document is already opened, that instance is returned and activated; otherwise, the best matching document template's **OpenDocumentFile** function is then called.

```
POSITION pos = m_templateList.GetHeadPosition();
CDocTemplate::Confidence bestMatch = CDocTemplate::noAttempt;
CDocTemplate* pBestTemplate = NULL;
CDocument* pOpenDocument = NULL;
while (pos != NULL) {
 CDocTemplate* pTemplate = (CDocTemplate*)m_templateList.GetNext(pos);
 CDocTemplate::Confidence match;
 match = pTemplate->MatchDocType(szPath, pOpenDocument);
 if (match > bestMatch) {
  bestMatch = match;
  pBestTemplate = pTemplate;
 }
 if (match == CDocTemplate::yesAlreadyOpen) break;
}

if (pOpenDocument != NULL) {
 POSITION pos = pOpenDocument->GetFirstViewPosition();
 if (pos != NULL) {
  CView* pView = pOpenDocument->GetNextView(pos); // get first one
  CFrameWnd* pFrame = pView->GetParentFrame();
  if (pFrame != NULL) pFrame->ActivateFrame();
  else
   TRACE0("Error: Can not find a frame for document to activate.\n");
  CFrameWnd* pAppFrame;
  if (pFrame != (pAppFrame = (CFrameWnd*)AfxGetApp()->m_pMainWnd))
   pAppFrame->ActivateFrame();
 }
 else TRACE0("Error: Can not find a view for document to activate.\n");
 }
 return pOpenDocument;
}
return pBestTemplate->OpenDocumentFile(szPath);
```

Thus, in those circumstances in which you know which document you wish to open, you could also code

```
ptrheadtmp->OpenDocumentFile (
                    "l:\\IntermediateMFC\\Pgm11a\\Game\\Battle.bth");
```

where **ptrheadtmp** is a pointer to the document template that you **know** matches this file.

This tells us that we must look at the **OpenDocumentFile** function of the document template class. In this chapter, I am examining only the multi document version. Again, stripped down to basics, the **CMultiDocTemplate**'s **OpenDocumentFile** does the following actions

```
CDocument* pDocument = CreateNewDocument();
CFrameWnd* pFrame = CreateNewFrame(pDocument, NULL);
if (lpszPathName == NULL)       {
 // create a new document - with default document name
 SetDefaultTitle(pDocument);
 pDocument->OnNewDocument();
}
else {
 // open an existing document
 pDocument->OnOpenDocument(lpszPathName)
 pDocument->SetPathName(lpszPathName);
}
InitialUpdateFrame(pFrame, pDocument, bMakeVisible);
return pDocument;
```

In our case in which the filename exists, **CreateNewDocument** and **CreateNewFrame** are called to prepare instances of both objects followed by a call to the new document's **OnOpenDocument** function. Finally, **InitialUpdateFrame** is invoked. The first two create functions build initial object instances and appear stripped down to basics as follows

```
CDocument* CDocTemplate::CreateNewDocument() {
 // default implementation constructs one from CRuntimeClass
 CDocument* pDocument = (CDocument*)m_pDocClass->CreateObject();
 AddDocument(pDocument);
 return pDocument;
}

CFrameWnd* CDocTemplate::CreateNewFrame(CDocument* pDoc,
                                        CFrameWnd* pOther) {
 CFrameWnd* pFrame = (CFrameWnd*)m_pFrameClass->CreateObject();
 pFrame->LoadFrame(m_nIDResource,
  WS_OVERLAPPEDWINDOW | FWS_ADDTOTITLE,   // default frame styles
   NULL, &context);
 return pFrame;
}
```

One footnote, notice that **FWS_ADDTOTITLE** is added to the frame window style; this is why so often **PreCreateWindow** is overridden just to remove this style.

The real work is therefore done in the **CDocument** class itself via **OnOpenDocument**. Here is where the serialization process is begun. Again, it is stripped down to basics

```
CFileException fe;
CFile* pFile = GetFile(lpszPathName,
                        CFile::modeRead|CFile::shareDenyWrite, &fe);
DeleteContents();
SetModifiedFlag();   // dirty during de-serialize
CArchive loadArchive(pFile, CArchive::load |
                       CArchive::bNoFlushOnDelete);
loadArchive.m_pDocument = this;
loadArchive.m_bForceFlat = FALSE;
Serialize(loadArchive);      // load me
loadArchive.Close();
ReleaseFile(pFile, FALSE);
SetModifiedFlag(FALSE);       // start off with unmodified
```

Finally, the document template's **InitialUpdateFrame** merely passes on the request to the **CFrameWnd**'s **InitialUpdateFrame** function. Here is the basics of that function

```
// if the frame does not have an active view, set to first pane
CView* pView = NULL;
if (GetActiveView() == NULL) {
 CWnd* pWnd = GetDescendantWindow(AFX_IDW_PANE_FIRST, TRUE);
 if (pWnd != NULL && pWnd->IsKindOf(RUNTIME_CLASS(CView)))  {
  pView = (CView*)pWnd;
  SetActiveView(pView, FALSE);
 }
}
if (bMakeVisible) {
 // send initial update to all views (and other controls) in the frame
 SendMessageToDescendants(WM_INITIALUPDATE, 0, 0, TRUE, TRUE);
 // give view a chance to save the focus (CFormView needs this)
 if (pView != NULL) pView->OnActivateFrame(WA_INACTIVE, this);
```

```
// finally, activate the frame
// (send the default show command unless the main desktop window)
int nCmdShow = -1;        // default
CWinApp* pApp = AfxGetApp();
if (this == pApp->m_pMainWnd) {
 nCmdShow = pApp->m_nCmdShow; // use the parameter from WinMain
 pApp->m_nCmdShow = -1; // set to default after first time
}
ActivateFrame(nCmdShow);
 if (pView != NULL) pView->OnActivateView(TRUE, pView, pView);
}
// update frame counts and frame title (may already have been visible)
pDoc->UpdateFrameCounts();
OnUpdateFrameTitle(TRUE);
```

Instructions for the Initial First Execution of Pgm11a

The major problem with this example is that the various document files contain filenames, particularly their paths. Since you may install the samples on a different drive or folder arrangement that I used, before you attempt to execute this application for the first time, you must use any text editor, such as Notepad, to alter the various filenames to your configuration.

Copy the file Battle.bakup to Battle.bth and open it with Notepad. It should appear as follows
```
The Battle for Paris between the Germans and French
D:\WindowsMFCProgrammingII\Pgm11a\Game\Paris.btl
0
The Battle for Sicily between the Italians and British
D:\WindowsMFCProgrammingII\Pgm11a\Game\Sicily.btl
0
```

Here the first line represents the description, the second, the filename of the control document, and the 0 is the status, meaning the battle has not yet begun. Please change the drive and pathname to where you have installed this sample.

The control documents assume that all other files are in the folder indicated in this header file.

Note that the application does use the Registry to find the path to the Battle.bth file as usual. Although one could easily store all the information contained in the bth battle header file in the Registry as well, it is not recommended. The players could have several battles on-going and your use of the Registry would have to include some kind of selection and identification process to determine which saved game they wished to resume. This makes it awkward for players to copy the game onto another computer and resume for the other computer's Registry would not be updated.

After you run the application one time, the save serialization process will rewrite the Battle.bth file as a binary file.

The Header Data Class

Obviously, the battle header document, .bth, contains arrays of the filenames of the various control documents along with the current status of each game. For example, if that particular game pointed to by a control document has been finished, no sense in permitting players to log on any more. Somehow these initial header document files must be created, presumably by another application. Also, since you may not have installed this sample into the same drive and directory structure as I did, some provision must be made to alter filenames and to edit these header files as text. Thus, I have made the serialization process of the header document more versatile. It attempts to serialize the bth file as binary data; should that fail, it then attempts to serialize it as a text file.

I created a class to store the array of battles, HeadData derived from **CObject** so that it can be serialized. Notice that the function Read is called should binary serialization fail and text is assumed. For convenience later on, should this particular battle be chosen for activation, I also store a pointer to the ControlDoc that is subsequently launched to control this battle.

Listing for File: HeadData.h

```
#pragma once
#include <fstream>
using namespace std;

class ControlDoc;


/**********************************************************************/
/*                                                                    */
/* HeadData: overall battle information class                         */
/*                                                                    */
/**********************************************************************/

#define Battle_NotStarted   0
#define Battle_InProgress   1
#define Battle_Completed    2

class HeadData : public CObject {
public:
  HeadData();          // constructor used by dynamic creation
  HeadData (char*, char*, long, ControlDoc*); // copy constr

  DECLARE_SERIAL(HeadData)

char          battle_descr [MAX_PATH];   // user description of battle
char          battle_file  [MAX_PATH];   // filename of battle data
char          battle_basefile [MAX_PATH];
long          battle_status;             // current battle status
ControlDoc    *ptrctldoc;                // will hold a ControlDoc ptr

virtual void Serialize(CArchive& ar);
virtual      ~HeadData();
virtual BOOL Read (CFile&);
...
};
```

```
/************************************************************************/
/*                                                                    */
/* HeaderDataArray: array container for header data objects            */
/*                                                                    */
/************************************************************************/

class HeadDataArray : public CObArray {
 DECLARE_SERIAL(HeadDataArray)
public:
   HeadDataArray () {}           // constructor for serialization
};
```

Listing for File: HeadData.cpp

```
...
IMPLEMENT_SERIAL (HeadData, CObject, 0)
IMPLEMENT_SERIAL (HeadDataArray, CObArray, 0)

HeadData::HeadData() { }
HeadData::~HeadData() { }

/************************************************************************/
/*                                                                    */
/* HeaderData: copy constructor                                        */
/*                                                                    */
/************************************************************************/

HeadData::HeadData (char *dname, char *fname, long st, ControlDoc *ptrdoc) {
 strcpy_s (battle_descr, sizeof(battle_descr), dname);
 strcpy_s (battle_basefile, sizeof(battle_basefile), fname);
 strcpy_s (battle_file, sizeof(battle_file), theApp.mainpath);
 strcat_s (battle_file, sizeof(battle_file), fname);
 battle_status = st;
 ptrctldoc = ptrdoc;
}

/************************************************************************/
/*                                                                    */
/* Serialize: attempt to I/O the bth file                              */
/*                                                                    */
/************************************************************************/

void HeadData::Serialize(CArchive& ar) {
 CObject::Serialize (ar);
 long i, j;
 BYTE b;
 if (ar.IsStoring ()) {
  j = strlen (battle_descr);
  ar << j;
  for (i=0; i<j; i++) ar << (BYTE) battle_descr[i];
  j = strlen (battle_basefile);
  ar << j;
  for (i=0; i<j; i++) ar << (BYTE) battle_basefile[i];
  ar << battle_status;
 }
 else {
  ar >> j;
```

```
  for (i=0; i<j; i++) {
   ar >> b;
   battle_descr[i] = b;
   }
  battle_descr[j] = 0;
  ar >> j;
  for (i=0; i<j; i++) {
   ar >> b;
   battle_basefile[i] = b;
   }
  battle_basefile[j] = 0;
  ar >> battle_status;
  strcpy_s (battle_file, sizeof(battle_file), theApp.mainpath);
  strcat_s(battle_file, sizeof(battle_file), battle_basefile);
  ptrctldoc = NULL;
 }
}


/***************************************************************************/
/*                                                                         */
/* Read: input text version of bth file                                    */
/*                                                                         */
/***************************************************************************/
BOOL HeadData::Read (CFile &file) {
 int i, count;
 char c;
 i=0;
 count = 1;
 while (count) { // read all file bytes, checking for new line codes
  count = file.Read (&battle_descr[i], 1);   // reads one byte
  if (!count) battle_descr[i] = 0;
  else if (battle_descr[i] == 0x0d) {
   battle_descr[i] = 0;
   file.Read (&c, 1);
   break;
  }
  i++;
 }
 if (!count) return FALSE;

 i=0;
 while (count) { // read all file bytes, checking for new line codes
  count = file.Read (&battle_basefile[i], 1);   // reads one byte
  if (!count) battle_basefile[i] = 0;
  else if (battle_basefile[i] == 0x0d) {
   battle_basefile[i] = 0;
   file.Read (&c, 1);
   break;
  }
  i++;
 }
 strcpy_s (battle_file, sizeof(battle_file), theApp.mainpath);
 strcat_s (battle_file, sizeof(battle_file), battle_basefile);
 if (!count) return FALSE;

 char s[80];
 i=0;
```

```
while (count) { // read all file bytes, checking for new line codes
 count = file.Read (&s[i], 1);    // reads one byte
 if (!count) s[i] = 0;
 else if (s[i] == 0x0d) {
  s[i]=0;
  file.Read (&c, 1);
  break;
 }
 i++;
}
battle_status = atol (s);

ptrctldoc = NULL;

return TRUE;
}
...
```

The coding is straight forward. But note one very important aspect. On input operations, I store a copy of the filename in the application class public member, **mainpath**. The assumption, here, is that the main path for the entire application is the folder in which these files are located. Thus, when the header data is being serialized, I can obtain a complete string to the folder of the game. Shortly, we shall see how this is used.

The Resource and Application Class of Pgm11a

Withe these basics understood, let's examine the different menus, resources and the application class to see how the initial Battle.bth header document is launched. In the resource file, Pgm11a.rc, I have shown the tool bar layout, the different menus for the different document-view classes, and the dialog form for the header document view which is derived from **CFormView**. Notice the very different menus of the three main doc-view classes. Only the View and Window pop-up menus remain constant. Clearly from the menus, the header class is responsible for choosing which control document is wanted. The control document is concerned with the actual log on process. The Player and Other documents are concerned with playing the game.

Notice also that the **CFormView** provides scrolling buttons to move forward and back in the pick list of control documents. It also provides an Activate button to launch this control document. And finally there is a high level Close this battle button. Pressing this high level Close button caused an enforced log off of all players, without their consent and terminate the game. View this termination as a "Server Shutting Down" type of closure.

Listing for File: Pgm11a.rc—Excerpts

```
...
/////////////////////////////////////////////////////////////////////////
//
```

```
// Toolbar
//

IDR_MAINFRAME TOOLBAR DISCARDABLE  16, 15
BEGIN
    BUTTON      CM_ACTIVATE_BATTLE
    BUTTON      CM_BATTLEDOC_ACTIONDONE
    SEPARATOR
    BUTTON      CM_PREV_BATTLE
    BUTTON      CM_NEXT_BATTLE
    SEPARATOR
    BUTTON      CM_BUTTON1
    BUTTON      CM_BUTTON2
END


/////////////////////////////////////////////////////////////////////////////
//
// Menu
//

IDR_MAINFRAME MENU PRELOAD DISCARDABLE
BEGIN
    POPUP "&File"
    BEGIN
        MENUITEM "&Connect to Battle Server",   CM_SERVER_CONNECT
        MENUITEM SEPARATOR
        MENUITEM "E&xit",                       ID_APP_EXIT
    END
    POPUP "&View"
    BEGIN
        MENUITEM "&View Administration Window", CM_VIEW_CONTROL
        MENUITEM SEPARATOR
        MENUITEM "&Toolbar",                    ID_VIEW_TOOLBAR
        MENUITEM "&Status Bar",                 ID_VIEW_STATUS_BAR
    END
END

IDR_HEADFRAME MENU PRELOAD DISCARDABLE
BEGIN
    POPUP "&File"
    BEGIN
        MENUITEM "Activate Battle for Play",    CM_ACTIVATE_BATTLE
        MENUITEM "Examine Next Battle",         CM_NEXT_BATTLE
        MENUITEM "Examine Previous Battle",     CM_PREV_BATTLE
        MENUITEM "Close This Battle Down",      CM_CLOSE_BATTLE
        MENUITEM "&Close - Suspend Game Here",  CM_FILE_CLOSE_SAVE
        MENUITEM "&Open Another Battle",        ID_FILE_OPEN
        MENUITEM SEPARATOR
        MENUITEM "E&xit",                       ID_APP_EXIT
    END
    POPUP "&View"
    BEGIN
        MENUITEM "&View Administration Window", CM_VIEW_CONTROL
        MENUITEM SEPARATOR
        MENUITEM "&Toolbar",                    ID_VIEW_TOOLBAR
        MENUITEM "&Status Bar",                 ID_VIEW_STATUS_BAR
    END
```

```
        POPUP "&Window"
        BEGIN
            MENUITEM "&Cascade",                        ID_WINDOW_CASCADE
            MENUITEM "&Tile Vertically",                ID_WINDOW_TILE_VERT
            MENUITEM "&Tile Horizontally",              ID_WINDOW_TILE_HORZ
            MENUITEM "&Arrange Icons",                  ID_WINDOW_ARRANGE
        END
END

IDR_CONTROLFRAME MENU PRELOAD DISCARDABLE
BEGIN
        POPUP "&File"
        BEGIN
            MENUITEM "Logon German Player",             CM_LOGON_GERMAN
            MENUITEM "Logon Italian Player",            CM_LOGON_ITALY
            MENUITEM "Logon Japanese Player",           CM_LOGON_JAPAN
            MENUITEM "Logon British Player",            CM_LOGON_BRITIAN
            MENUITEM "Logon French Player",             CM_LOGON_FRANCE
            MENUITEM "Logon USA Player",                CM_LOGON_USA
            MENUITEM "Logon Russian Player",            CM_LOGON_RUSSIA
            MENUITEM "Logon Minor Country Player",      CM_LOGON_MINOR
            MENUITEM "&Close Battle - Logoff players",  CM_FILE_CLOSE_BATTLE
            MENUITEM "&Open Another Battle",            ID_FILE_OPEN
            MENUITEM SEPARATOR
            MENUITEM "Recent File",                     ID_FILE_MRU_FILE1, GRAYED
            MENUITEM SEPARATOR
            MENUITEM "E&xit",                           ID_APP_EXIT
        END
        POPUP "&View"
        BEGIN
            MENUITEM "&Toolbar",                        ID_VIEW_TOOLBAR
            MENUITEM "&Status Bar",                     ID_VIEW_STATUS_BAR
        END
        POPUP "&Window"
        BEGIN
            MENUITEM "&Cascade",                        ID_WINDOW_CASCADE
            MENUITEM "&Tile Vertically",                ID_WINDOW_TILE_VERT
            MENUITEM "&Tile Horizontally",              ID_WINDOW_TILE_HORZ
            MENUITEM "&Arrange Icons",                  ID_WINDOW_ARRANGE
        END
END

IDR_PLAYERFRAME MENU PRELOAD DISCARDABLE
BEGIN
        POPUP "&File"
        BEGIN
            MENUITEM "&Save Game and Logoff Player",    CM_FILE_CLOSE_SAVE
            MENUITEM SEPARATOR
            MENUITEM "E&xit Battle - Logoff All Players", ID_APP_EXIT
        END
        POPUP "&Edit"
        BEGIN
            MENUITEM "&Undo Last Action",               CM_BATTLEDOC_UNDO
            MENUITEM "&DO IT! Completed All Actions",    CM_BATTLEDOC_ACTIONDONE
        END
        POPUP "&View"
        BEGIN
            MENUITEM "&Open Opponent Window",           CM_MAKE_OTHER_VIEW
```

```
        MENUITEM "&View Administration Window", CM_VIEW_CONTROL
        MENUITEM SEPARATOR
        MENUITEM "&Toolbar",                    ID_VIEW_TOOLBAR
        MENUITEM "&Status Bar",                 ID_VIEW_STATUS_BAR
    END
    POPUP "&Window"
    BEGIN
        MENUITEM "&Cascade",                    ID_WINDOW_CASCADE
        MENUITEM "&Tile Vertically",            ID_WINDOW_TILE_VERT
        MENUITEM "&Tile Horizontally",          ID_WINDOW_TILE_HORZ
        MENUITEM "&Arrange Icons",              ID_WINDOW_ARRANGE
    END
END

IDR_OTHERFRAME MENU PRELOAD DISCARDABLE
BEGIN
    POPUP "&File"
    BEGIN
        MENUITEM "Close &View of the Other Side", CM_FILE_CLOSE_OTHER
        MENUITEM "&Save Game and Logoff Player", CM_FILE_CLOSE_SAVE
        MENUITEM SEPARATOR
        MENUITEM "E&xit Battle - Logoff All Players", ID_APP_EXIT
    END
    POPUP "&View"
    BEGIN
        MENUITEM "&View Administration Window", CM_VIEW_CONTROL
        MENUITEM SEPARATOR
        MENUITEM "&Toolbar",                    ID_VIEW_TOOLBAR
        MENUITEM "&Status Bar",                 ID_VIEW_STATUS_BAR
    END
    POPUP "&Window"
    BEGIN
        MENUITEM "&Cascade",                    ID_WINDOW_CASCADE
        MENUITEM "&Tile Vertically",            ID_WINDOW_TILE_VERT
        MENUITEM "&Tile Horizontally",          ID_WINDOW_TILE_HORZ
        MENUITEM "&Arrange Icons",              ID_WINDOW_ARRANGE
    END
END
...
////////////////////////////////////////////////////////////////////////
//
// Dialog
//

IDD_HEAD DIALOG DISCARDABLE  0, 0, 380, 189
STYLE WS_CHILD
FONT 8, "MS Sans Serif"
BEGIN
    EDITTEXT            IDC_BATTLE_DESCR,75,10,290,13,ES_AUTOHSCROLL |
                        ES_READONLY
    EDITTEXT            IDC_BATTLE_FILE,75,30,290,13,ES_AUTOHSCROLL |
                        ES_READONLY
    EDITTEXT            IDC_BATTLE_STATUS,75,50,290,13,ES_AUTOHSCROLL |
                        ES_READONLY
    EDITTEXT            IDC_BATTLE_ACTIVE,75,70,290,13,ES_AUTOHSCROLL |
                        ES_READONLY
    PUSHBUTTON          "Show Next Battle",CM_NEXT_BATTLE,7,158,55,14
    PUSHBUTTON          "Show Previous Battle",CM_PREV_BATTLE,71,158,68,14
```

```
        PUSHBUTTON      "Activate This Battle",CM_ACTIVATE_BATTLE,148,158,62,14
        PUSHBUTTON      "Close This Battle",CM_CLOSE_BATTLE,219,158,56,14
        LTEXT           "Battle Description:",IDC_STATIC,10,15,55,8
        LTEXT           "Battle File:",IDC_STATIC,10,33,32,8
        LTEXT           "Battle Status:",IDC_STATIC,10,51,40,8
        LTEXT           "Battle Now Active:",IDC_STATIC,10,69,55,8
END
...
```

The App Class and More Registry Functions

The Pgm11aApp class defines the four document templates needed. Notice in particular that I am storing a pointer to the current HeadDoc instance that is currently activated. Other classes can then gain access to this top level document class easily when needed. Likewise, I store the main path to the folder containing the game files in **mainpath** for all other classes to utilize. I also made this application class instance available for convenience, the external **theApp**.

Listing for File: Pgm11a.h

```
...
class Pgm11aApp : public CWinApp {
public:

    char        mainpath[MAX_PATH]; // main path for all the other files
    HeadDoc     *ptrheaddoc;        // ptr to the head document class

    CMultiDocTemplate *ptrcontroltmp;
    CMultiDocTemplate *ptrheadtmp;
    CMultiDocTemplate *ptrplayertmp;
    CMultiDocTemplate *ptrothertmp;

            Pgm11aApp();
    CString RetrievePath ();  // retrieve the Registry path of last game bth
    bool    SavePath (CString& filename); // save this bth file in registry
    CString GetPaletteFile (CString& bthfile);

    virtual BOOL  InitInstance();
    virtual int   ExitInstance();

    // display error messages when no CWnd
    virtual long  DisplayMsg (long, long, UINT);

    afx_msg void  OnAppAbout();
        DECLARE_MESSAGE_MAP()
};
extern Pgm11aApp theApp;
```

Listing for File: Pgm11a.cpp

```
...
BEGIN_MESSAGE_MAP(Pgm11aApp, CWinApp)
```

```
        ON_COMMAND(ID_APP_ABOUT, OnAppAbout)
//      ON_COMMAND(ID_FILE_NEW, CWinApp::OnFileNew)
//      ON_COMMAND(ID_FILE_OPEN, CWinApp::OnFileOpen)
END_MESSAGE_MAP()

Pgm11aApp::Pgm11aApp() { }
Pgm11aApp theApp;

BOOL Pgm11aApp::InitInstance() {
 ptrheaddoc = NULL;
 SetRegistryKey ("WindowsMFCII"); // setup the higher level reg key
 LoadStdProfileSettings (10);     // load most recently used files

 ptrheadtmp = new CMultiDocTemplate(IDR_HEADFRAME,
                                RUNTIME_CLASS(HeadDoc),
                                RUNTIME_CLASS(HeadFrame),
                                RUNTIME_CLASS(HeadView));
 AddDocTemplate (ptrheadtmp);

 ptrcontroltmp = new CMultiDocTemplate(IDR_CONTROLFRAME,
                                    RUNTIME_CLASS(ControlDoc),
                                    RUNTIME_CLASS(ControlFrame),
                                    RUNTIME_CLASS(ControlView));
 AddDocTemplate (ptrcontroltmp);

 ptrplayertmp = new CMultiDocTemplate (IDR_PLAYERFRAME,
                                    RUNTIME_CLASS(GameDoc),
                                    RUNTIME_CLASS(GameFrame),
                                    RUNTIME_CLASS(PlayerView));
 AddDocTemplate (ptrplayertmp);

 ptrothertmp  = new CMultiDocTemplate (IDR_OTHERFRAME,
                                    RUNTIME_CLASS(GameDoc),
                                    RUNTIME_CLASS(GameFrame),
                                    RUNTIME_CLASS(OtherView));
 AddDocTemplate (ptrothertmp);

 MainFrame *ptrmainframe = new MainFrame;
 if (!ptrmainframe->LoadFrame (IDR_MAINFRAME)) return FALSE;
 ptrmainframe->ShowWindow (SW_SHOWMAXIMIZED);

 ptrmainframe->UpdateWindow ();
 m_pMainWnd = ptrmainframe;

 // automatic open of the game bth file
 CString bthfile = RetrievePath ();
 if (bthfile.IsEmpty()) {
  // here it was not found, so try the Game subfolder
  bthfile = "Game\\Battle.bth";
 }
 // build the filename for the Palette file
 CString palfile = GetPaletteFile (bthfile);
 if (!Palette::InitPalette (LPCSTR(palfile))) {
  AfxMessageBox ("Master.pal file failed to initialize", MB_OK);
  return FALSE;
 }
 OpenDocumentFile (LPCSTR(bthfile));
```

```
  // comment out the above series and uncomment this series if you want
  // to use the find dialog box
/* CWinApp::OnFileOpen();
  char pfile[MAX_PATH];
  strcpy (pfile, mainpath);
  strcat (pfile, "Master.pal");
  if (!Palette::InitPalette (pfile)) return FALSE;
*/
  return TRUE;
}


/*************************************************************************/
/*                                                                       */
/* RetrievePath: obtain the installed path from the system registry      */
/*                                                                       */
/*************************************************************************/

CString   Pgm11aApp::RetrievePath () {
  CString subkey = "SOFTWARE\\WindowsMFCII\\Pgm11a\\Settings";
  CString entry = "BthFile";
  CString filename = "";
  HKEY hkey;
  LONG ok;
  // attempt to make the Settings key, if it is not there yet
  ok = RegCreateKeyEx (HKEY_CURRENT_USER, subkey, 0, 0, 0, KEY_CREATE_SUB_KEY,
                    0, &hkey, 0);
  if (ok != ERROR_SUCCESS) return filename;

  // attempt to open the current user Settings key with our value
  ok = RegOpenKeyEx (HKEY_CURRENT_USER, subkey, 0, KEY_READ, &hkey);
  if (ok == ERROR_SUCCESS) {
   DWORD dwType, dwCount;
   // key exists, now verify BthFile entry is a string
   ok = RegQueryValueEx (hkey, entry, NULL, &dwType, NULL, &dwCount);
   if (ok == ERROR_SUCCESS && dwType == REG_SZ) {
    // now retrieve the actual path string
                 ok = RegQueryValueEx (hkey, entry, NULL, &dwType,
                        (LPBYTE) filename.GetBuffer (dwCount/sizeof(TCHAR)),
                        &dwCount);
     filename.ReleaseBuffer(); // release the CString buffer locked by GetBuffer
   }
   RegCloseKey (hkey);
  }
  return filename;
}


/*************************************************************************/
/*                                                                       */
/* SavePath: save path of bth file in registry                           */
/*                                                                       */
/*************************************************************************/

bool   Pgm11aApp::SavePath (CString& filename) {
  CString subkey = "SOFTWARE\\WindowsMFCII\\Pgm11a\\Settings";
  CString entry = "BthFile";
  HKEY hkey;
  LONG ok;
  // build Settings key, if it is not there yet
```

```
  ok = RegCreateKeyEx (HKEY_CURRENT_USER, subkey, 0, 0, 0, KEY_CREATE_SUB_KEY,
                       0, &hkey, 0);
  if (ok != ERROR_SUCCESS) return false;
  // attempt to open the current user Settings key with our value
  ok = RegOpenKeyEx (HKEY_CURRENT_USER, subkey, 0, KEY_WRITE, &hkey);
  if (ok == ERROR_SUCCESS) {
   // key exists, now store the value in BthFile
   ok = RegSetValueEx (hkey, entry, 0, REG_SZ,
                   (const BYTE*) filename.GetBuffer (), filename.GetLength ()+1);
   if (ok == ERROR_SUCCESS) {
    filename.ReleaseBuffer (); // release the CString buffer locked by GetBuffer
    RegCloseKey (hkey);
    return true;
   }
   RegCloseKey (hkey);
  }
  return false;
}


/***********************************************************************/
/*                                                                     */
/* GetPaletteFile: make the palette filename from the bth filename     */
/*                                                                     */
/***********************************************************************/

CString Pgm11aApp::GetPaletteFile (CString& bthfile) {
 char drive[_MAX_DRIVE];
 char dir[_MAX_PATH];
 char file[_MAX_PATH];
 char ext[_MAX_EXT];
 _splitpath_s ((LPCSTR) bthfile, drive, _MAX_DRIVE, dir, _MAX_PATH, file,
               _MAX_PATH, ext, _MAX_EXT);
 char answer[_MAX_PATH];
 _makepath_s (answer, _MAX_PATH, drive, dir, "Master", ".pal");
 return CString (answer);
}


/***********************************************************************/
/*                                                                     */
/* DisplayMsg: display a message box and return results                */
/*                                                                     */
/***********************************************************************/

long      Pgm11aApp::DisplayMsg (long id1, long id2, UINT flags) {
 CString msg1, msg2;
 msg1.LoadString (id1);
 msg2.LoadString (id2);
 return ::MessageBox (0, msg2, msg1, flags);
}


/***********************************************************************/
/*                                                                     */
/* ExitInstance: delete any palette, if running on older systems       */
/*                                                                     */
/***********************************************************************/

int Pgm11aApp::ExitInstance() {
 Palette::DeletePalette ();
```

```
        return CWinApp::ExitInstance();
}
```

Once the four document templates are allocated and the MainFrame constructed, the initial header document must be opened. Since you may have likely installed the sample on another drive and maybe even folder, I do not know where to look for you header document file. There are several ways this can be done. Here, I wish to illustrate further use of the registry.

In essence, a subkey called Settings stores a value called BthFile. The app tries to open this key to find the compete filespec of the last used game. If it finds one, then it opens it. If it does not find this registry entry, then it looks in the Games subfolder of this project. When the game is closed, the full filespec of the current .bth file in use is stored in the registry.

Alternatively, you could comment out these instructions and uncomment those indicated. This alternate approach calls **OnFileOpen** and let the framework open the dialog box for you to point to the folder containing Battle.bth. Experiment with the different ways of launching the application, using Battle.bth.

Registry Coding

Until now, we have just been making use of the normal MRU file entries that the framework automatically installs for us. Since several files are going to be opened in this application, the MRU list will contain them all, making it difficult to find the actual .bth file needed to launch the app. Hence, for this app, I want to store that filespec under its own key, here called Settings. The entry will be called BthFile.

Now we must deal with the real possibility that the first time the program is run, this subkey, Settings, has not yet been made. Thus, we must create the Settings subkey, if it is not present under the Pgm11a key. Next, we must write out our own value entry, BthFile=...

When a key might not be present and an app needs that key to be present in the registry, a different call must be made. Until now, we called **RegOpenKeyEx**, which fails if the key is not there. Here, we must use **RegCreateKeyEx**, which creates the key if it is not there, otherwise, it opens the key. The function prototype is

```
LONG RegCreateKeyEx (HKEY hKey, LPCTSTR lpSubKey, DWORD Reserved,
             LPTSTR lpClass, DWORD dwOptions, REGSAM samDesired,
             LPSECURITY_ATTRIBUTES lpSecurityAttributes,
             PHKEY phkResult, LPDWORD lpdwDisposition );
```

    Our call went thus:
```
CString subkey = "SOFTWARE\\WindowsMFCII\\Pgm11a\\Settings";
HKEY hkey;
LONG ok;
ok = RegCreateKeyEx (HKEY_CURRENT_USER, subkey, 0, 0, 0, KEY_CREATE_SUB_KEY,
```

```
                              0, &hkey, 0);
        if (ok != ERROR_SUCCESS) return false;
```

The subkey is the desired key to be opened or created, if it is not yet present in the registry. The Reserved parameter is 0 as is the class pointer because it is used for remote computers. The options value is also 0, which is the default and is the value given by the value **REG_OPTION_NON_VOLATILE**, saying that this is a permanent key, as opposed to temporary ones that are not saved when the app terminates.

The next parameter **KEY_CREATE_SUB_KEY** is what we are attempting to do with this function call. Some other possibilities consist of the following.

KEY_CREATE_SUB_KEY   Required to create a subkey of a registry key
KEY_ENUMERATE_SUB_KEYS Required to enumerate the subkeys of a registry key.
KEY_QUERY_VALUE   Required to query the values of a registry key
KEY_READ   Read this key
KEY_SET_VALUE   Required to create, delete, or set a registry value.
KEY_WRITE   Write this key

Once the key is built, the new value must be written using the **RegSetValueEx** function, whose prototype is

```
LONG RegSetValueEx (HKEY hKey, LPCTSTR lpValueName,
                DWORD Reserved, DWORD dwType,
                const BYTE* lpData, DWORD cbData );
```

Here I coded

```
CString entry = "BthFile";
ok = RegSetValueEx (hkey, entry, 0, REG_SZ,
    (const BYTE*) filename.GetBuffer(), filename.GetLength ()+1);
```

Notice that for strings, the function expects a constant BYTE pointer, not a char*.

The Reserved parameter must be 0. There are a number of different types that can be stored in the registry.

REG_BINARY   Binary data in any form.
REG_DWORD   A 32-bit number.
REG_EXPAND_SZ   Null-terminated string that contains unexpanded references to
                        environment variables (for example, "%PATH%"). It will be a Unicode
                        or ANSI string depending on whether you use the Unicode or ANSI
                        functions. To expand the environment variable references, use the
                        ExpandEnvironmentStrings function.
REG_MULTI_SZ   Array of null-terminated strings, terminated by two null characters.
REG_QWORD   A 64-bit number.
REG_SZ   Null-terminated string. It will be a Unicode or ANSI string, depending
                        on whether you use the Unicode or ANSI functions.

The Main Color Palette

Don't PANIC! This whole topic only applies if your computer is running in 256-color mode or lower. If you are running in the higher color modes, there is no color palette in use and the coding does nothing.

In this sample, all bitmaps use the same master palette. Thus, I have created a Palette class to encapsulate palette operations. The Master palette file consists of 256 **RGBQUAD** entries that are easily manipulated as desired. Notice that I have made use of static data members and static functions to handle the initial loading of the palette from the application class. The FillRgbColorTable function handles the alterations of the DIB color tables to force a identity palette when bitmaps are loaded.

Listing for File: Palette.h

```
...
/***************************************************************************/
/*                                                                         */
/* Palette Class: maintains the various identity palettes                  */
/*                                                                         */
/***************************************************************************/

class Palette {

   /***************************************************************************/
   /*                                                                         */
   /* Data Members                                                            */
   /*                                                                         */
   /***************************************************************************/

public:

CPalette      *ptrmainpal;                  // main map color palette

protected:

// the master set of all palettes
static RGBQUAD      pal[256];
static LOGPALETTE *ptrlogpal;               // common work area

// identity palette members
RGBQUAD       maincoltbl [256];             // main map color table for BITMAPINFO

   /***************************************************************************/
   /*                                                                         */
   /* Functions:                                                              */
   /*                                                                         */
   /***************************************************************************/

public:

         Palette (BOOL&);                   // makes a copy identity palette
```

```
            ~Palette ();                            // deletes the copy palette

static BOOL  InitPalette (const char*);            // load or build initial pals
static void  DeletePalette ();                     // remove common palette area
static void  ClearSystemPalette ();                // clear Palette Manager'sPal
static void  ClearSystemPalette (HDC&);
static void  ClearSystemPalette (CDC&);

CPalette*    GetPalette ();                         // member CPalette-not a copy
void         FillRgbColorTable (RGBQUAD*);          // copies RGBcolortbl for DIB
};
```

Listing for File: Palette.cpp

```
...
RGBQUAD      Palette::pal[256];
LOGPALETTE *Palette::ptrlogpal = NULL;


/**********************************************************************************/
/*                                                                              */
/* static InitPalette: loads the master palette                                 */
/*                                                                              */
/**********************************************************************************/

BOOL     Palette::InitPalette (const char *filename) {
 // allocate the common logical palette
 ptrlogpal = (LOGPALETTE*) malloc (sizeof(LOGPALETTE) +
                                   256 * sizeof (PALETTEENTRY));
 if (!ptrlogpal) {
  AfxMessageBox ("Palette Error: Unable to allocate memory for palette",
                 MB_OK);
  return FALSE;
 }
 ptrlogpal->palVersion = 0x300;        // set for Windows 3.0 and later
 ptrlogpal->palNumEntries = 256;       // set for 256-color

 CFileException file_err; // used if more info on errors is desired
 CFile palfile;
 palfile.Open (filename, CFile::modeRead, &file_err);
 UINT actsz = palfile.Read ((LPSTR) &pal[0], sizeof (pal));
 palfile.Close ();
 if (actsz != sizeof (pal)) {
   AfxMessageBox ("Palette Error: Unable to Load the .PAL file", MB_OK);
   return FALSE;
 }
 return TRUE;
}

/**********************************************************************************/
/*                                                                              */
/* static DeletePalette: remove the common palette work area                    */
/*                                                                              */
/**********************************************************************************/

void     Palette::DeletePalette () {
 if (ptrlogpal) free (ptrlogpal);
}
```

```
/*****************************************************************************/
/*                                                                         */
/* Palette: Constructor - setup the requested country palette              */
/*                                                                         */
/*****************************************************************************/

         Palette::Palette (BOOL &ok) {
ptrmainpal   = NULL;
ok = FALSE;

long i;
HDC hdc = CreateDC ("DISPLAY", NULL, NULL, NULL);
::GetSystemPaletteEntries (hdc, 0, 256, ptrlogpal->palPalEntry);

// now merge in the user's palette into the main map color table
for (i=10; i<246; i++) {
 ptrlogpal->palPalEntry[i].peBlue  = pal[i].rgbBlue;
 ptrlogpal->palPalEntry[i].peGreen = pal[i].rgbGreen;
 ptrlogpal->palPalEntry[i].peRed   = pal[i].rgbRed;
 ptrlogpal->palPalEntry[i].peFlags = PC_RESERVED;
}

// now copy these to the main map color table
for (i=0; i<256; i++) {
 maincoltbl[i].rgbBlue  = ptrlogpal->palPalEntry[i].peBlue;
 maincoltbl[i].rgbGreen = ptrlogpal->palPalEntry[i].peGreen;
 maincoltbl[i].rgbRed   = ptrlogpal->palPalEntry[i].peRed;
 maincoltbl[i].rgbReserved = 0;
}

// make our new main map palette
ptrmainpal = new CPalette ();
ptrmainpal->CreatePalette (ptrlogpal);
if (!ptrmainpal) {
 AfxMessageBox ("Palette Error: Unable to Create a Palette", MB_OK);
 DeleteDC (hdc);
 return;
}

// force Palette Manager to reset the master color table
// so the next palette that is realized gets its colors
// mapped into the order of use in the logical palette
// install our new palette, realize it to map the logical palette
// into the master palette, then remove the palette from the DC
ClearSystemPalette (hdc);
HPALETTE holdpal = SelectPalette (hdc,
                              (HPALETTE) ptrmainpal->GetSafeHandle (), FALSE);
RealizePalette (hdc);
SelectPalette (hdc, holdpal, FALSE);
DeleteDC (hdc);
ok = TRUE;
}

/*****************************************************************************/
/*                                                                         */
/* ~Palette: remove allocated objects                                      */
/*                                                                         */
```

```
/**********************************************************************/

   Palette::~Palette () {
 if (ptrmainpal)   delete ptrmainpal;
}


/**********************************************************************/
/*                                                                    */
/* ClearSystemPalette: force Palette Manager to reload colors - several forms*/
/*                                                                    */
/**********************************************************************/

void      Palette::ClearSystemPalette () {
 HDC hdc = CreateDC ("DISPLAY", NULL, NULL, NULL);
 SetSystemPaletteUse (hdc, SYSPAL_NOSTATIC);
 SetSystemPaletteUse (hdc, SYSPAL_STATIC);
 DeleteDC (hdc);
}

void      Palette::ClearSystemPalette (CDC &dc) {
 SetSystemPaletteUse (dc.GetSafeHdc (), SYSPAL_NOSTATIC);
 SetSystemPaletteUse (dc.GetSafeHdc (), SYSPAL_STATIC);
}

void      Palette::ClearSystemPalette (HDC &hdc) {
 SetSystemPaletteUse (hdc, SYSPAL_NOSTATIC);
 SetSystemPaletteUse (hdc, SYSPAL_STATIC);
}


/**********************************************************************/
/*                                                                    */
/* GetPalette: returns a ptr to the indicated identity palette        */
/*                                                                    */
/**********************************************************************/

CPalette* Palette::GetPalette () {
 return ptrmainpal ? ptrmainpal : NULL;
}


/**********************************************************************/
/*                                                                    */
/* FillRgbColorTable: copies the indicated identity color table to ptrdest */
/*                                                                    */
/**********************************************************************/

void      Palette::FillRgbColorTable (RGBQUAD *ptrdest) {
 if (!ptrmainpal) return; // defensive - not initied
 memcpy ((void*) ptrdest, (void*) maincoltbl, 256 * sizeof (RGBQUAD));
}
```

The MainFrame Class

The MainFrame class must handle the main application closure request, **OnClose**, by prompting the user that in doing so it will **forcibly** log off all players and games in progress. It manages the application wide palette by passing along palette change requests to the currently active view, if any.

However, two other problems are solved by MainFrame. The first is the unusual circumstance when all battle header files are closed down, leaving only the frame window active. Some provision must be made to open another battle header file to begin again. This is done via the member function CmServerConnect which calls the app's RetrievePath function to get the last used bth filename, then opens it. The enabler for this menu command is the absence of any application header document, contained in **ptrheaddoc**. You can improve on this as desired.

The other problem concerns the OtherPlayerView document, or the "god-mode" view. The circumstances are as follows. A player has logged on to a game and is in his Player View of the battle. If the Other View menu option is chosen, then an instance of the OtherView document class must be constructed. This additional construction is best done here in the MainFrame class, which can most easily manipulate all of the current views. For now, ignore this aspect. We will return to it when discussing the PlayerView class.

Listing for File: MainFrame.h

```
...
class MainFrame : public CMDIFrameWnd {
protected:  // control bar embedded members
 CStatusBar   m_wndStatusBar;
 CToolBar     m_wndToolBar;

public: // create from serialization only
 MainFrame();
 DECLARE_DYNCREATE(MainFrame)

 virtual BOOL   PreCreateWindow(CREATESTRUCT& cs);
 virtual        ~MainFrame();

protected:  // control bar embedded members
 afx_msg void   CmMakeOtherView ();          //  allocate opponent's view
 afx_msg void   CmCloseOtherView ();         //  close opponent's view
 afx_msg void   CmEnableServerConnect (CCmdUI*);
 afx_msg void   CmServerConnect ();
 afx_msg int    OnCreate(LPCREATESTRUCT lpCreateStruct);
 afx_msg void   OnClose();
 afx_msg void   OnPaletteChanged (CWnd*); // pass along palette change requests
 afx_msg BOOL   OnQueryNewPalette ();
 DECLARE_MESSAGE_MAP()

...
```

Listing for File: MainFrame.cpp—Excerpts

```
...
IMPLEMENT_DYNCREATE(MainFrame, CMDIFrameWnd)

BEGIN_MESSAGE_MAP(MainFrame, CMDIFrameWnd)
 ON_WM_CREATE()
 ON_WM_CLOSE()
 ON_WM_PALETTECHANGED ()
 ON_WM_QUERYNEWPALETTE ()
 ON_COMMAND (CM_SERVER_CONNECT,    CmServerConnect)
 ON_UPDATE_COMMAND_UI (CM_SERVER_CONNECT,  CmEnableServerConnect)
 ON_COMMAND (CM_MAKE_OTHER_VIEW,  CmMakeOtherView)
 ON_COMMAND (CM_FILE_CLOSE_OTHER, CmCloseOtherView)
END_MESSAGE_MAP()

static UINT indicators[] = {
 ID_SEPARATOR,              // status line indicator
 ID_INDICATOR_CAPS,
 ID_INDICATOR_NUM,
 ID_INDICATOR_SCRL,
};

MainFrame::MainFrame() { }
MainFrame::~MainFrame() { }

int MainFrame::OnCreate(LPCREATESTRUCT lpCreateStruct) {
 if (CMDIFrameWnd::OnCreate(lpCreateStruct) == -1)
  return -1;

 if (!m_wndToolBar.Create(this) ||
     !m_wndToolBar.LoadToolBar(IDR_MAINFRAME)) {
  TRACE0("Failed to create toolbar\n");
  return -1;       // fail to create
 }

 if (!m_wndStatusBar.Create(this) ||
     !m_wndStatusBar.SetIndicators(indicators,
      sizeof(indicators)/sizeof(UINT)))   {
  TRACE0("Failed to create status bar\n");
  return -1;       // fail to create
 }

 m_wndToolBar.SetBarStyle(m_wndToolBar.GetBarStyle() |
     CBRS_TOOLTIPS | CBRS_FLYBY | CBRS_SIZE_DYNAMIC);

 m_wndToolBar.EnableDocking(CBRS_ALIGN_ANY);
 EnableDocking(CBRS_ALIGN_ANY);
 DockControlBar(&m_wndToolBar);

 return 0;
}

/**************************************************************/
/*                                                          */
/* OnClose: query user about termination of whole battle    */
/*                                                          */
/**************************************************************/
```

```
void       MainFrame::OnClose () {
 CString msg1, msg2;
 msg1.LoadString (IDS_BATTLEMAIN_CLOSE);
 msg2.LoadString (IDS_BATTLEMAIN_QUERY);
 if (MessageBox (msg2, msg1, MB_YESNO | MB_ICONQUESTION) == IDYES) {
  if (theApp.ptrheaddoc &&
      theApp.ptrheaddoc->IsKindOf (RUNTIME_CLASS (HeadDoc))) {
   theApp.ptrheaddoc->OnCloseDocument ();
   theApp.ptrheaddoc = NULL;
   }
  CMDIFrameWnd::OnClose ();
  }
}

/**************************************************************************/
/*                                                                      */
/* CmEnableServerConnect: enabler for menu server connect item          */
/*                                                                      */
/**************************************************************************/

void       MainFrame::CmEnableServerConnect (CCmdUI *ptrui) {
 ptrui->Enable (theApp.ptrheaddoc ? 0 : 1);
}

/**************************************************************************/
/*                                                                      */
/* CmServerConnect: reconnect to the server to logon to battle games    */
/*                                                                      */
/**************************************************************************/

void       MainFrame::CmServerConnect () {
 if (!theApp.ptrheaddoc) {
  CString bthfile = theApp.RetrievePath ();
  if (bthfile.IsEmpty()) bthfile = "Game\\Battle.bth";
  theApp.ptrheadtmp->OpenDocumentFile (LPCSTR(bthfile));
  }
}

/**************************************************************************/
/*                                                                      */
/* CmMakeOtherView: create opponent view                                */
/*                                                                      */
/**************************************************************************/

void       MainFrame::CmMakeOtherView () {
 CMDIChildWnd *ptrMDIActive = MDIGetActive ();
 ASSERT(ptrMDIActive != NULL);
 if (!ptrMDIActive) return;

 CDocument *ptrdoc = ptrMDIActive->GetActiveDocument ();
 ASSERT(ptrdoc != NULL);
 if (!ptrdoc) return;

 CView *ptrview;
 POSITION pos = ptrdoc->GetFirstViewPosition ();
 while (pos != NULL) {
  ptrview = ptrdoc->GetNextView (pos);
  if (ptrview && ptrview->IsKindOf (RUNTIME_CLASS (OtherView))) {
```

```
   ptrview->GetParentFrame ()->ActivateFrame ();
   return;
  }
 }

 if (ptrdoc->IsKindOf (RUNTIME_CLASS (GameDoc))) {
  GameDoc *ptrbdoc = (GameDoc*) ptrdoc;
  long id = ptrbdoc->GetPlayerId ();
  if (id == -1) return;
  CMDIChildWnd *ptrNewFrame;
  ptrNewFrame = (CMDIChildWnd*) (theApp.ptrothertmp->CreateNewFrame (ptrdoc,
                                                                NULL));
  if (!ptrNewFrame) return;        // not created
  if (ptrNewFrame->IsKindOf (RUNTIME_CLASS (CMDIChildWnd)))
   theApp.ptrothertmp->InitialUpdateFrame (ptrNewFrame, ptrdoc);

  pos = ptrdoc->GetFirstViewPosition ();
  while (pos != NULL) {
   ptrview = ptrdoc->GetNextView (pos);
   if (ptrview && ptrview->IsKindOf (RUNTIME_CLASS (PlayerView))) {
    ptrview->GetParentFrame ()->ActivateFrame ();
    break;
   }
  }
  MDITile (MDITILE_VERTICAL);
 }
}

/****************************************************************************/
/*                                                                        */
/* CmCloseOtherView: close opponent view                                  */
/*                                                                        */
/****************************************************************************/

void     MainFrame::CmCloseOtherView () {
 CMDIChildWnd *ptrMDIActive = MDIGetActive ();
 ASSERT(ptrMDIActive != NULL);
 if (!ptrMDIActive) return;

 CDocument *ptrdoc = ptrMDIActive->GetActiveDocument ();
 ASSERT(ptrdoc != NULL);
 if (!ptrdoc) return;

 CView *ptrview;
 POSITION pos = ptrdoc->GetFirstViewPosition ();
 while (pos != NULL) {
  ptrview = ptrdoc->GetNextView (pos);
  if (ptrview && ptrview->IsKindOf (RUNTIME_CLASS (OtherView))) {
   ptrview->GetParentFrame ()->PostMessage (WM_CLOSE, 0, 0L);
   return;
  }
 }
}
```

The HeadDoc and HeadView Classes

The HeadDoc and HeadView classes combine to provide a **CFormView** of the array of control documents contained in the header document. Since the array of HeadData items is maintained in the document class, I have kept the actual form view message response handlers within the document class instead of the view class. The document member, **battle_array**, contains the array of HeadData objects serialized from the bth file. The member **selection** is the index of the current element in the array that has been given to the form view to display.

There are the usual document functions for opening, closing, serialization and deleting the document contents. Additionally, the functions CmNextBattle, CmPrevBattle, CmActivateBattle and CmCloseBattle respond to the for view buttons. I have command enablers to prevent their activation when not appropriate.

Functions GetNumBattles and GetThisBattle help the HeadView class display the next HeadData item, while GetHeadView provides a pointer to the associated view.

Inner-document communication functions, LogoffBattle and LogoffAllBattles, permit other documents and views to request termination of the current or all battles that have been started.

Listing for File: HeadDoc.h

```
...
/********************************************************************************/
/*                                                                          */
/* HeadDoc: Class to maintain lists of current battle to do                 */
/*                                                                          */
/********************************************************************************/

class HeadDoc : public CDocument {

public:
HeadDataArray    battle_array; // container of list of battle header objs
long             selection;    // currently selected header data

protected: // create from serialization only
 HeadDoc();
 DECLARE_DYNCREATE(HeadDoc)

public:
 virtual BOOL   OnNewDocument();
 virtual void   Serialize(CArchive& ar);
 virtual BOOL   CanCloseFrame(CFrameWnd* pFrame);
 virtual void   DeleteContents();
 virtual void   OnCloseDocument();
 virtual BOOL   OnOpenDocument(LPCTSTR lpszPathName);
 virtual        ~HeadDoc();

        long   GetNumBattles (); // gets number of battle header data objs
        void   GetThisBattle (char*, char*, char*, char*, long*, long*);
```

```
      void   LogoffBattle (long);
      void   LogoffAllBattles ();
   HeadView*  GetHeadView ();
afx_msg   void   OnFileClose ();
afx_msg   void   CmNextBattle ();
afx_msg   void   CmPrevBattle ();
afx_msg   void   CmActivateBattle ();
afx_msg   void   CmCloseBattle ();
afx_msg   void   CmEnableNextBattle (CCmdUI*);
afx_msg   void   CmEnablePrevBattle (CCmdUI*);
afx_msg   void   CmEnableActivateBattle (CCmdUI*);
afx_msg   void   CmEnableCloseBattle (CCmdUI*);
...
```

Listing for File: HeadDoc.cpp

```
...
IMPLEMENT_DYNCREATE(HeadDoc, CDocument)

BEGIN_MESSAGE_MAP(HeadDoc, CDocument)
 ON_COMMAND            (CM_NEXT_BATTLE,      CmNextBattle)
 ON_COMMAND            (CM_PREV_BATTLE,      CmPrevBattle)
 ON_COMMAND            (CM_ACTIVATE_BATTLE,  CmActivateBattle)
 ON_COMMAND            (CM_CLOSE_BATTLE,     CmCloseBattle)
 ON_UPDATE_COMMAND_UI  (CM_NEXT_BATTLE,      CmEnableNextBattle)
 ON_UPDATE_COMMAND_UI  (CM_PREV_BATTLE,      CmEnablePrevBattle)
 ON_UPDATE_COMMAND_UI  (CM_ACTIVATE_BATTLE,  CmEnableActivateBattle)
 ON_UPDATE_COMMAND_UI  (CM_CLOSE_BATTLE,     CmEnableCloseBattle)
END_MESSAGE_MAP()

HeadDoc::HeadDoc() {
  theApp.ptrheaddoc = this;
}

/****************************************************************************/
/*                                                                        */
/* GetNumBattles: returns the number of battles objects in the collection */
/*                                                                        */
/****************************************************************************/

long      HeadDoc::GetNumBattles () {
 return battle_array.GetSize ();
}

/****************************************************************************/
/*                                                                        */
/* GetHeadView: returns ptr to header view for minimize/normal msgs       */
/*                                                                        */
/****************************************************************************/

HeadView* HeadDoc::GetHeadView () {
 POSITION pos = GetFirstViewPosition ();
 CView *ptrview;
 while (pos != NULL) {
  ptrview = GetNextView (pos);
  if (ptrview && ptrview->IsKindOf (RUNTIME_CLASS (HeadView)))
   return (HeadView*) ptrview;
```

```
  }
  return NULL;
}

/***********************************************************************/
/*                                                                     */
/* GetThisBattle: returns a copy of the current Battle Header object    */
/*                                                                     */
/***********************************************************************/

void      HeadDoc::GetThisBattle (char *msg_descr,  char *msg_file,
                                   char *msg_status, char *msg_active,
                                   long *ptrsel, long *ptrnum) {
  if (battle_array.GetSize () == 0) {
   strcpy_s (msg_descr, _MAX_PATH, "No Battles are in this group");
   strcpy_s (msg_file, _MAX_PATH, "No file");
   strcpy_s (msg_status, 80, "None");
   strcpy_s (msg_active, 80, "None");
   *ptrsel = *ptrnum = 0;
  }
  else {
   HeadData *ptrdata = (HeadData*) battle_array.GetAt (selection);
   if (ptrdata && ptrdata->IsKindOf (RUNTIME_CLASS (HeadData))) {
    strcpy_s (msg_descr, _MAX_PATH, ptrdata->battle_descr);
    strcpy_s (msg_file, _MAX_PATH,  ptrdata->battle_file);
    if (ptrdata->battle_status == Battle_NotStarted)
     strcpy_s (msg_status, 80, "Battle has not been started");
    else if (ptrdata->battle_status == Battle_InProgress)
     strcpy_s (msg_status, 80, "Battle is in progress");
    else if (ptrdata->battle_status == Battle_Completed)
     strcpy_s (msg_status, 80, "Battle has been fully completed");
    else strcpy_s (msg_status, 80, "Unknown");
    if (ptrdata->ptrctldoc)
     strcpy_s (msg_active, 80,
              "Battle Administration Active - Battle can be played");
    else
     strcpy_s (msg_active, 80, "Battle Not Logged On Yet");
    *ptrsel = selection;
    *ptrnum = battle_array.GetSize ();
   }
  }
}

/***********************************************************************/
/*                                                                     */
/* DeleteContents: remove the array of BattleHeaderData objects         */
/*                                                                     */
/***********************************************************************/

void      HeadDoc::DeleteContents () {
  long i;
  selection = 0;
  if (battle_array.GetSize () !=0) {
   for (i=0; i<battle_array.GetSize (); i++)   // for each data object
    delete (HeadData*) battle_array.GetAt (i); // get at it and delete it
   battle_array.RemoveAll ();                  // now empty the array container
  }
}
```

```
/*******************************************************************************/
/*                                                                           */
/* OnNewDocument: launch a new BattleHeader document                         */
/*                                                                           */
/*******************************************************************************/

BOOL     HeadDoc::OnNewDocument () {
 selection = 0;
 if (!CDocument::OnNewDocument ()) return FALSE;
 HeadData *ptrdata = new HeadData ();
 strcpy_s (ptrdata->battle_descr, sizeof(ptrdata->battle_descr),
          "Denmark Battle between Germans and French");
 strcpy_s (ptrdata->battle_file, sizeof(ptrdata->battle_file),
          "D:\\WindowsMFCII\\Pgm11a\\Game\\BattleM.btl");
 ptrdata->battle_status = Battle_NotStarted;
 battle_array.Add (ptrdata);  // add the new object to the array
 ptrdata = new HeadData ();
 strcpy_s (ptrdata->battle_descr, sizeof(ptrdata->battle_descr),
          "Small Denmark Battle between Germans and French");
 strcpy_s (ptrdata->battle_file, sizeof(ptrdata->battle_file),
          "D:\\WindowsMFCII\\Pgm11a\\Game\\BattleS.btl");
 ptrdata->battle_status = Battle_InProgress;
 battle_array.Add (ptrdata); // add the new object to the array
 return TRUE;
}


/*******************************************************************************/
/*                                                                           */
/* OnOpenDocument: open existing BattleHeader document                       */
/*                                                                           */
/*                                                                           */
/*******************************************************************************/

BOOL     HeadDoc::OnOpenDocument (const char *filename) {
 selection = 0;
 CString path (filename);
 long i = path.ReverseFind ('\\');
 const char *pathc = (LPCTSTR) path;
 strcpy_s (theApp.mainpath, sizeof(theApp.mainpath), pathc);
 theApp.mainpath [i+1] = 0;
 BOOL retcd = CDocument::OnOpenDocument (filename);
 if (!retcd) {
  CFile file;                 // the file, will be binary I/O still
  CFileException file_err; // used if more info on errors is desired
  file.Open (filename, CFile::modeRead, &file_err);
  HeadData *ptrhead;
  ptrhead = new HeadData ();
  while (ptrhead->Read (file)) {
   battle_array.Add (ptrhead);   // and add it to the array
   ptrhead = new HeadData ();
  }
  delete ptrhead;
  file.Close ();
  if (battle_array.GetSize () > 0) {
   retcd = TRUE;
   SetModifiedFlag (TRUE);
   CDocument::SetPathName (filename, TRUE);
  }
```

```
 }
 SetModifiedFlag (TRUE);
 return retcd;
}

/*********************************************************************/
/*                                                                 */
/* Serialize: input or output the whole document - I/O binary data only  */
/*                                                                 */
/*********************************************************************/

void       HeadDoc::Serialize (CArchive &ar) {
 if (ar.IsStoring ()) {                        // save to .BTH file
  if (battle_array.GetSize () == 0) return;// none to save
  battle_array.Serialize (ar);               // output to container's serializer
 }
 else battle_array.Serialize (ar);            // input from container's serializer
}

/*********************************************************************/
/*                                                                 */
/* CmNextBattle: scroll to next battle group to examine            */
/*                                                                 */
/*********************************************************************/

void       HeadDoc::CmNextBattle () {
 if (selection + 1 >= battle_array.GetSize ()) {
  MessageBeep (0);
  return;
 }
 selection++;
 UpdateAllViews (NULL, 0, NULL);
}

/*********************************************************************/
/*                                                                 */
/* CmPrevBattle: scroll to previous battle to examine              */
/*                                                                 */
/*********************************************************************/

void       HeadDoc::CmPrevBattle () {
 if (selection - 1 < 0) {
  MessageBeep (0);
  return;
 }
 selection--;
 UpdateAllViews (NULL, 0, NULL);
}

/*********************************************************************/
/*                                                                 */
/* CmActivateBattle: open this battle for logon and playing        */
/*                                                                 */
/*********************************************************************/

void       HeadDoc::CmActivateBattle () {
 if (battle_array.GetSize ()) {
  HeadData *ptrdata = (HeadData*) battle_array.GetAt (selection);
```

```
  if (ptrdata->ptrctldoc == NULL) {
   CDocument *ptrdoc = theApp.ptrcontroltmp->
                         OpenDocumentFile (ptrdata->battle_file);
   ASSERT (ptrdoc->IsKindOf (RUNTIME_CLASS (ControlDoc)));
   if (ptrdoc && ptrdoc->IsKindOf (RUNTIME_CLASS (ControlDoc))) {
    ptrdata->ptrctldoc = (ControlDoc*) ptrdoc;
    ptrdata->ptrctldoc->SetHeaderAddr (this, selection, ptrdata->battle_descr);
    UpdateAllViews (NULL, 0, NULL);
    GetHeadView ()->GetParentFrame ()->ShowWindow (SW_MINIMIZE);
    return;
   }
  }
 }
 MessageBeep (0);
}

/******************************************************************************/
/*                                                                          */
/* LogoffBattle: BattleControlDoc view is terminating - kill whole battle   */
/*                                                                          */
/******************************************************************************/

void      HeadDoc::LogoffBattle (long id) {
 long num = battle_array.GetSize ();
 if (num && id >=0 && id < num) {
  HeadData *ptrdata = (HeadData*) battle_array.GetAt (id);
  if (ptrdata && ptrdata->IsKindOf (RUNTIME_CLASS (HeadData))) {
   ptrdata->ptrctldoc = NULL;
   GetHeadView ()->GetParentFrame ()->ShowWindow (SW_RESTORE);
   UpdateAllViews (NULL, 0, NULL);
  }
 }
}

/******************************************************************************/
/*                                                                          */
/* LogoffAllBattles: BattleHeaderDoc view is terminating - kill all battles*/
/*                                                                          */
/******************************************************************************/

void      HeadDoc::LogoffAllBattles () {
 long num = battle_array.GetSize ();
 for (long i = 0; i<num; i++) {
  HeadData *ptrdata = (HeadData*) battle_array.GetAt (i);
  if (ptrdata && ptrdata->IsKindOf (RUNTIME_CLASS (HeadData))) {
   ControlDoc *ptrdoc = ptrdata->ptrctldoc;
   if (ptrdoc && ptrdoc->IsKindOf (RUNTIME_CLASS (ControlDoc))) {
    ptrdoc->ServerClosesAdmin ();
    UpdateAllViews (NULL, 0, NULL);
   }
  }
 }
}

/******************************************************************************/
/*                                                                          */
/* OnFileClose: close all server docs and those below it                    */
/*                                                                          */
```

```
/*******************************************************************/

void      HeadDoc::OnFileClose () {
 OnCloseDocument ();
}

/*******************************************************************/
/*                                                               */
/* OnCloseDocument: close the server connection and all documents below it */
/*                                                               */
/*******************************************************************/

void      HeadDoc::OnCloseDocument () {
 LogoffAllBattles ();
 theApp.ptrheaddoc = NULL;
 CString s = GetPathName ();
 if (!s.IsEmpty ()) {
  // update registry with this bth file
  ((Pgm11aApp*) AfxGetApp ())->SavePath (s);
 }
 if (IsModified ()) {
  OnSaveDocument (s);
 }
 CDocument::OnCloseDocument ();
}

/*******************************************************************/
/*                                                               */
/* CanCloseFrame: respond to termination request                 */
/*                                                               */
/*******************************************************************/

BOOL      HeadDoc::CanCloseFrame (CFrameWnd *ptrwin) {
 if (!ptrwin) return TRUE;
 if (!ptrwin->IsKindOf (RUNTIME_CLASS (HeadFrame))) return FALSE;
 CView *ptrview = ((HeadFrame*) ptrwin)->GetActiveView ();
 if (ptrview && ptrview->IsKindOf (RUNTIME_CLASS (HeadView))) {
  CString msg1, msg2;
  msg1.LoadString (IDS_BATTLEHEAD_CLOSE);
  msg2.LoadString (IDS_BATTLEHEAD_QUERY);
  if (MessageBox (0, msg2, msg1, MB_YESNO | MB_ICONQUESTION) == IDYES) {
   LogoffAllBattles ();
   return CDocument::CanCloseFrame (ptrwin);//TRUE;
  }
  return FALSE;
 }
 return FALSE;
}

/*******************************************************************/
/*                                                               */
/* CmCloseBattle: terminate this battle and logoff all players   */
/*                                                               */
/*******************************************************************/

void      HeadDoc::CmCloseBattle () {
 if (battle_array.GetSize ()) {
  HeadData *ptrdata = (HeadData*) battle_array.GetAt (selection);
```

```
  if (ptrdata &&
      ptrdata->IsKindOf (RUNTIME_CLASS (HeadData)) &&
      ptrdata->ptrctldoc &&
      ptrdata->ptrctldoc->IsKindOf (RUNTIME_CLASS (ControlDoc))) {
   ptrdata->ptrctldoc->ServerClosesAdmin ();
   ptrdata->ptrctldoc = NULL;
   UpdateAllViews (NULL, 0, NULL);
  }
  else MessageBeep (0);
 }
 else MessageBeep (0);
}


/****************************************************************************/
/*                                                                        */
/* CmEnableNextBattle: enable or disable Next Battle menuitem             */
/*                                                                        */
/****************************************************************************/

void      HeadDoc::CmEnableNextBattle (CCmdUI *ptrui) {
 ptrui->Enable (selection + 2 > battle_array.GetSize () ? 0 : 1);
}


/****************************************************************************/
/*                                                                        */
/* CmEnablePrevBattle: enable or disable Previous Battle menuitem         */
/*                                                                        */
/****************************************************************************/

void      HeadDoc::CmEnablePrevBattle (CCmdUI *ptrui) {
 ptrui->Enable (selection > 0 ? 1 : 0);
}


/****************************************************************************/
/*                                                                        */
/* CmEnableActivateBattle: enable or disable Activate Battle menuitem     */
/*                                                                        */
/****************************************************************************/

void      HeadDoc::CmEnableActivateBattle (CCmdUI *ptrui) {
 ptrui->Enable (battle_array.GetSize () == 0 ? 0 :
               ((HeadData*) battle_array.GetAt (selection))->ptrctldoc
                ? 0 : 1);
}


/****************************************************************************/
/*                                                                        */
/* CmEnableCloseBattle: enable or disable Close Battle menuitem           */
/*                                                                        */
/****************************************************************************/

void      HeadDoc::CmEnableCloseBattle (CCmdUI *ptrui) {
 ptrui->Enable (battle_array.GetSize () == 0 ? 0 :
               ((HeadData*) battle_array.GetAt (selection))->ptrctldoc
                ? 1 : 0);
}
```

Notice that the constructor is responsible for installing a pointer to itself in the application class. I did this for convenience so that I did not have to continually dynamically locate this pointer.

In GetHeadView, I show the common coding for searching through all the views that have been opened on one document. The two functions, **GetFirstViewPosition** and **GetNextView**, work with a **POSITION** structure. Not only should you check for a NULL pointer, indicating no views, but also use the **IsKindOf** function to guarantee that the pointer is of the proper runtime class you desire

```
POSITION pos = GetFirstViewPosition ();
CView *ptrview;
while (pos != NULL) {
 ptrview = GetNextView (pos);
 if (ptrview && ptrview->IsKindOf (RUNTIME_CLASS (HeadView)))
   return (HeadView*) ptrview;
}
return NULL;
```

Next, examine **OnOpenDocument**. The first action is to extract the path from the file name and copy that path into the application's **mainpath** member. It is then concatenated to all other file names to form the full path. I construct a **CString** instance and use the **ReverseFind** function to find the last \ character

```
CString path (filename);
long i = path.ReverseFind ('\\');
const char *pathc = (LPCTSTR) path;
strcpy_s (theApp.mainpath, sizeof(theApp.mainpath), pathc);
theApp.mainpath [i+1] = 0;
```

Next, I assume the file is a binary bth file and try to serialize it by invoking the base class **OnOpenDocument**. This function will then call our **Serialize** function. Should the operation fail, I construct a **CFile** instance and try to use the text Read function

```
BOOL retcd = CDocument::OnOpenDocument (filename);
if (!retcd) {
 CFile file;              // the file, will be binary I/O still
 CFileException file_err; // used if more info on errors is
                          // desired
 file.Open (filename, CFile::modeRead, &file_err);
 HeadData *ptrhead;
 ptrhead = new HeadData ();
 while (ptrhead->Read (file)) {
  battle_array.Add (ptrhead);    // and add it to the array
  ptrhead = new HeadData ();
 }
 delete ptrhead;
 file.Close ();
```

How does a control document get launched? Via CmActivateBattle. Given the array index of the control document in the HeadData array, I launch the secondary document view classes by invoking the **OpenDocumentFile** function of the corresponding document template class. I have included a bit of runtime type checking to guarantee the launch is successful. Notice that I install the pointer to the newly launched control document class in the corresponding HeadData array member, **ptrctldoc**, so that I know which doc-view objects are associated with which control object. This way I can tell which one to shut down. Also, notice that I set a pointer to this HeadDoc in the control doc class as well. Rather like a double linked list. Now I can go forward or backwards between document classes. I have a parent child arrangement. After invoking **UpdateAllViews**, I then minimize this header view, leaving the control document the main active view on screen

```
    if (battle_array.GetSize ()) {
     HeadData *ptrdata = (HeadData*) battle_array.GetAt (selection);
     if (ptrdata->ptrctldoc == NULL) {
      CDocument *ptrdoc = theApp.ptrcontroltmp->
                            OpenDocumentFile (ptrdata->battle_file);
      ASSERT (ptrdoc->IsKindOf (RUNTIME_CLASS (ControlDoc)));
      if (ptrdoc && ptrdoc->IsKindOf (RUNTIME_CLASS (ControlDoc))) {
       ptrdata->ptrctldoc = (ControlDoc*) ptrdoc;
       ptrdata->ptrctldoc->SetHeaderAddr (
                            this,selection,ptrdata->battle_descr);
       UpdateAllViews (NULL, 0, NULL);
       GetHeadView ()->GetParentFrame ()->ShowWindow (SW_MINIMIZE);
       return;
      }
     }
    }
```

Since the framework has installed the **FWS_ADDTOTITLE** style and I want specific titles for the views, all of the frame windows for the view classes must have an overridden **PreCreateWindow** to remove that style. Since this is MDI, the view will have a child MDI frame window around it. Here is that simple class.

Listing for File: HeadFrame.cpp

```
...
/* PreCreateWindow: remove FWS_ADDTOTITLE so template name is used        */
/*                    not document file name                              */

BOOL HeadFrame::PreCreateWindow(CREATESTRUCT& cs) {
 cs.style &= ~(LONG) FWS_ADDTOTITLE;
 return CMDIChildWnd::PreCreateWindow (cs);
}
...
```

Since all of the major work has been done in the HeadDoc class, the HeadView class merely manages the transfer of the data to and from the **CFormView** controls.

Listing for File: HeadView.h

```
...
/******************************************************************************/
/*                                                                          */
/* HeadView Class: provide battle selection capabilities                    */
```

```
/*                                                                          */
/***************************************************************************/

class HeadView : public CFormView {
protected: // create from serialization only
 HeadView();
 DECLARE_DYNCREATE(HeadView)

enum {IDD = IDD_HEAD};

char msg_descr[MAX_PATH];
char msg_file[MAX_PATH];
char msg_status[80];
char msg_active[80];
long num_battles;
long selection;

public:
          HeadDoc* GetDocument();
 void     OnUpdate (CView*, LPARAM, CObject*);
 void     DoDataExchange (CDataExchange*);
 virtual ~HeadView();
...
};
#ifndef _DEBUG  // debug version in HeadView.cpp
inline HeadDoc* HeadView::GetDocument() { return (HeadDoc*)m_pDocument; }
#endif
```

Listing for File: HeadView.cpp

```
...
IMPLEMENT_DYNCREATE(HeadView, CFormView)

HeadView::HeadView() : CFormView (HeadView::IDD) {
 msg_descr[0]  = 0;
 msg_file[0]   = 0;
 msg_status[0] = 0;
 msg_active[0] = 0;
}

/***************************************************************************/
/*                                                                          */
/* OnUpdate: reacquire this battle information and redisplay it             */
/*                                                                          */
/***************************************************************************/

void     HeadView::OnUpdate (CView *ptrsender, LPARAM hint,
                               CObject *ptrdata) {
 HeadDoc *ptrdoc = GetDocument ();
 ptrdoc->GetThisBattle (msg_descr, msg_file, msg_status, msg_active,
                         &selection, &num_battles);
 UpdateData (FALSE);
 Invalidate ();
}

/***************************************************************************/
/*                                                                          */
```

```
/* DoDataExchange: transfer the battle information into the controls    */
/*                                                                       */
/*************************************************************************/

void       HeadView::DoDataExchange (CDataExchange *ptrdx) {
 GetDlgItem (IDC_BATTLE_DESCR)->SetWindowText (msg_descr);
 GetDlgItem (IDC_BATTLE_FILE)->SetWindowText (msg_file);
 GetDlgItem (IDC_BATTLE_STATUS)->SetWindowText (msg_status);
 GetDlgItem (IDC_BATTLE_ACTIVE)->SetWindowText (msg_active);
}
```

The ControlDoc and ControlView Classes

An id is defined for each of the possible eight players that could potentially be involved in a battle in the file PlayerId.h

```
enum Players {GermanPlayer, ItalianPlayer,  JapanesePlayer,
             BritishPlayer, FrenchPlayer, USAPlayer, RussianPlayer,
             MinorsPlayer};
```

All control documents are in text format for convenience. The Paris document file, Paris.btl, contains three integers. The first is the number of players that are required to play this battle. Next come a series of integers that identify the required players. Here 0 and 4 represent the German and French players. Finally, the bitmap file that contains the playing field for all sides is given.

```
2
0
4
Europe.bmp
```

To store this information, the control document class defines several structures. The Players structure contains two key **bool**s indicating whether this player is required for the battle and whether he is currently logged on. It also contains a pointer to that player's view so the control doc can quickly hide and show this player's view as the turns progress. The Game structure contains the basic information about this control doc, including the common background bitmap and the current player.

The ControlDoc class maintains an array of 8 Player structures, **players**. It has a pointer back to the HeadDoc that launched it.

There are the usual open and close document functions. The key functions for the control document lay in the launching and termination of the player documents and the processing of game turns. For each of the 8 possible players, there is a menu command function, such as CmLogonGerman, and a command enabler to enable only those players that are involved in this particular battle to be able to log on. Each of these command functions, simply calls the common helper function, LogonPlayer.

Similarly, there is a LogoffPlayer function as well as a LogoffAll function for a fast shut down. In other words, a player can voluntarily decide to log off or the game manager can force all to log off. AllLoggedOn returns true when all required players are currently logged on and triggers the game sequencing actions.

When a player has finished his turn and presses the Do It! button, ActionDone handles hiding that player and re-showing the next player. The actual hiding and showing of player views is done by ShowPlayer. NextPlayerIs returns the index of the which player get his turn next.

Serialization is handled via functions LoadBattle and SaveBattle while SetHeaderAddr provides a mechanism for the parent HeadDoc to install a pointer to itself in this ControlDoc instance.

Listing for File: ControlDoc.h

```
...
const int MAX_PLAYERS = 8;

struct Players {
 bool        isrequired;      // true when this player has forces
 bool        isloggedon;      // true when player is logged on
 PlayerView *ptrplayerview;   // the player's view
 GameDoc    *ptrgamedoc;      // the player's game doc
};

struct Game {
 long   active_phase;
 long   num_players_required;
 long   first_player;
 long   current_player;
 long   current_turn;
 char   bkgrndfile[MAX_PATH];
 char   bkgrndbasefile[MAX_PATH];
};

struct CurrentAction {
 BYTE done;
 BYTE type;
};

/***********************************************************************/
/*                                                                   */
/* ControlDoc: Container for one complete battle                     */
/*                                                                   */
/***********************************************************************/

class ControlDoc : public CDocument {
public:
          ControlDoc();
 virtual ~ControlDoc();
     DECLARE_DYNCREATE(ControlDoc)

/***********************************************************************/
/*                                                                   */
/* Data Members                                                      */
/*                                                                   */
```

```
/********************************************************************/

public:

HeadDoc    *ptrheaddoc;                // our head document
long        head_index;               // head index

char        descr[MAX_PATH];          // our battle description
char        controlfile[MAX_PATH];    // our filename to save into
bool        all_logged_on;            // true when all required are on

Players     players[MAX_PLAYERS];     // array of players to control
Game        game;

CurrentAction  current_action[MAX_PLAYERS];

virtual BOOL OnOpenDocument (LPCTSTR);         // open existing battle
virtual void OnCloseDocument ();
virtual void OnFileClose ();
virtual BOOL OnSaveDocument (LPCTSTR);         // save a battle
virtual void DeleteContents ();                // remove this battle
virtual void ServerClosesAdmin ();
virtual BOOL CanCloseFrame (CFrameWnd*);

virtual ControlView* GetControlView ();

virtual void LogonPlayer (long);
virtual void LogoffPlayer (long);
virtual void LogoffAll ();

virtual void SetHeaderAddr (HeadDoc*, long, char*);
virtual void ShowPlayer (long, bool);

virtual void ActionDone (long);

protected:

virtual long NextPlayerIs ();
virtual bool LoadBattle (LPCTSTR);             // load in a battle - setup view
virtual bool SaveBattle (LPCTSTR);             // save this battle
virtual void ClearControlValues ();
virtual void RemoveObjects ();                         // removes all allocated objects
virtual bool AllLoggedOn ();
virtual void CmLogonGerman ();
virtual void CmLogonItaly ();
virtual void CmLogonJapan ();
virtual void CmLogonBritian ();
virtual void CmLogonFrance ();
virtual void CmLogonUSA ();
virtual void CmLogonRussia ();
virtual void CmLogonMinor ();
virtual void CmEnableLogonGerman (CCmdUI*);
virtual void CmEnableLogonItaly (CCmdUI*);
virtual void CmEnableLogonJapan (CCmdUI*);
virtual void CmEnableLogonBritian (CCmdUI*);
virtual void CmEnableLogonFrance (CCmdUI*);
virtual void CmEnableLogonUSA (CCmdUI*);
virtual void CmEnableLogonRussia (CCmdUI*);
```

```
virtual void CmEnableLogonMinor (CCmdUI*);
...
```

The constructor sets all array values to NULL or 0 prior to the serialization process.

SetHeaderAddr does significant runtime checking on the pointers to verify they are correct class instances before storing them. It also builds the view frame's caption and calls **SetWindowText** to install the concatenated title. Thus, I am completely overriding normal document view filename titles.

Examine the process for launching the player documents, in LogonPlayer. Again, I use the application's player document template to launch the player document view objects. Then I runtime type check the results to guarantee a successful launch

```
CDocument *ptrcdoc =
                theApp.ptrplayertmp->OpenDocumentFile (game.bkgrndfile);
if (ptrcdoc) {
 if (ptrcdoc && ptrcdoc->IsKindOf (RUNTIME_CLASS (GameDoc))) {
  GameDoc *ptrdoc = (GameDoc*) ptrcdoc;
  CView *ptrcview;
  POSITION pos = ptrdoc->GetFirstViewPosition ();
  if (pos != NULL) {
   ptrcview = ptrdoc->GetNextView (pos);
   if (ptrcview && ptrcview->IsKindOf (RUNTIME_CLASS (PlayerView))) {
```

If all has gone ok, I store the pointer to the player view in the players structure along with a pointer to its document class. The player document also needs to be chained to its parent document, so I invoke the player's document's PostControlAddrs function to tell the player document which player ID it represents and who its parent control document and view are

```
PlayerView *ptrview = (PlayerView*) ptrcview;
players[id].ptrplayerview = ptrview;
players[id].ptrgamedoc  = ptrdoc;
players[id].isloggedon   = true;
ptrdoc->PostControlAddrs (this, id, descr, GetControlView ());
```

Finally, a check is made to see if all required players are now logged on. If so, the game sequencing can begin. The first player is made visible and all others hidden. Also now that all are logged on, the control view is also minimized

```
if ((all_logged_on = AllLoggedOn ()) == true) {
 game.current_player = game.first_player;
 for (long i=0; i<MAX_PLAYERS; i++) {  // start game
 if (players[i].isrequired) current_action[i].done = 0;
 else current_action[i].done = 1;
 if (i != game.current_player && players[i].isloggedon)
 ShowPlayer (i, FALSE);
 }
 GetControlView ()->GetParentFrame ()->ShowWindow (SW_MINIMIZE);
 GetControlView ()->Invalidate ();
 return;
```

In ActionDone, when a player has pressed Do It!, NextPlayerIs determines who goes next. The current player view is hidden and the next player view is made visible

```
current_action[id].done = 1;
long i = NextPlayerIs ();
...
ShowPlayer (game.current_player, false);
game.current_player = i;
ShowPlayer (game.current_player, true);
players[i].ptrplayerview->GetParentFrame ()->ActivateFrame ();
UpdateAllViews (NULL, 1, NULL);
```

Sometimes a player may need to quit for a while and logoff. When the player chooses the menu item to logoff, LogoffPlayer handles his request by resetting his entry in the players array, restoring the control view from its minimized state, and reshowing the next player's view

```
players[id].isloggedon = false;
players[id].ptrplayerview = NULL;
players[id].ptrgamedoc = NULL;
if (all_logged_on) all_logged_on = false;
GetControlView ()->GetParentFrame ()->ShowWindow (SW_RESTORE);
GetControlView ()->Invalidate ();
if (game.current_player == id) {
 game.current_player = -1;
 id = NextPlayerIs ();
 if (id != -1) {
  ShowPlayer (game.current_player, true);
  players[id].ptrplayerview->GetParentFrame ()->ActivateFrame ();
 }
}
UpdateAllViews (NULL, 1, NULL);
```

Should the ControlView be closed down, then LogoffAll is called. It resets all players values in the players array and then if the control document has bee modified, saves it. Then, it notifies the HeadDoc instance that this control document is terminating

```
if (IsModified ()) {
 SaveBattle (controlfile);
 SetModifiedFlag (FALSE);
}
all_logged_on = false;
if (ptrheaddoc && ptrheaddoc->IsKindOf (RUNTIME_CLASS (HeadDoc)))
 ptrheaddoc->LogoffBattle (head_index);
```

Listing for File: ControlDoc.cpp

```
...
IMPLEMENT_DYNCREATE(ControlDoc, CDocument)

ControlDoc::ControlDoc() {
 ClearControlValues ();
 controlfile[0] = 0;
```

```
}

ControlDoc::~ControlDoc() { }

BEGIN_MESSAGE_MAP(ControlDoc, CDocument)
 ON_COMMAND (CM_LOGON_GERMAN,   CmLogonGerman)
 ON_COMMAND (CM_LOGON_ITALY,    CmLogonItaly)
 ON_COMMAND (CM_LOGON_JAPAN,    CmLogonJapan)
 ON_COMMAND (CM_LOGON_BRITIAN,  CmLogonBritian)
 ON_COMMAND (CM_LOGON_FRANCE,   CmLogonFrance)
 ON_COMMAND (CM_LOGON_USA,      CmLogonUSA)
 ON_COMMAND (CM_LOGON_RUSSIA,   CmLogonRussia)
 ON_COMMAND (CM_LOGON_MINOR,    CmLogonMinor)
 ON_UPDATE_COMMAND_UI (CM_LOGON_GERMAN,   CmEnableLogonGerman)
 ON_UPDATE_COMMAND_UI (CM_LOGON_ITALY,    CmEnableLogonItaly)
 ON_UPDATE_COMMAND_UI (CM_LOGON_JAPAN,    CmEnableLogonJapan)
 ON_UPDATE_COMMAND_UI (CM_LOGON_BRITIAN,  CmEnableLogonBritian)
 ON_UPDATE_COMMAND_UI (CM_LOGON_FRANCE,   CmEnableLogonFrance)
 ON_UPDATE_COMMAND_UI (CM_LOGON_USA,      CmEnableLogonUSA)
 ON_UPDATE_COMMAND_UI (CM_LOGON_RUSSIA,   CmEnableLogonRussia)
 ON_UPDATE_COMMAND_UI (CM_LOGON_MINOR,    CmEnableLogonMinor)
END_MESSAGE_MAP()

/******************************************************************************/
/*                                                                            */
/* ClearControlValues: initialize beginning state                            */
/*                                                                            */
/******************************************************************************/

void      ControlDoc::ClearControlValues () {
 for (long i=0; i<MAX_PLAYERS; i++) {
  players[i].isrequired    = false;
  players[i].isloggedon    = false;
  players[i].ptrplayerview = NULL;
  players[i].ptrgamedoc    = NULL;
  current_action[i].done = 0;
  current_action[i].type = 0;
 }
 ptrheaddoc  = NULL;
 head_index = -1;
 all_logged_on = false;
 descr[0] = 0;
 game.num_players_required = 0;
 game.bkgrndfile[0] = 0;
 game.active_phase = 0;
 game.first_player = -1;
 game.current_player = -1;
 game.current_turn = 0;
}

/******************************************************************************/
/*                                                                            */
/* SetHeaderAddr: provides access to header doc, id, and our battle title  */
/*                                                                            */
/******************************************************************************/

void      ControlDoc::SetHeaderAddr (HeadDoc *ptrhdoc, long id, char *desc) {
 ASSERT (ptrhdoc->IsKindOf (RUNTIME_CLASS (HeadDoc)));
```

```
if (ptrhdoc && ptrhdoc->IsKindOf (RUNTIME_CLASS (HeadDoc))) {
 ptrheaddoc = ptrhdoc;
 head_index = id;
 strcpy_s (descr, sizeof(descr), desc);
 POSITION pos = GetFirstViewPosition ();
 if (pos != NULL) {
  CView *ptrview = GetNextView (pos);
  if (ptrview && ptrview->IsKindOf (RUNTIME_CLASS (ControlView))) {
   ControlView *ptrcview = (ControlView*) ptrview;
   CString msg;
   msg.LoadString (IDS_CONTROLLER_NAME);
   msg += descr;
   ptrcview->GetParentFrame ()->SetWindowText (msg);
  }
 }
}
}

/*************************************************************************/
/*                                                                     */
/* GetControlView: returns ptr to game control view for posting messages */
/*                                                                     */
/*************************************************************************/

ControlView*   ControlDoc::GetControlView () {
 POSITION pos = GetFirstViewPosition ();
 CView *ptrview;
 while (pos != NULL) {
  ptrview = GetNextView (pos);
  if (ptrview && ptrview->IsKindOf (RUNTIME_CLASS (ControlView)))
   return (ControlView*) ptrview;
 }
 return NULL;
}

/*************************************************************************/
/*                                                                     */
/* ShowPlayer: hides or shows a player's views                         */
/*                                                                     */
/*************************************************************************/

void     ControlDoc::ShowPlayer (long id, bool show) {
 if (id < 0 || id >= MAX_PLAYERS) return;
 if (players[id].isloggedon && players[id].ptrgamedoc &&
     players[id].ptrgamedoc->IsKindOf (RUNTIME_CLASS (GameDoc)))
  players[id].ptrgamedoc->ShowPlayer (show);
}

/*************************************************************************/
/*                                                                     */
/* ActionDone: active player done, so let other player do something    */
/*                                                                     */
/*************************************************************************/

void     ControlDoc::ActionDone (long id) {
 current_action[id].done = 1;
 long i = NextPlayerIs ();
 if (i == -1) {
```

```
 if (all_logged_on) {
  MessageBox (0, "Error - cannot find next player", "Game is confused",
              MB_OK);
  return;
 }
 else {
  MessageBox (0, "Your request has been accepted. Please Wait.",
              "Game is suspended until all players are logged on", MB_OK);
  return;
 }
}
ShowPlayer (game.current_player, false);
game.current_player = i;
ShowPlayer (game.current_player, true);
players[i].ptrplayerview->GetParentFrame ()->ActivateFrame ();
UpdateAllViews (NULL, 1, NULL);
return;
}

/****************************************************************************/
/*                                                                        */
/* NextPlayerIs: returns next player to have a turn                       */
/*                                                                        */
/****************************************************************************/

long     ControlDoc::NextPlayerIs () {
 long i;
 for (i=game.current_player + 1; i<MAX_PLAYERS; i++) {
  if (players[i].isrequired && players[i].isloggedon) return i;
 }
 for (i=0; i<game.current_player; i++) {
  if (players[i].isrequired && players[i].isloggedon) return i;
 }
 return -1;
}

/****************************************************************************/
/*                                                                        */
/* AllLoggedOn: returns TRUE when all players required are logged on       */
/*                                                                        */
/****************************************************************************/

bool     ControlDoc::AllLoggedOn () {
 for (long i=0; i<MAX_PLAYERS; i++)
  if (players[i].isrequired && !players[i].isloggedon) return false;
 return true;
}

/****************************************************************************/
/*                                                                        */
/* LogonPlayer: chains new player into controls and gives its doc access   */
/*                                                                        */
/****************************************************************************/

void     ControlDoc::LogonPlayer (long id) {
 CDocument *ptrcdoc = theApp.ptrplayertmp->OpenDocumentFile (game.bkgrndfile);
 if (ptrcdoc) {
  if (ptrcdoc && ptrcdoc->IsKindOf (RUNTIME_CLASS (GameDoc))) {
```

```
  GameDoc *ptrdoc = (GameDoc*) ptrcdoc;
  CView *ptrcview;
  POSITION pos = ptrdoc->GetFirstViewPosition ();
  if (pos != NULL) {
   ptrcview = ptrdoc->GetNextView (pos);
   if (ptrcview && ptrcview->IsKindOf (RUNTIME_CLASS (PlayerView))) {
     PlayerView *ptrview = (PlayerView*) ptrcview;
     players[id].ptrplayerview = ptrview;
     players[id].ptrgamedoc  = ptrdoc;
     players[id].isloggedon    = true;
     ptrdoc->PostControlAddrs (this, id, descr, GetControlView ());
     if ((all_logged_on = AllLoggedOn ()) == true) {
      game.current_player = game.first_player;
      for (long i=0; i<MAX_PLAYERS; i++) {  // start game
       if (players[i].isrequired) current_action[i].done = 0;
       else current_action[i].done = 1;
       if (i != game.current_player && players[i].isloggedon)
         ShowPlayer (i, false);
      }
      GetControlView ()->GetParentFrame ()->ShowWindow (SW_MINIMIZE);
      GetControlView ()->Invalidate ();
      return;
     }
     return;
    }
   }
  }
 }
 CString msg1, msg2;
 msg1.LoadString (IDS_BATTLCTRL_ERRH);
 msg2.LoadString (IDS_BATTLCTRL_ERR1);
 MessageBox (0, msg2, msg1, MB_OK);
}


/******************************************************************************/
/*                                                                          */
/* CmLogonXXXX: 8 logons for the possible players                           */
/*                                                                          */
/******************************************************************************/

void     ControlDoc::CmLogonGerman () {
 if (!players[GermanPlayer].isloggedon) LogonPlayer (GermanPlayer);
}

void     ControlDoc::CmLogonItaly () {
 if (!players[ItalianPlayer].isloggedon) LogonPlayer (ItalianPlayer);
}

void     ControlDoc::CmLogonJapan () {
 if (!players[JapanesePlayer].isloggedon) LogonPlayer (JapanesePlayer);
}

void     ControlDoc::CmLogonBritian () {
 if (!players[BritishPlayer].isloggedon) LogonPlayer (BritishPlayer);
}

void     ControlDoc::CmLogonFrance () {
 if (!players[FrenchPlayer].isloggedon) LogonPlayer (FrenchPlayer);
```

```
}

void      ControlDoc::CmLogonUSA () {
 if (!players[USAPlayer].isloggedon) LogonPlayer (USAPlayer);
}

void      ControlDoc::CmLogonRussia () {
 if (!players[RussianPlayer].isloggedon) LogonPlayer (RussianPlayer);
}

void      ControlDoc::CmLogonMinor () {
 if (!players[MinorsPlayer].isloggedon) LogonPlayer (MinorsPlayer);
}

/************************************************************************/
/*                                                                    */
/* CmEnableLogonXXXX: command enablers for the possible 8 players      */
/*                                                                    */
/************************************************************************/

void      ControlDoc::CmEnableLogonGerman (CCmdUI *ptrui) {
 ptrui->Enable (players[GermanPlayer].isrequired ?
              players[GermanPlayer].isloggedon ? 0 : 1 : 0);
}

void      ControlDoc::CmEnableLogonItaly (CCmdUI *ptrui) {
 ptrui->Enable (players[ItalianPlayer].isrequired ?
              players[ItalianPlayer].isloggedon ?  0 : 1 : 0);
}

void      ControlDoc::CmEnableLogonJapan (CCmdUI *ptrui) {
 ptrui->Enable (players[JapanesePlayer].isrequired ?
              players[JapanesePlayer].isloggedon ?  0 : 1 : 0);
}

void      ControlDoc::CmEnableLogonBritian (CCmdUI *ptrui) {
 ptrui->Enable (players[BritishPlayer].isrequired ?
              players[BritishPlayer].isloggedon ?  0 : 1 : 0);
}

void      ControlDoc::CmEnableLogonFrance (CCmdUI *ptrui) {
 ptrui->Enable (players[FrenchPlayer].isrequired ?
              players[FrenchPlayer].isloggedon ?  0 : 1 : 0);
}

void      ControlDoc::CmEnableLogonUSA (CCmdUI *ptrui) {
 ptrui->Enable (players[USAPlayer].isrequired ?
              players[USAPlayer].isloggedon ?  0 : 1 : 0);
}

void      ControlDoc::CmEnableLogonRussia (CCmdUI *ptrui) {
 ptrui->Enable (players[RussianPlayer].isrequired ?
              players[RussianPlayer].isloggedon ?  0 : 1 : 0);
}

void      ControlDoc::CmEnableLogonMinor (CCmdUI *ptrui) {
 ptrui->Enable (players[MinorsPlayer].isrequired ?
              players[MinorsPlayer].isloggedon ?  0 : 1 : 0);
```

```
}

/*************************************************************************/
/*                                                                       */
/* LogoffPlayer: remove player for active status and suspend game        */
/*                                                                       */
/*************************************************************************/
void       ControlDoc::LogoffPlayer (long id) {
 if (id < 0 || id >= MAX_PLAYERS) return;

 players[id].isloggedon = false;
 players[id].ptrplayerview = NULL;
 players[id].ptrgamedoc = NULL;

 if (all_logged_on) all_logged_on = false;
 GetControlView ()->GetParentFrame ()->ShowWindow (SW_RESTORE);
 GetControlView ()->Invalidate ();
 if (game.current_player == id) {
  game.current_player = -1;
  id = NextPlayerIs ();
  if (id != -1) {
   ShowPlayer (game.current_player, true);
   players[id].ptrplayerview->GetParentFrame ()->ActivateFrame ();
  }
 }
 UpdateAllViews (NULL, 1, NULL);
}

/*************************************************************************/
/*                                                                       */
/* LogoffAll: log all players off the battle                             */
/*                                                                       */
/*************************************************************************/
void       ControlDoc::LogoffAll () {
 for (long id=0; id<MAX_PLAYERS; id++) {
 if (players[id].isloggedon) players[id].ptrgamedoc->OnCloseDocument ();
  players[id].isloggedon = false;
  players[id].ptrplayerview = NULL;
  players[id].ptrgamedoc = NULL;
 }
 if (IsModified ()) {
  SaveBattle (controlfile);
  SetModifiedFlag (false);
 }
 all_logged_on = false;
 if (ptrheaddoc && ptrheaddoc->IsKindOf (RUNTIME_CLASS (HeadDoc)))
  ptrheaddoc->LogoffBattle (head_index);
 head_index = -1;
 ptrheaddoc = NULL;
 // halt game
}

/*************************************************************************/
/*                                                                       */
/* ServerClosesAdmin: the server requests closure of the game - log all off*/
```

```
/*                                                                           */
/***************************************************************************/


void        ControlDoc::ServerClosesAdmin () {
 CString msg1, msg2;
 msg1.LoadString (IDS_BATTLCTRL_SRVH);
 msg2.LoadString (IDS_BATTLCTRL_SRV1);
 MessageBox (0, msg2, msg1, MB_OK);
 OnCloseDocument ();
}


/***************************************************************************/
/*                                                                           */
/* OnFileClose: close the document which closes down all players             */
/*                                                                           */
/***************************************************************************/


void        ControlDoc::OnFileClose () {
 OnCloseDocument ();
}


/***************************************************************************/
/*                                                                           */
/* OnCloseDocument: fast close of the document and all players beneath        */
/*                                                                           */
/***************************************************************************/


void        ControlDoc::OnCloseDocument () {
 LogoffAll ();
 CDocument::OnCloseDocument ();
}


/***************************************************************************/
/*                                                                           */
/* CanCloseFrame: prompt user about shutting whole game down                  */
/*                                                                           */
/***************************************************************************/


BOOL        ControlDoc::CanCloseFrame (CFrameWnd *ptrwin) {
 if (!ptrwin) return TRUE;
 if (!ptrwin->IsKindOf (RUNTIME_CLASS (ControlFrame))) return FALSE;
 CView *ptrview = ((ControlFrame*) ptrwin)->GetActiveView ();
 if (ptrview->IsKindOf (RUNTIME_CLASS (ControlView))) {
  CString msg1, msg2;
  msg1.LoadString (IDS_BATTLCTRL_CLOSE);
  msg2.LoadString (IDS_BATTLCTRL_QUERY);
  if (MessageBox (0, msg2, msg1, MB_YESNO | MB_ICONQUESTION) == IDYES) {
   LogoffAll ();
   return TRUE;
  }
  return FALSE;
 }
 return FALSE;
}



/***************************************************************************/
/*                                                                           */
```

```
/* RemoveObjects: remove all allocated objects                                 */
/*                                                                             */
/*****************************************************************************/

void        ControlDoc::RemoveObjects () {
 // a place holder for you to insert deletion of game objects...
}

/*****************************************************************************/
/*                                                                             */
/* OnOpenDocument: open an existing battle                                     */
/*                                                                             */
/*****************************************************************************/

BOOL        ControlDoc::OnOpenDocument (LPCTSTR filename) {
 ClearControlValues ();
 RemoveObjects ();
 if (!CDocument::OnOpenDocument (filename)) return FALSE;
 return LoadBattle (filename);
}

/*****************************************************************************/
/*                                                                             */
/* OnSaveDocument: save this battle                                            */
/*                                                                             */
/*****************************************************************************/

BOOL        ControlDoc::OnSaveDocument (LPCTSTR filename) {
 return SaveBattle (filename);
}

/*****************************************************************************/
/*                                                                             */
/* LoadBattle: loads in a battle to play                                       */
/*                                                                             */
/*****************************************************************************/

bool        ControlDoc::LoadBattle (LPCTSTR filename) {
 strcpy_s (controlfile, sizeof(controlfile), filename);
 long i, j, k;
 char buf[MAX_PATH];        // the input buffer
 long count;                // 0 at EOF
 CFile file;                // the file, will be binary I/O still
 CFileException file_err;   // used if more info on errors is desired

 i = 0;
 file.Open (filename, CFile::modeRead, &file_err);
 while (true) { // read all file bytes, checking for new line codes
  count = file.Read (&buf[i], 1);     // reads one byte
  if (buf[i] == '\n') {
   buf[i]=0;                          // insert NULL terminator
   break;
  }
  else if (count==0) {
   buf[i] = 0;
   break;                            // also end when no more bytes
  }
  else i++;                          // get next byte in the line of data
```

```
 }
 sscanf_s (buf, "%ld", &k);  // convert into proper data types
 if (k < 2) {
  MessageBox (0, "Must have at least two players for a battle", "error", MB_OK);
  return false;
 }
 game.num_players_required = k;
 for (k=0; k<game.num_players_required; k++) {
  i = 0;
  while (true) { // read all file bytes, checking for new line codes
   count = file.Read (&buf[i], 1);      // reads one byte
   if (buf[i] == '\n') {
    buf[i]=0;                                // insert NULL terminator
    break;
   }
   else if (count==0) {
    buf[i] = 0;
    break;                                   // also end when no more bytes
   }
   else i++;                                 // get next byte in the line of data
  }
  sscanf_s (buf, "%ld", &j);
  if (j < 0 || j > 7) {
   MessageBox (0, "bad data in battle file","error", MB_OK);
   return false;
  }
  players[j].isrequired = true;
  if (game.first_player == -1) game.first_player = j;
 }
 i = 0;
 while (true) { // read all file bytes, checking for new line codes
  count = file.Read (&buf[i], 1);     // reads one byte
  if (buf[i] == '\n') {
   buf[i]=0;                                // insert NULL terminator
   break;
  }
  else if (count==0) {
   buf[i] = 0;
   break;              // also end when no more bytes
  }
  else i++;            // get next byte in the line of data
 }
 if (i>0 && buf[i-1] == '\r') buf[i-1]=0;
 strcpy_s (game.bkgrndbasefile, sizeof(game.bkgrndbasefile), buf);
 strcpy_s (game.bkgrndfile, sizeof(game.bkgrndfile), theApp.mainpath);
 strcat_s (game.bkgrndfile, sizeof(game.bkgrndfile), buf);
 file.Close ();
 return true;
}

/*********************************************************************/
/*                                                                   */
/* SaveBattle: saves a battle to disk                                */
/*                                                                   */
/*********************************************************************/

bool      ControlDoc::SaveBattle (LPCTSTR filename) {
 MessageBox (0, "Saving control battle file to be implemented", filename,
```

```
            MB_OK);
 // to be implemented
 return true;
}


/***************************************************************************/
/*                                                                         */
/* DeleteContents: remove this document's contents                         */
/*                                                                         */
/***************************************************************************/

void      ControlDoc::DeleteContents () {
 RemoveObjects ();
}
...
```

The ControlView displays the log on status of the players and the game turn information. All of its coding is straight forward.

Listing for File: ControlView.h

```
...
/***************************************************************************/
/*                                                                         */
/* ControlView: game controller view window                               */
/*                                                                         */
/***************************************************************************/
class ControlView : public CView {
protected:
 ControlView();
 DECLARE_DYNCREATE(ControlView)

protected:
 ControlDoc      *ptrdoc;
 Game            *ptrgame;
 CurrentAction   *action;
 Players         *players;

 long             char_width;
 long             char_height;

public:
virtual          void   OnInitialUpdate ();
afx_msg          int    OnCreate (LPCREATESTRUCT);   // make gray brush
virtual ControlDoc*  GetDocument ();

protected:
afx_msg    LRESULT   CmActionDone (WPARAM, LPARAM);
virtual          void   OnUpdate (CView*, LPARAM, CObject*);
virtual          void   GetAvgCharDims ();
virtual          void   RemoveObjects ();
virtual          void   OnDraw(CDC* pDC);           // overridden to draw this view
virtual               ~ControlView();
```

Listing for File: ControlView.cpp

```
...
IMPLEMENT_DYNCREATE(ControlView, CView)

ControlView::ControlView() {
 ptrdoc  = NULL;
 ptrgame = NULL;
 action  = NULL;
 players = NULL;
}

ControlView::~ControlView() {
 RemoveObjects ();
}

BEGIN_MESSAGE_MAP(ControlView, CView)
 ON_WM_CREATE ()
 ON_MESSAGE (CM_NOTIFY_BATDOC_ACTDONE,    CmActionDone)
END_MESSAGE_MAP()

/*******************************************************************************/
/*                                                                           */
/* RemoveObjects: delete all allocated objects                               */
/*                                                                           */
/*******************************************************************************/

void     ControlView::RemoveObjects () {
 // place holder
}

/*******************************************************************************/
/*                                                                           */
/* OnCreate: build the view with lt grey background brush                    */
/*                                                                           */
/*******************************************************************************/

int      ControlView::OnCreate (LPCREATESTRUCT lpCS) {
 int retcd = CView::OnCreate (lpCS); // pass along to base class
 // install new background color
 ::SetClassLong (m_hWnd, GCL_HBRBACKGROUND,
                 (long) (HBRUSH) ::GetStockObject (LTGRAY_BRUSH));
 return retcd;
}

/*******************************************************************************/
/*                                                                           */
/* OnInitialUpdate:                                                          */
/*                                                                           */
/*******************************************************************************/

void     ControlView::OnInitialUpdate () {
 ptrdoc = GetDocument ();
 if (ptrdoc) {
  ptrgame = &ptrdoc->game;
  action = ptrdoc->current_action;
  players = ptrdoc->players;
 }
 GetAvgCharDims (); // set average character dimensions
```

```
}

/*******************************************************************/
/*                                                                 */
/* CmActionDone: active player done, so let other player do something */
/*                                                                 */
/*******************************************************************/

LRESULT   ControlView::CmActionDone (WPARAM, LPARAM id) {
 ptrdoc->ActionDone (id);
 return 0;
}


/*******************************************************************/
/*                                                                 */
/* OnUpdate: respond to game status change                         */
/*                                                                 */
/*******************************************************************/

void      ControlView::OnUpdate (CView*, LPARAM hint, CObject*) {
 if (hint == 1) { // change in current player
  if (ptrdoc->all_logged_on) {
   players[ptrgame->current_player].ptrplayerview->PostMessage (
                 CM_NOTIFY_BATDOC_NEWACT, 0, 0);
  }
 }
 Invalidate (TRUE);
}


/*******************************************************************/
/*                                                                 */
/* GetAvgCharDims: retrieve current font's average dimensions      */
/*                                                                 */
/*******************************************************************/

void      ControlView::GetAvgCharDims () {
 TEXTMETRIC  tm;  // set the system font's characteristics in tm

 CClientDC *ptrdc = new CClientDC (this);      // acquire a DC
 ptrdc->GetTextMetrics (&tm);                  // get the font information
 delete ptrdc;                                 // delete the dc

 // calculate average character parameters
 char_width = tm.tmAveCharWidth;
 char_height = tm.tmHeight + tm.tmExternalLeading;
}


/*******************************************************************/
/*                                                                 */
/* OnDraw: Render the image onto the off screen DIB Section and Blit to dc */
/*                                                                 */
/*******************************************************************/

void      ControlView::OnDraw (CDC *ptrdc) {
 ptrdc->SetBkMode (TRANSPARENT);
 ptrdc->TextOut (char_width, char_height, ptrdoc->descr);
 char turnmsg[80], turnstr[80] = "Current Turn Number: %d";
 wsprintf (turnmsg, turnstr, ptrgame->current_turn);
```

```
ptrdc->TextOut (char_width, char_height*3, turnmsg);
ptrdc->TextOut (char_width, char_height*5, "Players in the Battle");
long linect = char_height *7;
for (long i=0; i<MAX_PLAYERS; i++) {
 if (players[i].isrequired) {
  CString msg;
  msg.LoadString (IDS_PLAYER_GERMAN + i);
  ptrdc->TextOut (char_width * 2, linect, msg);
  linect += char_height;
  if (players[i].isloggedon) {
   if (ptrgame->current_player == i)
    ptrdc->TextOut (char_width * 4, linect,
                    "Is Logged On  Is Currently Active Player");
   else ptrdc->TextOut (char_width * 4, linect, "Is Logged On");
   linect += char_height;
  }
  else {
   ptrdc->TextOut (char_width * 4, linect, "Not Logged On");
   linect += char_height;
  }
  linect += char_height * 3;
 }
}
}


/***************************************************************************/
/*                                                                         */
/* GetDocument: returns ptr to the associated CDocument                    */
/*                                                                         */
/***************************************************************************/

ControlDoc*  ControlView::GetDocument () {
 ControlDoc* ptrbdoc = (ControlDoc*) m_pDocument;
 ASSERT (ptrbdoc);
 ASSERT (ptrbdoc->IsKindOf (RUNTIME_CLASS (ControlDoc)));
 if (ptrbdoc && ptrbdoc->IsKindOf (RUNTIME_CLASS (ControlDoc)))
  return ptrbdoc;
 else return NULL;
}
```

The turn sequencing is handled through an **ON_MESSAGE**. When a player commits to his moves by pressing the Do It! button, the CM_NOTIFY_BATDOC_ACTDONE message is send. Here it is relayed to the ControlDoc class to permit switching players and their views. When the next player gets their turn, the ControlDoc uses a **hint** via the **OnUpdate** function to signal the other player's document-view classes that they are now active. When the hint is 1 and all players are logged on, the player's view that now can start their turn is sent the CM_NOTIFY_BATDOC_NEWACT message.

```
ON_MESSAGE (CM_NOTIFY_BATDOC_ACTDONE,    CmActionDone)
...
LRESULT   ControlView::CmActionDone (WPARAM, LPARAM id) {
 ptrdoc->ActionDone (id);
 return 0;
}
void      ControlView::OnUpdate (CView*, LPARAM hint, CObject*) {
 if (hint == 1) { // change in current player
  if (ptrdoc->all_logged_on) {
```

```
  players[ptrgame->current_player].ptrplayerview->PostMessage (
                  CM_NOTIFY_BATDOC_NEWACT, 0, 0);
   }
  }
  Invalidate (TRUE);
}
```

The Off Screen Buffer Class

One common approach with games and other graphic intensive applications is to utilize an off screen buffer to draw upon before actually bliting to the view. I constructed a BitmapDC class to encapsulate that off screen buffer. If the client machine is not in a higher color resolution mode, there is one common palette in use by the application. Thus, to maintain the identity palette, its colors must be mapped into this off screen buffer's color table.

The buffer is created by using **CreateDIBSection**. First the BitmapDC's Create function is called to construct a buffer of specific dimensions using the master palette for the color table entries. The user would then invoke the Read function to actually input the bits insert them into the buffer.

Listing for File: BitmapDC.h
```
...
/*****************************************************************************/
/*                                                                         */
/* BitmapDC Class: bitmap object in memory DC class                        */
/*                                                                         */
/*****************************************************************************/

class BitmapDC {

  /*****************************************************************************/
  /*                                                                         */
  /* Data Members                                                            */
  /*                                                                         */
  /*****************************************************************************/

public:
  HDC               hbmpdc;       // memory DC with DIB Section bitmap and palette

protected:
  HBITMAP           hbmp;         // Bitmap DIB Section style
  HBITMAP           holdbmp;      // old monochrome bitmap for deletion
  CPalette          *ptrpalette;  // palette for the bitmap
  BYTE              *ptrbits;     // ptr to the bits of the bitmap once drawn
  long              width;        // actual bitmap scanline dimensions
  long              height;

  /*****************************************************************************/
  /*                                                                         */
  /* Functions:                                                              */
  /*                                                                         */
```

```
/*******************************************************************/

public:
     BitmapDC ();          // constructor inits ptrs to NULL
    ~BitmapDC ();          // remove the DIB Section and TMemoryDC
                                // create the actual DIB Section and TMemoryDC
BOOL  Create (long w, long h, Palette*);
void  RealizePalette ();// complete Palette Manager reinitialization
void  RealizePalette (CDC&);// force Palette Manager reinit on anotherDC

BYTE* GetBits ();          // returns the address of the bitmap bits
long  Height ();          // returns real height of DIB Section bm
long  Width ();           // returns real width of DIB Section bm
long  TotalBits ();       // returns total bitmap bits in DIB Section
BOOL  Read (const char*, Palette*);  // construct bm from file in RLE
BYTE  GetPixel (CPoint&);            // retrieve color idx of this pel
                                // translate & update colors to green to id obj
protected:

void    RemoveBitmap ();  // removes a DIB Section
BITMAPINFO* MakeBITMAPINFO (long w, long h); // makes a BITMAPINFO structure
};
...
```

The constructor builds a NULL buffer. When a buffer is to be destroyed, notice that under Windows NT, we must wait until all other threads have finished using the buffer. This is done by calling **GdiFlush**. All queued actions for this buffer are then flushed and it is safe to destroy it or directly access its bits. It is not necessary to call **GdiFlush** under Windows 95.

In the Create function, notice that to get the requisite color table filled with the master color palette colors, I use the Palette class' FillRgbColorTable function before actually calling **CreateDIBSection** proper.

In the Read function, I construct a **CFile** instance for the bmp file. Once the bits are input, I then copy them into the DIB Section. Notice that the DIB Section width is a multiple of 32 bits, or four bytes, yet the bitmap file may not be such a multiple. Further, the bmp scan lines are upside down compared to the DIB Section. So I copy the bits one scan line at a time.

Listing for File: BitmapDC.cpp

...
```
/*****************************************************************************/
/*                                                                         */
/* BitmapDC: constructor initializes class to NULL - must use Create to use*/
/*                                                                         */
/*****************************************************************************/

BitmapDC::BitmapDC () {
 ptrpalette = NULL;
 hbmpdc     = 0;
 hbmp       = 0;
 height     = 0;
 width      = 0;
}


/*****************************************************************************/
/*                                                                         */
/* ~BitmapDC: destructor removes allocated objects                         */
/*                                                                         */
/*****************************************************************************/

BitmapDC::~BitmapDC () {
 RemoveBitmap ();
}


/*****************************************************************************/
/*                                                                         */
/* RemoveBitmap: removes the bitmap allocated objects                      */
/*                                                                         */
/*****************************************************************************/

void      BitmapDC::RemoveBitmap () {
 GdiFlush (); // NT synchronization let GDI finish any in progress actions
 if (hbmp) {
  SelectObject (hbmpdc, holdbmp);
  SelectPalette (hbmpdc, (HPALETTE) GetStockObject (DEFAULT_PALETTE), FALSE);
  DeleteObject (hbmp);
 }
 if (hbmpdc) DeleteDC (hbmpdc);

 hbmpdc     = 0;
 ptrpalette = NULL;
 hbmp       = 0;
 height     = 0;
 width      = 0;
}


/*****************************************************************************/
/*                                                                         */
/* Create: construct a DIB Section and MemoryDC with a specific palette    */
/*                                                                         */
/*****************************************************************************/

BOOL      BitmapDC::Create (long w, long h, Palette *ptrpalettes) {
 if (w<=0 || h<=0) w = h = 1;

 if (hbmpdc) RemoveBitmap ();
```

```
ptrpalette = ptrpalettes->GetPalette (); // insert the palette to be used
hbmpdc = ::CreateCompatibleDC (0);        // make a memory DC
if (hbmpdc) {
 RealizePalette ();                       // install identity palette
 BITMAPINFO* ptrinfo = MakeBITMAPINFO (w, h); // make the BITMAPINFO header
 if (ptrinfo) {
  width = ptrinfo->bmiHeader.biWidth;
  height = h;
  ptrpalettes->FillRgbColorTable (ptrinfo->bmiColors); // install color table
  hbmp = CreateDIBSection (hbmpdc, ptrinfo, DIB_RGB_COLORS,
                           (void**) &ptrbits, NULL, 0);
  free (ptrinfo);
  // if successful, install DIB Section bitmap into the memory DC
  if (hbmp) {
   holdbmp = (HBITMAP) SelectObject (hbmpdc, hbmp);
   // clear all DIB bits
   memset (ptrbits, 0, width * height);
  }
  else {
   RemoveBitmap ();
   return FALSE;
  }
 }
 else {
  RemoveBitmap ();
  return FALSE;
 }
}
else {
 RemoveBitmap ();
 return FALSE;
}
return TRUE;
}

/*********************************************************************/
/*                                                                   */
/* MakeBITMAPINFO: constructs a BITMAPINFO structure with DWORD rounded wid*/
/*                                                                   */
/*********************************************************************/

BITMAPINFO* BitmapDC::MakeBITMAPINFO (long w, long h) {
 BITMAPINFO *ptrinfo;
 ptrinfo = (BITMAPINFO*) malloc (sizeof(BITMAPINFO) + 256 * sizeof (RGBQUAD));
 if (ptrinfo) {
  w = w % 4 > 0 ? 4 - w % 4 + w : w; // force width onto 32-bit boundary
  ptrinfo->bmiHeader.biSize = sizeof (BITMAPINFOHEADER);
  ptrinfo->bmiHeader.biWidth = w;
  ptrinfo->bmiHeader.biHeight = -h;
  ptrinfo->bmiHeader.biPlanes = 1;
  ptrinfo->bmiHeader.biBitCount = 8;
  ptrinfo->bmiHeader.biCompression = BI_RGB;
  ptrinfo->bmiHeader.biSizeImage = 0;
  ptrinfo->bmiHeader.biXPelsPerMeter = 0;
  ptrinfo->bmiHeader.biYPelsPerMeter = 0;
  ptrinfo->bmiHeader.biClrUsed = 0;
  ptrinfo->bmiHeader.biClrImportant = 0;
  return ptrinfo;
```

```
 }
 else return NULL;
}

/***********************************************************************/
/*                                                                   */
/* RealizePalette: forces Palette Manager to completely reinstall new pal   */
/*                                                                   */
/***********************************************************************/

void      BitmapDC::RealizePalette () {
 if (hbmpdc) {
  // force Palette Manager to reset the master color table so the next palette
  // that is realized gets its colors mapped into the order of use in the
  // logpal
  Palette::ClearSystemPalette (hbmpdc);
  ::SelectPalette (hbmpdc, (HPALETTE) ptrpalette->GetSafeHandle (), FALSE);
  ::RealizePalette (hbmpdc);
 }
}

/***********************************************************************/
/*                                                                   */
/* RealizePalette: forces Palette Manager to reinstall new identity palette*/
/*                 on another DC - user must restore the DC's palette      */
/*                                                                   */
/***********************************************************************/

void      BitmapDC::RealizePalette (CDC &dc) {
 if (hbmpdc) {
  // force Palette Manager to reset the master color table so the next palette
  // that is realized gets its colors mapped into the order of use in the
  // logpal
  Palette::ClearSystemPalette (dc);
  dc.SelectPalette (ptrpalette, FALSE);
  dc.RealizePalette ();
 }
}

/***********************************************************************/
/*                                                                   */
/* GetBits: returns the address of the bitmap bits in the DIB Section     */
/*                                                                   */
/***********************************************************************/

BYTE*     BitmapDC::GetBits () {
 GdiFlush (); // NT synchronization let GDI finish any in progress actions
 if (hbmpdc) return ptrbits;
 else return NULL;
}

/***********************************************************************/
/*                                                                   */
/* Height: returns the actual height of this bitmap                        */
/*                                                                   */
/***********************************************************************/

long      BitmapDC::Height () {
```

```
 return height;
}

/****************************************************************************/
/*                                                                        */
/* Width: returns the actual width of this bitmap                         */
/*                                                                        */
/****************************************************************************/

long      BitmapDC::Width () {
 return width;
}

/****************************************************************************/
/*                                                                        */
/* TotalBits: returns the total number of bits in this bitmap             */
/*                                                                        */
/****************************************************************************/

long      BitmapDC::TotalBits () {
 return height * width;
}

/****************************************************************************/
/*                                                                        */
/* GetPixel: returns the bmp pixel color index                            */
/*                                                                        */
/****************************************************************************/

BYTE      BitmapDC::GetPixel (CPoint &p) {
 long r;

 if (p.y >= height || p.y <0) return 0;
 if (p.x >= width  || p.x <0) return 0;

 r  = p.y * width + p.x;
 return (r >= TotalBits ()) ? (BYTE) 0 : *(ptrbits + r);
}

/****************************************************************************/
/*                                                                        */
/* Read: input a bitmap and copy the bits into the DIB Section            */
/*                                                                        */
/****************************************************************************/

BOOL      BitmapDC::Read (const char *filename, Palette *ptrpalettes) {
 CFile file;
 CFileException file_err; // used if more info on errors is desired
 file.Open (filename, CFile::modeRead, &file_err);

 BITMAPFILEHEADER bmfh;
 UINT             actsz;

 HANDLE hdib = 0;
 // input the BITMAPFILEHEADER structure
 actsz = file.Read ((LPSTR) &bmfh, sizeof (BITMAPFILEHEADER));
 // verify it is a .BMP file
 if (actsz != sizeof (BITMAPFILEHEADER) || bmfh.bfType != * (WORD *) "BM") {
```

```
 AfxMessageBox ("Invalid bmp game file", MB_OK);
 file.Close ();
 return FALSE;
}

// calculate the size of the file less the file header
// and allocate memory for the dib
DWORD dwDibSize = bmfh.bfSize - sizeof (BITMAPFILEHEADER);
hdib = GlobalAlloc (GMEM_MOVEABLE, dwDibSize);
BYTE *ptrdib = (BYTE*) GlobalLock (hdib);
if (!ptrdib) {
 AfxMessageBox ("Cannot allocate memory for bmp file", MB_OK);
 file.Close ();
 if (hdib) GlobalFree (hdib);
 return FALSE;
}

// read in the rest of the DIB -
actsz = file.Read ((LPSTR) ptrdib, dwDibSize);
file.Close ();
if (actsz != dwDibSize) { // error, wrong number of bytes
 AfxMessageBox ("Invalid bmp game file", MB_OK);
 GlobalUnlock (hdib);
 GlobalFree (hdib);
 return FALSE;
 }

// check the validity of the size of the info header - fail OS2 bitmaps
if (((BITMAPINFOHEADER*) ptrdib)->biSize <= sizeof(BITMAPCOREHEADER)) {
 AfxMessageBox ("Invalid bmp game file", MB_OK);
 GlobalUnlock (hdib);
 GlobalFree (hdib);
 return FALSE;
}

WORD bitcount = ((BITMAPINFOHEADER*) ptrdib)->biBitCount;
DWORD numcolors = ((BITMAPINFOHEADER*) ptrdib)->biClrUsed;
if (numcolors == 0 && bitcount != 24) numcolors = 1L << bitcount;
if (numcolors == 0) {
 AfxMessageBox ("Invalid bmp game file", MB_OK);
 GlobalUnlock (hdib);
 GlobalFree (hdib);
 return FALSE;
}

width = ((BITMAPINFOHEADER*) ptrdib)->biWidth;
height = ((BITMAPINFOHEADER*) ptrdib)->biHeight;

if (!Create (width, height, ptrpalettes)) {
 GlobalUnlock (hdib);
 GlobalFree (hdib);
 return FALSE;
}

BYTE *ptrsrc = ptrdib + ((BITMAPINFOHEADER*) ptrdib)->biSize +
                                        numcolors * sizeof (RGBQUAD);
BYTE *ptrdes = GetBits ();
long i = 0;
```

```
ptrsrc += (height -1) * width;
while (i < height) {
 memcpy (ptrdes, ptrsrc, width);
 ptrsrc -= width;
 ptrdes += width;
 i++;
}
GlobalUnlock (hdib);
GlobalFree (hdib);
return TRUE;
}
```

The GameDoc, GameFrame, GameView Classes

Each player that logs on gets their individual GameDoc, GameFrame and PlayerView classes. It is
the responsibility of the GameDoc to encapsulate the game data. It maintains pointers to the
ControlDoc and ControlView parent classes, owns its local copy of the master palette and the off
screen buffer. When initially created the GameDoc instance does not know which player it is serving.
Instead, the PostControlAddrs function is subsequently called by the owning ControlDoc class to not
only post the owning class pointers but to also notify this instance of which player it represents.

Listing for File: GameDoc.h

```
...
/***************************************************************************/
/*                                                                         */
/* GameDoc: Container for one complete game                                */
/*                                                                         */
/***************************************************************************/

class GameDoc : public CDocument {
protected:
 GameDoc(); // protected constructor used by dynamic creation
 DECLARE_DYNCREATE(GameDoc)

   /***************************************************************************/
   /*                                                                         */
   /* Data Members                                                            */
   /*                                                                         */
   /***************************************************************************/

public:

ControlDoc  *ptrcontroldoc;        // our controlling document
ControlView *ptrcontrolview;

BitmapDC *ptrworldDC;              // the world bitmap
Palette  *ptrpalette;             // the player's palette

long     bmpw;                    // width and height of DIB Section
long     bmph;
```

```
CSize       world_size;              // dimensions of the world battle
CRect       world_rect;              // the world rectangle

long        playerid;                // the player id
char        descr[MAX_PATH];         // description of the battle for titlebar
char        docfilename[MAX_PATH];// the filename to save into

BOOL        isvisible;
BOOL        canundo;

public:

virtual BOOL OnOpenDocument (LPCTSTR);      // open existing battle
virtual BOOL OnSaveDocument (LPCTSTR);      // save a battle
virtual void DeleteContents ();             // remove this battle
virtual void OnCloseDocument ();            // closes this player doc down
virtual void OnFileClose ();                // handles closing this doc
virtual void LogoffPlayer ();               // notify game control when done
virtual long GetPlayerId ();                // returns player id

virtual BitmapDC* GetWorldDC ();                // provide access to world DC
virtual Palette*  GetWorldSizeAndPalette (CSize&);

            // sets our game control doc address
virtual void PostControlAddrs (ControlDoc*, long, char*, ControlView*);

virtual void LoginOtherView (OtherView*, long&);
virtual void LogoffOther ();

virtual void ShowPlayer (bool);             // true, show views, false, hide
virtual void ActionDone ();
virtual ControlDoc*  GetControlDoc ();
virtual ~GameDoc();

protected:

virtual bool LoadBattle (LPCTSTR);          // load in a battle - setup view
virtual bool SaveBattle (LPCTSTR);          // save this battle
virtual void RemoveObjects ();              // removes all allocated objects
...
```

There are only a few key functions that we need to examine. The constructor sets everything to NULL. The actual work in setting up the document instance is done by both the framework's opening of the document any by the subsequent call of the parent ControlDoc to this instance's PostControlAddrs.

First, **OnOpenDocument** calls LoadBattle which actually allocates the BitmapDC buffer and invokes its Read function, passing it the bitmap file to use. PostControlAddrs is a bit more complex since this document instance must now find its view class already launched. After verifying the passed ControlDoc and ControlView pointers are valid, the pointers to this doc's parents are saved along with the battle description. Then the correct view instance is located. **GetFirstViewPosition** initializes the **POSITION** member and **GetNextView** retrieves a pointer to the next view of this document. The returned pointer is checked to ensure the correct view class has been found.
```
    if (ptrcdoc && ptrcdoc->IsKindOf (RUNTIME_CLASS (ControlDoc)) &&
```

```
     ptrv    && ptrv->IsKindOf (RUNTIME_CLASS (ControlView))) {
 playerid = id;
 ptrcontroldoc = ptrcdoc;
 ptrcontrolview = ptrv;
 strcpy_s (descr, sizeof(descr), desc);
 POSITION pos = GetFirstViewPosition ();
 CView *ptrcview;
 while (pos != NULL) {
  ptrcview = GetNextView (pos);
  if (ptrcview && ptrcview->IsKindOf
                                 (RUNTIME_CLASS (PlayerView))) {
    PlayerView *ptrpview = (PlayerView*) ptrcview;
```

Finally, the PlayerView instance is given its player id number and the parent control view address. Based upon which player this instance represents, the correct title is then inserted into the player's view window

```
     ptrpview->PostPlayerIdAndAddr (id, ptrcontrolview);
     CString msg;
     msg.LoadString (IDS_PLAYER_GERMAN + id);
     msg += descr;
     ptrpview->GetParentFrame ()->SetWindowText (msg);
     break;
   }
  }
 }
```

The GameDoc's ShowPlayer function is responsible for the actual hiding and showing of its corresponding player view. LogoffPlayer notifies the ControlDoc when this player has quit by closing the view, say from the "X" button.

Should the player activate "god mode" and wish to launch the OtherView class instance to see what the other side is seeing, part of that launch processing calls LoginOtherView which sets that view's window title appropriately.

Listing for File: GameDoc.cpp

```
...
IMPLEMENT_DYNCREATE(GameDoc, CDocument)

GameDoc::GameDoc() {
 ptrworldDC     = NULL;
 ptrpalette     = NULL;
 ptrcontroldoc  = NULL;
 ptrcontrolview = NULL;
 playerid       = -1;
 world_size.cx = world_size.cy = 0;
 world_rect.SetRect (0, 0, 0, 0);
 descr[0] = 0;
 canundo  = FALSE;
}
```

```
GameDoc::~GameDoc() {
 RemoveObjects ();
}


BEGIN_MESSAGE_MAP(GameDoc, CDocument)
END_MESSAGE_MAP()

/*******************************************************************************/
/*                                                                             */
/* RemoveObjects: remove all allocated objects                                 */
/*                                                                             */
/*******************************************************************************/

void        GameDoc::RemoveObjects () {
 if (ptrworldDC) delete ptrworldDC;
 if (ptrpalette) delete ptrpalette;
 ptrworldDC = NULL;
 ptrpalette = NULL;
 ptrcontroldoc = NULL;
 ptrcontrolview = NULL;
 playerid = -1;
 world_size.cx = world_size.cy = 0;
 world_rect.SetRect (0, 0, 0, 0);
 descr[0] = 0;
}


/*******************************************************************************/
/*                                                                             */
/* PostControlAddrs: game controller installs player id and description        */
/*                   which is passed to our views and their titlebars          */
/*                                                                             */
/*******************************************************************************/

void        GameDoc::PostControlAddrs (ControlDoc *ptrcdoc, long id,
                                       char *desc, ControlView *ptrv) {
 ASSERT (ptrcdoc);
 ASSERT (ptrv);
 ASSERT (ptrcdoc->IsKindOf (RUNTIME_CLASS (ControlDoc)));
 ASSERT (ptrv->IsKindOf (RUNTIME_CLASS (ControlView)));
 if (ptrcdoc && ptrcdoc->IsKindOf (RUNTIME_CLASS (ControlDoc)) &&
     ptrv    && ptrv->IsKindOf (RUNTIME_CLASS (ControlView))) {
  playerid = id;
  ptrcontroldoc = ptrcdoc;
  ptrcontrolview = ptrv;
  strcpy_s (descr, sizeof(descr), desc);
  POSITION pos = GetFirstViewPosition ();
  CView *ptrcview;
  while (pos != NULL) {
   ptrcview = GetNextView (pos);
   if (ptrcview && ptrcview->IsKindOf (RUNTIME_CLASS (PlayerView))) {
    PlayerView *ptrpview = (PlayerView*) ptrcview;
    ptrpview->PostPlayerIdAndAddr (id, ptrcontrolview);
    CString msg;
    msg.LoadString (IDS_PLAYER_GERMAN + id);
    msg += descr;
    ptrpview->GetParentFrame ()->SetWindowText (msg);
    break;
   }
```

```
   }
  }
}

/****************************************************************************/
/*                                                                        */
/* GetPlayerId: returns the current player ID number                      */
/*                                                                        */
/****************************************************************************/

long     GameDoc::GetPlayerId () {
 return playerid;
}

/****************************************************************************/
/*                                                                        */
/* ShowPlayer: when TRUE, shows all windows, FALSE hides all windows       */
/*                                                                        */
/****************************************************************************/

void     GameDoc::ShowPlayer (bool which) {
 POSITION pos = GetFirstViewPosition ();
 CView *ptrview;
 while (pos != NULL) {
  ptrview = GetNextView (pos);
  if (ptrview && ptrview->IsKindOf (RUNTIME_CLASS (GameView)))
   if (which) (GameView*)ptrview->GetParentFrame()->ShowWindow (SW_SHOW);
   else (GameView*)ptrview->GetParentFrame()->ShowWindow (SW_HIDE);
 }
 isvisible = which;
}

/****************************************************************************/
/*                                                                        */
/* ActionDone: clear canundo flag                                         */
/*                                                                        */
/****************************************************************************/

void     GameDoc::ActionDone () {
 canundo = false;
}

/****************************************************************************/
/*                                                                        */
/* GetControlDoc: returns the ptr to the control doc                      */
/*                                                                        */
/****************************************************************************/

ControlDoc*   GameDoc::GetControlDoc () {
 if (ptrcontroldoc &&
     ptrcontroldoc->IsKindOf (RUNTIME_CLASS (ControlDoc)))
  return ptrcontroldoc;
 else return NULL;
}

/****************************************************************************/
/*                                                                        */
/* LoginOtherView: notify other view of player id and sets it titlebar    */
```

```
/*                                                                          */
/**************************************************************************/

void        GameDoc::LoginOtherView (OtherView *ptrview, long &id) {
 id = playerid;
 CString msg;
 msg.LoadString (IDS_OTHER_GERMAN + id);
 msg += descr;
 ptrview->GetParentFrame ()->SetWindowText (msg);
}

/**************************************************************************/
/*                                                                          */
/* LogoffPlayer: notify game controller of player departure                 */
/*                                                                          */
/**************************************************************************/

void        GameDoc::LogoffPlayer () {
 if (IsModified ()) {
  SaveBattle (docfilename);
  SetModifiedFlag (FALSE);
 }
 ptrcontroldoc->LogoffPlayer (playerid);
}

/**************************************************************************/
/*                                                                          */
/* LogoffOther: notification of closure of other view                       */
/*                                                                          */
/**************************************************************************/

void        GameDoc::LogoffOther () {
}

/**************************************************************************/
/*                                                                          */
/* OnFileClose: handle file close messages - should not be needed           */
/*                                                                          */
/**************************************************************************/

void        GameDoc::OnFileClose () {
 LogoffPlayer ();
 CDocument::OnCloseDocument ();
}

/**************************************************************************/
/*                                                                          */
/* OnCloseDocument: usually called from game controller document to quit    */
/*                                                                          */
/**************************************************************************/

void        GameDoc::OnCloseDocument () {
 if (IsModified ()) {
  SaveBattle (docfilename);
  SetModifiedFlag (FALSE);
 }
 CDocument::OnCloseDocument ();
}
```

```
/*************************************************************/
/*                                                           */
/* GetWorldDC: returns a ptr to the background DIB Section DC */
/*                                                           */
/*************************************************************/

BitmapDC*  GameDoc::GetWorldDC () {
 return ptrworldDC;
}

/*************************************************************/
/*                                                           */
/* GetWorldSizeAndPalette: give view world size and current palette */
/*                                                           */
/*************************************************************/

Palette*  GameDoc::GetWorldSizeAndPalette (CSize &viewworld) {
 viewworld = world_size;
 return ptrpalette;
}



/*************************************************************/
/*                                                           */
/* OnOpenDocument: open an existing battle                   */
/*                                                           */
/*************************************************************/

BOOL     GameDoc::OnOpenDocument (LPCTSTR filename) {
 if (!CDocument::OnOpenDocument (filename)) return FALSE;
 return LoadBattle (filename);
}

/*************************************************************/
/*                                                           */
/* OnSaveDocument: save this battle                          */
/*                                                           */
/*************************************************************/

BOOL     GameDoc::OnSaveDocument (LPCTSTR filename) {
 return SaveBattle (filename);
}

/*************************************************************/
/*                                                           */
/* LoadBattle: loads in a battle to play                     */
/*                                                           */
/*************************************************************/

bool     GameDoc::LoadBattle (LPCTSTR filename) {
 SetModifiedFlag (TRUE);
 strcpy_s (docfilename, sizeof(docfilename), filename);
 RemoveObjects ();
 BOOL ok;

 ptrpalette = new Palette (ok);
 ptrworldDC = new BitmapDC ();
 if (!ptrpalette || !ok || !ptrworldDC) {
```

```
CString msg1, msg2;
msg1.LoadString (IDS_GAMEDOC_FILERRH);
msg1 += filename;
msg2.LoadString (IDS_GAMEDOC_FILERR1);
MessageBox (0, msg2, msg1, MB_OK);
return false;
}

if (!ptrworldDC->Read (filename, ptrpalette)) return false;

world_rect.SetRect (0, 0, ptrworldDC->Width (), ptrworldDC->Height ());
world_size.cx = ptrworldDC->Width ();
world_size.cy = ptrworldDC->Height ();

return true;
}

/*********************************************************************/
/*                                                                   */
/* SaveBattle: saves a battle to disk                                */
/*                                                                   */
/*********************************************************************/

bool     GameDoc::SaveBattle (LPCTSTR filename) {
MessageBox (0, "Saving a battle", filename, MB_OK);
return true;
}

/*********************************************************************/
/*                                                                   */
/* DeleteContents: remove this document's contents                   */
/*                                                                   */
/*********************************************************************/

void     GameDoc::DeleteContents () {
RemoveObjects ();
}
...
```

All player views use instances of the GameFrame class. This **CMDIChildWnd** derived class has as its purpose to differentiate between the player closing the OtherView or closing the actual PlayerView. If it is a request to close the true PlayerView, a query message is given. **GetActiveView** returns a pointer to the view class this frame contains. The **GetDocument** function of the view class returns the GameDoc pointer. The GameDoc instance is then notified via LogoffPlayer or LogoffOther.

Listing for File: GameFrame.h

```
...class GameFrame : public CMDIChildWnd {
DECLARE_DYNCREATE(GameFrame)
protected:
GameFrame(); // protected constructor used by dynamic creation
protected:
virtual ~GameFrame();
BOOL  PreCreateWindow (CREATESTRUCT&); // override to use template title
```

```
afx_msg void  OnClose ();                    // process other view close requests
...
```

Listing for File: GameFrame.cpp

```
...
IMPLEMENT_DYNCREATE (GameFrame, CMDIChildWnd)

GameFrame::GameFrame () { }
GameFrame::~GameFrame () { }

/****************************************************************************/
/*                                                                          */
/* PreCreateWindow: remove FWS_ADDTOTITLE so template name is used          */
/*                  not document file name                                  */
/*                                                                          */
/****************************************************************************/

BOOL      GameFrame::PreCreateWindow (CREATESTRUCT &cs) {
 cs.style &= ~(LONG) FWS_ADDTOTITLE;
 return CMDIChildWnd::PreCreateWindow (cs);
}

BEGIN_MESSAGE_MAP (GameFrame, CMDIChildWnd)
 ON_WM_CLOSE ()
END_MESSAGE_MAP ()

/****************************************************************************/
/*                                                                          */
/* OnClose: query user only for closing player views                       */
/*                                                                          */
/****************************************************************************/

void      GameFrame::OnClose () {
 CString msg1, msg2;
 CView *ptrview = GetActiveView ();
 CView *ptrcview;
 if (ptrview && ptrview->IsKindOf (RUNTIME_CLASS (PlayerView))) {
  msg1.LoadString (IDS_PLAYER_QUIT);
  msg2.LoadString (IDS_PLAYER_QUITMSG);
  if (MessageBox (msg2, msg1, MB_YESNO | MB_ICONQUESTION) == IDYES) {
   GameDoc *ptrdoc = ((PlayerView*) ptrview)->GetDocument ();
   if (ptrdoc && ptrdoc->IsKindOf (RUNTIME_CLASS (GameDoc)))
    ptrdoc->LogoffPlayer ();
   POSITION pos = ptrdoc->GetFirstViewPosition ();
   while (pos != NULL) {
    ptrcview = ptrdoc->GetNextView (pos);
    if (ptrcview != ptrview)
     ptrcview->GetParentFrame ()->PostMessage (WM_CLOSE, 0, 0L);
   }
   CMDIChildWnd::OnClose ();
  }
 }
 else if (ptrview && ptrview->IsKindOf (RUNTIME_CLASS (OtherView))) {
   GameDoc *ptrdoc = ((OtherView*) ptrview)->GetDocument ();
   if (ptrdoc && ptrdoc->IsKindOf (RUNTIME_CLASS (GameDoc)))
    ptrdoc->LogoffOther ();
```

```
      CMDIChildWnd::OnClose ();
   }
else CMDIChildWnd::OnClose ();
}
...
```

The GameView, PlayerView, and OtherView Classes

When circumstances allow, do not hesitate to define a base class for functionality and then derive working classes from them. In this sample program, there are two views that utilize the off screen buffer, the player's view and the "god mode" other player view. Thus, it makes sense to define a common base class, GameView, for these two views that includes the basic functionality. Then, derive specific classes, PlayerView and OtherView from GameView.

GameView provides the basic functionality of providing a **CScrollView** in which the basic background bitmap is displayed as needed. It maintains the off screen buffer and the palette. Data members also contain the current off screen dimensions. When the bool **must_render** is true, the off screen buffer must be rendered to the screen.

The document contains the master background BitmapDC. The GameView class maintains its own BitmapDC to be blited to the screen. Rendering consists of copying that portion of the document's bitmap into the view's off screen BitmapDC, adding all of the various game sprites representing the playing counters and so forth. When the image is constructed, it is blited to the view screen.

Complexity enters when the user wishes to resize the view. Our off screen buffer dimensions should then change. Thus, we need to dynamically respond. **OnGetMinMaxInfo** is overridden to force the view to never exceed the maximum size of the actual background world bitmap. **OnSize** responds to resizing by re-creating the off screen buffer to match the new view size.

Listing for File: GameView.h

```
...
/***************************************************************************/
/*                                                                         */
/* GameView: Basic Offscreen Buffer Scrolled View                          */
/*                                                                         */
/***************************************************************************/

class GameView : public CView {
protected:
 GameView();             // protected constructor used by dynamic creation
 DECLARE_DYNCREATE(GameView)

public:
BitmapDC *ptroffscreenDC;  // the offscreen DIB Section bitmap
Palette  *ptrpalette;      // the palette in use
```

```
bool        must_render;       // TRUE when view must redraw its BitmapDC from map
CSize       world_size;        // the dimensions of the world

protected:
CRect       offscreen_rect;    // the offscreen DIB Section bitmap rect
CPoint      offscreen_offset;  // the offscreen World X,Y offset
CSize       offscreen_size;    // the dimensions of the off screen buffer
bool        lbtndown;          // TRUE when left button is down
GameDoc     *ptrdoc;

virtual void    OnDraw(CDC* pDC);        // overridden to draw this view
virtual bool    CreateOffScreenBuffer ();        // create off the screen buffer
virtual void    Draw (CDC *ptrdc);               // place holder for derived class
virtual void    Render (CRect *ptrclip = NULL);// place holder for derived class
virtual void    OnInitialUpdate ();              // place holder for derived class
afx_msg int     OnCreate (LPCREATESTRUCT);       // install gray background brush
afx_msg void    OnGetMinMaxInfo (MINMAXINFO*);
afx_msg void    OnSize (UINT, int, int);         // recreate new sized buffer
afx_msg void    OnVScroll (UINT, UINT, CScrollBar*); // scroll screen in X dir
afx_msg void    OnHScroll (UINT, UINT, CScrollBar*); // scroll screen in Y dir
virtual void    SetOurScrollRange ();            // sets the scrolling range
virtual void    CreateFailure (long);            // show why and set to NULL
virtual void    RemoveObjects ();                // remove offscreen objects
virtual         ~GameView();
afx_msg void    OnPaletteChanged (CWnd*);        // respond to palette change
afx_msg BOOL    OnQueryNewPalette ();            // respond to palette change

public:
virtual GameDoc*  GetDocument ();                // get access to our document
virtual BitmapDC* GetOffScreenBuffer ();   // provide access to our buffer
...
```

The constructor sets all data members to NULL, implying no off screen buffer has yet been installed. In **OnInitialUpdate** I wish to initially make the view about 600 pixels square and positioned in the upper left of the screen. So I acquire the client rectangle of the frame window which houses this view and obtain any area occupied by any controls. These combined with the height of the main menu, and scroll bars for the view added to the total dimensions of the main background image are then compared to the 600 pixel value. I use the smaller of the two. Finally, **CalcWindowRect** gives me the dimensions of the window and I then use **SetWindowPos** to reposition the frame window which in turn repositions the view

```
CFrameWnd *ptrframe = GetParentFrame ();
CRect rf, rc, rq;
ptrframe->GetClientRect (&rc);
ptrframe->RepositionBars (AFX_IDW_CONTROLBAR_FIRST,
          AFX_IDW_CONTROLBAR_LAST, NULL, reposQuery, &rf, NULL);
long menuht = GetSystemMetrics (SM_CYMENU);
long xsb = GetSystemMetrics (SM_CXVSCROLL);
long ysb = GetSystemMetrics (SM_CYHSCROLL);
long ht = rc.Height () - rf.Height ();// + menuht;
rq.SetRect (0, 0, world_size.cx + xsb, world_size.cy + ht + ysb);
if (rq.Width () > 600) rq.right = 600;
if (rq.Height() > 600) rq.bottom = 600;
```

```
ptrframe->CalcWindowRect (&rq, 0);
ptrframe->SetWindowPos (NULL, 0, 0, rq.Width (), rq.Height (),
                   SWP_NOZORDER | SWP_NOACTIVATE);
```

OnSize is responsible for actually constructing the off screen buffer. The current width is forced onto a 32-bit boundary. If there is no change in the size, I return. If the palette is not yet present, I save the size values and leave. This avoids the early calls to **OnSize** before the view is actually ready to be used. If all is ok, the buffer is created

```
w = w % 4 > 0 ? 4 - w % 4 + w : w;
// force width onto 32-bit boundary
// first avoid doing anything for initial call with no size
if (ptroffscreenDC && w == offscreen_size.cx &&
    h == offscreen_size.cy) return;
// if not yet attached to document, save the current size for
// later use
if (!ptrpalette) {
 offscreen_rect.SetRect (0, 0, w, h); // save for real build
 offscreen_size.cx = w;
 offscreen_size.cy = h;
 offscreen_offset.x = offscreen_offset.y = 0;
 return;
}
else { // all ok, so build the off screen buffer
 offscreen_size.cx = w;
 offscreen_size.cy = h;
 CreateOffScreenBuffer ();
}
```

Actual rendering functions do nothing. Such functionality must be provided by the derived classes for only they know what would be appropriate to render for each type of view. My intention is to have the Render function draw all the sprites representing the counters onto the off screen buffer while Draw copies the final image to the screen.

Listing for File: GameView.cpp
```
...
IMPLEMENT_DYNCREATE(GameView, CView)

GameView::GameView() {
 ptroffscreenDC      = NULL;
 ptrpalette          = NULL;
 lbtndown            = false;
 must_render         = false;
 world_size.cx       = world_size.cy = 0;
 offscreen_size.cx   = offscreen_size.cy  = 0;
 offscreen_offset.x  = offscreen_offset.y = 0;
 offscreen_rect.SetRect (0, 0, 0, 0);
 ptrdoc              = NULL;
}

GameView::~GameView() {
```

```
RemoveObjects ();
}

BEGIN_MESSAGE_MAP(GameView, CView)
 ON_WM_GETMINMAXINFO ()
 ON_WM_CREATE ()
 ON_WM_PALETTECHANGED ()
 ON_WM_QUERYNEWPALETTE ()
 ON_WM_HSCROLL ()
 ON_WM_VSCROLL ()
 ON_WM_SIZE ()
END_MESSAGE_MAP()

/***************************************************************************/
/*                                                                         */
/* RemoveObjects: delete all allocated objects                             */
/*                                                                         */
/***************************************************************************/

void      GameView::RemoveObjects () {
 if (ptroffscreenDC) delete ptroffscreenDC;
 ptroffscreenDC = NULL;
 ptrpalette     = NULL;
 world_size.cx  = world_size.cy = 0;
 offscreen_rect.SetRect (0, 0, 0, 0);
 offscreen_size.cx = offscreen_size.cy = 0;
 offscreen_offset.x = offscreen_offset.y = 0;
}

/***************************************************************************/
/*                                                                         */
/* OnCreate: build the view with lt grey background brush                  */
/*                                                                         */
/***************************************************************************/

int       GameView::OnCreate (LPCREATESTRUCT lpCS) {
 int retcd = CView::OnCreate (lpCS); // pass along to base class
 // install new background color
  ::SetClassLong (m_hWnd, GCL_HBRBACKGROUND,
                  (long) (HBRUSH) ::GetStockObject (LTGRAY_BRUSH));
 return retcd;
}

/***************************************************************************/
/*                                                                         */
/* OnInitialUpdate: initial create of the DIB Section off screen buffer    */
/*                                                                         */
/***************************************************************************/

void      GameView::OnInitialUpdate () {
 CFrameWnd *ptrframe = GetParentFrame ();
 CRect rf, rc, rq;
 ptrframe->GetClientRect (&rc);
 ptrframe->RepositionBars (AFX_IDW_CONTROLBAR_FIRST, AFX_IDW_CONTROLBAR_LAST,
                           NULL, reposQuery, &rf, NULL);
 long menuht = GetSystemMetrics (SM_CYMENU);
 long xsb = GetSystemMetrics (SM_CXVSCROLL);
 long ysb = GetSystemMetrics (SM_CYHSCROLL);
```

```
long ht = rc.Height () - rf.Height () + menuht;
rq.SetRect (0, 0, world_size.cx + xsb, world_size.cy + ht + ysb);
if (rq.Width () > 600) rq.right = 600;
if (rq.Height() > 600) rq.bottom = 600;
ptrframe->CalcWindowRect (&rq, 0);
ptrframe->SetWindowPos (NULL, 0, 0, rq.Width (), rq.Height (),
                           SWP_NOZORDER | SWP_NOACTIVATE);
CView::OnInitialUpdate ();
}


/**************************************************************************/
/*                                                                        */
/* CreateOffScreenBuffer: create the DIB Section and save the Palette     */
/*                                                                        */
/**************************************************************************/

bool        GameView::CreateOffScreenBuffer () {
 if (!ptrpalette) {
  CreateFailure (1); // no palette
  return false;
 }
 if (ptroffscreenDC) delete ptroffscreenDC;
 ptroffscreenDC = new BitmapDC ();
 if (ptroffscreenDC)
  if (ptroffscreenDC->Create (offscreen_size.cx, offscreen_size.cy,
      ptrpalette)) {
   offscreen_rect.SetRect (0, 0, ptroffscreenDC->Width (),
                                   ptroffscreenDC->Height ());
   offscreen_size.cx = ptroffscreenDC->Width ();
   offscreen_size.cy = ptroffscreenDC->Height ();
   if (offscreen_offset.x + offscreen_size.cx > world_size.cx) {
    offscreen_offset.x = world_size.cx - offscreen_size.cx;
    if (offscreen_offset.x < 0) offscreen_offset.x = 0;
   }
   if (offscreen_offset.y + offscreen_size.cy > world_size.cy) {
    offscreen_offset.y = world_size.cy - offscreen_size.cy;
    if (offscreen_offset.y < 0) offscreen_offset.y = 0;
   }
   must_render = true;
   SetOurScrollRange ();
   Invalidate(FALSE);                   // force repainting of window
  }
  else {
   CreateFailure (2);
   return false;
  }
 else {
  CreateFailure (3);
  return false;
 }
 return true;
}


/**************************************************************************/
/*                                                                        */
/* CreateFailure: Display why cannot create the offscreen buffer - set NULL*/
/*                                                                        */
/**************************************************************************/
```

```
void      GameView::CreateFailure (long why) {
 CString msg1, msg2;
 msg1.LoadString (IDS_GAMEVIEW_ERRHD);
 if (why == 1) msg2.LoadString (IDS_GAMEVIEW_ERR1);
 else if (why == 2) msg2.LoadString (IDS_GAMEVIEW_ERR2);
 else if (why == 3) msg2.LoadString (IDS_GAMEVIEW_ERR3);
 MessageBox (msg2, msg1, MB_OK);
 RemoveObjects ();
 must_render = TRUE;
 SetOurScrollRange ();
 Invalidate (FALSE);
}

/*******************************************************************/
/*                                                               */
/* OnSize: respond to new size of the view window - adjust size of DIB buf */
/*                                                               */
/*******************************************************************/

void      GameView::OnSize (UINT a, int w, int h) {
 CView::OnSize    (a, w, h);
 w = w % 4 > 0 ? 4 - w % 4 + w : w; // force width onto 32-bit boundary
 // first avoid doing anything for initial call with no size
 if (ptroffscreenDC && w == offscreen_size.cx &&
    h == offscreen_size.cy) return;
 // if not yet attached to document, save the current size for later use
 if (!ptrpalette) {
  offscreen_rect.SetRect (0, 0, w, h); // save for real build
  offscreen_size.cx = w;
  offscreen_size.cy = h;
  offscreen_offset.x = offscreen_offset.y = 0;
  return;
 }
 else { // all ok, so build the off screen buffer
  offscreen_size.cx = w;
  offscreen_size.cy = h;
  CreateOffScreenBuffer ();
 }
}

/*******************************************************************/
/*                                                               */
/* OnGetMinMaxInfo: force window to not exceed size of world coordinates   */
/*                                                               */
/*******************************************************************/

void      GameView::OnGetMinMaxInfo (MINMAXINFO *ptrinfo) {
 if (world_size.cx == 0 || world_size.cy == 0) return;
 ptrinfo->ptMaxTrackSize.x = world_size.cx;
 ptrinfo->ptMaxTrackSize.y = world_size.cy;
}

/*******************************************************************/
/*                                                               */
/* SetOurScrollRange: sets up the new scroll range in World coordinates    */
/*                                                               */
/*******************************************************************/
```

```
void      GameView::SetOurScrollRange () {
 long x = world_size.cx - offscreen_size.cx;
 if (x < 0) x = 0;
 long y = world_size.cy - offscreen_size.cy;
 if (y < 0) y = 0;
 SetScrollRange (SB_VERT, 0, y, FALSE);
 SetScrollPos (SB_VERT, offscreen_offset.y, TRUE);
 SetScrollRange (SB_HORZ, 0, x, FALSE);
 SetScrollPos (SB_HORZ, offscreen_offset.x, TRUE);
}


/***************************************************************************/
/*                                                                       */
/* Draw: override to display background DIB Section to screen            */
/*                                                                       */
/***************************************************************************/

void      GameView::Draw (CDC *ptrdc) {
}


/***************************************************************************/
/*                                                                       */
/* Render: override to copy world map and draw sprites onto offscreen DIB */
/*                                                                       */
/***************************************************************************/

void      GameView::Render (CRect*) {
}


/***************************************************************************/
/*                                                                       */
/* OnDraw: Render the image onto the off screen DIB Section and Blit to dc */
/*                                                                       */
/***************************************************************************/

void      GameView::OnDraw (CDC *ptrdc) {
}


/***************************************************************************/
/*                                                                       */
/* OnVScroll: process world Y direction scroll                           */
/*                                                                       */
/***************************************************************************/

void      GameView::OnVScroll (UINT type, UINT pos, CScrollBar *ptrsb) {
 long max_pels = world_size.cy - offscreen_size.cy;
 if (max_pels < 0) max_pels = 0;
 long page = offscreen_size.cy / 2 > max_pels ? max_pels :
                                               offscreen_size.cy / 2;
 long at = offscreen_offset.y;

 if (type == SB_LINEUP) {      // scroll up 1 pel
  if (at > 0) at--;
 }
 else if (type == SB_LINEDOWN) {   // scroll 1 pel down
  if (at <= max_pels) at++;
 }
 else if (type == SB_PAGEUP) {     // scroll 1 page up
```

```
  if (at > 0)
    if (at > page) at -= page;
    else at = 0;
}
else if (type == SB_PAGEDOWN) {    // scroll 1 page down
  if (at <= max_pels) {
    at += page;
    if (at > max_pels) at = max_pels;
  }
}
else if (type == SB_THUMBTRACK) { // follow thumb bar
  at = pos;
}

if (at != offscreen_offset.y) {
  SetScrollPos (SB_VERT, at, TRUE); // set new scroll position
  offscreen_offset.y = at;
  must_render = TRUE;
  Invalidate (FALSE);
}
}

/******************************************************************************/
/*                                                                          */
/* OnHScroll: process world X direction scroll                              */
/*                                                                          */
/******************************************************************************/

void       GameView::OnHScroll (UINT type, UINT pos, CScrollBar *ptrsb) {
  long max_pels = world_size.cx - offscreen_size.cx;
  if (max_pels < 0) max_pels = 0;
  long page = offscreen_size.cx / 2 > max_pels ? max_pels :offscreen_size.cx/2;
  long at = offscreen_offset.x;

  if (type == SB_LINEUP) {            // scroll left 1 pel
    if (at > 0) at--;
  }
  else if (type == SB_LINEDOWN) {    // scroll right 1 pel
    if (at <= max_pels) at++;
  }
  else if (type == SB_PAGEUP) {      // scroll 1 page left
    if (at > 0)
      if (at > page) at -= page;
      else at = 0;
  }
  else if (type == SB_PAGEDOWN) {    // scroll 1 page right
    if (at <= max_pels) {
      at += page;
      if (at > max_pels) at = max_pels;
    }
  }
  else if (type == SB_THUMBTRACK) { // follow thumb bar
    at = pos;
  }

  if (at != offscreen_offset.x) {
    SetScrollPos (SB_HORZ, at, TRUE); // set new scroll position
    offscreen_offset.x = at;
```

```
  must_render = TRUE;
  Invalidate (FALSE);
 }
}


/**************************************************************************/
/*                                                                      */
/* GetDocument: returns ptr to the associated CDocument                 */
/*                                                                      */
/**************************************************************************/

GameDoc*  GameView::GetDocument () {
 GameDoc* ptrbdoc = (GameDoc*) m_pDocument;
 ASSERT (ptrbdoc);
 if (ptrbdoc && ptrbdoc->IsKindOf (RUNTIME_CLASS (GameDoc))) return ptrbdoc;
 else return NULL;
}


/**************************************************************************/
/*                                                                      */
/* GetOffScreenBuffer: returns a ptr to the off screen BitmapDC         */
/*                                                                      */
/**************************************************************************/

BitmapDC*  GameView::GetOffScreenBuffer () {
 return ptroffscreenDC;
}


/**************************************************************************/
/*                                                                      */
/* OnPaletteChanged: we are inactive, so make the best of it            */
/*                                                                      */
/**************************************************************************/

void      GameView::OnPaletteChanged (CWnd *ptrwin) {
 if (ptrwin != this) OnQueryNewPalette ();
}


/**************************************************************************/
/*                                                                      */
/* OnQueryNewPalette: we are going active so realize our palette        */
/*                                                                      */
/**************************************************************************/

BOOL      GameView::OnQueryNewPalette () {
 if (ptrpalette) {
  CDC *ptrdc = GetDC ();
  CPalette *ptroldpal = ptrdc->SelectPalette (ptrpalette->GetPalette(),
                                              FALSE);
  UINT num = ptrdc->RealizePalette ();
  ReleaseDC (ptrdc);
  if (num) {
   InvalidateRect (NULL, TRUE);
   return TRUE;
  }
 }
 return FALSE;
}
```

...

The PlayerView is the main view the players use to carry out their game actions. Two data members hold the pointer to the ControlDoc and the player id number. The base class render functions are overridden to actually blit the off screen image. And some member functions provide the user interface, here quite small. Just add in the rest of the game.

Listing for File: PlayerView.h

```
...
class PlayerView : public GameView {
protected:
 PlayerView(); // protected constructor used by dynamic creation
 DECLARE_DYNCREATE(PlayerView)

public:
long playerid; // the player id which is ties into the country numbers

protected:
ControlView  *ptrcontrolview;

virtual void OnDraw(CDC* pDC); // overridden to draw this view
virtual      ~PlayerView();

public:
virtual void   PostPlayerIdAndAddr (long, ControlView*);
virtual void   Draw (CDC *ptrdc);
virtual void   Render (CRect *ptrclip = NULL);
virtual void   OnInitialUpdate ();
virtual void   OnUpdate (CView*, LPARAM, CObject*);

protected:
afx_msg void   OnKeyDown (UINT, UINT, UINT);
afx_msg void   OnChar (UINT, UINT, UINT);
afx_msg void   CmActionDone ();
afx_msg void   CmUndo ();
afx_msg void   CmEnableUndo (CCmdUI*);
...
```

PostControlAddrs makes the view active by providing the control view address for turn sequencing and the player id number. **OnInitialUpdate** obtains the world size and master palette from the document and can then create the off screen buffer after the GameView base class has handled its actions. Remember that the base class' **OnSize** from here on handles resizing situations automatically.

Currently, **OnDraw** installs the palette into the Paint DC and blits the off screen buffer onto the screen. In the real game, sprites must be rendered onto the off screen buffer first before the final results are blitted to the screen.

OnChar provides the Undo option, a Ctl-Z while **OnKeyDown** handles the Do It! short cut.

Notice one important feature. The view cannot respond directly to the menu item to open the OtherView on the document! Rather opening a second view on a document must be handled by the MainFrame window of the application.

Listing for File: PlayerView.cpp

```
...
IMPLEMENT_DYNCREATE(PlayerView, GameView)

PlayerView::PlayerView() : GameView () {
 playerid = -1; // indicates no player id yet installed
 ptrcontrolview = NULL;
}

PlayerView::~PlayerView() { }

BEGIN_MESSAGE_MAP(PlayerView, GameView)
 ON_WM_CHAR ()
 ON_WM_KEYDOWN ()
 ON_COMMAND (CM_BATTLEDOC_ACTIONDONE,    CmActionDone)
 ON_COMMAND (CM_BATTLEDOC_UNDO,          CmUndo)
 ON_UPDATE_COMMAND_UI(CM_BATTLEDOC_UNDO, CmEnableUndo)
END_MESSAGE_MAP()

/**************************************************************************/
/*                                                                        */
/* PostPlayerIdAndAddr: call back from document to install player number  */
/*                      and game controller view for message posting      */
/*                                                                        */
/**************************************************************************/

void      PlayerView::PostPlayerIdAndAddr (long id, ControlView *ptrv) {
 playerid = id;
 ptrcontrolview = ptrv;
}

/**************************************************************************/
/*                                                                        */
/* OnInitialUpdate: set the initial size of the view                      */
/*                                                                        */
/**************************************************************************/

void      PlayerView::OnInitialUpdate () {
 GameDoc *ptrbdoc = GetDocument ();
 if (ptrbdoc && ptrbdoc->IsKindOf (RUNTIME_CLASS (GameDoc))) {
  ptrdoc = ptrbdoc;
  ptrpalette = ptrdoc->GetWorldSizeAndPalette (world_size);
  GameView::OnInitialUpdate ();
  CreateOffScreenBuffer (); // let base handle errors
 }
}

/**************************************************************************/
```

```
/*                                                                     */
/* OnUpdate: Process hints from document                               */
/*                                                                     */
/**********************************************************************/

void      PlayerView::OnUpdate(CView *ptrsender, LPARAM lhint,
                               CObject* /*ptrhint*/) {
 ASSERT(ptrsender != this);                // avoid repaint if it's us
 if (lhint == 0) Invalidate (TRUE);        // force repaint, erase background
 else if (lhint == 1) Invalidate (FALSE);  // force repaint, no erase on scroll
}

/**********************************************************************/
/*                                                                     */
/* Draw:                                                               */
/*                                                                     */
/**********************************************************************/

void      PlayerView::Draw (CDC *ptrdc) {
 if (!ptroffscreenDC) return;

 CRect drawrect = offscreen_rect;
 CRect cliprect;
 ptrdc->GetClipBox (cliprect);
 CPalette *ptroldpal = NULL;  // install our palette
 if (ptrpalette) {
  ptroldpal = ptrdc->SelectPalette (ptrpalette->GetPalette (), FALSE);
  ptrdc->RealizePalette ();
 }
 // copy our offscreen buffer to the screen
 BitBlt (ptrdc->GetSafeHdc (), drawrect.left, drawrect.top, drawrect.Width (),
         drawrect.Height (), ptroffscreenDC->hbmpdc, drawrect.left,
         drawrect.top, SRCCOPY);
 if (ptroldpal) ptrdc->SelectPalette (ptroldpal, 0);
}

/**********************************************************************/
/*                                                                     */
/* Render:                                                             */
/*                                                                     */
/**********************************************************************/

void      PlayerView::Render (CRect*) {
 GameDoc *ptrdoc = GetDocument ();
 BitmapDC *ptrmemdc = ptrdoc->GetWorldDC (); // get access to the world map DC
 if (!ptrmemdc || !ptroffscreenDC) return;
 // copy the portion of the world map to our offscreen buffer
 BitBlt (ptroffscreenDC->hbmpdc, 0, 0, offscreen_rect.Width (),
         offscreen_rect.Height (), ptrmemdc->hbmpdc, offscreen_offset.x,
         offscreen_offset.y, SRCCOPY);
 CDC dc;
 dc.Attach (ptroffscreenDC->hbmpdc);
 CPalette *ptroldpal = NULL;  // install our palette
 if (ptrpalette) {
  ptroldpal = dc.SelectPalette (ptrpalette->GetPalette (), FALSE);
  dc.RealizePalette ();
 }
 if (ptroldpal) dc.SelectPalette (ptroldpal, 0);
```

```
 dc.Detach ();
}

/**********************************************************************/
/*                                                                    */
/* OnDraw:                                                            */
/*                                                                    */
/**********************************************************************/

void      PlayerView::OnDraw (CDC *ptrdc) {
 if (must_render) Render ();
 Draw (ptrdc);
}

/**********************************************************************/
/*                                                                    */
/* OnChar: get hot key actions                                       */
/*                                                                    */
/**********************************************************************/

void      PlayerView::OnChar (UINT c, UINT a, UINT b) {
 switch (c) {
  case 0x1b: // escape
  case 26:   // ^Z
   // undo
   break;
  default:
   GameView::OnChar (c, a, b);
 };
}

/**********************************************************************/
/*                                                                    */
/* OnSysKeyDown: get hot key actions                                 */
/*                                                                    */
/**********************************************************************/

void      PlayerView::OnKeyDown (UINT c, UINT a, UINT b) {
 switch (c) {
  case VK_F2:
   CmActionDone ();
   break;
  default:
   GameView::OnKeyDown (c, a, b);
 };
}

/**********************************************************************/
/*                                                                    */
/* CmActionDone: post done to control doc                            */
/*                                                                    */
/**********************************************************************/

void      PlayerView::CmActionDone () {
 if (ptrdoc) ptrdoc->ActionDone ();
 if (ptrcontrolview)
  ptrcontrolview->PostMessage (CM_NOTIFY_BATDOC_ACTDONE, 0, playerid);
}
```

```
/****************************************************************************/
/*                                                                        */
/* CmUndo: undo last action                                               */
/*                                                                        */
/****************************************************************************/

void      PlayerView::CmUndo () {
 if (ptrdoc && ptrdoc->canundo) {
  //...
 }
}

/****************************************************************************/
/*                                                                        */
/* CmEnableUndo: enable undo menuitem                                     */
/*                                                                        */
/****************************************************************************/

void      PlayerView::CmEnableUndo (CCmdUI *ptrui) {
 ptrui->Enable (ptrdoc ? ptrdoc->canundo ? 1 : 0 : 0);
}
```

Back to the MainFrame Implementation and the OtherView

So we are finally ready to look at that coding in the MainFrame class given far above! MainFrame then responds to each logged on player's request to open the OtherView. First, the main frame must find the currently active view's **CMDIChildWnd** frame window using the **MDIGetActive** function. If there is an active view, obtain a pointer to its document class

```
void      MainFrame::CmMakeOtherView () {
 CMDIChildWnd *ptrMDIActive = MDIGetActive ();
 ASSERT(ptrMDIActive != NULL);
 if (!ptrMDIActive) return;

 CDocument *ptrdoc = ptrMDIActive->GetActiveDocument ();
 ASSERT(ptrdoc != NULL);
 if (!ptrdoc) return;
```

Next, realize that the OtherView could have already been created by the player. In such a case, we need only to activate that view and bring it to the forefront

```
 CView *ptrview;
 POSITION pos = ptrdoc->GetFirstViewPosition ();
 while (pos != NULL) {
  ptrview = ptrdoc->GetNextView (pos);
  if (ptrview && ptrview->IsKindOf (RUNTIME_CLASS (OtherView))) {
   ptrview->GetParentFrame ()->ActivateFrame ();
   return;
  }
 }
```

If the OtherView does not exist, then we must create a second view on the current document. Obtain a pointer to the active view's GameDoc and get the player's id number. To create another view on this document, call the application template's **CreateNewFrame** for the other document view. This new frame should be an instance of the **CMDIChildWnd**. If successful, call the **InitialUpdateFrame**, tying this new frame and the current document to which this second view is being attached together

```
if (ptrdoc->IsKindOf (RUNTIME_CLASS (GameDoc))) {
 GameDoc *ptrbdoc = (GameDoc*) ptrdoc;
 long id = ptrbdoc->GetPlayerId ();
 if (id == -1) return;
 CMDIChildWnd *ptrNewFrame;
 ptrNewFrame =
(CMDIChildWnd*) (theApp.ptrothertmp->CreateNewFrame (ptrdoc, NULL));
 if (!ptrNewFrame) return;       // not created
 if (ptrNewFrame->IsKindOf (RUNTIME_CLASS (CMDIChildWnd)))
  theApp.ptrothertmp->InitialUpdateFrame (ptrNewFrame, ptrdoc);
```

Finally, since the player cannot perform any actions in the other view, I wish the original player view to remain activated

```
 pos = ptrdoc->GetFirstViewPosition ();
 while (pos != NULL) {
  ptrview = ptrdoc->GetNextView (pos);
  if (ptrview && ptrview->IsKindOf(RUNTIME_CLASS (PlayerView))) {
   ptrview->GetParentFrame ()->ActivateFrame ();
   break;
  }
 }
 MDITile (MDITILE_VERTICAL);
```

Using the **MDITile** function makes the two views look quite nice on screen with the player view (currently active) on the left and the other view on the right. Note if I did not make the player view the active view, then the other view would have been on the left.

Whenever the player wishes to close the other view, the MainFrame must also handle the operation. Again, find the active MDI child window and then its document. From the document, find the other view, if any. If found, post the WM_CLOSE message to remove that view

```
void      MainFrame::CmCloseOtherView () {
 CMDIChildWnd *ptrMDIActive = MDIGetActive ();
 ASSERT(ptrMDIActive != NULL);
 if (!ptrMDIActive) return;

 CDocument *ptrdoc = ptrMDIActive->GetActiveDocument ();
 ASSERT(ptrdoc != NULL);
 if (!ptrdoc) return;

 CView *ptrview;
 POSITION pos = ptrdoc->GetFirstViewPosition ();
 while (pos != NULL) {
  ptrview = ptrdoc->GetNextView (pos);
```

```
    if (ptrview && ptrview->IsKindOf (RUNTIME_CLASS (OtherView))) {
     ptrview->GetParentFrame ()->PostMessage (WM_CLOSE, 0, 0L);
     return;
    }
   }
  }
```

The OtherView simply overrides the main rendering functions to blit the correct image to the screen. So it is a relatively simple class here.

Listing for File: OtherView.h

```
...
class OtherView : public GameView {
protected:
 OtherView();  // protected constructor used by dynamic creation
 DECLARE_DYNCREATE(OtherView)

public:
long playerid; // player id which ties into the country

protected:
        virtual void OnDraw(CDC* pDC);        // overridden to draw this view
virtual void  Draw (CDC *ptrdc);
virtual void  Render (CRect *ptrclip = NULL);
virtual void  OnInitialUpdate ();
virtual void  OnUpdate (CView*, LPARAM, CObject*);
virtual       ~OtherView();
...
```

OnDraw calls Render and then Draw. Render constructs the sprites (here none) and Draw blits the results to the screen. **OnUpdate** uses hints to control whether to force the background to be repainted or not.

Listing for File: OtherView.cpp

```
...
IMPLEMENT_DYNCREATE(OtherView, GameView)

OtherView::OtherView() : GameView () {
 playerid = -1; // indicate no player installed yet
}

OtherView::~OtherView() { }

BEGIN_MESSAGE_MAP(OtherView, GameView)
END_MESSAGE_MAP()

/************************************************************************/
/*                                                                      */
/* OnInitialUpdate: set the initial size of the view                    */
/*                                                                      */
/************************************************************************/
```

```
void        OtherView::OnInitialUpdate () {
 GameDoc *ptrdoc = GetDocument ();
 ptrdoc->LoginOtherView (this, playerid);
 ptrpalette = ptrdoc->GetWorldSizeAndPalette (world_size);
 GameView::OnInitialUpdate ();
 CreateOffScreenBuffer (); // let base handle errors
}


/****************************************************************************/
/*                                                                        */
/* OnUpdate: Process hints from document                                  */
/*                                                                        */
/****************************************************************************/

void        OtherView::OnUpdate(CView *ptrsender, LPARAM lhint,
                                CObject* /*ptrhint*/) {
 ASSERT(ptrsender != this);                 // avoid if its us
 if (lhint == 0) Invalidate (TRUE);         // force repaint, erase background
 else if (lhint == 1) Invalidate (FALSE); // force repaint, no erase on scroll
}


/****************************************************************************/
/*                                                                        */
/* Draw:                                                                  */
/*                                                                        */
/****************************************************************************/

void        OtherView::Draw (CDC *ptrdc) {
 if (!ptroffscreenDC) return;

 CRect drawrect = offscreen_rect;
 CRect cliprect;
 ptrdc->GetClipBox (cliprect);

 CPalette *ptroldpal = NULL;
 if (ptrpalette) {
  ptroldpal = ptrdc->SelectPalette (ptrpalette->GetPalette (), FALSE);
  ptrdc->RealizePalette ();
 }
 BitBlt (ptrdc->GetSafeHdc (), drawrect.left, drawrect.top, drawrect.Width(),
         drawrect.Height (), ptroffscreenDC->hbmpdc, drawrect.left,
         drawrect.top, SRCCOPY);
 if (ptroldpal) ptrdc->SelectPalette (ptroldpal, 0);
}


/****************************************************************************/
/*                                                                        */
/* Render:                                                                */
/*                                                                        */
/****************************************************************************/

void        OtherView::Render (CRect*) {
 GameDoc *ptrdoc = GetDocument ();
 BitmapDC *ptrmemdc = ptrdoc->GetWorldDC ();
 if (!ptrmemdc || !ptroffscreenDC) return;
 BitBlt (ptroffscreenDC->hbmpdc, 0, 0, offscreen_rect.Width (),
         offscreen_rect.Height (), ptrmemdc->hbmpdc, offscreen_offset.x,
         offscreen_offset.y, SRCCOPY);
```

```
}

/******************************************************************/
/*                                                              */
/* OnDraw:                                                      */
/*                                                              */
/******************************************************************/

void        OtherView::OnDraw (CDC *ptrdc) {
 Render ();
 Draw (ptrdc);
}
```

So now the next step is to add in some sprites to represent the counters and implement some game rules. Have fun.

Chapter 12 Enhanced Metafiles and Printing

What is an enhanced metafile? It is a collection of GDI functions which when executed creates an image. Such images range in complexity from simple lines and rectangles to complete photographic quality bitmaps. Because enhanced metafiles contain only the GDI function calls, they take up far less space than device-independent bitmaps. Once created, an enhanced metafile can be played back (at which time, the GDI function calls are executed) on the screen or printer in a wide variety of ways. They can be played back positioned anywhere on the display surface and can be scaled to any dimensions and retain their shape and proportions. Enhanced metafiles yield significant device independent rendering.

More precisely, the enhanced metafile consists of an array of a variable number of varying length records, each of which contains data specific to that record type. The first record is always the enhanced metafile header which contains crucial data needed for playback, including the size of the metafile, the dimensions of the picture, any user color palette, and the resolution of the original device upon which the metafile was modeled.

The MFC encapsulates enhanced metafile operations, simplifying their usage. In the simplest situation, only four short steps are required. First, an instance of the **CMetaFileDC** class is created and **CreateEnhanced** invoked to create the metafile device context. If all is successful, a DC is returned. Second, the desired image is rendered onto the metafile DC. Third, when the initial rendering is complete, the metafile is closed and made ready for playback using **CloseEnhanced**. Finally, at any time desired, the image can be displayed on any **CDC** by using the **PlayMetaFile CDC** function. One valuable feature of enhanced metafiles is that the same code path can be used to both render initially to the metafile as well as to the screen or printer. That is, there can be one common shared code path for all drawing. We do not need to special case draw. **OnDraw** can be used to perform the initial rendering of the metafile as well as to the screen or printer. Of course, there are many other options available with enhanced metafiles. For instance, enhanced metafiles can be cut and pasted on the Clipboard, saved only in memory, or saved as a file on disk with the emf extension.

This chapter explores quite a number of the basic actions that can be done using metafiles to illustrate their power and device independence. Rather than just use some simple rectangles and lines for metafiles, I have opted to add some spice to the images, real graphs of several functions found in engineering and mathematics applications which are an improvement over the simple sales bar chart from Pgm05a. When we finally arrive at the printing portion of the code, you will find that it is almost trivial to handle print, preview and page setup operations.

Printing Situation #6: (Pgm12a)

a. Images to be printed are contained in an enhanced metafile

b. Printing is done within the doc-view architecture

c. Both App and Class Wizards are used

d. Printing and Preview are done in MM_ANISOTROPIC mode

e. Printing can be done from PlayMetaFile or by direct rendering

f. OnDraw controls the rendering process

g. User margins are supported

Program Pgm12a in Operation

Let's begin by observing the application in operation. The shell is MDI; in Figure 12.1, I have constructed the default instances of each graph type and tiled them. More importantly, the graphs are being drawn on-screen using the same render coding that built the four enhanced metafiles.

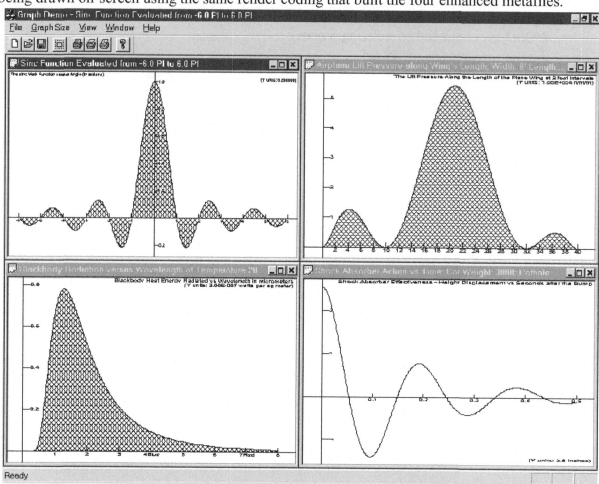

Figure 12.1 Pgm12a with One Instance of Each of the Four Graph Types Rendered Directly On-screen

In Figure 12.2, I have switched the display options so that all four graphs are being rendered from the metafiles using only the **PlayMetaFile** function. You should see little or no differences.

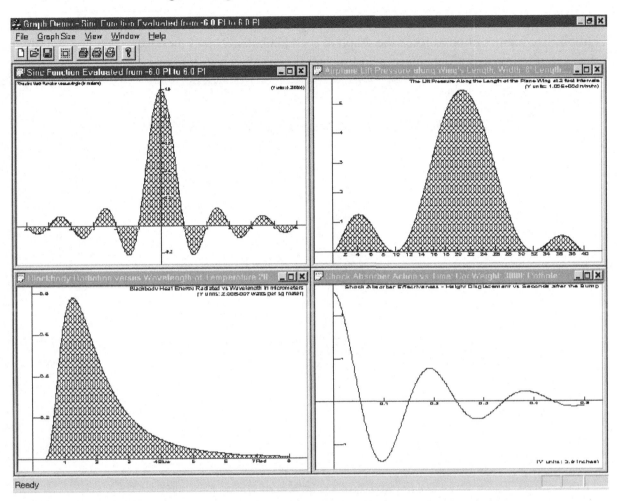

Figure 12.2 Pgm12a with One Instance of Each of the Four Graph Types Rendered From the Metafiles

Next, I minimized three views and enlarged the Sinc Function window. Then I used the Set Graph Size menu option to force the graph to be scaled always to 5 inches by 3 inches and dragged the scaled image to a more central window location as shown in Figure 12.3.

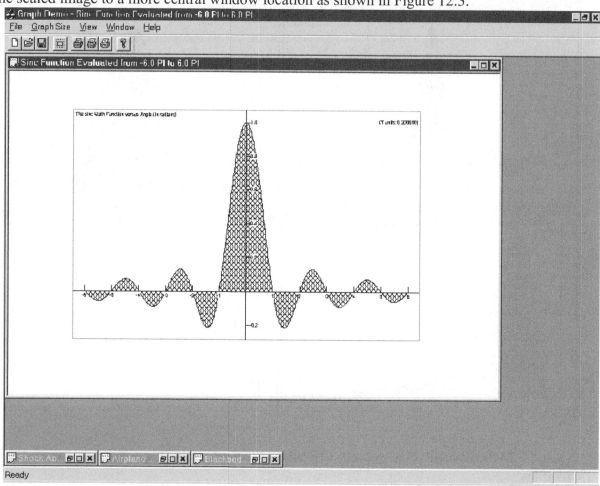

Figure 12.3 The Sinc Function Scaled to 5 by 3 inches and Dragged to a Central Location

Next, I printed the graphs in several forms. Figure 12.4 shows the sinc mathematical function graph constrained to a uniform one inch margin in the preview window.

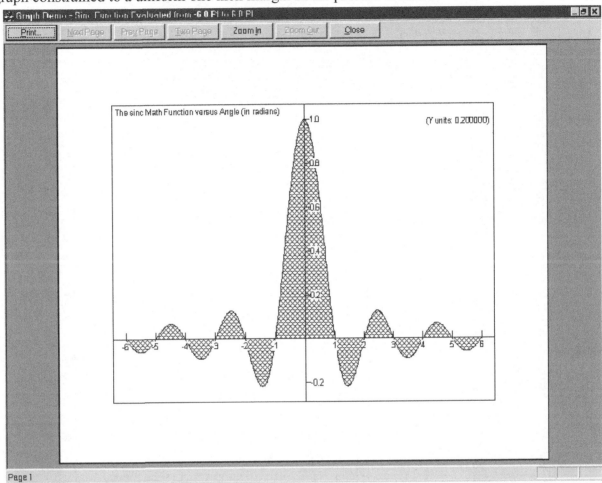

Figure 12.4 The Sinc Math Function with One Inch Margins as Seen in the Preview Window

Figure 12.5 shows the printed page with two inch margins containing a graph of the automobile shock absorber effectiveness when a 10 inch pothole is hit.

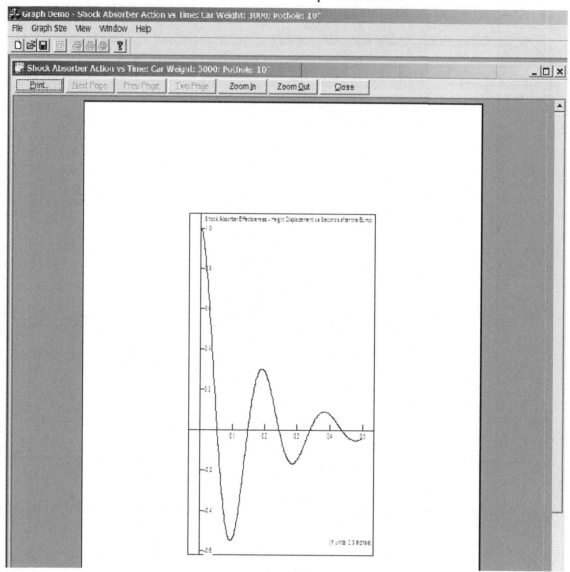

Figure 12.5 Print Preview with Two Inch Margins Showing Shock Absorber Effectiveness

Figure 12.6 shows the printed full page graph of the air lift pressure along the length of an airplane's wing.

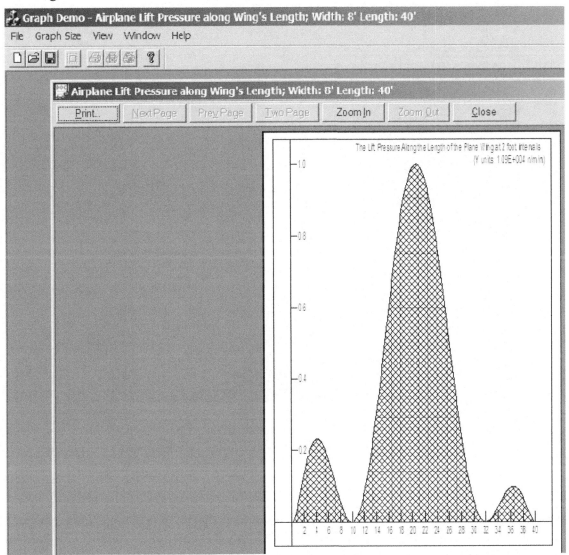

Figure 12.6 Print Preview of Airplane Lift Pressure Along the Length of the Wing

Figure 12.6 shows the full page graph of the black body radiation emitted by an object at 2000 degrees with the visible light portion of the spectrum indicated.

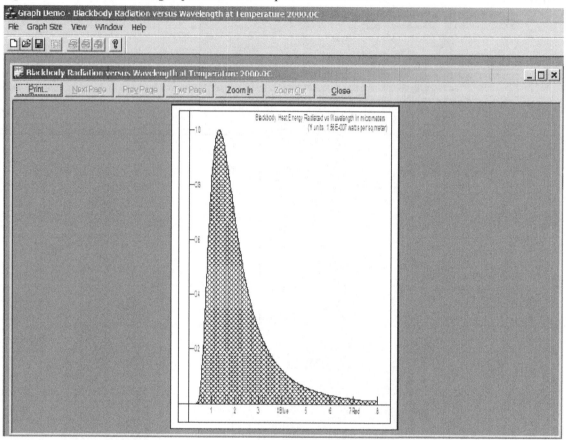

Figure 12.7 The Printed Full Page Graph of Black body Radiation — Visible Wavelengths Indicated

Note that all these displays, whether to the screen, printer or preview window can be rendered directly by performing the drawing on a DC or simply by playing the enhanced metafile onto that device. Which method is used is controlled by the check marked menu item View|Display View from Metafile.

Actually, the sample program Pgm12a is not limited to creating and displaying variations of these four graphs. Using File|Open, any enhanced metafile can be opened, scaled, and played back onto either the screen or printer. I have included the Bird32.emf demo file from one of the Microsoft sample programs, EMFDCODE; it draws a black and white stylized bird. Also from the View|View Enh Metafile Header menu item, the current enhanced metafile's header record can be displayed in a dialog box. So before proceeding into all of the details, I suggest that you familiarize yourself with the functionality provided by the application. Get a feel for what is being done with the enhanced metafile.

Overall Design Principles for Constructing Enhanced Metafiles

The most difficult aspect of enhanced metafiles really lies at the design stage, preparatory to the **CreateEnhanced** function call. Within an enhanced metafile, any mapping mode can be used; other enhanced metafiles can even be embedded within one. And it is with the choice of mapping mode that the design process begins, for the enhanced metafile adds yet another layer to the mapping process. And perhaps the best way to grasp how they work is to consider the enhanced metafile as if it were a "real device" such as a screen or printer instead of an abstract.

An enhanced metafile, like a real device, has a given set of physical characteristics. Resolution (pixels per inch, for example) and page or canvas size (8-1/2 by 10 inches, for example) define the metafile surface. Notice that these measurements are in real inches. So if the metafile surface is in real inches with a known number of pixels per inch, correct scaling to any other device and dimensions can be accurately done by mapping the real inches of the enhanced metafile to the real inches of the device on which the image is to be rendered. I shall refer to this initial mapping as the "metafile to device" mapping mode. When an enhanced metafile is to be played back onto a real device, the metafile to device mapping is done first. Then normal mapping modes that were used to render the image into the metafile are applied.

For example, suppose that when the enhanced metafile was initially created and rendered, the drawing process began by installing the **MM_ANISOTROPIC** mode and then set up window and viewport extents to scale the image on both axis. When playback of the enhanced metafile occurs, first the metafile to device mapping occurs and then the **MM_ANISOTROPIC** mode is applied within the constraints of the metafile to device mapping. Yes, it is one more layer of mapping to consider. That is why I said the initial design process is the most difficult part of enhanced metafile operations.

But just how does an enhanced metafile, which is an abstract, come to have a resolution and page size when it is not a real device? When they are created, enhanced metafiles borrow the resolution and page size from a real device known as the **reference DC** and from a passed rectangle, known as **rclFrame**, that specifies the real page size in real physical units. While for some of us, it would be convenient if the real physical units were in inches (or thousandths), the real physical units are in .01 millimeters, or **HIMETRIC** units. The reference DC must be a real device, such as the screen or printer, for example. When the enhanced metafile is created, it borrows the resolution of the reference DC to fix the number of pixels per .01 millimeters in both the x and y axis, found by dividing the width in pixels of the reference DC by the width in .01 mm of the reference DC and by dividing the length in pixels by the length in .01 mm. This is combined with the passed rectangle, **rclFrame**, that specifies the image size given in .01 mm (**HIMETRIC** units) to yield the enhanced metafile device units according to the following formula

```
ref_w_pels   - reference DC's total width in pixels
ref_w_mm     - reference DC's total width in .01 mm
ref_h_pels   - reference DC's total height in pixels
```

```
ref_h_mm      - reference DC's total height in .01 mm
rclFrame      - the passed image size definition rectangle in .01
                mm units
meta_w_pels - the metafile's width in pixels
meta_h_pels - the metafile's height in pixels

meta_w_pels = rclFrame.Width ()  * ref_w_pels / ref_w_mm
meta_h_pels = rclFrame.Height () * ref_h_pels / ref_h_mm
```

Please note that the **rclFrame** rectangle's width and height by virtue of being in **HIMETRIC** units actually define the **real** size of the image in .01 mm units. Say for example that one wished to draw a line one inch long (as in showing a ruler). One inch is 25.4 (mm/inch) * 100 **HIMETRIC** units. When drawing the horizontal one inch line on the enhanced metafile, use the following

```
x_meta_pels = 2540 * ref_w_pels / ref_w_mm;
```

Remember that **GetDeviceCaps** is used to obtain the reference DC values

```
ref_w_pels = refdc.GetDeviceCaps (HORZRES);
ref_w_mm   = refdc.GetDeviceCaps (HORZSIZE) * 100;
ref_y_pels = refdc.GetDeviceCaps (VERTRES);
ref_y_mm   = refdc.GetDeviceCaps (VERTSIZE) * 100;
```

From a design standpoint, the **rclFrame** rectangle with the total dimensions in .01mm based on the reference DC is the key. The original size of the image can then be specified as 4x5 inches, 8.5x10.5 inches, or any other size desired. If the enhanced metafile playback is going to always be full size or the original size, then create the image with a specific image size in inches in mind. On the other hand, if the metafile will always be scaled to fit a specific output size, then the original design size can be nearly anything desired.

However there is one catch! The enhanced metafile **always** has the resolution of the reference DC. If the reference DC has a small dpi (dots per inch resolution) and the playback DC has a significantly higher dpi resolution, loss of detail occurs, or a general fuzziness occurs.

Design Rule: If playback quality is a design factor, always use the highest resolution real device for the reference DC.

In other words, if the application can reasonably expect the user to playback the metafile onto a 600 dpi printer, then when the enhanced metafile is created, use a DC based on the 600 dpi printer as the reference DC.

The second half of the metafile to device mapping is provided by the application when the metafile is to be played back onto a real DC. When invoking the PlayMetaFile function, the playRect or drawRect provides the desired image position on the page or screen as well as its dimensions or size. For convenience, the units of the playRect are in logical units of the playback DC, usually client screen pixel coordinates or pixels on the printed page. Since the playback DC is passed as the **this** parameter, the enhanced metafile playback function can internally convert from playback logical units into real physical units such as inches or **HIMETRIC**. Thus, the highest level mapping involved with enhanced metafiles maps the metafile real dimension in, say inches, to the playRect dimensions in real inches. Thus, device independence is realized. Of course, within this high level mapping, normal GDI mapping subsequently occurs, such as **MM_ANISOTROPIC** scaling.

Often times, if a common code path is used to both render the metafile upon creation as well as render directly to the screen or printer, the scaling factor of the metafile to device mapping is needed to convert values for GDI functions. For common code path rendering, the logical units formula consist of multiplying by the ratio of the metafile size over the render or viewport size

```
double y_lu_per_inch =
    ((double) GetDeviceCaps (hdc, LOGPIXELSY) *
                    meta_h_pels / view_rect.Height () ;
```

When performing the initial render to create the metafile, the view rectangle's height is the same as the metafile's; thus, one is left with just the **LOGPIXELSY** factor, the logical number of pixels per inch. On the other hand, when this same code is use to render to a client rectangle on the screen, the view rectangle's height is likely quite different from the metafile's created size; scaling occurs.

Font height could then be converted from point size in tens as follows

```
font_height = (int) (pointsztens * y_lu_per_inch / 720);
```

The Use of Fonts in Enhanced Metafiles

Fonts can be created and used in enhanced metafiles as normally. Usually the user font interface via the Choose Fonts Common Dialog uses point size (often in tens) as the means of font height selection. A zero width is used permitting the GDI to best render the font for legibility.

Design Rule: When using fonts in an enhanced metafile, if the image is not going to always be played back at its original dimensions, consider using a non-zero width so the font can be scaled in width as well.

Otherwise, if the height is held constant (which pins the font size scaling for zero widths) and the width of the playback image is varied, then the font remains at that height dictated by the playback window height. As the playback window width shrinks, the characters remain fixed in size, yielding quite undesirable effects. Conceivably text can be lost if the window is too small.

I use a width of 1/3 the height because it closely approximates the GDI provided width when the font is created with a zero width.

Converting a real font point size (in tens) to the requisite height for font creation is another story. Point size (in tens) is a real world measurement. That is, point size (in tens) divided by 720 is the height in real number of inches (a point is 1/72 of an inch).

Design Rule: **If the font point size is to remain the real size of the font, then that point size must be converted into metafile device units before the font is created.**

That is, the height requested in the font creation process must be converted into metafile device units following the above conversions

```
font height = points (in tens) / 720 *
                                    refdc->GetDeviceCaps (LOGPIXELSY);
```

If we use the above formula to calculate the desired font height, in the metafile image, the font would be a true representation of a font with that point size. But is this necessarily what we want? Well it all depends. If we have rendered the metafile at a size of say 4x5 inches and used a 10 point font and IF that image is always going to be rendered at 4x5 inches, then the font will always be a true 10 point font. However, if the image is actually played back with other dimensions, then the font is scaled by the metafile to device mapping and is not on the rendered canvas a true real 10 points. Obviously, if the playback size to sufficiently small, then the scaled font might even become invisible. Similarity, if the playback size if sufficiently large, the font might be huge. But it will always be in proportion to the rest of the image as the whole image is mapped to the device. Again, unless absolute point size on the playback surface is desired, this effect is precisely what we want to occur.

Design Rule Corollary: **If point size does not have to be communicated to the user, arbitrary font heights can be used, chosen so that they look the best for the given situation.**

But consider yet another situation. Suppose that the application has a fixed length title to display in the enhanced metafile and further suppose that the **rclFrame** dimensions (the total image size in HIMETRIC units) is NOT known at compile time. And yet the application desires to have the user select font sizes using the usual common dialog which uses point sizes. This is precisely the problem faced in this sample program. The user controls the range over which all of these graphs, except the shock absorber graph, is plotted. I have then two choices: fix the overall image size to some arbitrary value or letting the image size vary according to the desired range the user selects. The sinc function graph epitomizes the problem. The default plots the function from -6 PI radians to +6 PI radians. Yet the user could choose to see the function plotted from 0 to 1 PI radians, one-twelfth the x range. If I were to use a fixed real point size to determine font height and width, the title which fits nicely in the default case does not come remotely close to fitting the second case. Thus, I must somehow scale fonts chosen on point size to map to the actual area available for display. Scaling can be done in a number of ways.

Design Rule: **If point size must be retained and the font is to really be scaled to the metafile size, then use some converting scale factor.**

One method would be to ignore point size entirely and scale the height to fit the metafile width. To get the character width in metafile logical units (pixels), take the total metafile width in logical units and divide by the number of characters to be placed withing that space; scale the height to three times that amount.

Since I want to tie the font height back to point size in tens, I have opted to first convert the point size in tens into real logical units following the above formula based upon **LOGPIXELSY** and then to scale that value to best fit the total image size. In Pgm12a, I used the following to scale the fonts from a given point size in tens

```
double y_lu_per_inch =
                   ((double) GetDeviceCaps (hdc, LOGPIXELSY) *
                            meta_h_pels / view_rect.Height () ;
double scale = ((double) view_rect.Height ()) /
                   (GetDeviceCaps (hdc, LOGPIXELSY) *10);
font_height = (int) (pointsztens *y_lu_per_inch / 720 * scale);
```

Creating an Enhanced Metafile using the CMetaFileDC

The **CMetaFileDC** constructor takes no parameters as expected. Only two functions are required to build the metafile. The enhanced metafile is created using the **CreateEnhanced** function and after it is rendered, the **CloseEnhanced** function is called to close the construction and return a handle to the global memory version of the enhanced metafile which is used for all further operations, such as playback. When the application is completely done using the metafile, the API function **DeleteEnhMetaFile** is called to remove the global memory instance; otherwise a memory leak results. The functions are defined as follows

```
BOOL CreateEnhanced (CDC *ptrrefdc, LPCSTR filename,
                     LPRECT rclFrame, LPCSTR description);

HENHMETAFILE CloseEnhanced ();

dc.PlayMetaFile (HENHMETAFILE handle, LPCRECT draw_rect);

::DeleteEnhMetaFile (HENHMETAFILE handle);
```

The **CreateEnhanced** is passed a pointer to the reference DC and the **rclFrame** rectangle which contains the dimensions of the total metafile in **HIMETRIC** or .01mm units. Enhanced metafiles can contain a description. It consists of two null-terminated strings followed by an additional null code. By convention, the first string identifies the application that created the metafile and the second is an application specific description. A constant version of the description could be created by coding

```
"Pgm12a\0Shock Absorber Graph\0\0"
```

In Pgm12a, whenever the enhanced metafile header record's contents are displayed in a dialog box, I also extract the description string and display both embedded strings.

The filename string parameter to **CreateEnhanced** can be either NULL or a real filename. If it is a real filename, then a file is created for permanent storage of the metafile. However, if it is

NULL, then the enhanced metafile is created only in memory and is not permanent, existing for the life of the application instance.

Once the enhanced metafile is closed, a handle to the metafile is returned for our playback usage. The handle is typically stored in a member variable. In the **CDC PlayMetaFile** function, remember that the draw_rect rectangle contains normal client coordinates in pixels and represents the area to be filled by the metafile. draw_rect is usually found by using **GetClientRect**. draw_rect provides the second half of the metafile to device mapping process.

When the document or application terminates, **DeleteEnhMetaFile** is called to destroy the global memory copy. If a filename was provided, the metafile resides still on disk; only the global memory copy is destroyed.

How does one open an existing enhanced metafile stored on disk? Use the **GetEnhMetaFile** API function which creates a global instance of the metafile, returning its handle.

```
HENHMETAFILE ::GetEnhMetaFile (filename);
```

The following illustrates the general sequences to create, use, and destroy an enhanced metafile.

```
CRect          rclFrame;
CRect          view_rect;
CDC            refdc;
CMetaFileDC dc;
```

1. Install total pixel dimensions in **rclFrame** and in view_rect.

2. Obtain a reference DC, here the screen

```
refdc.CreateDC ("DISPLAY", NULL, NULL, NULL);
```

3. Convert the pixel dimensions to .01mm units on the reference dc the easy way

```
CSize szul (rclFrame.left, rclFrame.top);
CSize szlr (rclFrame.right, rclFrame.bottom);
dcref.DPtoHIMETRIC (&sz1);    // convert to .01 mm units
dcref.DPtoHIMETRIC (&sz2);    // convert to .01 mm units
rclFrame.left   = sz1.cx;
rclFrame.top    = sz1.cy;
rclFrame.right  = sz2.cx;
rclFrame.bottom = sz2.cy;
```

4. Construct a description string

```
char desc[200];
strcpy_s (desc, sizeof(desc),
          "\\PrintMFC\\Pgm12a\\Debug\\Pgm12a.exe");
int i = strlen (desc);
char des[100];
strcpy_s (des, sizeof(des), our_description);
strcpy_s (&desc[strlen (desc) + 1], sizeof(des), des);
desc[i + 1 + strlen (des) + 1]=0;
```

5. Invoke **CreateEnhanced**, and if all is OK, go render the image to the metafile, and close it

```
if (dc.CreateEnhanced (&dcref, filename, rclFrame, desc)) {
 OurRenderFunction (&dc, view_rect);
 hMetafile = dc.CloseEnhanced ();

}
```

6. In **OnDraw**, play the metafile on the screen DC, **pDC**

```
GetClientRect (draw_rect);
pDC->PlayMetaFile (hMetafile, &draw_rect);
```

7. When application is done, delete the global memory instance of the enhanced metafile

```
::DeleteEnhMetaFile (hMetafile);
```

The Rendering Process—Drawing on the Enhanced Metafile Surface—Pitfalls to Avoid

When rendering to the created enhanced metafile, usually the mapping mode and the window/viewport extents and the window/viewport origins are set first, as desired by the application. Then draw as normal. However, there are several pitfalls to avoid. The first one applies solely to MFC applications.

Design Rule: When using CMetaFileDC, the various get information functions fail; use API calls.

The **CDC** class encapsulates the actual real DC on which drawing occurs, but it also attaches another DC, the attribute DC to which all references to Get information type functions are directed. **GetTextMetrics**, for example is directed to the attribute DC, not the real DC. Likewise for **GetTextExt** calls. In the **CMetaFileDC** class, there is no attribute DC; it is NULL. Thus, all get information type of **CDC** function calls fail. Therefore, when the get information type of calls are needed, make API style calls using the real DC

```
dc.GetTextMetrics (&tm);                    // fails
::GetTextMetrics (dc.GetSafeHdc (), &tm); // works correctly
```

Because of this, many choose to perform all of the rendering in API calls. I prefer to only use API calls when required.

Design Rule: No clipping is done by the GDI when rendering on the enhanced metafile; perform your own clipping.

In other words, after all the careful planning and initialization of the various mappings, the metafile DC permits one to draw anywhere, even completely outside the space. When the metafile is played back and scaled, whatever lies outside what should have been the **rclFrame** area is drawn, producing unexpected and undesirable results. Thus, within the render coding, we must manually ensure that drawing is constrained to the **rclFrame**.

Design Rule: **To ensure lines of width 1 always appear during playback, create pens with a width of zero.**

If pens are created with a width of 1 or more pixels, when the metafile is played back and undergoes both metafile to device mapping as well as any normal mapping, finite width lines can end up being scaled to a zero width and therefore appear missing, depending upon the scale. Conversely, if the pen with a width of one pixel could be scaled to a fairly thick line! (Note that the width is scaled only when the image is scaled in the x direction.) However, if the pen is created with a width of zero, the GDI ensures that that line will appear with a width of one pixel on all renderings. In Pgm12a this effect is quite observable. I draw a rectangle around the total graph frame, the **rclFrame**. If you change the pen width to one pixel, when displaying from the metafile, you can observe the bottom and/or right side disappear, depending upon the size of the client area.

It is worth repeating a previous design rule given above. When using **TextOut**, the x-placement of each character varies or scales with the metafile; the font width does not scale if the font has a zero width. This can result in overlapping characters. Use a non-zero font width.

Design Rule: **SelectObject returns either 1 for successful recording in the metafile or 0 for failed recording; it does not return the previously selected object (HGDIOBJ).**

Avoid coding such as the following.
```
::DeleteObject (::SelectObject (hdc, hnewpen));

HPEN holdpen = SelectObject (hdc, hnewpen);
::SelectObject (hdc, holdpen);
```

Coordinate Mappings and World Transformations

In this sample program, I do not have the luxury of knowing in advance how many inches the graphs will be. The user often controls the x-axis length by virtue of specifying a range over which to evaluate the function. The functions themselves often dictate the range of y-axis values. For example, the sinc function has a maximum y value of +1; significantly less in the -y direction. On the other hand, the black body radiation peak intensity value can vary over a wide range of powers of 10 depending upon the temperature chosen by the user. As a result, these graphs present an opportunity to examine coordinate mappings and scaling.

Under Windows NT, there is a World-Space coordinate transformation system that is not yet available under Windows 95. Therefore, since it is not universally available, I will handle the transformations manually. The World-Space coordinate system offers great flexibility. In essence, when I plot one of the functions from x start through x end, I end up with an array of x and y coordinates, all doubles. These real coordinates are referred to as World-Space coordinates. They can be anything. Here, depending upon the function evaluated, the magnitude of the coordinates can be huge! And likely are in the case of the black body radiation y values. To obtain the World-Space coordinates, I have divided the x range into 1000 uniform pieces. Thus the arrays x and y contain 1000 world coordinates. The member variable num_pts is set to 1000 as a default. In some cases, the world y coordinates can be both positive and negative; in others, the world x coordinates can also be both positive and negative. The airplane lift pressure and the black body radiation graphs only plot positive x and y values. The shock absorber function plots positive and negative y values, while the sinc function can have both y and x values be positive and negative. In other words, the graph can lie in any one or combination of the four quadrants.

However, the range from maximum to minimum values in both x and y become crucial to the final image size. One just cannot arbitrarily use the World-Space coordinates to display the graph. Suppose the y values range from 0.0 to 0.5 in one graph and from 0.0 to 10000000. in the next graph. These World-Space coordinates must be mapped into Page-Space coordinates appropriately scaled. Page-Space coordinates are given in integers for plotting.

I have chosen to create one common Page-Space coordinate system for all graphs. The dimensions of Page-Space have been chosen sufficiently large so that no detail is lost in the transformation process. How big is Page-Space? Well, here the Windows 95's 16-bit legacy GDI differs from NT. Under NT, the values can be longs, but under Windows 95, coordinates are truncated to 16-bits. Thus, I chose the Page-Space dimensions to range from 16,000 to –16,000 units in both x and y. (32,767 is the total range maximum.)

The World-Space to Page-Space transformation consists of mapping the the maximum y dimension to 16,000; likewise for the x axis. Actually, it is a bit more involved. If the maximum y value in World-Space is positive and the minimum World-Space value is zero or above, then the yscale value is just 16,000 divided by the maximum y value. Similarly, if all the y values were negative, they would map to –16,000. However, if the graph extends into both + and –y quadrants, then I use the biggest absolute value: either + y max or absolute value of – y min.

To allow for titles and values placed by the tick marks on the axis, I remove 2,000 units from the total Page-Space size for borders of 1,000 units on either side. Thus, if draw_quad_size contains 14,000 units, the scaling factors to convert from World-Space to Page-Space become

```
if (ymax > 0)
 if (fabs (ymin) > ymax) ysz = fabs (ymin);
 else ysz = ymax;
else ysz = fabs (ymin);
yscale = draw_quad_size / ysz;

if (xe > 0)
 if (fabs (xs) > xe) xsz = fabs (xs);
 else xsz = xe;
else xsz = fabs (xs);
```

```
xscale = draw_quad_size / xsz;
```

To convert any point in World-Space to Page-Space, use the following formula.
```
x_page = x_world * xscale;
y_page = y_world * yscale;
```

Next, Page-Space coordinates must be mapped into Device-Space either onto the metafile space or directly onto the screen or printer space. This transformation is done through the **MM_ANISOTROPIC** mode. The graph extents in Page-Space define both the window extent and window origin. If the graph lies in one quadrant only, say for example in +y and +x quadrant, then the window extent would range from 0 to 16,000 in both the x and y direction. However, if the graph fell into both positive and negative portions of the same axis, then the window extent becomes the actual max y point + border size less the quantity of the minimum y – border size. Glance back at Figure 12.1 to see why I have followed this method. In the sinc function plot, the maximum y value is +1 which was scaled to 15,000 Page-Space units. However, the –y portion of the graph does not extent to the corresponding –1 point. Rather it is only slightly negative. If I arbitrarily also included –16,000 (including the border), the graph's bottom one half would be blank, visually distracting at best. Thus, the window extent becomes only the maximum to minimum range plus borders.

The window origin is that point that maps to the upper left of the viewport. This would be the minimum x less borders and the largest y value plus borders. Thus, the following define the first half of the transformation from Page-Space into Device-Space

```
xpmin = (int) (xs * xscale);
xpmax = (int) (xe * xscale);
ypmin = (int) (ymin * yscale);
ypmax = (int) (ymax * yscale);

// set up the scaling to convert from Page-Space coords into
// Device-Space window extent includes true drawing size plus
// borders on either end
window_ext_y = (ypmax - ypmin) + 2 * border_size;
window_ext_x = (xpmax - xpmin) + 2 * border_size;

// window origin is that point in Page-Space that becomes the
// upper left point in Device-Space
window_org_x = xpmin - border_size;
window_org_y = ypmax + border_size;
```

The other half of the transformation, the viewport, can come from several sources, but **only** at the time the actual rendering is to occur: initial rendering to the metafile, screen repaint, printing and preview options. Note that the latter three invoke the render code with a paint or printer DC when not playing the metafile. When the metafile is in use, the direct render code is not called.

When rendering to the metafile, the Render function is passed the **CMetaFileDC** instance and the view_rect rectangle which contains the total metafile image size in pixels. Recall that these are the values that are converted into **HIMETRIC** units and passed to the **CreateEnhanced** function. Thus, in this case, rendering on the metafile, the viewport extents are the maximum size of the metafile itself. So if both x-axis quadrants are shown fully, the width is 32,000 metafile units. If a 600 dpi printer is used as the reference DC, that would translate to an image of about 53 inches wide! In other words, I have really super resolution; the graph will not fuzz-out on any current physical device. I negate the viewport y extent to force the positive y at the top of the screen. The viewport origin is also set to the view_rect's left-top point so no offsetting occurs.

When rendering to a real device such as the screen or printer, the view_rect now becomes the dimensions of the desired rendering and its offset position. Once again the viewport extents become the width and negative height of the rectangle. However, the rectangle's left-top point might not be 0,0. In the case of the screen, the user may have chosen a fixed size in inches for the rendering and then moved its on-screen location. Similarly, when printing, if the user has selected page margins, then the left-top point reflects those margins.

Thus, the Render coding handles the Page-Space to Device-Space transformation using **MM_ANISOTROPIC** mode. For example, 16,000-0 Page-Space units map to 400-0 pixels of the client window on-screen. PlayMetaFile likewise does the same functionality when playing back the enhanced metafile. Here the metafile to device mapping maps the 16,000-0 metafile units onto the 400-0 pixels of the client window.

One of the fastest methods that I know of to really learn the ins and outs of mapping modes is to work a while with enhanced metafiles!

The Implementation of Pgm12a

With these basics understood, we can explore the implementation of Pgm12a. The resource file, although long, contains only basic simple dialogs and menus. However, as an aid to following the program structure, the main menu and the registration string are shown.

Listing for File: Pgm12a.rc

```
...
IDR_GRAPHTYPE MENU PRELOAD DISCARDABLE
BEGIN
    POPUP "&File"
    BEGIN
        MENUITEM "&New\tCtrl+N",               ID_FILE_NEW
        MENUITEM "&Open...\tCtrl+O",            ID_FILE_OPEN
        MENUITEM "&Close",                      ID_FILE_CLOSE
        MENUITEM "&Save\tCtrl+S",               ID_FILE_SAVE
        MENUITEM "Save &As...",                 ID_FILE_SAVE_AS
        MENUITEM SEPARATOR
        MENUITEM "&Print...\tCtrl+P",           ID_FILE_PRINT
        MENUITEM "Print Page &Setup",           CM_PAGESETUP
        MENUITEM "Print Pre&view",              ID_FILE_PRINT_PREVIEW
        MENUITEM "P&rint Setup...",             ID_FILE_PRINT_SETUP
        MENUITEM SEPARATOR
```

```
        MENUITEM "Recent File",                        ID_FILE_MRU_FILE1, GRAYED
        MENUITEM SEPARATOR
        MENUITEM "E&xit",                              ID_APP_EXIT
    END
    POPUP "&Graph Size"
    BEGIN
        MENUITEM "&Set Graph Size",                    CM_SET_GRAPH_SIZE
    END
    POPUP "&View"
    BEGIN
        MENUITEM "&Display View from Metafile",  CM_VIEW_FROM_EMF
        MENUITEM SEPARATOR
        MENUITEM "&View Enh Metafile Header",    CM_VIEWHEADER
        MENUITEM SEPARATOR
        MENUITEM "&Toolbar",                           ID_VIEW_TOOLBAR
        MENUITEM "&Status Bar",                        ID_VIEW_STATUS_BAR
    END
    POPUP "&Window"
    BEGIN
        MENUITEM "&New Window",                        ID_WINDOW_NEW
        MENUITEM "&Cascade",                           ID_WINDOW_CASCADE
        MENUITEM "&Tile",                              ID_WINDOW_TILE_HORZ
        MENUITEM "&Arrange Icons",                     ID_WINDOW_ARRANGE
    END
    POPUP "&Help"
    BEGIN
        MENUITEM "&About Pgm12a...",                   ID_APP_ABOUT
    END
END
...
STRINGTABLE PRELOAD DISCARDABLE
BEGIN
    IDR_MAINFRAME              "Graph Demo"
    IDR_GRAPHTYPE
"\nGraph\nGraph\nEnhanced    Metafiles    (*.emf)\n.emf\nGraph.Document\nGraph
Document"
END
...
```

The Pgm12aApp Class

Saving the printer defaults we have seen before. What's new here is that when a temporary enhanced metafile must be created, a folder must be supplied. Here, I have installed a folder called Emfs beneath the project folder.

Sometimes when an application starts, it needs to know the precise path to the folder in which it is installed. The **CWinApp** class automatically constructs a full filespec to where it thinks any corresponding help (.hlp) file is located, in the same folder as the exe. It is stored in the member **m_pszHelpFilePath**.

As the app begins, LocateEmfsFolder is called to extract this path, appending the Emfs folder to it, and then trying to build the folder. That way, when the document class tries to build a temporary emf file, it has a folder available.

Once the path is created, that path is then passed on to SavePath to install it into the system registry under the Settings key, Emfs= value. Thus when the document class needs to make a temporary emf file, it calls RetrievePath, which returns the **CString** of the path stored in the registry.

` If you are not sure how folders are made, refer to the LocateEmfsFolder function below.

Listing for File: Pgm12a.cpp

```
...
BOOL Pgm12aApp::InitInstance() {
 SetRegistryKey ("WindowsMFCII"); // setup the higher level reg key
 LoadStdProfileSettings(10);  // Load MRU

 CMultiDocTemplate* pDocTemplate;
 pDocTemplate = new CMultiDocTemplate(
       IDR_GRAPHTYPE,
       RUNTIME_CLASS(GraphDoc),
       RUNTIME_CLASS(ChildFrame),
       RUNTIME_CLASS(GraphView));
 AddDocTemplate(pDocTemplate);

 // create main MDI Frame window
 MainFrame* pMainFrame = new MainFrame;
 if (!pMainFrame->LoadFrame(IDR_MAINFRAME))
  return FALSE;
 m_pMainWnd = pMainFrame;

 // find and/or make the temp folder for emf files
 CString emfs = LocateEmfsFolder ();
 SavePath (emfs);

 // Enable drag/drop open
 m_pMainWnd->DragAcceptFiles();

 // Enable DDE Execute open
 EnableShellOpen();
 RegisterShellFileTypes(TRUE);

 // Parse command line for standard shell commands, DDE, file open
 CCommandLineInfo cmdInfo;
 ParseCommandLine(cmdInfo);

 // Dispatch commands specified on the command line
 if (!ProcessShellCommand(cmdInfo))
  return FALSE;
 pMainFrame->ShowWindow(SW_SHOWMAXIMIZED);
 pMainFrame->UpdateWindow();

 return TRUE;
}

/******************************************************************/
/*                                                                */
/* LocateEmfsFolder: locate the Emfs folder                       */
```

```
/*                                                                    */
/*********************************************************************/

CString   Pgm12aApp::LocateEmfsFolder () {
 char drive[_MAX_DRIVE];
 char dir[_MAX_PATH];
 char filen[_MAX_PATH];
 char ext[_MAX_EXT];
 char cl[_MAX_PATH];
 char cl2[_MAX_PATH];
 // m_pszHelpFilePath has the full path to where the .hlp file might be
 // if running from the ide, may have the Debug or Release folder as part
 // of the path string, so remove that portion
 strcpy_s (cl, _MAX_PATH, theApp.m_pszHelpFilePath);
_splitpath_s (cl, drive, _MAX_DRIVE, dir, _MAX_PATH, filen, _MAX_PATH, ext,
            _MAX_EXT);
 strcpy_s (cl2, _MAX_PATH, dir);
 CString s = cl2;
 s.MakeUpper ();
 int i = s.Find ("DEBUG\\");
 if (i != -1) cl2[i] = 0;
 else i = s.Find ("RELEASE\\");
 if (i != -1) cl2[i] = 0;
 CString filename = drive;
 filename += cl2;
 filename += "Emfs";
 // attempt to make this directory
 if (_mkdir (filename) == -1) { // try to make Emfs folder
  if (errno != EEXIST) {        // failed because it exists? then is ok too
   AfxMessageBox (
  "Error: The Emfs folder cannot be created. Cannot make temporary metafiles",
    MB_ICONSTOP | MB_OK);
   filename = "";
   return filename;
  }
 }
 filename += "\\";
 return filename;
}

/*********************************************************************/
/*                                                                    */
/* RetrievePath: obtain the installed path from the system registry   */
/*                                                                    */
/*********************************************************************/

CString   Pgm12aApp::RetrievePath () {
 CString subkey = "SOFTWARE\\WindowsMFCII\\Pgm12a\\Settings";
 CString entry = "Emfs";
 CString filename = "";
 HKEY hkey;
 LONG ok;
 // attempt to make the Settings key, if it is not there yet
 ok = RegCreateKeyEx (HKEY_CURRENT_USER, subkey, 0, 0, 0, KEY_CREATE_SUB_KEY,
                 0, &hkey, 0);
 if (ok != ERROR_SUCCESS) return filename;

 // attempt to open the current user Settings key with our value
```

```
 ok = RegOpenKeyEx (HKEY_CURRENT_USER, subkey, 0, KEY_READ, &hkey);
 if (ok == ERROR_SUCCESS) {
  DWORD dwType, dwCount;
  // key exists, now verify BthFile entry is a string
  ok = RegQueryValueEx (hkey, entry, NULL, &dwType, NULL, &dwCount);
  if (ok == ERROR_SUCCESS && dwType == REG_SZ) {
   // now retrieve the actual path string
   ok = RegQueryValueEx (hkey, entry, NULL, &dwType,
                            (LPBYTE) filename.GetBuffer (dwCount/sizeof(TCHAR)),
                            &dwCount);
    filename.ReleaseBuffer(); // release the CString buffer locked by GetBuffer
  }
  RegCloseKey (hkey);
 }
 return filename;
}


/*****************************************************************************/
/*                                                                         */
/* SavePath: save path of Emfs temp files in registry                      */
/*                                                                         */
/*****************************************************************************/

bool   Pgm12aApp::SavePath (CString& filename) {
 CString subkey = "SOFTWARE\\WindowsMFCII\\Pgm12a\\Settings";
 CString entry = "Emfs";
 HKEY hkey;
 LONG ok;
 // build Settings key, if it is not there yet
 ok = RegCreateKeyEx (HKEY_CURRENT_USER, subkey, 0, 0, 0, KEY_CREATE_SUB_KEY,
                      0, &hkey, 0);
 if (ok != ERROR_SUCCESS) return false;
 // attempt to open the current user Settings key with our value
 ok = RegOpenKeyEx (HKEY_CURRENT_USER, subkey, 0, KEY_WRITE, &hkey);
 if (ok == ERROR_SUCCESS) {
  // key exists, now store the value in BthFile
  ok = RegSetValueEx (hkey, entry, 0, REG_SZ,
                 (const BYTE*) filename.GetBuffer(), filename.GetLength ()+1);
  if (ok == ERROR_SUCCESS) {
   filename.ReleaseBuffer(); // release the CString buffer locked by GetBuffer
   RegCloseKey (hkey);
   return true;
  }
  RegCloseKey (hkey);
 }
 return false;
}


/*****************************************************************************/
/*                                                                         */
/* SavePrinterDefaults: saves printer setup results                        */
/*                                                                         */
/*****************************************************************************/

void Pgm12aApp::SavePrinterDefaults (HGLOBAL hdevmode, HGLOBAL hdevnames) {
 // remove previous copies, if any
 if (m_hDevNames) GlobalFree (m_hDevNames);
 if (m_hDevMode) GlobalFree (m_hDevMode);
```

```
// lock the new instances from the document results
LPDEVNAMES ptrnewdevnames = (LPDEVNAMES) GlobalLock (hdevnames);
LPDEVMODE  ptrnewdevmode  = (LPDEVMODE)  GlobalLock (hdevmode);
// allocate and lock our copies of the new results
m_hDevNames = GlobalAlloc (GPTR, GlobalSize (hdevnames));
m_hDevMode  = GlobalAlloc (GPTR, GlobalSize (hdevmode));
LPDEVNAMES ptrdevnames = (LPDEVNAMES) GlobalLock (m_hDevNames);
LPDEVMODE  ptrdevmode  = (LPDEVMODE)  GlobalLock (m_hDevMode);
// copy user selections into our copies
memcpy (ptrdevnames, ptrnewdevnames, (size_t) GlobalSize (hdevnames));
memcpy (ptrdevmode,  ptrnewdevmode,  (size_t) GlobalSize (hdevmode));
GlobalUnlock (ptrdevmode);
GlobalUnlock (ptrnewdevmode);
GlobalUnlock (ptrdevnames);
GlobalUnlock (ptrnewdevnames);
}
```

The MainFrame class is just the default class that the Application Wizard built to manage the toolbar and statusbar. It is not shown in the text. Similarly, the MDI child frame windows are not shown here, they are also the default coding from the wizard.

The Document Class of Pgm12a—GraphDoc

The "documents" that Pgm12a use are enhanced metafiles themselves which commonly have the emf file extension. Therefore, using File|Open should allow **any** emf file to be retrieved and displayed. And that is just what **OnOpenDocument** does. However, when File|New is chosen, one of the four graph types is constructed and used. Thus, the GraphDoc class primary purpose is to provide a handle to the enhanced metafile. Its secondary purpose is to construct enhanced metafiles representing one of the four graph types done in response to File|New.

When a new enhanced metafile is to be created, the user is presented with a series of three dialog boxes, the third of which is graph-type specific supplying the parameters for that specific graph. Figure 12.8 shows the first two dialogs common to all four graphs. The user must select the resolution of the reference DC for the enhanced metafile creation and then which of the four types of graphs to construct. Then the third dialog box, dependent upon which graph type is selected, is shown to obtain the specifics for each graph, as shown in Figure 12.8.

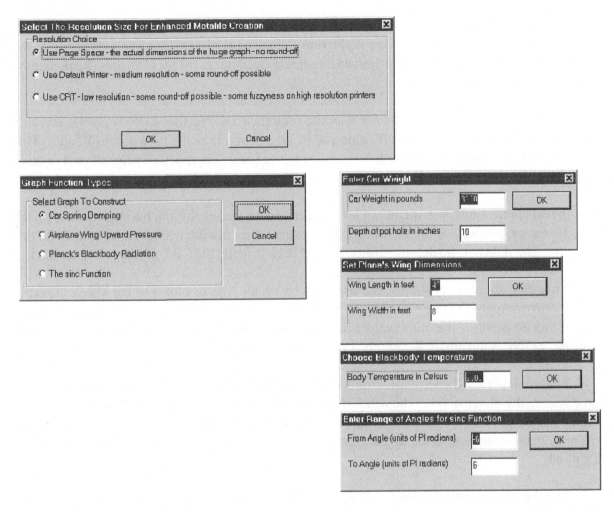

Figure 12.8 The Choose Resolution, Choose Function Dialogs, and the Four Parameter Entry Dialogs

The first choice is the resolution of the reference DC. The default choice is Use Page Space in which the graph's total Page-Space dimensions are used. With this option, the Page-Space dimensions are converted to .01mm units and passed as **rclFrame** to **CreateEnhanced**. The Render function is then given a viewport that contains the total Page-Space dimensions. The result is probably over-kill in terms of resolution which is higher than all normal display devices. Note that the choice of resolution make **no** difference in the file size of the emf file itself. Remember, what is stored in the emf file are a series of GDI drawing commands. The only drawback of such a high resolution is that an application cannot playback the enhanced metafile at its original size for in the worst case, it is likely to be nearly 50x50 inches. For the reference DC, since I am still limited by the dpi of the reference device, I compare the dpi of both the CRT and default printer, choosing whichever device has the highest resolution.

The second choice is to use the default printer as the reference DC. Here the printed page dimensions in .01mm units is used as the **rclFrame** and the page dimensions in pixels becomes the viewport to Render. Thus, the image original size should be about 8-1/2 by 11 inches. Realistically, this may often be the optimum choice.

The third choice is to use the CRT as the reference DC. In this case, I use the screen's dimensions in .01mm units for the **rclFrame** and its size in pixels as the viewport to Render. This choice, referred to as the low resolution case, can result in image degradation when played back on substantially higher resolution devices.

In real applications, you might not let the user choose the resolution, basing it always on the printer. However, be alert for the possibility that the user does not have any default printer. In this sample program, if there is no default printer, I revert back to using the CRT for the reference device.

After choosing the resolution, the user picks a graph type to plot. For car shock absorber damping, the parameters are the car's weight and the depth of the pothole. I hold the spring or shock absorber data constant. If the car's weight becomes too large, the shock absorber's effectiveness fails. If the weight is too small, the bump is smoothed out at once.

When calculating the airplane wing's take-off lift pressure along the length of the wing, the parameters are the dimensions of the wing. If you are curious, experiment with short stubby wings and long wings; observe the point when the maximum lift force is occurring. Various secondary points appear and disappear as the length changes, rather like water ripples when a stone is dropped into a pond.

The black body radiation intensity function requires only the temperature to be input. As the temperature rises, more total radiation is emitted; the peak emission progressively moves toward the blue end, ultraviolet, of the spectrum. Temperatures above 2000 degrees begin to approach the surface temperature of stars. Compare the peak and intensity levels at the red end of the spectrum for boiling water (100 degrees Celsius) and say 500 degrees. As you gradually raise the temperature from 100 degrees, notice that the intensity at the red point of the spectrum increases and then decreases as the peak moves toward the blue end of the spectrum.

Finally, the mathematical sinc function, which is sin (x) / x, requires the range of angles over which to evaluate the function. The angles, for convenience, are in units of PI radians.

Reflecting upon these four distinct graphs, realize that they have much in common. Each graph has a set of World-Space x,y double values that must be converted into Page-Space x,y integer values. Each must be rendered either to the metafile or to the screen or printer. Thus, I factored out all of the commonality and placed such into an abstract base class called Function. Function owns all of the x,y data, is responsible for destroying the dynamically allocated arrays of data, and renders the data as required. Function has one pure virtual function, Create, which derived classes must provide. Create actually calculates the x,y values. The derived class' constructor provides the unique graph title strings.

Let us begin the examination of the document class with Function and its four derived classes. Data members include a detailed caption as well as a description string, title, that is placed at the top of the graph. title_on_right controls right justifying the title on the graph while use_hatch_brush controls whether a hatch brush pattern fills the area under the curve or not. Hatch fill works well for three of the graphs. The total number of points to plot is kept in num_pts; it defaults to 1,000 points. Next, a series of World-Space values define the plot; these are computed by the derived class' Create function. The x and y arrays are dynamically allocated in the Create function. The maximum and minimum values of both a and y values are kept. Next a series of Page-Space values are maintained; they are similarly calculated in the Create function. The **CPoint** array pts contains the x,y values to be plotted in the Render function. Page-Space is defined by the quadrant size, max_quad_size, which is set to 16,000 units. The member draw_quad_size contains 15,000 which is the largest plotted value. A border_size of 1,000 units allows room for titles and potentially the scale values on the two axis. The pair of doubles, xscale and yscale, are the scaling factors to convert from World-Space to Page-Space.

The conversion factors for the transformation from Page-Space to Device-Space are those values required for the **MM_ANISOTROPIC** mode. Only the window values are maintained, since the viewport values are known only at render time. These include the window's extent and origin point to be mapped to the device's upper left corner: window_ext_x, window_ext_y, window_org_x, and window_org_y. The **bool**s xvisible and yvisible are true when that axis is visible in the resultant plot. If an axis is visible in the plot, the scale tick marks and corresponding text values can be placed beside the visible axis. If the axis is not visible, they are placed along the extreme edge of the graph.

Font data include font_height and pointsztens. The font height is calculated once and used in all subsequent render operations. Finally, data and arrays are kept that define the x and y axis tick marks and their corresponding text. Create calculates the uniform tick mark spacing and the text to display beside each tick. Computing the x axis tick spacing is quite straight forward in these graphs. But the y axis tick marks is perhaps the most complex bit of coding in the entire application. At compile time, the magnitude of y axis values is not known. When the graph is plotted, the y range can be small (say from 0-.5) or enormous (say from 0 to 1,000,000,000). If you are in to graphics, you may find the coding to determine the uniform y axis tick marks interesting. If not, you can safely skip over it.

In contrast to the many data members, the member functions are few in number. The constructor provides common initializations, such as setting the size of Page-Space and the various array pointers to NULL. The destructor removes all allocated arrays. GetTitle returns the graph's title which we need when constructing the metafile description string. GetGraphSize fills up the passed integer references with the graph's Page-Space dimensions which we need to have to construct the **rclFrame** rectangle. Render draws the graph either to the enhanced metafile or to a real device, the screen or printer. ScaleYAxis calculates the tick mark locations and text along the highly variable y axis. Create is the pure virtual function which makes Function an abstract base class. The derived classes must provide their own Create function. All functions are virtual. This is extremely important. In the actual document class which allocates instances of the four derived classes maintains only a pointer to the common Function base class. All calls to member function are made via the base class pointer.

Listing for File: Function.h

```
...
/****************************************************************************/
/*                                                                        */
/* Function: Abstract Base Class for all four Function classes            */
/*                                                                        */
/****************************************************************************/

class Function {

    /****************************************************************************/
    /*                                                                        */
    /* Class Data:                                                            */
    /*                                                                        */
    /****************************************************************************/

public:

    char    caption[80];        // the graph's title to be used in the caption
    char    title[80];          // the graph's title to be used in the metafile
    bool    title_on_right;     // when TRUE, right justify title
    bool    use_hatch_brush;    // when TRUE, hatch brush highlights area under curve

    double  parm1;              // user range variable 1
    double  parm2;              // user range variable 2, if any

    int     num_pts;            // the total number of points to plot

// world space values
    double  *x;                 // array of plotted x values in world space
    double  *y;                 // array of plotted y values in world space

    double  ymax;               // y max value in world space
    double  ymin;               // y min value in world space
    double  xs;                 // x start or min value
    double  xe;                 // x end or max value

    double  dx;                 // x axis increment between x points

// page space definition values
    int     max_quad_size;      // full size quadrant
    int     draw_quad_size;     // drawing's reduced size
    int     border_size;        // border size on all sides
    double  xscale;             // scaling factors to convert from world to page space
    double  yscale;

    CPoint  *pts;               // the graph of plotted points in page space
    int     xpmin;              // the x,y min and max plotted values in page space
    int     xpmax;
    int     ypmin;
```

```
int       ypmax;

// device space conversion values
int       window_ext_x; // the window's extent in page space
int       window_ext_y;
int       window_org_x; // the window origin - that point in page space
int       window_org_y; // that is to map to the upper left corner of device space

bool      xvisible;      // TRUE when the x axis is visible in device space
bool      yvisible;      // TRUE when the y axis is visible in device space

// font data
int       font_height;   // rendered font height
int       pointsztens;   // point size in tens for titles

// x axis definition values in page space
int       ticksize;      // length/width of ticks
int       num_xtics_tot;// array size for ticks, some might be clipped
int       num_xtics;     // actual number of ticks on x axis to draw
int       *xtics_x;      // array of x axis tick points
char      **xtics_msg;   // caption for each tick
int       xtics_ys;      // x axis ticks start y position
int       xtics_ye;      // x axis ticks end y position

// y axis definition values in page space
double    ybase;         // y axis base values for ticks
bool      istenths;      // TRUE when using tenths units for scale
bool      yscale_msg_up;// TRUE when y scale message in in upper rt corner
char      yscale_msg[50]; // the scale on the y axis message
int       num_ytics_tot;// array size for ticks, some might be clipped
int       num_ytics;     // actual number of ticks on y axis to draw
int       *ytics_y;      // array of y axis tick points
char      **ytics_msg;   // caption for each tick
int       ytics_xs;      // y axis ticks start x position
int       ytics_xe;      // y axis ticks end x position

    /**********************************************************************/
    /*                                                                    */
    /* Class Functions:                                                   */
    /*                                                                    */
    /**********************************************************************/

public:
            Function (int, double&, double&); // set defaults
virtual     ~Function ();                      // deletes the arrays
virtual char* GetTitle ();                     // returns the graph's title
virtual void  GetGraphSize (int&, int&); // return graph's page space size

virtual bool  Create () = 0;               // calculates the plot
virtual void  Render (CDC*, CRect&);       // draws the plot
virtual void  ScaleYAxis ();               // calc Y axis scale for tick marks
};

const int YSTRLEN = 10; // length of y axis messages
...
```

In Function.cpp, the constructor sets all array pointers to NULL. The destructor removes all allocated arrays whose pointers are not NULL. Remember that the Create function which allocates the arrays can fail (out of memory, for example). The text arrays of x and y axis tick values are really two-dimensional arrays, that is an array of strings. Note that the graph size returned by GetGraphSize is simply the Device-Space window extents.

Focus your attention onto the Render code. Recall that this function represents a single code path that renders to the enhanced metafile, to the screen, and to the printer. Yes, what I am saying is if you can paint your "image" on-screen, you can use that same code to save the image in a metafile for later use!

Except for a few enhanced metafile quirks, the render coding appears much like normal coding you would expect to find to draw the graph on-screen. When **OnDraw** calls Render, the passed DC is the paint DC amd the draw_rect is the client rectangle (or a smaller rectangle if the image is being sized). The quirks for metafile rendering include using pen widths of 0 and using the real DC in API style calls for the get information functions. Thus, the first action is to acquire the real DC encapsulated by the **CDC** class

```
HDC hdc = ptrdc->GetSafeHdc ();
```

Then the **MM_ANISOTROPIC** mode is set up. The window extents use the full Page-Space dimensions. The window origin is that point to map to the upper left corner of the viewport window. These values are assigned in the derived class' Create function. The viewport is set to the size of the passed rectangle; notice that the y value is negated so that positive y values are at the top and negative ones at the bottom. Finally, since when printing and displaying the image can be positioned other than at 0,0, the viewport origin is set to the upper left point of the view rectangle

```
ptrdc->SetMapMode (MM_ANISOTROPIC);
ptrdc->SetWindowExt (window_ext_x, window_ext_y);
ptrdc->SetViewportExt (view_rect.Width (), -view_rect.Height ());
ptrdc->SetWindowOrg (window_org_x, window_org_y);
ptrdc->SetViewportOrg (view_rect.left, view_rect.top);
```

Next I draw a rectangle around the complete image. While this provides a nice border, drawing around the extreme edge is a good debugging aid to help verify the enhanced metafile and screen renderings are working correctly.

If the area under the curve should be filled with the hatch brush, draw the filled curve at this point, before drawing the axis and tick marks and text. Why? So that these items are visible over the top of the filled in area. Otherwise, such information can be overlain by the hatch pattern. However, if a single line curve is to be drawn, then to avoid overlaying the curve, draw in the axis and tick marks and titles before plotting the curve. To display the hatch filled plot, the **Polygon** function is used with a hatch background brush. There is one slight detail to handle. The **Polygon** function requires the last point in the array of points should join up with the first point. If it does not, **Polygon** joins them for you, completing the polygon. In the Create function, if the hatch pattern is used, I reserve the last two points of the array of points to force polygon closure as we shall see shortly.

The x and y axis are then drawn. The font height is calculated as described above when the enhanced metafile is first created. The font height is saved and used in all subsequent renderings to the screen or printer. Notice that the textmetrics are obtained using an API function call; similarly, the several text extents use **GetTextExtentPoint32**.

After displaying the tick marks on the axis and their corresponding text, the graph title is shown. If only a single line curve is to be plotted, the last action is to use **Polyline** to draw the curve, which potentially could overlay the ticks, their text values, and even the titles. The single line curve should always be visible. Presumably one can adjust the titles.

Listing for File: Function.cpp

```
...
/***************************************************************************/
/*                                                                         */
/* Function: base class for all graph functions                            */
/*                                                                         */
/***************************************************************************/

/***************************************************************************/
/*                                                                         */
/* Function: constructor saves parms and NULLs the array pointers          */
/*                                                                         */
/***************************************************************************/

Function::Function (int num, double &p1, double &p2) {
 num_pts = num;                // save initial calues
 parm1 = p1;
 parm2 = p2;

 use_hatch_brush = true;       // use hatch marks under curve

 x = NULL;                     // set no arrays allocated yet
 y = NULL;
 pts = NULL;
 xtics_x = NULL;
 xtics_msg = NULL;
 ytics_y = NULL;
 ytics_msg = NULL;

 max_quad_size  = 16000;       // full size quadrant
 draw_quad_size = 14000;       // drawing's reduced size
 border_size = (max_quad_size - draw_quad_size) /2; // border size
 font_height = 0;              // indicate no font yet installed
 pointsztens = 160;            // default point size in tens for titles
 strcpy_s (title, sizeof(title), "No Graph");   // indicate no graph yet done
 strcpy_s (caption, sizeof(caption), "No Graph");
 title_on_right = false;       // place title left justified
 ticksize = 400;               // length of ticks on both axis
}

/***************************************************************************/
/*                                                                         */
/* ~Function: deletes any arrays                                           */
/*                                                                         */
```

```
/******************************************************************/

            Function::~Function () {
 if (x)          delete [] x;
 if (y)          delete [] y;
 if (pts)        delete [] pts;
 if (xtics_x)    delete [] xtics_x;
 if (ytics_y)    delete [] ytics_y;
 int i;
 if (xtics_msg) {
  for (i=0; i<num_xtics_tot; i++) delete [] xtics_msg[i];
  delete [] xtics_msg;
 }
 if (ytics_msg) {
  for (i=0; i<num_ytics_tot; i++) delete [] ytics_msg[i];
  delete [] ytics_msg;
 }
}


/******************************************************************/
/*                                                              */
/* GetTitle: returns graph's title                              */
/*                                                              */
/******************************************************************/

char*       Function::GetTitle () {
 return caption;
}


/******************************************************************/
/*                                                              */
/* GetGraphSize: returns page space dimensions                  */
/*                                                              */
/******************************************************************/

void        Function::GetGraphSize (int &xx, int &yy) {
 xx = window_ext_x;
 yy = window_ext_y;
}


/******************************************************************/
/*                                                              */
/* Render: display function on a DC                             */
/*                                                              */
/******************************************************************/

void        Function::Render (CDC *ptrdc, CRect &view_rect) {
 HDC hdc = ptrdc->GetSafeHdc ();
 CPen black_pen (PS_SOLID, 0, RGB (0,0,0));

 // now set the device mapping mode for screen or printer
 ptrdc->SetMapMode (MM_ANISOTROPIC);
 ptrdc->SetWindowExt (window_ext_x, window_ext_y);
 ptrdc->SetViewportExt (view_rect.Width (), -view_rect.Height ());
 ptrdc->SetWindowOrg (window_org_x, window_org_y);
 ptrdc->SetViewportOrg (view_rect.left, view_rect.top);

 // if not printing, let's use some color so we can differentiate some
```

```
// drawn items for better understanding of the coordinate mappings
if (!ptrdc->IsPrinting ()) {
 CPen p1 (PS_SOLID, 0, RGB (255, 0, 0));
 ptrdc->SelectObject (&p1);
}
else ptrdc->SelectObject (&black_pen);

// first, draw a rectangle around the complete total display area
ptrdc->Rectangle (window_org_x, window_org_y, window_ext_x + window_org_x,
                  window_org_y - window_ext_y);
ptrdc->SelectObject (&black_pen);

// if using hatch shading, draw curve first and overlay with ticks and axis
// otherwise, show ticks and then draw curve
if (use_hatch_brush) {
 CBrush br (HS_DIAGCROSS, RGB (0,0,0));
 ptrdc->SelectObject (&br);
 ptrdc->Polygon (pts, num_pts);
}

// now draw the two axis
ptrdc->MoveTo (window_org_x, 0);
ptrdc->LineTo (window_org_x + window_ext_x, 0);
ptrdc->MoveTo (0, window_org_y);
ptrdc->LineTo (0, window_org_y - window_ext_y);

// construct a reasonable scaleable font based on a point size
// but really scaled to the drawing by the double scale
CFont *ptrfont = new CFont ();
if (font_height == 0) {
 double luperinch = ((double) window_ext_y) * GetDeviceCaps (hdc, LOGPIXELSY)
                    / view_rect.Height () ;
 double scale = ((double) view_rect.Height ()) /
                                   (GetDeviceCaps (hdc, LOGPIXELSY) *10);
 font_height = (int) (pointsztens * luperinch / 720 * scale);
}
ptrfont->CreateFont (font_height, font_height / 3, 0, 0, FW_NORMAL, 0, 0, 0,
                 DEFAULT_CHARSET, OUT_DEFAULT_PRECIS, CLIP_DEFAULT_PRECIS,
                 PROOF_QUALITY, TMPF_TRUETYPE, "Arial");
ptrdc->SelectObject (ptrfont);

// obtain text metrics for text display actions
TEXTMETRIC  tm;
GetTextMetrics (hdc, &tm);
int avg_char_width  = (int) tm.tmAveCharWidth;
int avg_char_height = (int) ((tm.tmHeight + tm.tmExternalLeading));

// display the title in the upper border zone, right or left justified
if (title_on_right) {
 CSize sz;
 ::GetTextExtentPoint32 (hdc, title, strlen (title), &sz);
 ptrdc->TextOut (window_org_x + window_ext_x - avg_char_width - sz.cx,
             window_org_y - avg_char_height / 6, title);
}
else ptrdc->TextOut (window_org_x + avg_char_width,
                     window_org_y - avg_char_height / 6, title);

// display x axis ticks that are visible
```

```
int i;
for (i=0; i<num_xtics; i++) {
 ptrdc->MoveTo (xtics_x[i], xtics_ys);
 ptrdc->LineTo (xtics_x[i], xtics_ye);
 ptrdc->TextOut (
   xtics_x[i] - avg_char_width / 2
               - avg_char_width * (strlen (xtics_msg[i]) -1) / 2,
   xtics_ye - avg_char_height / 6, xtics_msg[i]);
}

// display all the y axis ticks that are visible
for (i=0; i<num_ytics; i++) {
 ptrdc->MoveTo (ytics_xs, ytics_y[i]);
 ptrdc->LineTo (ytics_xe, ytics_y[i]);
 ptrdc->TextOut (ytics_xs + avg_char_width / 6,
                ytics_y[i] + avg_char_height / 2, ytics_msg[i]);
}

CSize sz;
// now display the y units scale in the lower right corner or upper right
if (yscale_msg_up) {
  ::GetTextExtentPoint32 (hdc, yscale_msg, strlen (yscale_msg), &sz);
  ptrdc->TextOut (window_org_x + window_ext_x - avg_char_width - sz.cx,
                window_org_y - avg_char_height / 6 - avg_char_height,
                yscale_msg);
}
else {
  ::GetTextExtentPoint32 (hdc, yscale_msg, strlen (yscale_msg), &sz);
  ptrdc->TextOut (window_org_x + window_ext_x - avg_char_width - sz.cx,
                window_org_y - window_ext_y + avg_char_height * 2,
                yscale_msg);
}

// now draw the graph - it may overlay some ticks, axis, and text
if (!use_hatch_brush) ptrdc->Polyline (pts, num_pts);
delete ptrfont;
}

/****************************************************************************/
/*                                                                          */
/* ScaleYAxis: calculate uniform Y axis scale for tick marks                */
/*                                                                          */
/****************************************************************************/

void        Function::ScaleYAxis () {
double yrange = ymax > fabs (ymin) ? ymax : fabs (ymin);
// extract the exponent and convert back into a power of ten
// if range was 9000, ybase becomes 1000
// the number of ticks would then be 9
ybase = pow (10., log10 (yrange));
num_ytics_tot = (int) (yrange / ybase + .5);
// however, if the range was 1000, ybase is also 1000 with one tick
// so if only one tick, divide into 5 2-tenths units
istenths = false;
if (num_ytics_tot == 1) {
 ybase /= 5;
 num_ytics_tot = 5;
 istenths = true;
```

```
}
// further, if the number of ticks is 0, the range is between 0 and 1
// reduce the base by 10 and recalculate
else if (num_ytics_tot == 0) {
 ybase /= 10;
 num_ytics_tot = (int) (yrange / ybase + .5);
}
num_ytics_tot *= 2;
}

// MUST derive from this abstract base class and provide for the
// pure virtual function: Create
```

Next, four classes are derived from this Function base class. Create must be coded, since it is a pure virtual function

Listing for File: SincFunction.h

```
#include "Function.h"

/******************************************************************************/
/*                                                                            */
/* SincFunction: Plot sinc function over user angle range                     */
/*                                                                            */
/******************************************************************************/

class SincFunction : public Function {

// base class defines all the data members
public:
             SincFunction (int, double&, double&);
virtual bool  Create ();  // calculates the plot
};
```

The constructor installs the title, caption and point size in tens. Create must allocate the arrays and evaluate the function. I used try-catch logic around all array allocations, just in case of trouble. The x-axis interval is divided into num_pts equally spaced points. Actually, if the hatch brush is used, I reserved the last two points to force polygon closure. The main loop calculates the new x[i] value and the corresponding sinc value, stored in y[i]. To avoid making another pass through the array, I also find the maximum and minimum y values within this same loop.

When the main calculation loop is done, to force polygon closure, from the last calculated point, a line must be brought down to the x axis and then joined with the x axis value of the first point of the array. If you don't see why, run Pgm12a building a sinc plot from .5 to 2.3 radians. Note that I am letting **Polygon** add the line from the last point of the array to the first point. If you still cannot visualize what is occurring, comment out this joining code and the reduction coding that sets num_pts to two less than num_pts and rerun the above range.

The plot is then converted from World-Space to Page-Space coordinates exactly as discussed above. There are no additions to that process. Then the Page-Space to Device-Space conversion factors are calculated

```
window_ext_y = (ypmax - ypmin) + 2 * border_size;
window_ext_x = (xpmax - xpmin) + 2 * border_size;
window_org_x = xpmin - border_size;
window_org_y = ypmax + border_size;
```

These are the crucial values that are used in the **MM_ANISOTROPIC** mode set up. Finally, the uniform x and y axis tick marks and their corresponding text are calculated. What is important here is that clipping must be done to ensure that nothing is drawn outside the Page-Space area. If xx and yy represent the current Page-Space coordinates of the tick marks, clipping is done by only storing these values in the ticks and text arrays if they lie within the valid region

```
if (xx >= window_org_x && xx <= window_org_x + window_ext_x && i) {
    ...
```

```
if (yy <= window_org_y && yy >= window_org_y - window_ext_y && i) {
    ...
```

Also, avoid displaying ticks and text at the origin point; such would clutter the graph. The other three derived classes are coded similarly, differing in the actual function used to calculate the y values and in the x axis scaling. With these basic function classes understood, let's examine the coding of the document class, GraphDoc.

Listing for File: SincFunction.cpp

```
...
/*******************************************************************/
/*                                                                 */
/* SincFunction: Plot sinc function over user angle range          */
/*                                                                 */
/*******************************************************************/

SincFunction::SincFunction (int num, double &p1, double &p2)
            : Function (num, p1, p2) {
 sprintf_s (caption, sizeof(caption),
         "Sinc Function Evaluated from %.1f PI to %.1f PI",
         p1, p2);
 pointsztens = 200;
 strcpy_s (title, sizeof(title),
            "The sinc Math Function versus Angle (in radians)");
}


/*******************************************************************/
/*                                                                 */
/* Create: construct the plot                                      */
/*                                                                 */
/*******************************************************************/

bool      SincFunction::Create () {
 try {
  x = new double [num_pts];     // x,y are world space coords
  y = new double [num_pts];
  pts = new CPoint [num_pts];  // the page space coords
```

```
}
catch (...) {
 MessageBeep (0);
 AfxMessageBox ("Out of Memory", MB_OK | MB_ICONSTOP);
 return false;
}

double pi = acos (-1.);
xs = parm1 * pi;
xe = parm2 * pi;

// if using hatch brush, reserve 2 points for polygon closure
int numpts = num_pts;
if (use_hatch_brush) numpts = num_pts - 2;
dx = (xe - xs) / (numpts - 1);

int i;
// construct the graph in world coordinates
for (i=0; i<numpts; i++) {
 x[i] = xs + dx * i;
 if (fabs (x[i]) <= .00001) y[i] = 0.; // at 0, avoid dividing by 0
 else y[i] = sin (x[i]) / x[i];
 // find the max and min values as points are created
 if (i) {
  if (y[i] > ymax) ymax = y[i];
  if (y[i] < ymin) ymin = y[i];
 }
 else {
  ymax = y[i];
  ymin = y[i];
 }
}

// if using hatch brush, force curve polygon closure
if (use_hatch_brush) {
 i = numpts;
 x[i] = x[i-1];
 y[i] = 0;
 i++;
 x[i] = x[0];
 y[i] = 0;
}

double ysz, xsz;

// scale image in world space coords to page space coords of draw_quad_size
// so that the graph always is a reasonable physical size
// by using the larger quadrant extent should the image lie in two quadrants
if (ymax > 0)
 if (fabs (ymin) > ymax) ysz = fabs (ymin);
 else ysz = ymax;
else ysz = fabs (ymin);
yscale = draw_quad_size / ysz;

if (xe > 0)
 if (fabs (xs) > xe) xsz = fabs (xs);
 else xsz = xe;
else xsz = fabs (xs);
```

```
xscale = draw_quad_size / xsz;

// scale all plotted points to get from world space to page space
for (i=0; i<num_pts; i++) {
 pts[i].x = (int) (x[i] * xscale);
 pts[i].y = (int) (y[i] * yscale);
}
// and scale the bounds as well
xpmin = (int) (xs * xscale);
xpmax = (int) (xe * xscale);
ypmin = (int) (ymin * yscale);
ypmax = (int) (ymax * yscale);

// now set up the scaling to convert from page space coords into device space
//the window extent includes the true drawing size plus borders on either end
window_ext_y = (ypmax - ypmin) + 2 * border_size;
window_ext_x = (xpmax - xpmin) + 2 * border_size;
// the window origin is that point in page space that becomes the upper left
// point in device space
window_org_x = xpmin - border_size;
window_org_y = ypmax + border_size;

// now determine which axis are visible in device space
xvisible = false;
yvisible = false;
if (window_ext_x + window_org_x >= 0 && window_org_x <= 0) yvisible = true;
if (window_org_y >= 0 && window_org_y - window_ext_y <= 0) xvisible = true;

delete [] x;
delete [] y;
x = NULL;
y = NULL;

// now we must display the tick marks and the text values represented by them
// in case an axis is not actually visible, place the info on the
// left or bottom line outlining the entire window

// print the x axis ticks and scale
// if not visible, use the bottom edge as the position to base the ticks
xtics_ys = xvisible ? ticksize : window_org_y - window_ext_y - ticksize;
xtics_ye = xvisible ? 0 : window_org_y - window_ext_y;

// here use PI as the units
int xcts = (int) (xs / pi); // obtain starting number
int xcte = (int) (xe / pi); // and ending number
num_xtics_tot = xcte - xcts + 1;

// allocate arrays for x axis coords and scale messages
try {
 xtics_x = new int [num_xtics_tot];
 xtics_msg = new char* [num_xtics_tot];
 for (i=0; i<num_xtics_tot; i++) xtics_msg[i] = new char [YSTRLEN];
}
catch (...) {
 MessageBeep (0);
 AfxMessageBox ("Out of Memory", MB_OK | MB_ICONSTOP);
 return false;
}
```

```
int j = 0;
for (i=xcts; i<=xcte; i++) {
 int xx = (int) (i * pi * xscale); // calc x in page space
 // clip and avoid printing at x = 0
 if (xx >= window_org_x && xx <= window_org_x + window_ext_x && i) {
  xtics_x[j]= xx;
  sprintf_s (xtics_msg[j], YSTRLEN, "%d", i);
  j++;
 }
}
num_xtics = j;

// now calculate the y axis ticks and scale values
// if the y axis is not visible, use the left edge
ytics_xs = yvisible ? ticksize : window_org_x + ticksize;
ytics_xe = yvisible ? 0 : window_org_x;

// come up with a reasonable set of evenly spaced ticks even though the
// range of values could be anything - first use the the larger
// portion, if the image lies in the two y quadrants
ScaleYAxis ();

// allocate arrays for y axis coord and scale message
try {
 ytics_y = new int [num_ytics_tot];
 ytics_msg = new char* [num_ytics_tot];
 for (i=0; i<num_ytics_tot; i++) ytics_msg[i] = new char [YSTRLEN];
}
catch (...) {
 MessageBeep (0);
 AfxMessageBox ("Out of Memory", MB_OK | MB_ICONSTOP);
 return false;
}

// now calc the y axis - handle clipping
j = 0;
// calc the ticks on the y axis - handle clipping an don't prnt at y = 0
for (i=-num_ytics_tot/2; i<=num_ytics_tot/2; i++) {
 // calculate the y position in page space coords
 int yy = (int) (ybase * i * yscale);
 if (yy <= window_org_y && yy >= window_org_y - window_ext_y && i) {
  ytics_y[j] = yy;
  if (!istenths) sprintf_s (ytics_msg[j], YSTRLEN, "%d", i);
  else sprintf_s (ytics_msg[j], YSTRLEN, "%.1f", i * .2);
  j++;
 }
}
num_ytics = j;

// now set the y units scale in the upper right corner
sprintf_s (yscale_msg, sizeof(yscale_msg), "(Y units: %f)", ybase);
yscale_msg_up = true;

 return true;
}
```

The three **bool**s assist the views in knowing what option can be done on a specific document instance. When an emf file is opened in response to File|Open, use_metafile_only is true, signifying that there is no graph class instance associated with this metafile. Render cannot be called. A view can only play back the metafile. When constructing a new graph, isnew is true. However, it is possible that the graph construction fails and no enhanced metafile is created. Thus, metafile_available is true whenever there is a valid metafile available for use. If a shortage of disk space arises, the graph could still be displayed directly from Render.

When creating a new graph, I construct a new enhanced metafile on disk. Since the user might not want to save that metafile, I use the API functions to acquire a temporary disk file in the current folder. File|Save operations merely copy or move this temporary file. Member tempname contains the temporary file name so that I can delete the file if the user does not wish to save the metafile. If the file is saved or the user has opened a real metafile, I store the file name in tempname as well.

The real metafile global object is stored in **hMetafile**, which can be accessed by the view classes. Page setup margins are stored as has been done in previous sample programs.

When I save one of our graphs in an enhanced metafile, I store the full path to the program and also the compete title including the parameters that define the graph in the metafile description string. When that metafile is then opened via File|Open, I retrieve the description string and use the description as the view window's title, passing it to **SetTitle**. However, the framework during later stages of the document open process calls **SetTitle** to install the filename as the title, eliminating my title. A simple solution without overriding other doc-view architecture functions, is to override **CDocument's SetTitle** and bypass the second call.

The key action member is ptrfn, a pointer to the base class Function for all of the derived graph classes. I use it to invoke all of the graph class member functions instead of maintaining an explicit pointer to the desired derived class. C++ power at work!

Listing for File: RadiationFunction.cpp

...
```
/*****************************************************************/
/*                                                               */
/* RadiationFunction: Plot blackbody radiation over the visible spectrum   */
/*                                                               */
/*****************************************************************/

RadiationFunction::RadiationFunction (int num, double &p1,
                    double &p2) : Function (num, p1, p2) {
 sprintf_s (caption, sizeof(caption),
         "Blackbody Radiation versus Wavelength at Temperature %.1fC",
         p1);
 pointsztens = 200;
 strcpy_s (title, sizeof(title),
  "Blackbody Heat Energy Radiated vs Wavelength in micrometers");
```

```
  title_on_right = true;
}

/******************************************************************************/
/*                                                                          */
/* Create: construct the plot                                               */
/*                                                                          */
/******************************************************************************/

bool        RadiationFunction::Create () {
 try {
  x = new double [num_pts];    // world space coords
  y = new double [num_pts];
  pts = new CPoint [num_pts]; // page space coords
 }
 catch (...) {
  MessageBeep (0);
  AfxMessageBox ("Out of Memory", MB_OK | MB_ICONSTOP);
  return false;
 }

 double t = parm1 + 273.;      // convert to Kelvin degrees

 double a = 3.7415E-4;          // watts - micrometer squared
 double b = 14388.;             // micrometer - degrees Kelvin
 double c = b / t;

 xs = 0.1;                      // wavelength in micrometers
 xe = 8.;                       // infrared area

 // if using hatch brush, reserve 2 points for polygon closure
 int numpts = num_pts;
 if (use_hatch_brush) numpts = num_pts - 2;
 dx = (xe - xs) / (numpts - 1);

 int i;
 // plot the graph in world space
 for (i=0; i<numpts; i++) {
  x[i] = xs + dx * i;
  double l = x[i];
  y[i] = a / (l * l * l * l * l) / (exp (c / l) - 1.);
  // find the max and min values as points are created
  if (i) {
   if (y[i] > ymax) ymax = y[i];
   if (y[i] < ymin) ymin = y[i];
  }
  else {
   ymax = y[i];
   ymin = y[i];
  }
 }

 // if using hatch brush, force curve polygon closure
 if (use_hatch_brush) {
  i = numpts;
  x[i] = x[i-1];
  y[i] = 0;
  i++;
```

```
  x[i] = x[0];
  y[i] = 0;
}


double ysz, xsz;

// scale image in world space coords to page space coords of draw_quad_size
// so that the graph always is a reasonable physical size
// by using the larger quadrant extent should the image lie in two quadrants
if (ymax > 0)
  if (fabs (ymin) > ymax) ysz = fabs (ymin);
  else ysz = ymax;
else ysz = fabs (ymin);
yscale = draw_quad_size / ysz;

if (xe > 0)
  if (fabs (xs) > xe) xsz = fabs (xs);
  else xsz = xe;
else xsz = fabs (xs);
xscale = draw_quad_size / xsz;

// scale all plotted points to get from world space to page space
for (i=0; i<num_pts; i++) {
  pts[i].x = (int) (x[i] * xscale);
  pts[i].y = (int) (y[i] * yscale);
}
// and scale the bounds as well
xpmin = (int) (xs * xscale);
xpmax = (int) (xe * xscale);
ypmin = (int) (ymin * yscale);
ypmax = (int) (ymax * yscale);

// now set up the scaling to convert from page space coords into device space
// the window extent includes the true drawing size plus borders on either end
window_ext_y = (ypmax - ypmin) + 2 * border_size;
window_ext_x = (xpmax - xpmin) + 2 * border_size;
// the window origin is that point in page space that becomes the upper left
// point in device space
window_org_x = xpmin - border_size;
window_org_y = ypmax + border_size;

// now determine which axis are visible in device space
xvisible = false;
yvisible = false;
if (window_ext_x + window_org_x >= 0 && window_org_x <= 0) yvisible = true;
if (window_org_y >= 0 && window_org_y - window_ext_y <= 0) xvisible = true;

delete [] x;
delete [] y;
x = NULL;
y = NULL;

// now we must display the tick marks and the text values represented by them
// in case an axis is not actually visible, place the info on the
// left or bottom line outlining the entire window

// print the x axis ticks and scale
// if not visible, use the bottom edge as the position to base the ticks
```

```
xtics_ys = xvisible ? ticksize : window_org_y - window_ext_y - ticksize;
xtics_ye = xvisible ? 0 : window_org_y - window_ext_y;

//get total x axis tics and allocate arrays for x coords and scale messages
num_xtics_tot = (int) (xe);
try {
 xtics_x = new int [num_xtics_tot];
 xtics_msg = new char* [num_xtics_tot];
 for (i=0; i<num_xtics_tot; i++) xtics_msg[i] = new char [YSTRLEN];
}
catch (...) {
 MessageBeep (0);
 AfxMessageBox ("Out of Memory", MB_OK | MB_ICONSTOP);
 return false;
}

int j = 0;
double ix;
for (ix=1.; ix<=xe; ix+=1.) {
 int xx = (int) (ix * xscale); // calc x in page space
 if (xx >= window_org_x && xx <= window_org_x + window_ext_x) { // clip
  xtics_x[j] = xx;
  sprintf_s (xtics_msg[j], YSTRLEN, "%.0f", ix);
  if (ix == 4.) strcat_s (xtics_msg[j], YSTRLEN, "Blue");
  else if (ix == 7.) strcat_s (xtics_msg[j], YSTRLEN, "Red");
  j++;
 }
}
num_xtics = j;

// now calculate the y axis ticks and scale values
// if the y axis is not visible, use the left edge
ytics_xs = yvisible ? ticksize : window_org_x + ticksize;
ytics_xe = yvisible ? 0 : window_org_x;

// come up with a reasonable set of evenly spaced ticks even though the
// range of values could be anything - first use the the larger
// portion, if the image lies in the two y quadrants
ScaleYAxis ();

// allocate arrays for y axis coord and scale message
try {
 ytics_y = new int [num_ytics_tot];
 ytics_msg = new char* [num_ytics_tot];
 for (i=0; i<num_ytics_tot; i++) ytics_msg[i] = new char [YSTRLEN];
}
catch (...) {
 MessageBeep (0);
 AfxMessageBox ("Out of Memory", MB_OK | MB_ICONSTOP);
 return false;
}

// now calc the y axis - handle clipping
j = 0;
// calc the ticks on the y axis - handle clipping an don't prnt at y = 0
for (i=-num_ytics_tot/2; i<=num_ytics_tot/2; i++) {
 // calculate the y position in page space coords
 int yy = (int) (ybase * i * yscale);
```

```
  if (yy <= window_org_y && yy >= window_org_y - window_ext_y && i) {
   ytics_y[j] = yy;
   if (!istenths) sprintf_s (ytics_msg[j], YSTRLEN, "%d", i);
   else sprintf_s (ytics_msg[j], YSTRLEN, "%.1f", i * .2);
   j++;
  }
 }
 num_ytics = j;

 // now display the y units scale in the upper right corner below title
 sprintf_s (yscale_msg, sizeof(yscale_msg),
            "(Y units: %.2E watts per sq meter)", ybase);
 yscale_msg_up = true;

 return true;
}
```

Listing for File: SpringFunction.cpp

```
...
/****************************************************************/
/*                                                              */
/* SpringFunction: Car shock absorber effectiveness             */
/*                                                              */
/****************************************************************/

SpringFunction::SpringFunction (int num, double &p1, double &p2)
                : Function (num, p1, p2) {
 sprintf_s (caption, sizeof(caption),
            "Shock Absorber Action vs Time: Car Weight: %.0f; Pothole: %.0f\"",
            p1, p2);
 pointsztens = 160;
 strcpy_s (title, sizeof(title),
   "Shock Absorber Effectiveness - Height Displacement vs Seconds after the
Bump");
 title_on_right = true;
 use_hatch_brush = false;
}


/****************************************************************/
/*                                                              */
/* Create: construct the plot                                   */
/*                                                              */
/****************************************************************/

bool       SpringFunction::Create () {
 try {
  x = new double [num_pts];      // the plotted world coords
  y = new double [num_pts];
  pts = new CPoint [num_pts];    // the page space coords
 }
 catch (...) {
  MessageBeep (0);
  AfxMessageBox ("Out of Memory", MB_OK | MB_ICONSTOP);
  return false;
 }
```

```
double m = parm1 * 373.24172;    // convert to grams
double x0 = parm2 / 12. * .3048; // convert inches to meters
double c = 1.4E7;                // spring damping coefficient grams/second
double k = 1.25E9;               // spring constant grams/second/second
double n = c / (2. * m);
double t1 = k / m;
double t2 = c * c / (4. * m * m);
if (t1 < t2) {                   // validity check
 MessageBeep (0);
 AfxMessageBox ("Error: cannot use this car weight - try another",
                MB_OK | MB_ICONSTOP);
 return false;
}
double p = sqrt (t1 - t2);       // valid so calc sqrt

xs = 0;                          // time 0
xe = .5;                         // half second later

dx = (xe - xs) / (num_pts - 1);
int i;

// plot the graph in world space
for (i=0; i<num_pts; i++) {
 x[i] = xs + dx * i;
 y[i] = exp (-n * x[i]) * (x0 * cos (p * x[i]) + x0 * n / p *
                                               sin (p * x[i]));
 // find the max and min values as points are created
 if (i) {
  if (y[i] > ymax) ymax = y[i];
  if (y[i] < ymin) ymin = y[i];
 }
 else {
  ymax = y[i];
  ymin = y[i];
 }
}

double ysz, xsz;

// scale image in world space coords to page space coords of draw_quad_size
// so that the graph always is a reasonable physical size
// by using the larger quadrant extent should the image lie in two quadrants
if (ymax > 0)
 if (fabs (ymin) > ymax) ysz = fabs (ymin);
 else ysz = ymax;
else ysz = fabs (ymin);
yscale = draw_quad_size / ysz;

if (xe > 0)
 if (fabs (xs) > xe) xsz = fabs (xs);
 else xsz = xe;
else xsz = fabs (xs);
xscale = draw_quad_size / xsz;

// scale all plotted points to get from world space to page space
for (i=0; i<num_pts; i++) {
 pts[i].x = (int) (x[i] * xscale);
 pts[i].y = (int) (y[i] * yscale);
```

```
}
// and scale the bounds as well
xpmin = (int) (xs * xscale);
xpmax = (int) (xe * xscale);
ypmin = (int) (ymin * yscale);
ypmax = (int) (ymax * yscale);

// now set up the scaling to convert from page space coords into device space
//the window extent includes the true drawing size plus borders on either end
window_ext_y = (ypmax - ypmin) + 2 * border_size;
window_ext_x = (xpmax - xpmin) + 2 * border_size;
// the window origin is that point in page space that becomes the upper left
// point in device space
window_org_x = xpmin - border_size;
window_org_y = ypmax + border_size;

// now determine which axis are visible in device space
xvisible = false;
yvisible = false;
if (window_ext_x + window_org_x >= 0 && window_org_x <= 0) yvisible = true;
if (window_org_y >= 0 && window_org_y - window_ext_y <= 0) xvisible = true;

delete [] x;
delete [] y;
x = NULL;
y = NULL;

// calculate the x axis tick marks and the text values represented by them
// in case an axis is not actually visible, place the info on the
// left or bottom line outlining the entire window

// if not visible, use the bottom edge as the position to base the ticks
xtics_ys = xvisible ? ticksize : window_org_y - window_ext_y - ticksize;
xtics_ye = xvisible ? 0 : window_org_y - window_ext_y;

// here .1 second units - allocate arrays for x coord and x scale msgs
num_xtics_tot = (int) (xe * 10);
try {
 xtics_x = new int [num_xtics_tot];
 xtics_msg = new char* [num_xtics_tot];
 for (i=0; i<num_xtics_tot; i++) xtics_msg[i] = new char [YSTRLEN];
}
catch (...) {
 MessageBeep (0);
 AfxMessageBox ("Out of Memory", MB_OK | MB_ICONSTOP);
 return false;
}

int j = 0;
double ix;
for (ix=.1; ix<=xe; ix+=.1) {
 // calc position of x axis ticks in world coords and convert to page space
 int xx = (int) (ix * xscale);
 // clip any outside page space
 if (xx >= window_org_x && xx <= window_org_x + window_ext_x) {
  xtics_x[j] = xx;
  sprintf_s (xtics_msg[j], YSTRLEN, "%.1f", ix);
  j++;
```

```
  }
}
num_xtics = j;

// now calculate the y axis ticks and scale values
// if the y axis is not visible, use the left edge
ytics_xs = yvisible ? ticksize : window_org_x + ticksize;
ytics_xe = yvisible ? 0 : window_org_x;

// come up with a reasonable set of evenly spaced ticks even though the
// range of values could be anything - first use the the larger
// portion, if the image lies in the two y quadrants
ScaleYAxis ();

// allocate arrays for y axis coord and scale message
try {
 ytics_y = new int [num_ytics_tot];
 ytics_msg = new char* [num_ytics_tot];
 for (i=0; i<num_ytics_tot; i++) ytics_msg[i] = new char [YSTRLEN];
}
catch (...) {
 MessageBeep (0);
 AfxMessageBox ("Out of Memory", MB_OK | MB_ICONSTOP);
 return false;
}

// now calc the y axis - handle clipping
j = 0;
for (i=-num_ytics_tot/2; i<=num_ytics_tot/2; i++) {
 // calculate the y position in world coords and convert to page space coords
 int yy = (int) (ybase * i * yscale);
 // clip if outside page space and avoid printing at y = 0
 if (yy <= window_org_y && yy >= window_org_y - window_ext_y && i) {
  ytics_y[j] = yy;
  if (!istenths) sprintf_s (ytics_msg[j], YSTRLEN, "%d", i);
  else sprintf_s (ytics_msg[j], YSTRLEN, "%.1f", i * .2);
  j++;
 }
}
num_ytics = j;

// now install the y units scale message in the lower right corner
yscale_msg_up = false;
sprintf_s (yscale_msg, sizeof(yscale_msg),
          "(Y units: %.1f inches)", ybase * 12 / .3048);

return true;
}
```

Listing for File:
...

```
/**********************************************************************/
/*                                                                    */
/* PlaneFunction: Plane Wing Air Lift Pressure Function               */
/*                                                                    */
/**********************************************************************/

PlaneFunction::PlaneFunction (int num, double &p1, double &p2)
                : Function (num, p1, p2) {
 sprintf_s (caption, sizeof(caption),
  "Airplane Lift Pressure along Wing's Length; Width: %.0f' Length: %.0f'",
  p1, p2);

 pointsztens = 200;
 strcpy_s (title, sizeof(title),
  "The Lift Pressure Along the Length of the Plane Wing at 2 foot intervals");
 title_on_right = true;
}


/**********************************************************************/
/*                                                                    */
/* Create: construct the plot                                         */
/*                                                                    */
/**********************************************************************/

bool PlaneFunction::Create () {
 try {
  x = new double [num_pts];    // world space coords
  y = new double [num_pts];
  pts = new CPoint [num_pts];  // page space coords
 }
 catch (...) {
  MessageBeep (0);
  AfxMessageBox ("Out of Memory", MB_OK | MB_ICONSTOP);
  return false;
 }

 double w = parm1 * .3048;    // convert width to meters
 double l = parm2 * .3048;    // convert length to meters
 double x0 = l - w;
 double p0 = 6.0E8;                // init air pressure newtons per meter squared
 double l2 = l * l;
 double l4 = l2 * l2;
 double l8 = l4 * l4;
 double p1 = p0 / (l8 * w * w);
 double yp = w / 2.;          // find pressure down the middle of the wing width
 double ef = yp / 4. - w / 6.;
 double yf = yp * (w - yp) / exp (ef * ef);
 double x1, x2, x3;
 xs = 0.;                          // begin at fuselage edge
 xe = l;                           // end at wing tip

 // if using hatch brush, reserve 2 points for polygon closure
 int numpts = num_pts;
 if (use_hatch_brush) numpts = num_pts - 2;
 dx = (xe - xs) / (numpts - 1);
```

```
int i;
// plot the graph in world space
for (i=0; i<numpts; i++) {
 x[i] = xs + dx * i;
 x1 = x[i] - 1;
 x2 = x[i] - 3.;
 x3 = x[i] - x0;
 y[i] = p1 * x[i] * x[i] * x1 * x1 * x2 * x2 * x3 * x3 * yf;
 // find the max and min values as points are created
 if (i) {
  if (y[i] > ymax) ymax = y[i];
  if (y[i] < ymin) ymin = y[i];
 }
 else {
  ymax = y[i];
  ymin = y[i];
 }
}

// if using hatch brush, force curve polygon closure
if (use_hatch_brush) {
 i = numpts;
 x[i] = x[i-1];
 y[i] = 0;
 i++;
 x[i] = x[0];
 y[i] = 0;
}

double ysz, xsz;

// scale image in world space coords to page space coords of draw_quad_size
// so that the graph always is a reasonable physical size
// by using the larger quadrant extent should the image lie in two quadrants
if (ymax > 0)
 if (fabs (ymin) > ymax) ysz = fabs (ymin);
 else ysz = ymax;
else ysz = fabs (ymin);
yscale = draw_quad_size / ysz;

if (xe > 0)
 if (fabs (xs) > xe) xsz = fabs (xs);
 else xsz = xe;
else xsz = fabs (xs);
xscale = draw_quad_size / xsz;

// scale all plotted points to get from world space to page space
for (i=0; i<num_pts; i++) {
 pts[i].x = (int) (x[i] * xscale);
 pts[i].y = (int) (y[i] * yscale);
}
// and scale the bounds as well
xpmin = (int) (xs * xscale);
xpmax = (int) (xe * xscale);
ypmin = (int) (ymin * yscale);
ypmax = (int) (ymax * yscale);

// now set up the scaling to convert from page space coords into device space
```

```
//the window extent includes the true drawing size plus borders on either end
window_ext_y = (ypmax - ypmin) + 2 * border_size;
window_ext_x = (xpmax - xpmin) + 2 * border_size;
// the window origin is that point in page space that becomes the upper left
// point in device space
window_org_x = xpmin - border_size;
window_org_y = ypmax + border_size;

// now determine which axis are visible in device space
xvisible = false;
yvisible = false;
if (window_ext_x + window_org_x >= 0 && window_org_x <= 0) yvisible = true;
if (window_org_y >= 0 && window_org_y - window_ext_y <= 0) xvisible = true;

delete [] x;
delete [] y;
x = NULL;
y = NULL;

// now we must display the tick marks and the text values represented by them
// in case an axis is not actually visible, place the info on the
// left or bottom line outlining the entire window

// print the x axis ticks and scale
// if not visible, use the bottom edge as the position to base the ticks
xtics_ys = xvisible ? ticksize : window_org_y - window_ext_y - ticksize;
xtics_ye = xvisible ? 0 : window_org_y - window_ext_y;

// here use 2 feet as the units - get total possible number x ticks
num_xtics_tot = (int) (parm2 / 2.);
// allocate arrays for x axis coords and scale messages
try {
 xtics_x = new int [num_xtics_tot];
 xtics_msg = new char* [num_xtics_tot];
 for (i=0; i<num_xtics_tot; i++) xtics_msg[i] = new char [YSTRLEN];
}
catch (...) {
 MessageBeep (0);
 AfxMessageBox ("Out of Memory", MB_OK | MB_ICONSTOP);
 return false;
}

int j = 0;
for (i=1; i<=num_xtics_tot; i++) {
 int xx = (int) (i * 2 * .3048 * xscale); // cals x in page space
 if (xx >= window_org_x && xx <= window_org_x + window_ext_x) {// clip
  xtics_x[j] = xx;
  sprintf_s (xtics_msg[j], YSTRLEN, "%d", i * 2);
  j++;
 }
}
num_xtics = j;

// now calculate the y axis ticks and scale values
// if the y axis is not visible, use the left edge
ytics_xs = yvisible ? ticksize : window_org_x + ticksize;
ytics_xe = yvisible ? 0 : window_org_x;
```

```
// come up with a reasonable set of evenly spaced ticks even though the
// range of values could be anything - first use the the larger
// portion, if the image lies in the two y quadrants
ScaleYAxis ();

// allocate arrays for y axis coord and scale message
try {
 ytics_y = new int [num_ytics_tot];
 ytics_msg = new char* [num_ytics_tot];
 for (i=0; i<num_ytics_tot; i++) ytics_msg[i] = new char [YSTRLEN];
}
catch (...) {
 MessageBeep (0);
 AfxMessageBox ("Out of Memory", MB_OK | MB_ICONSTOP);
 return false;
}

// now calc the y axis - handle clipping
j = 0;
// calc the ticks on the y axis - handle clipping an don't print at y = 0
for (i=-num_ytics_tot/2; i<=num_ytics_tot/2; i++) {
 // calculate the y position in page space coords
 int yy = (int) (ybase * i * yscale);
 if (yy <= window_org_y && yy >= window_org_y - window_ext_y && i) {
  ytics_y[j] = yy;
  if (!istenths) sprintf_s (ytics_msg[j], YSTRLEN, "%d", i);
  else sprintf_s (ytics_msg[j], YSTRLEN, "%.1f", i * .2);
  j++;
 }
}
num_ytics = j;

// now display the y units scale in the upper right corner , second line
sprintf_s (yscale_msg, sizeof(yscale_msg), "(Y units: %.2E n/m/m)", ybase);
yscale_msg_up = true;

return true;
}
```

Notice how easily these four derived classes reuse the common base coding. At last, we can examine GraphDoc itself.

Listing for File: GraphDoc.h

```
...
class Function;

class GraphDoc : public CDocument {
protected: // create from serialization only
 GraphDoc();
 DECLARE_DYNCREATE(GraphDoc)

public:
 bool        isnew;              // TRUE for a new document
 bool        metafile_available; // TRUE when metafile exists
 bool        use_metafile_only;  // TRUE when no graph instance exists
```

```
char            tempname[MAX_PATH];  // new metafile name
CMetaFileDC     dc;                  // the DC for the metafile creates
HENHMETAFILE    hMetafile;           // the metafile proper

int             which_graph;         // which graph to construct
int             num_pts;             // the number of points to use in the graph
double          parm1;               // the graph construction parameters
double          parm2;
Function        *ptrfn;              // graph base class

bool            is_open_title_call;  // patch to retain Open doc title
int             num_calls;           // count of SetTitle calls - bypass #2

RECT            *ptrmargins;         // saved PageSetup's margins

public:
        void    SetMargins (PAGESETUPDLG*);  // install our page margins
        void    SaveMargins (RECT*);         // save page setup margins
        RECT*   GetMargins ();               // returns the margins

        virtual BOOL OnNewDocument();                    // open new graph
        virtual BOOL OnOpenDocument(LPCTSTR lpszPathName);// open existing EMF
        virtual void DeleteContents();                   // remove objects
        virtual BOOL OnSaveDocument(LPCTSTR lpszPathName);// save as EMF file
        virtual void SetTitle(LPCTSTR lpszTitle);        // install caption
        virtual      ~GraphDoc();
...
```

In the implementation file, let's look at the lengthy sequence of **OnNewDocument** first because the remaining functions refer to results from the creation process. Although in MDI docview, the document class is not reused, under SDI the document is emptied and reused on subsequent new or open document requests. Thus, I begin by invoking **DeleteContents** so that you could place this coding into an SDI example. Next the controlling BOOLs are initialized, assuming the worst—failure to create the metafile. Thus, at key points when failure occurs, I can simply return FALSE and leave. The default graph is the shock absorber plot. The integer which_graph can range from 0 to 3. One could use an enum, if desired. Here I set the number of points to 1,000. You can increase or decrease this as desired; or let the user enter this value. Since no graph type has yet been selected, ptrfn is set to NULL. The integer resolution is set for the default highest resolution, using Page-Space values. And the user is then presented with the Choose Resolution dialog followed at once by the Choose Function to graph dialog. If a graph is chosen, the enter parameters dialog specific to the chosen function is then allocated. I install default parameters to appear in each dialog as an aid. If the user does not cancel the dialog, I then allocate an instance of the appropriate derived graph class, assigning a pointer to its base class to ptrfn. Then I use that pointer to invoke the derived class' **Create** function and install the document's title

```
if (!ptrfn->Create ()) {
  delete ptrfn;  // plot failed, so remove attempt
  ptrfn = NULL;
  return FALSE;  // set doc new failed
}
SetTitle (ptrfn->GetTitle ());
```

Next, based on the resolution, I must make a reference DC for the enhanced metafile and fill in the **rclFrame** and viewFrame rectangles for **CreateEnhanced**. If the highest resolution is used, I construct both a printer and screen DC and use the one with the largest resolution, dpi. The Page-Space dimensions are retrieved and scaled to **HIMETRIC** units.

```
int w, h;
ptrfn->GetGraphSize (w, h);
CSize sz (w, h);
dcref.DPtoHIMETRIC (&sz);     // convert to .01 mm units
rclFrame.right   = sz.cx;     // bounding rect in .01 mm units
rclFrame.bottom  = sz.cy;
viewFrame.right  = w;         // render viewport in pixels
viewFrame.bottom = h;
```

If the printer or screen is used to obtain the resolution, then the image rectangles use that device's total size.

```
rclFrame.right    = dcref.GetDeviceCaps (HORZSIZE) * 100;
rclFrame.bottom   = dcref.GetDeviceCaps (VERTSIZE) * 100;
viewFrame.right   = dcref.GetDeviceCaps (HORZRES);
viewFrame.bottom  = dcref.GetDeviceCaps (VERTRES);
```

Next, the description string is built, joining a string containing the full path to Pgm12a.exe with the complete graph title that includes the parameters used to construct the graph. Do not forget to append an additional \0 on the end.

```
char desc[200];
strcpy (desc, sizeof(desc),
                  "\\WindowsMFCII\\Pgm12a\\Debug\\Pgm12a.exe");
int i = strlen (desc);
char des[100];
strcpy (des, ptrfn->GetTitle ());
strcpy (&desc[strlen (desc) + 1], des);
desc[i + 1 + strlen(des) + 1]=0;
```

To acquire a temporary file, the API function **GetTempFileName** is used. The function is passed the default folder to use or NULL if the system temporary folder would suffice, the filename prefix to be used—here "TMP," a 0 to request that Windows should construct a temporary name from the date and time, and our string to be filled with the temporary filename.

```
CString emfsPath = ((Pgm12aApp*) AfxGetApp ())->RetrievePath ();
// have Windows build a unique temporary file name
// if it is not saved, when the doc is closed, the temp file is
// deleted
::GetTempFileName(emfsPath, "TMP", 0, tempname);
```

Now the enhanced metafile can be built following the sequences given previously

```
if (dc.CreateEnhanced (&dcref, tempname, rclFrame, desc)) {
  ptrfn->Render (&dc, viewFrame);// draw the graph on the metafile
  hMetafile = dc.CloseEnhanced ();//finish drawing, get its handle
  metafile_available = true;     // flag as usable if desired
  SetModifiedFlag (TRUE);        // indicate must be saved
```

```
}
```

By setting the modified flag, if the user does not use File|Save or SaveAs, when the document is closed, the framework prompts the user. When save is selected, the framework invokes **OnSaveDocument**. Here if the metafile exists, I use the API **CopyFile** function to copy the metafile to the new filename

```
if (metafile_available) {
 CopyFile (tempname, lpszPathName, FALSE);
 SetTitle (lpszPathName);
}
```

Then in **DeleteContents**, if a temporary file was built, the API **DeleteFile** is invoked to delete the temporary file. Also any existing global memory metafile instance is also deleted

```
if (isnew) DeleteFile (tempname);
if (hMetafile) ::DeleteEnhMetaFile (hMetafile);
```

OnOpenDocument sets use_metafile_only to true since no instance of the graph classes exist. If the enhanced metafile can be acquired and if it is one of ours, the description portion of the description string which contains the graph specific title is extracted and used as the document title. If not ours and a title does exist, it is used. Otherwise, the filename becomes the document title. The API function **GetEnhMetaFileDescription** function is used to obtain the description string which contains the two embedded strings. Since the framework calls **SetTitle** after calling **OnOpenDocument**, I set the flag is_open_title_call and set the num_calls to 0. The overridden **SetTitle** then bypasses the second **SetTitle** framework call

```
DeleteContents ();
isnew = FALSE;
metafile_available = FALSE;
use_metafile_only = TRUE;
is_open_title_call = TRUE;
num_calls = 0;
hMetafile = ::GetEnhMetaFile (lpszPathName);
if (hMetafile) {
 metafile_available = true;
 strcpy_s (tempname, sizeof(tempname), lpszPathName);
 SetModifiedFlag (FALSE);        // indicate not altered
 char desc[200];
 int len = GetEnhMetaFileDescription (hMetafile, 200, desc);
 if (len > 0 ) {
  int i = strlen (desc);
  if (len > i + 1) SetTitle (&desc[i+1]);
  else SetTitle (desc); // not there, so use application name
 }
 else SetTitle (lpszPathName); // nothing, so use filename
```

Listing for File: GraphDoc.cpp

```
...
/**************************************************************************/
/*                                                                        */
/* GraphDoc: set initial defaults                                         */
/*                                                                        */
/**************************************************************************/

GraphDoc::GraphDoc () {
 ptrfn = NULL;
 ptrmargins = NULL;
 is_open_title_call = false;
 hMetafile = 0;
}

/**************************************************************************/
/*                                                                        */
/* ~GraphDoc: remove allocated objects                                    */
/*                                                                        */
/**************************************************************************/

GraphDoc::~GraphDoc () {
 if (ptrfn) delete ptrfn;
 if (hMetafile) ::DeleteEnhMetaFile (hMetafile);
 if (ptrmargins) delete ptrmargins;
}

/**************************************************************************/
/*                                                                        */
/* DeleteContents: remove all allocated objects                           */
/*                                                                        */
/**************************************************************************/

void      GraphDoc::DeleteContents () {
 if (ptrfn) delete ptrfn;
 if (hMetafile) ::DeleteEnhMetaFile (hMetafile);
 if (ptrmargins) delete ptrmargins;
 hMetafile = 0;
 ptrfn = NULL;
 ptrmargins = NULL;
 if (isnew) DeleteFile (tempname);
 CDocument::DeleteContents();
}

/**************************************************************************/
/*                                                                        */
/* SetMargins: copy our saved margins to PageSetup Dlg                    */
/*                                                                        */
/**************************************************************************/

void      GraphDoc::SetMargins (PAGESETUPDLG *ptrpd) {
 if (ptrmargins) ptrpd->rtMargin = *ptrmargins;
}

/**************************************************************************/
/*                                                                        */
/* GetMargins: returns the margins                                        */
/*                                                                        */
```

```
/****************************************************************************/

RECT*      GraphDoc::GetMargins () {
 return ptrmargins;
}

/****************************************************************************/
/*                                                                        */
/* SaveMargins: save page setup margins                                   */
/*                                                                        */
/****************************************************************************/

void       GraphDoc::SaveMargins (RECT *ptrrect) {
 if (ptrmargins) delete ptrmargins;
 ptrmargins = new RECT;
 *ptrmargins = *ptrrect;
}


/****************************************************************************/
/*                                                                        */
/* OnNewDocument: Construct a new graph from user's choice                 */
/*                                                                        */
/****************************************************************************/

BOOL       GraphDoc::OnNewDocument () {
 DeleteContents ();
 isnew               = true;  // indicate new file, create as a temporary file
 use_metafile_only   = false; // indicate graph function can render
 metafile_available  = false; // indocate no metafile exists yet

 which_graph = 0;                // set the default graph type
 num_pts = 1000;                 // number of points to plot
 ptrfn = NULL;                   // no graph class instance yet

 int resolution = 0;             // set for Page Space huge resolution
 // get user's choice of resolution with which to construct the metafile
 ChooseResolutionDlg cdlg (NULL, &resolution);
 cdlg.DoModal ();

 // get user's choice of function
 ChooseFunction dlg (NULL, &which_graph);
 if (dlg.DoModal () == IDOK) {
  // have a choice, so construct a document
  if (!CDocument::OnNewDocument()) return FALSE;
  if (which_graph == 0) { // car shock absorber case
   parm1 = 3000.0;        // set dafault car weight in pounds
   parm2 = 10.;           // set default depth of pot hole in inches
   // get user's choices for weight and depth
   GetSpringDlg dlg (NULL, &parm1, &parm2);
   if (dlg.DoModal () == IDOK) {
    // got user's choices, so allocate the spring instance
    ptrfn = new SpringFunction (num_pts, parm1, parm2);
    if (!ptrfn) return FALSE;
   }
   else return FALSE;
  }
  else if (which_graph == 1) { // plane lift pressure case
   parm1 = 8.0;                 // set default wing width in feet
```

```
  parm2 = 40.0;                          // set default wing length in feet
  // get user's wing dimension choices
  GetPlaneDlg dlg (NULL, &parm1, &parm2);
  if (dlg.DoModal () == IDOK) {
   // got the user's choices, so allocate the plane instance
   ptrfn = new PlaneFunction (num_pts, parm1, parm2);
   if (!ptrfn) return FALSE;
  }
  else return FALSE;
 }
 else if (which_graph == 2) { // blackbody radiation case
  parm1 = 2000.0;                        // set default temperature in Celsius
  // get user's temperature
  GetTempDlg dlg (NULL, &parm1);
  if (dlg.DoModal () == IDOK) {
   // got the user's choice, so allocate the blackbody instance
   ptrfn = new RadiationFunction (num_pts, parm1, parm2);
   if (!ptrfn) return FALSE;
  }
  else return FALSE;
 }
 else {                 // the sinc function case
  parm1 = -6.0;         // set default angle range in PI radian units
  parm2 = +6.0;
  GetAnglesDlg dlg (NULL, &parm1, &parm2);
  if (dlg.DoModal () == IDOK) {
   // got user's choices, so allocate the sinc instance
   ptrfn = new SincFunction (num_pts, parm1, parm2);
   if (!ptrfn) return FALSE;
  }
  else return FALSE;
 }

 // here one of the four is allocated, so actually go create the plot
 if (!ptrfn->Create ()) {
  delete ptrfn;   // plot failed, so remove attempt
  ptrfn = NULL;
  return FALSE;   // set doc new failed
 }
 // install the graph's title
 SetTitle (ptrfn->GetTitle ());

 // make reference DC for Enhanced Metafile creation to model
 // and fill in the two rects defining the metafile mapping
 CDC dcref;
 CRect rclFrame (0, 0, 0, 0);  // the rclFrame for CreateEnhanced
 CRect viewFrame (0, 0, 0, 0); // the viewport rect for render to metafile

 static char   printer[80];    // for printer DC acquisition
 char          *device, *driver, * output, *next;

 if (resolution == 0) {        // use full Page Space for the resolution
  // first find the highest resolution device - default printer or screen
  bool use_printer = TRUE;     // assume it is the printer
  // get access to a printer DC from the ini file installed printer
  GetProfileString ("windows", "device", "...", printer, 80);
  if ((device = strtok_s (printer, ",", &next)) != NULL &&
      (driver = strtok_s (NULL,    ",", &next)) != NULL &&
```

```
     (output = strtok_s (NULL,     ",", &next)) != NULL) {
   // a default printer exists, so get a DC for it
   CDC *ptrprdc = new CDC;
   ptrprdc->CreateDC (driver, device, output, NULL);
   CDC *ptrscrdc = new CDC;
   ptrscrdc->CreateDC ("DISPLAY", NULL, NULL, NULL);
   if (ptrprdc->GetDeviceCaps (LOGPIXELSX) <
       ptrscrdc->GetDeviceCaps (LOGPIXELSX)) use_printer = false;
   delete ptrprdc;
   delete ptrscrdc;
  }
 else use_printer = false;
 if (use_printer) dcref.CreateDC (driver, device, output, NULL);
 else dcref.CreateDC ("DISPLAY", NULL, NULL, NULL);
 // construct total graph bounding rectangle in HIMETRIC .01 mm units
 // by getting the graph's width and height in pixels and converting
 int w, h;
 ptrfn->GetGraphSize (w, h);
 CSize sz (w, h);
 dcref.DPtoHIMETRIC (&sz);     // convert to .01 mm units
 rclFrame.right    = sz.cx;    // bounding rect in .01 mm units
 rclFrame.bottom   = sz.cy;
 viewFrame.right   = w;        // render viewport in pixels
 viewFrame.bottom  = h;
}
else if (resolution == 1) { // use the default printer as a model
 // get access to a printer DC from the ini file installed printer
 GetProfileString ("windows", "device", "...", printer, 80);
 if ((device = strtok_s (printer, ",", &next)) != NULL &&
     (driver = strtok_s (NULL,    ",", &next)) != NULL &&
     (output = strtok_s (NULL,    ",", &next)) != NULL)
  // a default printer exists, so get a DC for it
  dcref.CreateDC (driver, device, output, NULL);
 else dcref.CreateDC ("DISPLAY", NULL, NULL, NULL);
 rclFrame.right    = dcref.GetDeviceCaps (HORZSIZE) * 100;
 rclFrame.bottom   = dcref.GetDeviceCaps (VERTSIZE) * 100;
 viewFrame.right   = dcref.GetDeviceCaps (HORZRES);
 viewFrame.bottom  = dcref.GetDeviceCaps (VERTRES);
}
else {
 dcref.CreateDC ("DISPLAY", NULL, NULL, NULL);
 rclFrame.right    = dcref.GetDeviceCaps (HORZSIZE) * 100;
 rclFrame.bottom   = dcref.GetDeviceCaps (VERTSIZE) * 100;
 viewFrame.right   = dcref.GetDeviceCaps (HORZRES);
 viewFrame.bottom  = dcref.GetDeviceCaps (VERTRES);
}

// make the description string: file\0descr\0\0 format
char desc[_MAX_PATH*2];
strcpy_s (desc, sizeof(desc), "\\WindowsMFCII\\Pgm12a\\Debug\\Pgm12a.exe");
int i = strlen (desc);
char des[100];
strcpy_s (des, sizeof(des), ptrfn->GetTitle ());
strcpy_s (&desc[strlen (desc) + 1], sizeof(des)-1, des);
desc[i + 1 + strlen(des) + 1]=0;

CString emfsPath = ((Pgm12aApp*) AfxGetApp ())->RetrievePath ();
// have Windows build a unique temporary file name
```

```
    // if it is not saved, when the doc is closed, the temp file is deleted
    ::GetTempFileName (emfsPath, "TMP", 0, tempname);

    // build the metafile based on the ref dc and the bound rect in .01mm units
    if (dc.CreateEnhanced (&dcref, tempname, rclFrame, desc)) {
     // to draw on it, must use a viewport size of the bound rect in pixels
     ptrfn->Render (&dc, viewFrame);   // draw the graph on the metafile
     hMetafile = dc.CloseEnhanced (); // finish drawing, get a handle to it
     metafile_available = true;        // flag as usable if desired
     SetModifiedFlag (TRUE);           // indicate must be saved
    }
    else {
     MessageBeep (0);
     AfxMessageBox ("Can't create metafile", MB_OK | MB_ICONSTOP);
     ::DeleteFile (tempname);
    }
    return TRUE;
   }
  return FALSE;
}


/**************************************************************************/
/*                                                                        */
/* OnOpenDocument: open ANY .EMF file as the document                     */
/*                                                                        */
/**************************************************************************/

BOOL       GraphDoc::OnOpenDocument (LPCTSTR lpszPathName) {
 DeleteContents ();                    // remove any existing items - if used in SDI
 isnew = FALSE;                        // set not a new document
 metafile_available = false;   // assume the worst and assume not valid emf
 use_metafile_only = true;     // set must use the metafile - no graph object
 is_open_title_call = true;    // handle extra set title call from framework
 num_calls = 0;

 // attempt to open the metafile
 hMetafile = ::GetEnhMetaFile (lpszPathName);
 if (hMetafile) {
  // it exists, so flag as available for use
  metafile_available = true;
  strcpy_s (tempname, sizeof(tempname), lpszPathName); // save the filename
  SetModifiedFlag (FALSE);          // indicate not altered
  // now see if this is one of our 4 types of graphs
  // by retrieving the documentation string, if any is present
  char desc[200];
  int len = GetEnhMetaFileDescription (hMetafile, 200, desc);
  if (len > 0 ) {
   // a description string is present
   // skip over program string and use the description portion if it's there
   int i = strlen (desc);
   if (len > i + 1) SetTitle (&desc[i+1]);
   else SetTitle (desc); // not there, so use application name
  }
  else SetTitle (lpszPathName); // nothing present, so use filename
  return TRUE;
 }
 else {
  MessageBeep (0);
```

```
  AfxMessageBox ("Unable to open requested metafile", MB_OK | MB_ICONSTOP);
  return FALSE;
  }
}


/**************************************************************************/
/*                                                                      */
/* SetTitle: override to prevent framework's second call to set filename */
/*           as the title; instead use our names as titles              */
/*                                                                      */
/**************************************************************************/
void        GraphDoc::SetTitle(LPCTSTR lpszTitle) {
 if (is_open_title_call) {
  num_calls ++;
  // only prevent the second call by the framework from replacing our title
  if (num_calls != 2) CDocument::SetTitle(lpszTitle);
 }
 else CDocument::SetTitle(lpszTitle);
}


/**************************************************************************/
/*                                                                      */
/* OnSaveDocument: save document by copying the metafile                 */
/*                                                                      */
/**************************************************************************/
BOOL        GraphDoc::OnSaveDocument (LPCTSTR lpszPathName) {
 BOOL ok = CDocument::OnSaveDocument(lpszPathName);
 if (metafile_available) {
  CopyFile (tempname, lpszPathName, FALSE);
  SetTitle (lpszPathName);
 }
 else {
  MessageBeep (0);
  AfxMessageBox ("No metafile exists to save", MB_OK | MB_ICONSTOP);
 }
 return ok;
}
...
```

The GraphView Class

The **CView** class, GraphView, is fairly simple in comparison to the document class. It maintains a **bool** usemetafile to toggle between using the metafile to display to the screen and printer and to use the graph class' Render function. The draw_rect defines the rectangle in which to place the image. It can be the screen client area or the printer page. When printing, the dimensions of the page are used to define draw_rect. If the user has selected page margins, the upper left corner of draw_rect must be offset to accommodate the top and left margins; similarly for the bottom right corner of draw_rect. In a similar manner, if the user has chosen to set the graph size for display purposes, ptrgraph_rect is allocated ans contains the user's requested size. Later on, if the image is then dragged, ptrgraph_rect is offset to the dragged location. If ptrgraph_rect exists, it is used as the draw rectangle. The **bool** dragging is true only during an actual drag operation. During the drag operation, init_pt contains the current initial point of dragging.

Along with the usual **CView** member functions, **OnFilePageSetup** responds to the page margins setup menu item. OnViewFromEmf toggles between rendering from the metafile and from the graph's Render function. Its command enabler verifies that there is a valid enhanced metafile available. OnSetGraphSize displays a dialog enabling the user to size the image on-screen. OnViewHeader extracts the enhanced metafile header record and displays its key values in a dialog box. Figure 12.9 shows both the Set Graph Size dialog box and the Enhanced Metafile Header dialog box. Notice that the graph size is given in inches and that there is a check box to revert back to the default of sizing to the client window dimensions.

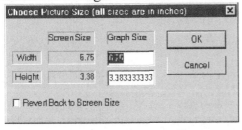

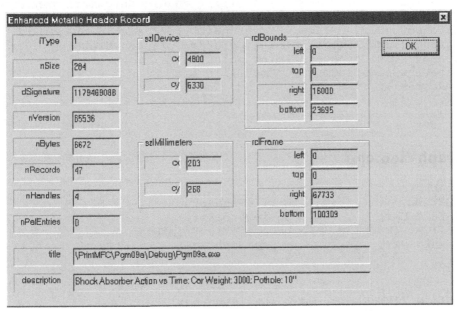

Figure 12.9 The Set Graph Size and Display Enhanced Metafile Header Dialog Boxes

Listing for File: GraphView.h

```
...
class GraphView : public CView {
protected:
 GraphView();              // protected constructor used by dynamic creation
 DECLARE_DYNCREATE(GraphView)

 bool    useMetafile;      // true when view is using the metafile to render
 CRect   draw_rect;        // the rect in which to place the graph
 CRect *ptrgraph_rect;     // the graph's size when on-screen
 bool    dragging;         // true while user drags image about the client area
 CPoint init_pt;           // initial point for dragging

public:
    GraphDoc* GetDocument();
 virtual void OnDraw(CDC* pDC); // draws from emf or render
 virtual      ~GraphView();

protected:
 virtual BOOL OnPreparePrinting(CPrintInfo* pInfo);// set total pages, margins
 virtual void OnPrint(CDC* pDC, CPrintInfo* pInfo);// set drawing rect
 afx_msg void OnFilePageSetup ();                 // do page setup for margins
 afx_msg void OnViewFromEmf();                    // switch between Render and EMF
 afx_msg void OnUpdateViewFromEmf(CCmdUI* pCmdUI);// enable checkmark menuitem
 afx_msg void OnSetGraphSize();                   // get user graph size
 afx_msg void OnLButtonDown(UINT nFlags, CPoint point); // enable dragging
 afx_msg void OnLButtonUp(UINT nFlags, CPoint point);   // end dragging
 afx_msg void OnMouseMove(UINT nFlags, CPoint point);   // move graph
 afx_msg void OnUpdateViewHeader(CCmdUI* pCmdUI);
 afx_msg void OnViewHeader();
...
```

Listing For File: GraphView.cpp

```
...
BEGIN_MESSAGE_MAP(GraphView, CView)
 ON_COMMAND(CM_PAGESETUP,              OnFilePageSetup)
 ON_COMMAND(CM_VIEW_FROM_EMF,          OnViewFromEmf)
 ON_UPDATE_COMMAND_UI(CM_VIEW_FROM_EMF, OnUpdateViewFromEmf)
 ON_COMMAND(CM_SET_GRAPH_SIZE,         OnSetGraphSize)
 ON_WM_LBUTTONDOWN()
 ON_WM_LBUTTONUP()
 ON_WM_MOUSEMOVE()
 ON_UPDATE_COMMAND_UI(CM_VIEWHEADER, OnUpdateViewHeader)
 ON_COMMAND(CM_VIEWHEADER, OnViewHeader)
 ON_COMMAND(ID_FILE_PRINT,             CView::OnFilePrint)
 ON_COMMAND(ID_FILE_PRINT_DIRECT,      CView::OnFilePrint)
 ON_COMMAND(ID_FILE_PRINT_PREVIEW,     CView::OnFilePrintPreview)
END_MESSAGE_MAP()

/*******************************************************************************/
/*                                                                           */
/* GraphView: initialization                                                 */
/*                                                                           */
/*******************************************************************************/

GraphView::GraphView () {
```

```
 useMetafile = false;
 ptrgraph_rect = NULL;
 dragging = false;
}

/**********************************************************************/
/*                                                                    */
/* ~GraphView: remove any graph size rectangle in use                 */
/*                                                                    */
/**********************************************************************/

GraphView::~GraphView () {
 if (ptrgraph_rect) delete ptrgraph_rect;
}

/**********************************************************************/
/*                                                                    */
/* OnDraw: display graph from its Render or from EMF directly         */
/*                                                                    */
/**********************************************************************/

void      GraphView::OnDraw (CDC* pDC) {
 GraphDoc* pDoc = GetDocument ();
 ASSERT_VALID(pDoc);
 //setup the drawing rect when not printing by using client area or graph size
 if (!pDC->IsPrinting ())
  if (!ptrgraph_rect) GetClientRect (draw_rect);
  else draw_rect = *ptrgraph_rect;

 if (!pDoc->use_metafile_only && !useMetafile && pDoc->ptrfn)
  pDoc->ptrfn->Render (pDC, draw_rect);
 else if (pDoc->metafile_available)
  pDC->PlayMetaFile (pDoc->hMetafile, &draw_rect);
}

/**********************************************************************/
/*                                                                    */
/* OnPreparePrinting: set the page numbers to 1 for the Print dlg and prevw*/
/*                                                                    */
/**********************************************************************/

BOOL      GraphView::OnPreparePrinting (CPrintInfo* pInfo) {
 if (pInfo->m_bPreview) pInfo->m_nNumPreviewPages = 1;
 pInfo->SetMaxPage (1);
 return DoPreparePrinting(pInfo);
}

/**********************************************************************/
/*                                                                    */
/* OnPrint: apply any user margins to the page rectangle              */
/*                                                                    */
/**********************************************************************/

void      GraphView::OnPrint (CDC* pDC, CPrintInfo* pInfo) {
 OnPrepareDC (pDC, pInfo);              // fix up the DC for rendering

 // retrieve any user margins
 RECT *ptrmargins = GetDocument ()->GetMargins ();
```

```
 // construct the working rectangle by applying margins to full page rect
 draw_rect = pInfo->m_rectDraw;

 // apply margins, if present
 if (ptrmargins) {
  // retrieve the printer's pixels per inch for scaling margins
  int logpixelsx = pDC->GetDeviceCaps (LOGPIXELSX);
  int logpixelsy = pDC->GetDeviceCaps (LOGPIXELSX);
  // I am ignoring the physical margins effect - see Pgm06a
  // scale and add in margins top form final drawing rectangle
  draw_rect.left   += MulDiv (ptrmargins->left,   logpixelsx, 1000);
  draw_rect.right  -= MulDiv (ptrmargins->right,  logpixelsx, 1000);
  draw_rect.top    += MulDiv (ptrmargins->top,    logpixelsx, 1000);
  draw_rect.bottom -= MulDiv (ptrmargins->bottom, logpixelsx, 1000);
 }
 CView::OnPrint(pDC, pInfo);        // go print the page
}

/****************************************************************************/
/*                                                                          */
/* OnFilePageSetup: setup the page margins for printing                     */
/*                                                                          */
/****************************************************************************/

void      GraphView::OnFilePageSetup () {
 CPageSetupDialog pd (PSD_DEFAULTMINMARGINS | PSD_MARGINS |
                      PSD_INTHOUSANDTHSOFINCHES, this);
 GetDocument ()->SetMargins (&pd.m_psd);              // install saved margins
 if (pd.DoModal () == IDOK)                           // get user choices
   ((Pgm12aApp*)AfxGetApp ())->SavePrinterDefaults (
                              pd.m_psd.hDevMode, pd.m_psd.hDevNames);
  GetDocument ()->SaveMargins (&pd.m_psd.rtMargin); // save user margins
}

/****************************************************************************/
/*                                                                          */
/* OnViewFromEmf: toggle between viewing from EMF and from Render           */
/*                                                                          */
/****************************************************************************/

void      GraphView::OnViewFromEmf () {
 GraphDoc* pDoc = GetDocument();
 ASSERT_VALID(pDoc);
 if (!pDoc->use_metafile_only && pDoc->metafile_available) {
  useMetafile = !useMetafile;
  Invalidate ();
 }
}

/****************************************************************************/
/*                                                                          */
/* OnUpdateViewFromEmf: enable or checkmark View from EMF menu option       */
/*                                                                          */
/****************************************************************************/

void      GraphView::OnUpdateViewFromEmf (CCmdUI* pCmdUI) {
 GraphDoc* pDoc = GetDocument();
 ASSERT_VALID(pDoc);
```

```
 if (pDoc->use_metafile_only || !pDoc->metafile_available)
  pCmdUI->Enable (FALSE);
 else
  pCmdUI->SetCheck (useMetafile);
}


/**************************************************************************/
/*                                                                      */
/* OnSetGraphSize: get user's choice for display graph size             */
/*                                                                      */
/**************************************************************************/

void      GraphView::OnSetGraphSize () {
 CClientDC dc (this);
 // get the pixels per inch
 double logpixelsx = dc.GetDeviceCaps (LOGPIXELSX);
 double logpixelsy = dc.GetDeviceCaps (LOGPIXELSY);
 // get the current window size and convert to inches
 GetClientRect (draw_rect);
 GRAPHSIZE gsz;
 char msg[20];
 sprintf_s (msg, sizeof(msg), "%.2f", draw_rect.Width () / logpixelsx);
 gsz.scrn_width  = msg;
 sprintf_s (msg, sizeof(msg), "%.2f", draw_rect.Height () / logpixelsy);
 gsz.scrn_height = msg;
 gsz.revert_screen = FALSE;
//if there is a previous graph size, use its values; otherwise use window size
 if (ptrgraph_rect) {
  gsz.graph_width  = ptrgraph_rect->Width ()  / logpixelsx;
  gsz.graph_height = ptrgraph_rect->Height () / logpixelsy;
 }
 else {
  gsz.graph_width  = draw_rect.Width () / logpixelsx;
  gsz.graph_height = draw_rect.Height () / logpixelsy;
 }
      GraphSizeDlg dlg (this, &gsz);
 if (dlg.DoModal () == IDOK) {
  // implement user's choices
  if (!ptrgraph_rect) ptrgraph_rect = new CRect (0,0,0,0);
  ptrgraph_rect->right  = ptrgraph_rect->left +
                                    (int) (gsz.graph_width * logpixelsx);
  ptrgraph_rect->bottom = ptrgraph_rect->top +
                                    (int) (gsz.graph_height * logpixelsy);
  // if revert is requested, delete the graph size rectangle so graph follows
  // the window resizing operations once more
  if (gsz.revert_screen) {
   delete ptrgraph_rect;
   ptrgraph_rect = NULL;
  }
  Invalidate ();
 }
}


/**************************************************************************/
/*                                                                      */
/* OnLButtonDown: begin user dragging of the graph around the client area  */
/*                                                                      */
/**************************************************************************/
```

```
void        GraphView::OnLButtonDown (UINT nFlags, CPoint point) {
 CView::OnLButtonDown(nFlags, point);
 if (ptrgraph_rect && !dragging) {
  dragging = true;   // enable dragging
  init_pt = point;   // save current mouse location
 }
}


/**********************************************************************/
/*                                                                  */
/* OnLButtonUp: halt moving the graph around the client area        */
/*                                                                  */
/**********************************************************************/

void        GraphView::OnLButtonUp (UINT nFlags, CPoint point) {
 dragging = false;
 CView::OnLButtonUp(nFlags, point);
}


/**********************************************************************/
/*                                                                  */
/* OnMouseMove: move graph image to new location within client window */
/*                                                                  */
/**********************************************************************/

void        GraphView::OnMouseMove (UINT nFlags, CPoint point) {
 CView::OnMouseMove(nFlags, point);
 if (ptrgraph_rect && dragging) {
  CPoint pt (point - init_pt);     // calculate the offset for this movement
  ptrgraph_rect->OffsetRect (pt); // offset the drawing rect this amount
  init_pt = point;                 // save current mouse location for next move
  Invalidate ();                   // force painting at this spot
 }
}


/**********************************************************************/
/*                                                                  */
/* OnUpdateViewHeader: enable view enhanced metafile header menuitem */
/*                                                                  */
/**********************************************************************/

void        GraphView::OnUpdateViewHeader (CCmdUI* pCmdUI) {
 GraphDoc* pDoc = GetDocument();
 ASSERT_VALID(pDoc);
 pCmdUI->Enable (pDoc->metafile_available);
}


/**********************************************************************/
/*                                                                  */
/* OnViewHeader: view the contents of the metafile header record     */
/*                                                                  */
/**********************************************************************/

void        GraphView::OnViewHeader () {
 GraphDoc* pDoc = GetDocument();
 ASSERT_VALID(pDoc);
 if (!pDoc->metafile_available) return; // avoid doing nothing
 ENHMETAHEADER eh;
```

```
if (GetEnhMetaFileHeader (pDoc->hMetafile, sizeof (eh), &eh) == 0) return;
char title[256];
char desc[256];
int len = GetEnhMetaFileDescription (pDoc->hMetafile, sizeof(title), title);
if (len > 0 ) { // a description string is present
 //skip over the program string and use the description portion if it's there
 int i = strlen (title);
 if (len > i + 1) strcpy_s (desc, sizeof(desc), &title[i+1]);
 else strcpy_s (desc, sizeof(desc), "No Description");
}
else {
 strcpy_s (desc, sizeof(desc), "No description present");
 strcpy_s (title, sizeof(title), "No title present");
}
ViewHeaderDlg dlg (this, &eh, title, desc);
dlg.DoModal ();
}
...
```

The constructor sets useMetafile to false forcing the default of rendering from the graph function. ptrgraph_rect is set to NULL implying that the image is to follow the client rectangle. The destructor removes and ptrgraph_rect rectangle.

In **OnDraw** if we are not printing, the drawing rectangle is based on either the client rectangle or on the explicit values of ptrgraph_rect. Then either Render or **PlayMetaFile** is invoked to paint the image. If we are printing, then draw_rect has already been set up

```
if (!pDC->IsPrinting ())
 if (!ptrgraph_rect) GetClientRect (draw_rect);
 else draw_rect = *ptrgraph_rect;
 if (!pDoc->use_metafile_only && !useMetafile && pDoc->ptrfn)
 pDoc->ptrfn->Render (pDC, draw_rect);
 else if (pDoc->metafile_available)
 pDC->PlayMetaFile (pDoc->hMetafile, &draw_rect);
```

In OnViewHeader, the enhanced metafile's header record is retrieved using **GetEnhMetaFileHeader** which must be passed the global handle to the enhanced metafile and an instance of the **ENHMETAHEADER** structure and its size. The description record is retrieved by using the function **GetEnhMetaFileDescription**. It is passed the global handle and our title string and its maximum length to be filled. There are numerous other enhanced metafile functions. All of the records in the metafile can be retrieved if desired. Usually the only functions needed are those used in Pgm12 with the possible addition of retrieving a color palette

```
ENHMETAHEADER eh;
if (GetEnhMetaFileHeader (pDoc->hMetafile, sizeof (eh), &eh) == 0)
 return;
char title[256];
char desc[256];
int len=GetEnhMetaFileDescription(pDoc->hMetafile, sizeof(title),
                                          title);
if (len > 0 ) { // a description string is present
  ...
```

The layout of the **ENHMETAHEADER** record is as follows.

```
struct ENHMETAHEADER {
  DWORD iType;              // the record type.
  DWORD nSize;              // the structure size, in bytes
  RECTL rclBounds;         // the dimensions, in device units, of the
                           // smallest rectangle that can be drawn around
                           // the picture. This rectangle is supplied by
                           // graphics device interface (GDI). Its
                           // dimensions include the right and bottom
                           // edges
  RECTL rclFrame;          // dimensions, in .01 millimeter units, of a
                           // rectangle surrounding the picture stored in
                           // the metafile. Its dimensions include the
                           // right and bottom edges
  DWORD dSignature;        // must specify the value assigned to the
                           // ENHMETA_SIGNATURE constant
  DWORD nVersion;          // metafile version, currently the value is
                           // 0x10000
  DWORD nBytes;            // size of the enhanced metafile, in bytes
  DWORD nRecords;          // number of records in the enhanced metafile
  WORD  nHandles;          // number of handles in the enh-metafile handle
                           // table
  WORD  sReserved;         // Reserved - must be zero
  DWORD nDescription;      // number of characters in the array that
                           // contains the description of the enhanced
                           // metafile's contents.
  DWORD offDescription;    // offset from the beginning of the
                           // ENHMETAHEADER structure to the array that
                           // contains the description of the enhanced
                           // metafile's contents
  DWORD nPalEntries;       // number of entries in the enh metafile's
                           // palette
  SIZEL szlDevice;         // resolution of the ref device, in pixels
  SIZEL szlMillimeters;    // resolution of the ref device, in millimeters
};
```

Printing Enhanced Metafiles

OnPreparePrinting becomes extremely simple; set the pages to print at one. In **OnPrint**, draw_rect must be filled with the page dimensions and any user margins installed. As usual, the margins are stored in one thousandths of an inch

```
RECT *ptrmargins = GetDocument ()->GetMargins ();
draw_rect = pInfo->m_rectDraw;
if (ptrmargins) {
  int logpixelsx = pDC->GetDeviceCaps (LOGPIXELSX);
  int logpixelsy = pDC->GetDeviceCaps (LOGPIXELSX);
  // scale and add in margins top form final drawing rectangle
  draw_rect.left  += MulDiv (ptrmargins->left, logpixelsx, 1000);
  draw_rect.right -= MulDiv (ptrmargins->right, logpixelsx,1000);
```

```
  draw_rect.top    += MulDiv (ptrmargins->top,   logpixelsx, 1000);
  draw_rect.bottom -= MulDiv(ptrmargins->bottom,logpixelsx, 1000);
}
CView::OnPrint(pDC, pInfo);        // go print the page
```

That completely handles all printing and print preview operations! It is almost trivial. The pages can be rendered from the metafile or directly from the graph's Render function. I have not shown here the many little dialog classes, since these are very simple in nature.

Chapter 13 Introduction to the Internet Classes Making an FTP File Browser with Download Capabilities

The MFC support for Internet access spans a wide spectrum of needs. The MFC supports those programming the server side including construction of ActiveX controls for inclusion on a web page. The client side of Internet programming is equally well supported with classes and methods to add E-mail to any Windows application, to browse html pages, to perform FTP and Gopher file transfers. The classes and methods span the gamut of programmer experience with web programming, ranging from the beginner to the advanced level. Entire books are devoted to Internet programming. What can be done in one chapter? The basic potentials are examined first. Then, these are applied to a fairly common application need to transfer files. File transfer is done using a crude FTP browser. Additionally, the FTP browser illustrates how to use a **CListCtrl** in report view mode with column sorting.

Adding E-mail support to an application

The simplest action an application can perform is to provide E-mail access to an application. The framework provides the method to E-mail the active document. Using the Class Wizard or by hand, add a new File pop up menuitem with the built-in ID of ID_FILE_SEND_MAIL

```
        MENUITEM "Send",    ID_FILE_SEND_MAIL
```
The Class Wizard adds the following for the flyby hint and tool tip
```
    ID_FILE_SEND_MAIL
            "Send the active document through electronic mail\nSend Mail"
```

      When this menuitem is chosen, the framework automatically searches the System Registry and loads the default E-mail system to send the contents of the current active document.

The Internet MFC Classes

This chapter examines the client side of Internet programming only. Typically, an application needs html, ftp or gopher support. The basic underlying API is WinInet which is encapsulated in several MFC classes. The basic cycle of action for each of these is to establish a connection to the desired site, make requests of the web server and to close the connection when done. The Internet file encapsulations closely parallel those of normal stdio file operations using the **CStdio** class. This means that you can even use a Console Application program to perform your Internet access.

The **CInternetSession** class encapsulates all types of actual proto call connections. When you construct an instance of **CInternetSession**, it creates and initializes one or more simultaneous Internet sessions. By default, it uses the normal Internet setup that is stored in the System registry. (Of course, the defaults can be overridden if needed.) Once the session has been created, you have several options. Member functions can open a URL or establish an http, ftp or gopher connection. With the connection established, you can then perform the various actions you need such as enumerating all the files in all folders, retrieving a file, sending a file, or simply viewing a web page in html format. Each of the three main protocols are encapsulated in **CFtpConnection**, **CGopherConnection** and **CHttpConnection** classes. The **CInternetSession** class provides three functions to make an instance of each of these three protocol connections, **GetFtpConnection**, **GetGopherConnection**, **GetHttpConnection**.

The connection classes are all derived from the common base class **CInternetConnection** which provides a uniform connection mechanism. Additionally, an error class, **CInternetException**, encapsulates error situations thrown by the various Internet classes.

Suppose that you just want to quickly download a specific file from a site. A simple Console Application might be

```
#include <afxinet.h>
#include <stdio.h>
int main () {
 char server[] = "ftp.thesite.com";
 char getfile[] = "\\somefolder\\somefile.dat";
 char mydir[] = "c:\\download";
 CInternetSession the_session ("MyFastSession");
 CFtpConnection *ptrftp = NULL;
 ptrftp = the_session.GetFtpConnection (server);
 if (ptrftp)
  if (ptrftp->GetFile (getfile, mydir))
   printf ("successful download");
  else
   printf ("cannot download the file");
 else
  printf ("cannot make the ftp connection at this time");
 delete ptrftp;
 the_session.Close ();
 return 0;
}
```
Yes, it really can be this easy!

CInternetSession Details

When performing Internet access, often one of two approaches are used, one time only sequential operations and on-going net access. The one time only approach is used whenever an application might need to download or upload a file or document, usually in response to a user's menuitem choice. In the menuitem's handler function, one would use a sequence similar to the above Console application. If you need to provide specific connection information, the constructor allows you to pass proxies and so on, not just a session name to identify this session. But when on-going net access is required, the **CInternetSession** object becomes a class member used as needed. Thus, there is a default constructor that takes no parameters. In this case, it uses the application's name along with the default System registry values. If you need to initialize the session to use various proxies and the like, then in **OnCreate** or **OnInitDialog**, after the call to the base class, call the **SetOption** member function to setup your specific needs. Quite often, the defaults work just fine.

When completely done with the session, call the **Close** function which takes no parameters.

Beginning applications usually call one of three member functions, **GetFtpConnection**, **GetGopherConnection** or **GetHttpConnection**. Let's examine how each of these are called.

The prototype for **GetFtpConnection** is
```
CFtpConnection*    GetFtpConnection (LPCTSTR serverstring,
                                     LPCTSTR username,
                                     LPCTSTR password,
                                     INTERNET_PORT portnum,
                                     BOOL passive);
```

The **serverstring** identifies the URL of the site, such as "ftp.microsoft.com". The strings, **username** and **password**, default to NULL. If both the **username** and **password** are NULL strings, then the server is sent the user name of "anonymous" with a password of the user's E-mail name. This is very often the desired choices when surfing the net. If only the **username** is not NULL, then the user name string is sent along with a NULL password. If both strings are present, both are sent. However, you cannot specify a password without specifying a user name; this raises an error. The **portnum** specifies which TCP/IP port to use. **passive** defaults to FALSE. (When TRUE, it uses passive FTP semantics.)

The function then connects with the FTP server and returns a pointer to that connection. Now you are ready to request operations on that site. If the function fails to connect, it raises a **CInternetException** which you should catch to display error information.

The prototype for **GetGopherConnection** is
```
CGopherConnection*    GetGopherConnection (LPCTSTR serverstring,
                                           LPCTSTR username,
                                           LPCTSTR password,
                                           INTERNET_PORT portnum);
```

The prototype for **GetHttpConnection** is
```
CHttpConnection*    GetHttpConnection (LPCTSTR serverstring,
                                       INTERNET_PORT portnum,
```

```
                                        LPCTSTR username,
                                        LPCTSTR password);
```
(Don't ask why the parameters are in a different order.)

If you wish to directly download a file given the complete URL specification, then use the **OpenURL** function whose prototype is
```
CStdioFile*   OpenURL (LPCTSTR urlstring, DWORD context,
                       DWORD flags, LPCTSTR headerstring,
                       DWORD lengthheader);
```
The **urlstring** must begin with file:, ftp:, gopher:, or http:. Note that file: is used to open local files. The **context** defaults to 1 and is an application defined value that is passed back to call-back functions when status information, for example, is desired. The **flags** default to **INTERNET_FLAG_TRANSFER_ASCII** indicating an ASCII text transfer. You could OR in **INTERNET_FLAG_RELOAD** if you wish to force it to reload the file from the net and not use a local copy if one exists. (See the documentation for other lesser used flags.)

The return pointer varies depending upon the type of data
```
URL type     return pointer
file://      CStdioFile*
http://      CHttpFile*
ftp://       CInternetFile*
gopher://    CGopherFile*
```

All four of these functions throw a **CInternetException** if the connection cannot be made. The exception class has a member, **m_dwError**, that contains the error code. The error code possibilities include normal system errors, defined in winerror.h or Internet errors defined in wininet.h.

The CFtpConnection Class

Since the sample application for this chapter is an FTP Browser, let's examine the corresponding **CFtpConnection** class. Note that we never allocate an instance of this class, rather the **CInternetSession::GetFtpConnection** actually creates our instance for us, returning a pointer to the object for our use. Member functions exist for getting and setting the current directory on the remote site, reading and writing files, creating and removing directories, renaming and removing files, and closing the connection. Let's look at the more commonly used function prototypes.

Frequently, the current directory must be set or retrieved.
```
BOOL   GetCurrentDirectory (CString &dirstring) const;
```
or
```
BOOL GetCurrentDirectory (LPTSTR dirstring,
                          LPDWORD stringlength) const;
```
The function will return the current directory in use in either the **CString** reference or in the provided character string (**stringlength** provides the maximum size of the char buffer). It returns TRUE if it successfully returns the current directory. (Note the function does not return the current directory in URL format, such as ftp://ftp.microsoft.com/mstools; **GetCurrentDirectoryAsURL** does and this function has the same parameters as **GetCurrentDirectory**.)

```
BOOL   SetCurrentDirectory (LPCTSTR dirstring);
```
This function sets the current directory to the value given in **dirstring**. The value can be fully qualified or partially qualified relative to the current directory. Either \ or / can be used as the separators and will be automatically converted to the appropriate values by the function.

Often, an application desires to download a file or perhaps less frequently upload a file. **GetFile** and **PutFile** handles the entire file transfer operation.
```
BOOL   GetFile (LPCTSTR remotefilename, LPCTSTR localfilename,
               BOOL fail_if_exists, DWORD attributes,
               DWORD flags, DWORD context);
```
If the function fails, you can call the Win32 function **GetLastError** to determine the cause of the error. See the error codes in winerror.h. The filenames can be fully or partially qualified relative to the current subdirectory. The parameter, **fail_if_exists**, handles the problem of what to do if the file you want to download already exists on the local machine. The default, TRUE, causes the function to fail when the file already exists on the local machine. Using FALSE replaces the existing file. Normally, the attribute flags are left as the default, **FILE_ATTRIBUTE_NORMAL**, unless you are downloading hidden, read only type files. The next download flags default to **FTP_TRANSFER_TYPE_BINARY**. The alternative is ASCII. The context identifier is used in call-back functions when ongoing status information is required.

```
BOOL   PutFile (LPCTSTR localfilename, LPCTSTR remotefilename,
               DWORD flags, DWORD context);
```
Again, the filenames can be fully or partially qualified. The flags default to binary transfer; however, ASCII can be used.

If you wish to manually handle the reading and writing of the file, use

```
CInternetFile*   OpenFile (LPCTSTR filename, DWORD access,
                            DWORD flag, DWORD context);
```

The **filename** on the remote site can be fully or partially qualified. The **access** flag is either **GENERIC_READ** or **GENERIC_WRITE**; updates are not allowed (that is, open for both reading and writing). The transfer **flag** is either binary or ASCII. Next given the **CInternetFile** pointer, you can then issue your own read and write requests directly.

The CFtpFindFile Class

Typically, when using FTP to browse a site, applications must enumerate the files present in the current directory, often displaying the files and directories in a view. The user typically selects which directory to expand next. And once that folder is make the current directory, it is then enumerated. When the user finds the file to be downloaded, for example, he/she then begins the file transfer for the selected file. The file enumeration functions are encapsulated into the **CFtpFindFile** class. This small class has a constructor and three member functions.

```
CFtpFindFile (CFtpConnection *ptrftp, DWORD context);
```
The constructor takes a pointer to the current FTP connection and a context call-back number that defaults to 1 for normal use.

Enumeration is initialized by calling
```
BOOL    FindFile (LPCTSTR filename, DWORD flags);
```
The **filename** can be NULL in which case a wildcard search in the current directory is assumed. Normal wildcard variations are permitted. For example, *. yields all subdirectories only. Usually when surfing a site, *.* is used to find both subdirectories and actual files. The **flags** default to **INTERNET_FLAG_RELOAD** which forces the enumeration to obtain its data from the site as opposed to using a local cached copy. (Other flags are seldom used.)

Subsequent files are located using
```
BOOL    FindNextFile ();
```

So how does one get access to the found item? The **CFtpFindFile** class is derived from the **CFindFile** class. Use member functions of the base class to obtain information on the found file. These simple functions include, **GetLength** to obtain the filesize in bytes, **GetFileName** to get the filename.extension, **GetFilePath** to get the fully qualified **filename, GetCreationTime**, and **IsDots** and **IsDirectory** return TRUE if the found item is ., .., or a folder. **GetCreationTime** needs an explanation. Its prototype is
```
BOOL    GetCreationTime (CTime &time);
```

Not all systems use the same format of date and time as a PC. Thus, this **CTime** class handles the conversions for us. Conveniently, **CTime** has a **Format** function to easily format the encapsulated date-time stamp into whatever string view we desire. Typical coding here might be
```
CTime t;
ftpfind.GetCreationTime (t);
CString datetime = t.Format ("%m/%d/%Y   %H:%M");
```
which yields the obvious date-time result.

Armed with these basics, let's write an FTP Browser and File Downloader program.

Pgm13a—FTP Browser and File Download Program

Figure 13.1 shows the browser just after it is launched. I have used the normal File|Open tool bar image to represent the command "Make a Connection." The URL **CEdit** box in the tool bar holds the URL. The default is for Microsoft's site. But it is not a simple **CEdit** control in a tool bar. Rather, I am too used to the commercial browsers; after entering the URL, I press the Enter Key to make the connection. Thus, the edit URL control must trap carriage return key presses and send back the launch URL command. Notice that the "CD" and the "<-" buttons are grayed. The former changes the directory while the latter downloads the file.

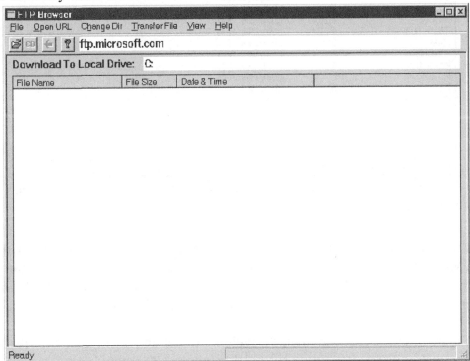

Figure 13.1 The FTP Browser — Initial View Before Connecting

Notice that there is also another **CEdit** control to enter the local machine path for storing download files. The status bar has two panes. The first pane shows the flyby hints and short action messages such as shown in Figure 13.2. The second pane shows the current directory on the remote site. The main screen is the viewer area which is a **CListCtrl** object. Yes, I could have used a **CListView** class instead, however, here I wanted to also illustrate additional tips when placing controls into a window instead of a dialog. Notice that the list view is in report mode only. By pressing on the header controls (containing the column headings), the control can sort the files into either ascending or descending order. For example, the first time you click on "File Size", the files are sorted into ascending order; the second time, descending. A toggle switch flips between ascending and descending.

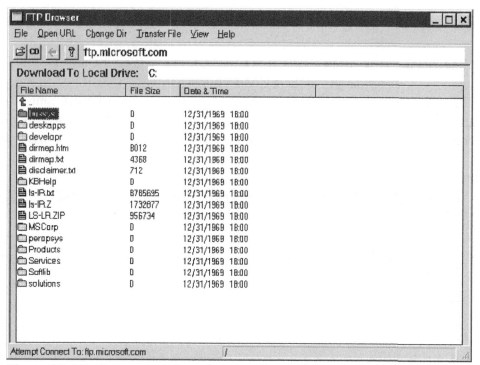

Figure 13.2 FTP Browser Now Connected to Microsoft.com with Folder
Selected

In Figure 2, I have made the connection to the site and files have been listed in the order they
came from Microsoft.com. The bottom right status bar pane shows the current directory as the root,
/. Additionally, I have clicked on the bussys folder. Notice that since it is a folder, the "CD" or
Change Directory button is not active; the file transfer button is still grayed.

In Figure 3, I have changed to the "Developr" folder and highlighted the "readme.txt" file.
Notice now that the file transfer button is available but the CD button is not.

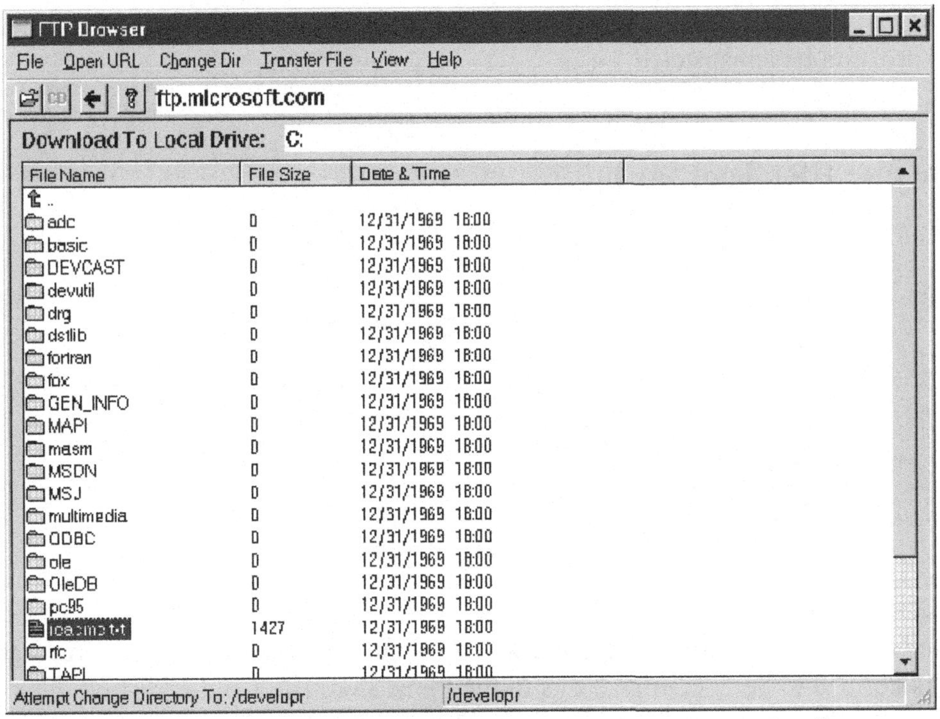

Figure 13.3 FTP Browser with File Selected Ready for Downloading

The Implementation of Pgm13a—FTP Browser

The application class has no new coding. **InitInstance** simply defines a simple document template and launches the application normally.

The CMainFrame class which normally just creates and loads the tool bar and status bar is slightly modified for convenience in handling the tool bar's edit control. In the CMainFrame header file I have defined the following

```
...
protected:    // control bar embedded members
 CStatusBar   m_wndStatusBar;
 URLToolBar   m_wndToolBar;

public:
 void    SetURL (CString&);
 CString GetURL ();
```

The GetURL and SetURL functions provide a convenient method for a view to access the text in the **CEdit** control embedded in the tool bar.

The URLToolBar class is derived from **CToolBar** in order to embed the URLEdit control within it. Member **editURL**, an instance of the URLEdit class, is needed so that the Enter Key can be used to signal opening the URL. The URLToolBar also has GetURL and SetURL functions to relay the information on down to the actual control proper. **OnCreate** is overridden so that the actual URLEdit control can be constructed.

Listing for file: URLToolBar.h

```
...
class URLToolBar : public CToolBar {
public:

  URLEdit editURL; // the embedded CEdit URL control

          URLToolBar ();
 virtual  ~URLToolBar();
 void      SetURL (CString&);
 CString   GetURL ();

protected:
afx_msg int OnCreate(LPCREATESTRUCT lpCreateStruct);
...
```

In the URLToolBar implementation file, the separator that is going to be replaced with the edit control is defined to be 7. Compare this to the Pgm13a.rc file's button array:

```
IDR_MAINFRAME TOOLBAR DISCARDABLE  16, 15
BEGIN
     BUTTON       CM_ACTIVATEURL
     BUTTON       CM_CHANGEDIR
     SEPARATOR
     BUTTON       CM_COPY_FILE
     SEPARATOR
     BUTTON       ID_APP_ABOUT
     SEPARATOR
     SEPARATOR
END
```

Listing for file: URLToolBar.cpp

```
// the 0-based index of the separator to be replaced by this control
#define EDIT_INDEX 7

URLToolBar::URLToolBar () { }
URLToolBar::~URLToolBar () { }

BEGIN_MESSAGE_MAP(URLToolBar, CToolBar)
 ON_WM_CREATE()
END_MESSAGE_MAP()

/******************************************************************/
/*                                                                */
/* OnCreate: allocate the actual CEdit control in the toolbar     */
/*                                                                */
/******************************************************************/

int URLToolBar::OnCreate (LPCREATESTRUCT lpCreateStruct) {
 if (CToolBar::OnCreate(lpCreateStruct) == -1)   return -1;
 if (!LoadToolBar (IDR_MAINFRAME)) return -1;
```

```
// determine a good position and width for the control based on total
// window width
CRect rr;
GetParent()->GetClientRect (&rr);
int x = rr.Width () - 22 * 6;
// install the new button ID for the CEdit control
SetButtonInfo (EDIT_INDEX, IDC_EDITURL, TBBS_SEPARATOR, x);
// now create the control
CRect r;
GetItemRect (EDIT_INDEX, &r);
r.right = r.left + x;
if (!editURL.Create (this, r))
  return -1;
return 0;
}


/**********************************************************************/
/*                                                                    */
/* SetURL: move a URL string into the CEdit control                   */
/*                                                                    */
/**********************************************************************/

void URLToolBar::SetURL (CString &msg) {
 editURL.SetWindowText (msg);
}


/**********************************************************************/
/*                                                                    */
/* GetURL: retrieve the URL from the CEdit control                    */
/*                                                                    */
/**********************************************************************/

CString URLToolBar::GetURL () {
 CString url;
 editURL.GetWindowText (url);
 return url;
}
```

The URLEdit class, derived from **CEdit**, is quite simple. Only two functions are needed, **Create** and **OnKeyDown**. The multi line option is required so that the Enter key is accepted. When the Enter key is pressed, the control posts the command message CM_ACTIVATEURL.

Listing for file: URLEdit.cpp

```
/**********************************************************************/
/*                                                                    */
/* Create: construct the control with the passed dimensions           */
/*                                                                    */
/**********************************************************************/

BOOL URLEdit::Create(CWnd *ptrpar, CRect &r) {
 return CEdit::Create (ES_AUTOHSCROLL | ES_MULTILINE | WS_CHILD | WS_VISIBLE,
                       r, ptrpar, IDC_EDITURL);
}


/**********************************************************************/
```

```
/*                                                                            */
/* OnKeyDown: Post the Activate URL message                                   */
/*                                                                            */
/****************************************************************************/

void URLEdit::OnKeyDown (UINT nChar, UINT nRepCnt, UINT nFlags) {
 if (nChar == VK_RETURN)
  AfxGetApp ()->m_pMainWnd->PostMessage (WM_COMMAND, CM_ACTIVATEURL, 0);
 else CEdit::OnKeyDown(nChar, nRepCnt, nFlags);
}
```

The View and CListCtrl Classes

The document class is just the default App Wizard generated class in this sample. All the action takes place in the FTPView and associated **CListCtrl** class, SiteList. By splitting the workload, both classes become more streamlined. SiteList, derived from **CListCtrl**, handles the internal **CListCtrl** events, such as sorting on filename or filesize. Additionally, when the user double clicks on an entry, SiteList posts a message to it's parent, FTPView, CM_CHANGEDIR or CM_COPY_FILE. The FTPView can then change to a new directory or begin to download a file.

Since the list control is going to potentially sort the files and folders, a method must be established to be able to tie a selected item in the control back to the actual site information it represents. Thus, I created the basic structure FILEITEM which is defined in the file FileItem.h

```
struct FILEITEM {
 BOOL     isfolder;
 int      imagenum;
 CString filename;
 DWORD    filesize;
 CString datetime;
 CString fullfilename;
};
```

For convenience, I store an indicator of whether this entry is a folder or a file. Since I am going to provide an image to the left of the filename in the list view (a folder or a text icon or an arrow), I store the image list index to the correct bitmap image. The usual date to be displayed come next, the filename, filesize and the formatted date-time. Finally, again for my convenience, I also store the complete path; if the user downloads this file, I immediately have the filename to use.

FTPView uses a **CPtrArray** to store the file items as they are received during the FtpFileFind process. Whenever the user changes the current directory, the **CPtrArray** is emptied and refilled with the new data. Then the SiteList control is updated. So from the **CListCtrl**'s point of view, it begins empty of items and periodically its SetList helper function is called to install a new set of file items to be shown.

The FTPView class then maintains the **CPtrArray** and handles all the Internet events.

The SiteList (CListCtrl) Class

Some additional complexities arise when dealing with a report view. Specifically, how does the control handle columns of data? By using subitems. When adding an entry to the list control, only one bit of text can be entered per entry. So if a line has four columns, then four separate calls must be made to the **InsertItem** function. **iItem** refers to the line index while **iSubItem** refers to the zero-based index of which column the data resides in. The user **lParam** value holds the **CPtrArray** subscript so at any time the original file item entry can be found.

Next if sorting is supported, then a call-back comparison function is required. Because the user **lParam** value holds the **CPtrArray** subscript, the data can be sorted in any manner desired. However, if the control owns the strings, the sorting process duplicates those strings several times. Thus for both speed and memory usage, the **LPSTR_TEXTCALLBACK** option is used when **InsertItem** is invoked to add each item to the control. Whenever the list view needs to display the text in a specific column of a specific row, it sends a message, **LVN_GETDISPINFO**. SiteList must then respond to that message in **OnGetDispInfo** and deliver up the requisite text to be shown. Again, since the **lParam** value holds the subscript into the **CPtrArray**, we have immediate access to the file item. **OnGetDispInfo** can determine which column is needed by examining the **iSubItem** member from the passed **LV_DISPINFO**.

The **LV_DISPINFO** structure contains the data needed to display an item in a list view control. It is basically an **LV_ITEM** structure after the common header information:

```
struct LV_DISPINFO {
    NMHDR   hdr;
    LV_ITEM item;
};
```

The **code** member of the header identifies is either **LVN_GETDISPINFO** or **LVN_SETDISPINFO**. Here we only need to respond to getting the text to display. The **LV_ITEM**, **item**'s **mask** member tells us what is needed. The **mask** contains the **LVIF_TEXT** flag when text is needed for the subitems. We merely need to create the string for the indicated column.

Listing for file: SiteList.h

```
class SiteList : public CListCtrl {
public:
            SiteList();
    void    SetList (CPtrArray *);
virtual BOOL Create(CWnd*);
virtual     ~SiteList();

static int CALLBACK Compare (LPARAM, LPARAM, LPARAM);

protected:
static CPtrArray *ptrfileitems;
static int          direction[3];

 afx_msg void OnDblclk(NMHDR* pNMHDR, LRESULT* pResult);
```

```
afx_msg void OnColumnClick(NMHDR* pNMHDR, LRESULT* pResult);
afx_msg void OnGetDispInfo(NMHDR* pNMHDR, LRESULT* pResult);
...
```

Sorting requires a call-back function similar to **qsort**. Additionally, since subsequent clicks on the same column header ought to toggle between sorted in ascending and then descending order, an array of the current order for each column must be maintained. Here it is called **direction**. The other static item is the pointer to the **CPtrArray** of items. It is NULL until items are added to the control. **CString** conveniently provides a **CompareNoCase** function making the sorting exceptionally easy. The only complicating factor is the presence of the requisite up to the previous folder or back up arrow. It must always remain the very first item. Only this one item uses the image number 7. Thus, by checking to see which bitmap image index the item uses, one can tell if an item is this back arrow. Simply force this item to always be at the top of the list as it sorts or displays. When the SetList function is called, the first item must be this back up arrow item. When sorting, SiteList keeps it first in the list.

Listing for file: SiteList.cpp

```
...

/*********************************************************************/
/*                                                                   */
/* static members: the CPtrArray pointer and the sort direction array */
/*                                                                   */
/*********************************************************************/

CPtrArray *   SiteList::ptrfileitems = NULL;
int           SiteList::direction[3] = {1, 1, 1};


SiteList::SiteList () { }
SiteList::~SiteList () { }

BEGIN_MESSAGE_MAP(SiteList, CListCtrl)
 ON_NOTIFY_REFLECT(NM_DBLCLK, OnDblclk)
 ON_NOTIFY_REFLECT(LVN_COLUMNCLICK, OnColumnClick)
 ON_NOTIFY_REFLECT(LVN_GETDISPINFO, OnGetDispInfo)
END_MESSAGE_MAP()

/*********************************************************************/
/*                                                                   */
/* Create: construct the CListCtrl object in report style            */
/*                                                                   */
/*********************************************************************/

BOOL SiteList::Create(CWnd *ptrpar) {
 return CListCtrl::Create (LVS_REPORT | WS_BORDER | WS_VISIBLE |
                           WS_EX_STATICEDGE, CRect (0,0, 500, 500),
                           ptrpar, IDC_LISTCTRL);
}


/*********************************************************************/
/*                                                                   */
```

```
/* SetList: install a new set of items in the control                      */
/*                                                                          */
/****************************************************************************/

void SiteList::SetList (CPtrArray *ptrar) {
 ptrfileitems = ptrar;
 DeleteAllItems ();
 int num = ptrfileitems->GetSize ();
 int i;
 for (i=0; i<num; i++) {
  FILEITEM *ptritem = (FILEITEM*) ptrfileitems->GetAt (i);
  LV_ITEM lvi;
  lvi.mask = LVIF_TEXT | LVIF_IMAGE | LVIF_PARAM;
  lvi.iItem = i;
  lvi.iSubItem = 0;
  lvi.iImage = ptritem->imagenum;
  lvi.pszText = LPSTR_TEXTCALLBACK;
  lvi.lParam = i;
  InsertItem (&lvi);
 }
}


/****************************************************************************/
/*                                                                          */
/* OnDblclk: Post a change dir command - let receiver sort out which        */
/*                                                                          */
/****************************************************************************/

void SiteList::OnDblclk (NMHDR* pNMHDR, LRESULT* pResult) {
 if (GetSelectedCount () == 1) {
  int i = GetNextItem (-1, LVNI_ALL | LVNI_SELECTED);
  if (i != -1) {
   i = GetItemData (i);
   FILEITEM *ptrfi = (FILEITEM*) ptrfileitems->GetAt (i);
   if (ptrfi->isfolder)
    GetParent ()->PostMessage (WM_COMMAND, CM_CHANGEDIR, 0);
   else
    GetParent ()->PostMessage (WM_COMMAND, CM_COPY_FILE, 0);
  }
 }
 *pResult = 0;
}


/****************************************************************************/
/*                                                                          */
/* OnColumnClick: sort column                                               */
/*                                                                          */
/****************************************************************************/

void SiteList::OnColumnClick (NMHDR* pNMHDR, LRESULT* pResult) {
 NM_LISTVIEW* pNMListView = (NM_LISTVIEW*)pNMHDR;
 SortItems (Compare, pNMListView->iSubItem);
 // now toggle the ascending/decsending value for the next time
 int i = pNMListView->iSubItem;
 direction[i] = direction[i] == 1 ? -1 : 1;
}


/****************************************************************************/
```

```
/*                                                                         */
/* Compare: determine which column text is larger                         */
/*                                                                         */
/***************************************************************************/

int CALLBACK SiteList::Compare (LPARAM lp1, LPARAM lp2, LPARAM sortcol) {
 FILEITEM *ptr1 = (FILEITEM*) ptrfileitems->GetAt (lp1);
 FILEITEM *ptr2 = (FILEITEM*) ptrfileitems->GetAt (lp2);
 // if either one is the "up to higher directory" entry, force it to top
 if (ptr1->imagenum == 7) return -1;
 if (ptr2->imagenum == 7) return -1;
 switch (sortcol) {
 case 0:
  return (ptr1->filename.CompareNoCase (ptr2->filename)) * direction[sortcol];
 case 1:
  return (ptr1->filesize - ptr2->filesize) * direction[sortcol];
 case 2:
  return (ptr1->datetime.CompareNoCase (ptr2->datetime)) * direction[sortcol];
 }
 return 0;
}


/***************************************************************************/
/*                                                                         */
/* OnGetDispInfo: provide the text for the specific column                 */
/*                                                                         */
/***************************************************************************/

void SiteList::OnGetDispInfo (NMHDR* pNMHDR, LRESULT* pResult) {
 // convert the header pointer into the DISPINFO type pointer
 LV_DISPINFO *ptrlvdi = (LV_DISPINFO*) pNMHDR;
 // handle only the requests for text to display
 if (ptrlvdi->item.mask & LVIF_TEXT) {
  // retrieve the subscript into the array for this item
  int i = ptrlvdi->item.lParam;
  // get the actual file item
  FILEITEM *ptrfi = (FILEITEM*) ptrfileitems->GetAt (i);
  // provide the text for the indicated column
  switch (ptrlvdi->item.iSubItem) {
  case 0: // filename
   ::lstrcpy (ptrlvdi->item.pszText, (LPCSTR) ptrfi->filename);
   break;
  case 1: // filesize
   if (ptrfi->imagenum == 7) break; // bypass text for up to prev dir arrow
   char sz[20];
   wsprintf (sz, "%ld", ptrfi->filesize);
   ::lstrcpy (ptrlvdi->item.pszText, sz);
   break;
  case 2: // date-time
   if (ptrfi->imagenum == 7) break; // bypass text for up to prev dir arrow
   ::lstrcpy (ptrlvdi->item.pszText, (LPCSTR) ptrfi->datetime);
   break;
  }
 }
 *pResult = 0;
}
```

The FTPView Class

The FTPView class contains an instance of the SiteList control, **sitelist**, and a **CEdit** control, **localedit**, to contain the user's local folder in which to copy files. It also has the bitmap images for the various items in the list control. The **fileitems CPtrArray** houses the file items in this current directory. File items are created during the **FtpFindFile** enumeration process. Member **inet_session** is our instance of **CInternetSession** while **ptrftp**, when not NULL, represents our **CFtpConnection**.

Listing for file: FTPView.h

```
#pragma once
#include "FileItem.h"
#include "SiteList.h"

class FTPView : public CView {
protected:
 FTPView();
 DECLARE_DYNCREATE(FTPView)

 SiteList    sitelist;  // the CListCtrl object
 CImageList  images;    // the image bitmaps
 CPtrArray   fileitems; // the array of folders and files in this directory
 CEdit       localedit; // the edit control containing the local path

 CString     localpath;
 CString     downloadmsg;

 int height;
 int width;
 int avg_char_height;
 int avg_char_width;

 CInternetSession inet_session;
 CFtpConnection   *ptrftp;

 CString           curdir;
 CString           url;

public:
      FTPDoc* GetDocument();
 virtual void OnDraw(CDC* pDC);   // overridden to draw this view
 virtual BOOL PreCreateWindow(CREATESTRUCT& cs);
 virtual void OnInitialUpdate();
 virtual     ~FTPView();

protected:
         void UpdateStatusBar (int, CString&);
         void RepositionControls ();
         void RemoveFileItems ();
         void Populate (CFtpConnection*);
 afx_msg void OnSize(UINT nType, int cx, int cy);
 afx_msg void OnDestroy();
 afx_msg void OnAppExit();
 afx_msg void OnCopyFile();
```

```
afx_msg void OnUpdateCopyFile(CCmdUI* pCmdUI);
afx_msg void OnActivateURL ();
afx_msg void OnUpdateActivateURL(CCmdUI* pCmdUI);
afx_msg void OnChangeDir();
afx_msg void OnUpdateChangeDir(CCmdUI* pCmdUI);
...
```

OnInitialUpdate must allocate the controls and initialize them. Specifically, it must set the number of columns in the **CListCtrl** and the text for the headings. When the view is resized, helper function RepositionControls is called to move and resize the various controls.

The helper function Populate does the actual **FtpFindFile** enumeration process, creating the file items to be shown. **OnDestroy** and **OnAppExit** must handle proper termination of any on-going Internet actions. OnActivateURL attempts the connection to the user's specified URL, while OnChangeDir attempts to change to the requested folder. OnCopyFile downloads the selected file(s) to the current local directory.

Since text messages are to appear in both panes of the status bar, I created the UpdateStatusBar function which takes as its parameters the pane index and the text. In RepositionControls the width of the second pane is established.

Since there is no document really, I do not want the usual document name and "Untitled" appearing as the caption. Hence, in **PreCreateWindow**, the **FWS_ADDTOTITLE** style is removed before the real window creation begins.

Listing for file: FTPView.cpp

```
...
/***********************************************************************/
/*                                                                     */
/* FTPView: Handle FPT actions                                         */
/*                                                                     */
/***********************************************************************/

IMPLEMENT_DYNCREATE(FTPView, CView)

BEGIN_MESSAGE_MAP(FTPView, CView)
 ON_WM_SIZE()
 ON_WM_DESTROY()
 ON_COMMAND(CM_COPY_FILE, OnCopyFile)
 ON_UPDATE_COMMAND_UI(CM_COPY_FILE, OnUpdateCopyFile)
 ON_COMMAND (CM_ACTIVATEURL, OnActivateURL)
 ON_UPDATE_COMMAND_UI(CM_ACTIVATEURL, OnUpdateActivateURL)
 ON_COMMAND(CM_CHANGEDIR, OnChangeDir)
 ON_UPDATE_COMMAND_UI(CM_CHANGEDIR, OnUpdateChangeDir)
 ON_COMMAND(ID_APP_EXIT, OnAppExit)
END_MESSAGE_MAP()

/***********************************************************************/
/*                                                                     */
/* FTPView: constructor and destructor                                 */
```

```
/*                                                                      */
/**********************************************************************/

FTPView::FTPView (){
 ptrftp = NULL;
 curdir = "";
 localpath = "C:";
 downloadmsg = "Download To Local Drive: ";
}


FTPView::~FTPView () {  }

/**********************************************************************/
/*                                                                      */
/* PreCreateWindows: remove add to title                                */
/*                                                                      */
/**********************************************************************/

BOOL FTPView::PreCreateWindow (CREATESTRUCT& cs) {
 cs.style &= ~(LONG) FWS_ADDTOTITLE;
 cs.style |= WS_CLIPCHILDREN;
 return CView::PreCreateWindow (cs);
}


/**********************************************************************/
/*                                                                      */
/* OnDraw: display a header for local edit control                      */
/*                                                                      */
/**********************************************************************/

void FTPView::OnDraw (CDC* pDC) {
 FTPDoc* pDoc = GetDocument ();
 ASSERT_VALID (pDoc);
 pDC->SetBkColor (RGB(192,192,192));
 pDC->TextOut (avg_char_width, 4, downloadmsg);
}


/**********************************************************************/
/*                                                                      */
/* UpdateStatusBar: update the indicated pane text                      */
/*                                                                      */
/**********************************************************************/

void  FTPView::UpdateStatusBar (int pane, CString &msg) {
 CStatusBar *ptrbar = ((CStatusBar*) AfxGetApp()->m_pMainWnd->
                     GetDescendantWindow (AFX_IDW_STATUS_BAR));
 if (ptrbar) ptrbar->SetPaneText (pane, msg, TRUE);
}


/**********************************************************************/
/*                                                                      */
/* OnSize: reposition the controls to adapt to the new size             */
/*                                                                      */
/**********************************************************************/

void FTPView::OnSize (UINT nType, int cx, int cy) {
 CView::OnSize (nType, cx, cy);
 height = cy;
```

```
 width  = cx;
 // controls must exist to be moved safely
 if (cx && cy && sitelist.GetSafeHwnd() && localedit.GetSafeHwnd())
  RepositionControls ();
}


/************************************************************************/
/*                                                                    */
/* RepositionControls: based on current view dimensions, position controls */
/*                                                                    */
/************************************************************************/

void FTPView::RepositionControls () {
 // position the list view
 sitelist.MoveWindow (avg_char_width, 30,
                      width - 2*avg_char_width, height - 30);
 // position the local edit control
 int x = downloadmsg.GetLength ();
 localedit.MoveWindow (x * avg_char_width, 4,
                       width - (x + 1) * avg_char_width, 20);

 // setup the second pane size on the status bar
 UINT id, style;
 int sz;
 CStatusBar *ptrbar = ((CStatusBar*) AfxGetApp()->m_pMainWnd->
                       GetDescendantWindow (AFX_IDW_STATUS_BAR));
 ptrbar->GetPaneInfo (1, id, style, sz);
 ptrbar->SetPaneInfo (1, ID_INDICATOR_SITE, style, width/2);
}


/************************************************************************/
/*                                                                    */
/* OnInitialUpdate: create controls and setup list control headers    */
/*                                                                    */
/************************************************************************/

void FTPView::OnInitialUpdate () {
 CView::OnInitialUpdate ();
 // install new background color
 ::DeleteObject ((HBRUSH)::SetClassLong (m_hWnd, GCL_HBRBACKGROUND,
                 (long) (HBRUSH) ::GetStockObject (LTGRAY_BRUSH)));

 // get text metrics to aid in placement of controls
 TEXTMETRIC  tm;
 CClientDC dc (this);
 dc.GetTextMetrics (&tm);
 avg_char_width  = tm.tmAveCharWidth;
 avg_char_height = tm.tmHeight + tm.tmExternalLeading;

 // install the default URL in the toolbar
    ((CMainFrame*)   (AfxGetApp()->m_pMainWnd))->SetURL   (CString
("ftp.microsoft.com"));

 // create the local edit control
 if (!localedit.Create (ES_AUTOHSCROLL | WS_CHILD | WS_VISIBLE,
     CRect (0,0,20,20), this, IDC_LOCALEDIT)) {
  AfxMessageBox ("Error - unable to create edit control", MB_OK);
  AfxGetApp ()->m_pMainWnd->PostMessage(WM_CLOSE);
```

```
  return;
 }
 localedit.SetWindowText (localpath);

 // create the list view control
 if (!sitelist.Create (this)) {
  AfxMessageBox ("Error - unable to create list control", MB_OK);
  AfxGetApp ()->m_pMainWnd->PostMessage(WM_CLOSE);
  return;
 }
 // install the image bitmap strip
 images.Create (IDB_IMAGES, 16, 0, RGB(0,0,255));
 images.SetBkColor (GetSysColor (COLOR_WINDOW));
 sitelist.SetImageList (&images, LVSIL_SMALL);

 // install the column headers
 sitelist.InsertColumn (0, "File Name", LVCFMT_LEFT, 20*avg_char_width, 0);
 sitelist.InsertColumn (1, "File Size", LVCFMT_LEFT, 10*avg_char_width, 1);
 sitelist.InsertColumn (2, "Date & Time", LVCFMT_LEFT, 25*avg_char_width, 2);

 // initialize the listview with no file items
 sitelist.SetList (&fileitems);
 RepositionControls ();
 UpdateStatusBar (1, CString (""));
}

void FTPView::RemoveFileItems () {
 int num = fileitems.GetSize ();
 if (num) {
  for (int i=0; i<num; i++) {
   FILEITEM *ptrfi = (FILEITEM*) fileitems[i];
   delete ptrfi;
  }
  fileitems.RemoveAll ();
 }
}

/******************************************************************************/
/*                                                                          */
/* OnDestroy: close the internet session and clean up allocated items       */
/*                                                                          */
/******************************************************************************/

void FTPView::OnDestroy() {
 delete ptrftp;
 inet_session.Close ();
 RemoveFileItems ();
 CView::OnDestroy ();
}

/******************************************************************************/
/*                                                                          */
/* OnAppExit: onstruct the window object                                    */
/*                                                                          */
/******************************************************************************/

void FTPView::OnAppExit() {
 if (AfxMessageBox ("Terminate current file transfer?", MB_YESNO) == IDYES)
```

```
  AfxGetApp ()->m_pMainWnd->PostMessage(WM_CLOSE);
}

/******************************************************************************/
/*                                                                          */
/* OnUpdateActivateURL: enable when there is text in the URL edit control   */
/*                                                                          */
/******************************************************************************/

void FTPView::OnUpdateActivateURL(CCmdUI* pCmdUI) {
 CString s = ((CMainFrame*) (AfxGetApp()->m_pMainWnd))->GetURL ();
 pCmdUI->Enable (s.GetLength () > 0 ? 1 : 0);
}

/******************************************************************************/
/*                                                                          */
/* OnActivateURL: open a connection to this URL                             */
/*                                                                          */
/******************************************************************************/

void FTPView::OnActivateURL () {
 url = ((CMainFrame*) (AfxGetApp()->m_pMainWnd))->GetURL ();
 CWaitCursor cursor;
 try {
  CString msg = "Attempt Connect To: " + url;
  UpdateStatusBar (0, msg);
  ptrftp = NULL;
  ptrftp = inet_session.GetFtpConnection (url);
 }
 catch (CInternetException *ptrex) {
  AfxMessageBox ("Cannot get an ftp connection to this site.", MB_OK);
  ptrex->Delete ();
  return;
 }
 // now remove all previous file items and repopulate the file list
 RemoveFileItems ();
 sitelist.SetList (&fileitems);
 ptrftp->GetCurrentDirectory (curdir);
 Populate (ptrftp);
 sitelist.SetList (&fileitems);
 UpdateStatusBar (1, curdir);
}

/******************************************************************************/
/*                                                                          */
/* Populate: enumerate all files and folders in this directory             */
/*                                                                          */
/******************************************************************************/

void FTPView::Populate (CFtpConnection *ptrftp) {
 // insert up arrow item as the first item always
 FILEITEM *fi = new FILEITEM;
 fi->isfolder = TRUE;
 fi->imagenum = 7;
 fi->filename = "..";
 fi->filesize = 0;
 fi->fullfilename = "";
 fi->datetime = "";
```

```
 fileitems.Add (fi);

 // construct a search string by adding wild cards to end of current dir
 CString searchdir;
 if (curdir.CompareNoCase (CString ("/")) == 0) searchdir = _T("/*");
 else searchdir = curdir + _T("/*");
 // construct instance to find files
 CFtpFileFind ftpfind (ptrftp);
 BOOL ok = ftpfind.FindFile (searchdir);
 if (!ok) {
  ftpfind.Close ();
  return;
 }
 // for each found item, add it to the file items list
 while (ok) {
  ok = ftpfind.FindNextFile ();
  // do not add . .. and temporary files
  if (ftpfind.IsDots () || ftpfind.IsHidden () || ftpfind.IsTemporary ())
   break;
  if (ftpfind.IsDirectory ()) {
   fi = new FILEITEM;
   fi->isfolder = TRUE;
   fi->imagenum = 0;
   fi->filename = ftpfind.GetFileName ();
   fi->fullfilename = ftpfind.GetFilePath ();
   fi->filesize = 0;
   CTime t;
   ftpfind.GetCreationTime (t);
   fi->datetime = t.Format ("%m/%d/%Y   %H:%M");
   fileitems.Add (fi);
  }
  else {
   fi = new FILEITEM;
   fi->isfolder = FALSE;
   fi->imagenum = 6;
   fi->filename = ftpfind.GetFileName ();
   fi->fullfilename = ftpfind.GetFilePath ();
   fi->filesize = (DWORD) ftpfind.GetLength ();
   CTime t;
   ftpfind.GetCreationTime (t);
   fi->datetime = t.Format ("%m/%d/%Y   %H:%M");
   fileitems.Add (fi);
  }
 }
 ftpfind.Close ();
}

/**********************************************************************************/
/*                                                                              */
/* OnCopyFile: download selected files to local dir                             */
/*                                                                              */
/**********************************************************************************/

void FTPView::OnCopyFile() {
 CWaitCursor cursor;                    // show wait cursor
 localedit.GetWindowText (localpath); // get current local dir to use
 int num, j;
 if ((num = sitelist.GetSelectedCount ()) > 0) {
```

```
  int i = sitelist.GetNextItem (-1, LVNI_ALL | LVNI_SELECTED);
  while (i != -1) {
   j = sitelist.GetItemData (i);
   FILEITEM *ptrfi = (FILEITEM*) fileitems.GetAt (j);
   if (!ptrfi->isfolder) {
    CString msg = "Copying file: " + ptrfi->filename + " to " + localpath;
    UpdateStatusBar (0, msg);
    CString toname = localpath + "\\" + ptrfi->filename;
    ptrftp->GetFile (ptrfi->fullfilename, toname, FALSE);
   }
   i = sitelist.GetNextItem (i, LVNI_BELOW | LVNI_SELECTED);
  }
 }
}


/***********************************************************************/
/*                                                                     */
/* OnUpdateCopyFile: enable if a file is selected                      */
/*                                                                     */
/***********************************************************************/

void FTPView::OnUpdateCopyFile(CCmdUI* pCmdUI) {
 int num, j;
 if ((num = sitelist.GetSelectedCount ()) > 0) {
  int i = sitelist.GetNextItem (-1, LVNI_ALL | LVNI_SELECTED);
  while (i != -1) {
   j = sitelist.GetItemData (i);
   FILEITEM *ptrfi = (FILEITEM*) fileitems.GetAt (j);
   if (!ptrfi->isfolder) {
    pCmdUI->Enable (TRUE);
    return;
   }
   i = sitelist.GetNextItem (i, LVNI_BELOW | LVNI_SELECTED);
  }
 }
 pCmdUI->Enable (FALSE);
}


/***********************************************************************/
/*                                                                     */
/* OnChangeDir: respond to dir change requests                         */
/*                                                                     */
/***********************************************************************/

void FTPView::OnChangeDir () {
 // must be single selected item to CD to
 if (sitelist.GetSelectedCount () == 1) {
  int i = sitelist.GetNextItem (-1, LVNI_ALL | LVNI_SELECTED);
  if (i != -1) {
   i = sitelist.GetItemData (i);
   FILEITEM *ptrfi = (FILEITEM*) fileitems.GetAt (i);
   // now check to see it it is the back to previous dir item or a folder
   if (ptrfi->isfolder && ptrfi->imagenum != 7) {
    // here it is a folder, so make up a new curdir name by appending folder
    if (curdir.CompareNoCase (CString ("/")) !=0) curdir += "/";
    curdir += ptrfi->filename;
    // display an attempt message on the status bar
    CString msg = "Attempt Change Directory To: " + curdir;
```

```
        UpdateStatusBar (0, msg);
        CWaitCursor cursor; // show wait cursor
        RemoveFileItems (); // empty the file items array
        sitelist.SetList (&fileitems); // and update the listview
        // attempt the ftp action
        ptrftp->SetCurrentDirectory (curdir);
        // enumerate the files under this folder
        Populate (ptrftp);
        // install the new file items list in the listview
        sitelist.SetList (&fileitems);
        UpdateStatusBar (1, curdir);
      }
    else if (ptrfi->isfolder) {
      // here the back up arrow was selcted
      // verify we are not already at the root dir
      if (curdir.CompareNoCase (CString ("/")) == 0) return;
      i = curdir.ReverseFind ('/');
      char *string = curdir.GetBuffer (1);
      string[i] = 0;
      curdir.ReleaseBuffer (-1);
      CString msg = "Attempt Change Directory To: " + curdir;
      UpdateStatusBar (0, msg);
      CWaitCursor cursor;
      RemoveFileItems ();
      sitelist.SetList (&fileitems);
      ptrftp->SetCurrentDirectory (curdir);
      Populate (ptrftp);
      sitelist.SetList (&fileitems);
      UpdateStatusBar (1, curdir);
      }
    }
  }
 }
}


/*********************************************************************************/
/*                                                                             */
/* OnUpdateChangeDir: enable CD button if a folder is selected                 */
/*                                                                             */
/*********************************************************************************/

void FTPView::OnUpdateChangeDir (CCmdUI* pCmdUI) {
 // cannot handle multiple selected items
 if (sitelist.GetSelectedCount () == 1) {
  int i = sitelist.GetNextItem (-1, LVNI_ALL | LVNI_SELECTED);
  if (i != -1) { // here an item is selected
   i = sitelist.GetItemData (i);
   FILEITEM *ptrfi = (FILEITEM*) fileitems.GetAt (i);
   if (ptrfi->isfolder) { // can only CD if it is a folder
    pCmdUI->Enable (TRUE);
    return;
   }
  }
 }
 pCmdUI->Enable (FALSE);
}
```

First, some general notes. **OnSize** responds to changes in the main window size by calling RepositionControls. However, if the list view and local edit controls have not yet been created, the repositioning will fail. Perhaps the best test for the existence of the controls is to check if they have a valid HWND.

```
if (cx && cy && sitelist.GetSafeHwnd() &&
    localedit.GetSafeHwnd())
  RepositionControls ();
```

Next, in **OnInitialUpdate** the default FTP site URL is inserted into the tool bar edit control as follows

```
((CMainFrame*) (AfxGetApp()->m_pMainWnd))->SetURL (
                             CString ("ftp.microsoft.com"));
```

The local edit control is created

```
    if (!localedit.Create (ES_AUTOHSCROLL | WS_CHILD |
        WS_VISIBLE, CRect (0,0,20,20), this, IDC_LOCALEDIT)) {
    ...
    localedit.SetWindowText (localpath);
```

The list view control creation process goes as follows

```
    if (!sitelist.Create (this)) {
    ...
    images.Create (IDB_IMAGES, 16, 0, RGB(0,0,255));
    images.SetBkColor (GetSysColor (COLOR_WINDOW));
    sitelist.SetImageList (&images, LVSIL_SMALL);
```

The column headers are added

```
  sitelist.InsertColumn (0, "File Name", LVCFMT_LEFT, 20*avg_char_width, 0);
  sitelist.InsertColumn (1, "File Size", LVCFMT_LEFT, 10*avg_char_width, 1);
  sitelist.InsertColumn (2, "Date & Time", LVCFMT_LEFT, 25*avg_char_width,2);
```

And the list view is given its initial empty list

```
    sitelist.SetList (&fileitems);
```

Now let's examine the Internet coding. The first action must be to connect to a site; OnActivateURL is called. After obtaining the contents of the URL edit control in the tool bar, a wait cursor is shown. A clever way to have the wait cursor appear is simply to allocate an instance of the **CWaitCursor** on the stack. When the function terminates, this instance is then destroyed and the normal arrow cursor appears automatically. Since the **GetFtpConnection** can raise an exception, that code is wrapped in a try-catch block

```
url = ((CMainFrame*) (AfxGetApp()->m_pMainWnd))->GetURL ();
CWaitCursor cursor;
try {
 CString msg = "Attempt Connect To: " + url;
 UpdateStatusBar (0, msg);
 ptrftp = NULL;
 ptrftp = inet_session.GetFtpConnection (url);
}
catch (CInternetException *ptrex) {
 AfxMessageBox ("Cannot get an ftp connection to this site.", MB_OK);
 ptrex->Delete ();
```

```
  return;
}
```

Next, any existing file items in the **CPtrArray** are removed and the list view is updated with the empty list.

```
RemoveFileItems ();
sitelist.SetList (&fileitems);
```

The current directory is retrieved from the remote site and the remote site is queried to find all the files and folders contained in this directory via Populate and then added to the list view.

```
ptrftp->GetCurrentDirectory (curdir);
Populate (ptrftp);
sitelist.SetList (&fileitems);
UpdateStatusBar (1, curdir);
```

Populate is passed our instance of **CFtpConnection**. Now while the list view when sorting on a user requested column always sorts the "up arrow" or back to the previous directory file item as the top item in the view, initially the file items will be in the order they are found on the remote site. Thus, we must add the up arrow as the first file item before beginning to enumerate the files in this directory.

```
    FILEITEM *fi = new FILEITEM;
    fi->isfolder = TRUE;
    fi->imagenum = 7;
    fi->filename = "..";
    fi->filesize = 0;
    fi->fullfilename = "";
    fi->datetime = "";
    fileitems.Add (fi);
```

The search process begins with the construction of the search pattern, here *.*

```
CString searchdir;
if (curdir.CompareNoCase (CString ("/")) == 0)
  searchdir=_T("/*");
else
  searchdir = curdir + _T("/*");
```

Next an instance of the **CFtpFindFile** class is allocated passing it the current FTP connection and the **FindFile** function invoked to prime the loop

```
    CFtpFileFind ftpfind (ptrftp);
    BOOL ok = ftpfind.FindFile (searchdir);
```

For each found item, we want to add it to the file items list. Avoid adding the entries representing this folder and its parent folder as well as any temporary files on the host. Use the **IsDots**, **IsHidden** and **IsTemporary** member functions

```
    while (ok) {
      ok = ftpfind.FindNextFile ();
```

```
  if (ftpfind.IsDots () || ftpfind.IsHidden ()
      || ftpfind.IsTemporary ())
  break;
```

Folders are added
```
  if (ftpfind.IsDirectory ()) {
  fi = new FILEITEM;
  fi->isfolder = TRUE;
  fi->imagenum = 0;
  fi->filename = ftpfind.GetFileName ();
  fi->fullfilename = ftpfind.GetFilePath ();
  fi->filesize = 0;
  CTime t;
  ftpfind.GetCreationTime (t);
  fi->datetime = t.Format ("%m/%d/%Y   %H:%M");
  fileitems.Add (fi);
```

While actual files are added
```
  fi = new FILEITEM;
  fi->isfolder = FALSE;
  fi->imagenum = 6;
  fi->filename = ftpfind.GetFileName ();
  fi->fullfilename = ftpfind.GetFilePath ();
  fi->filesize = ftpfind.GetLength ();
  CTime t;
  ftpfind.GetCreationTime (t);
  fi->datetime = t.Format ("%m/%d/%Y   %H:%M");
  fileitems.Add (fi);
```
Do not forget to close the find connection when done
```
  ftpfind.Close ();
```

The next likely user action is to change the current directory. OnChangeDir responds by checking for the number of selected items in the list view. If one item is selected and that item is a folder or the special back up arrow, the current directory change can be requested.
```
  if (sitelist.GetSelectedCount () == 1) {
  int i = sitelist.GetNextItem (-1, LVNI_ALL |
                                LVNI_SELECTED);
  if (i != -1) {
  i = sitelist.GetItemData (i);
  FILEITEM *ptrfi = (FILEITEM*) fileitems.GetAt (i);
  if (ptrfi->isfolder && ptrfi->imagenum != 7) {
```

At this point, a directory has been selected so the **curdir** member has the selected folder appended to it. For convenience, a short message is sent to the status bar, the file items list is emptied as well as the list view.
```
    if (curdir.CompareNoCase (CString ("/")) !=0)
    curdir += "/";
```

```
curdir += ptrfi->filename;
CString msg = "Attempt Change Directory To: " + curdir;
UpdateStatusBar (0, msg);
CWaitCursor cursor; // show wait cursor
RemoveFileItems (); // empty the file items array
sitelist.SetList (&fileitems); // and update the listview
```

Now the FTP actions begin. First, try to change the current directory using **SetCurrentDirectory** and then call Populate to recreate the list of file items contained in this new folder. And then transfer them to the list view to be shown to the user.

```
ptrftp->SetCurrentDirectory (curdir);
Populate (ptrftp);
sitelist.SetList (&fileitems);
```

If the back up arrow was chosen, we must guard against any attempt to back up beyond the root. If we are at the root, simply return and ignore this request. To back up, use the **CString** member function **ReverseFind** to find the previous / separator. Once that has been done, the remainder of the coding is the same.

```
else if (ptrfi->isfolder) {
  if (curdir.CompareNoCase (CString ("/")) == 0) return;
  i = curdir.ReverseFind ('/');
  char *string = curdir.GetBuffer (1);
  string[i] = 0;
  curdir.ReleaseBuffer (-1);
```

Finally, the user may wish to download one or more selected files. OnCopyFiles handles such requests. The **GetFile** function handles all of the transfer actions for one file. We merely need to wrap a loop around it, obtaining the selected files from the list view using **GetNextItem**. Just make sure we bypass any accidentally selected folders. The abbreviated sequence is

```
localedit.GetWindowText (localpath);
if ((num = sitelist.GetSelectedCount ()) > 0) {
 int i = sitelist.GetNextItem(-1, LVNI_ALL | LVNI_SELECTED);
 while (i != -1) {
  j = sitelist.GetItemData (i);
  FILEITEM *ptrfi = (FILEITEM*) fileitems.GetAt (j);
  if (!ptrfi->isfolder) {
   CString toname = localpath + "\\" + ptrfi->filename;
   ptrftp->GetFile (ptrfi->fullfilename, toname, FALSE);
  }
  i = sitelist.GetNextItem (i, LVNI_BELOW | LVNI_SELECTED);
 }
}
```

And so we have our initial FTP browser operational.

Improvements to the Browser

After you run the browser for a few minutes, you should be able to see its major deficiencies. High on the list are the following. All of the FTP functions called go off and do their actions before ever returning to our application. Some method must be provided to cancel or abort an action in progress. Further, during the actual file transfer operation, a progress window with a cancel button should be present.

As a first approach, you might try to replace the **GetFile** function with the **OpenFile** function and use **CInternetFile** class functions to perform the I/O in smaller portions. The **Seek** function can be used to initially determine the total filesize and reposition back to the beginning of the file. Now calculate how many actual input requests are needed to input the whole file. Construct a progress dialog with a slider to show the progress. Then loop using the **Read** function to input blocks. As each read completes, write that block to the local file and update the progress control. The dialog could also handle the Cancel operation.

Another design issue is that the FTP actions are synchronous. That is, once started they do not return until that action is completed, whether a few seconds or an hour. Frequently, this may not be a desirable approach. If you wish to make use of the FTP call-back status functions, then a number of changes to the design and use of the classes must be made. Sometimes connection and change directory commands can take several minutes on the busy net. The user need a way to be able to cancel these operations as well. If, for example, they decide to change directories, there ought to be a way for them to cancel that operation, for them to change their minds.

The **CInternetSession** class provides for asynchronous searches and downloading, allowing the user to perform other tasks in the interim period. Many status call-backs are available that can be used to report the progress of requests. However, asynchronous operations are more difficult to program. In the **CInternetSession** class constructor, use the flag **INTERNET_FLAG_ASYNC** and set the context word to 1. Then call **EnableStatusCallback**; it will then call-back to the pure virtual function **OnStatusCallback**. Your implementation of **OnStatusCallback** must sort out the different call-back events. However, the real problem is that in order to use the call-back scheme, you must derive your own class from **CInternetSession** to provide the **OnStatusCallback** function.

The final improvement would be to present the local side of the machine in a similar manner as the remote side, permitting the user to select files and folders, to change local directories and drives, much like other ftp client programs do. Add in an arrow button to transfer files from the local machine to the remote site. To do this, consider reworking the sample to use a pair of **CListViews** instead of the **CListCtrl** class. Use a splitter window to house the pair of views. Perhaps even place a tool bar with left and right arrows between the two views, indicating file transfer operations (removing the arrow button from the main tool bar).

Once you have a good feel for how the simple FTP functions operate, you can then expand into other realms, such as making your own http browser or robots. Good luck.

Chapter 14 Fancy Controls, Property Pages, Owner-drawn Controls

In this chapter, let's look over some fancier controls that can often be found in dialogs and how to work with property pages.

Property Sheets or Tabbed Dialogs

A property sheet is basically a container for multiple pages, each of which is akin to a separate dialog. In a complex application, provision for setting many options must be made, all too often in a tangled jumble of nested dialogs. Property sheets offer a very convenient wrapper that is exceedingly easy for users to manipulate. So make your users happy; give them property sheets.

Pgm14a represents the simple conversion from a menu of dialogs to a property sheet. Figures 14.1 through 14.4 show the different property pages of the Options Dialog. Each property page is a separate dialog class with all its own features. However, several additional functions are added to turn them into a unified whole and support the Apply Now button.

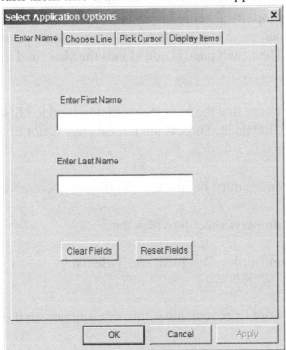

Figure 14.1 Names Property Page

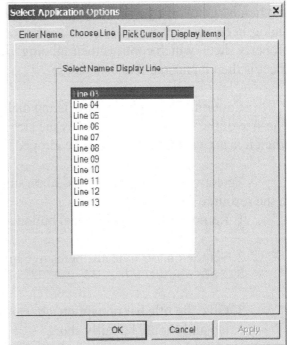

Figure 14.2 Listbox Property Page

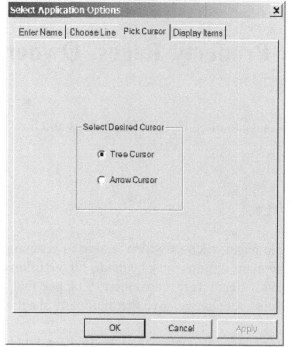

Figure 14.3 Cursors Property Page

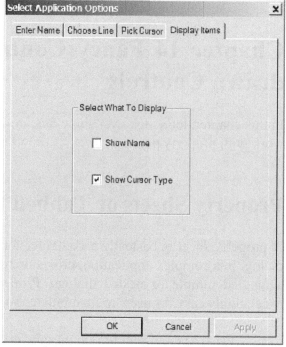

Figure 14.4 Checkbox Property Page

To create a uniform look between the pages, each of the dialogs should have the same width and height. Converting a series of dialogs into one property sheet is surprisingly easy to do! Each dialog becomes a property page. An instance of each page is allocated and one instance of the property sheet, which controls their tabbing views. Then each page is added into the sheet and the sheet is then launched. It is that simple.

Caution, when converting existing dialogs, be sure that the largest size dialog is added first. The size of the sheet is determined by the size of the first page. Thus, if the largest page is not first, when it is activated, portions may be clipped.

To convert to property pages, some small changes must be made to the dialogs themselves in the resource file.

1. Remove all OK and Cancel buttons—the property sheet provides these.

2. Set the dialog style attributes to Child, Thin Border, Disabled, and Title bar:
```
STYLE WS_CHILD | WS_VISIBLE | WS_DISABLED | WS_CAPTION
```

3. Give the title bar or caption a one or two word title; remember this title appears on the tab and should be fairly short.

4. Alter the menu. Remove all of the menu items for the dialogs that are now a part of the property sheet. Add a new menu item to launch the property sheet.

5. Add another include for afxcmn.h which contains the Windows common controls

Listing for File: Pgm14a.rc

```
...
MAINMENU MENU DISCARDABLE
BEGIN
    POPUP "&Dialogs"
    BEGIN
        MENUITEM "&Set Options",                CM_PROPERTYSHEET
        MENUITEM "Show &Location of Cursor",     CM_LOCATION_DLG
    END
    POPUP "&Help"
    BEGIN
        MENUITEM "Help &About",                  CM_ABOUT
    END
END
... modeless locate dialog is not part of the property pages

IDD_RADIO DIALOG DISCARDABLE  20, 40, 200, 200
STYLE WS_CHILD | WS_VISIBLE | WS_DISABLED | WS_CAPTION
CAPTION "Pick Cursor"
FONT 8, "MS Sans Serif"
BEGIN
    CONTROL         "Tree Cursor",IDC_RADIOBUTTON_TREE,"Button",
                    BS_AUTORADIOBUTTON | WS_GROUP | WS_TABSTOP,66,78,52,13
    CONTROL         "Arrow Cursor",IDC_RADIOBUTTON_ARROW,"Button",
                    BS_AUTORADIOBUTTON | WS_TABSTOP,66,97,52,13
    GROUPBOX        "Select Desired Cursor",IDC_GRPBTN,49,60,87,66,WS_GROUP
END


IDD_CHECKBOX DIALOG DISCARDABLE  20, 40, 200, 200
STYLE WS_CHILD | WS_VISIBLE | WS_DISABLED | WS_CAPTION
CAPTION "Display Items"
FONT 8, "MS Sans Serif"
BEGIN
    CONTROL         "Show Name",IDC_CHECK_NAME,"Button",BS_AUTOCHECKBOX |
                    WS_TABSTOP,64,70,69,15
    CONTROL         "Show Cursor Type",IDC_CHECK_CURSOR,"Button",
                    BS_AUTOCHECKBOX | WS_TABSTOP,64,97,69,15
    GROUPBOX        "Select What To Display",IDC_STATIC,48,47,96,83
END


IDD_LISTBOX DIALOG DISCARDABLE  20, 40, 200, 200
STYLE WS_CHILD | WS_VISIBLE | WS_DISABLED | WS_CAPTION
CAPTION "Choose Line"
FONT 8, "MS Sans Serif"
BEGIN
    LISTBOX         IDC_LISTBOX,44,33,102,125,LBS_SORT |
                    LBS_NOINTEGRALHEIGHT | WS_VSCROLL | WS_TABSTOP
    GROUPBOX        "Select Names Display Line",IDC_STATIC,32,15,129,158
END


IDD_EDITDLG DIALOG DISCARDABLE  20, 40, 200, 200
STYLE WS_CHILD | WS_VISIBLE | WS_DISABLED | WS_CAPTION
CAPTION "Enter Name"
```

```
FONT 8, "MS Sans Serif"
BEGIN
    CTEXT             "Enter First Name",-1,36,35,56,10
    EDITTEXT          IDC_FIRSTNAME,36,48,110,14
    LTEXT             "Enter Last Name",-1,36,80,56,10
    EDITTEXT          IDC_LASTNAME,36,94,110,14
    PUSHBUTTON        "Clear Fields",IDC_CLEARBUTTON,39,144,46,14
    PUSHBUTTON        "Reset Fields",IDC_RESETBUTTON,99,144,46,14
END

...
```

MFC Property Sheet Pgm14a

The new MFC classes are **CPropertySheet** and **CPropertyPage**. After converting the resource file, be sure that your stdafx.h header includes the header file that defines the new Windows common controls.

```
        #include <afxcmn.h>   // MFC support for Windows Common Controls
```

Next, modify the message response map to include a property sheet menu item command handler and remove all of the dialog command launchers.

```
    BEGIN_MESSAGE_MAP(MainFrame, CFrameWnd)
     ON_WM_SIZE ()
     ON_WM_PAINT ()
     ON_WM_CREATE ()
     ON_WM_CLOSE ()
     ON_WM_DESTROY ()
     ON_WM_MOUSEMOVE ()
     ON_COMMAND(CM_PROPERTYSHEET,CmPropertySheet)
     ON_COMMAND(CM_LOCATION_DLG,  CmLocationDlg)
     ON_COMMAND(CM_ABOUT,         CmAbout)
    END_MESSAGE_MAP()
```

The four dialogs must now be derived from the **CPropertyPage** class. Begin with the simpler cases. Here, I assume that you may be converting the sample dialogs from Chapter 7 of the Windows MFC Programming I samples. CRadioBtnsDlg is altered to RadioBtnsPP. The base constructor only requires the ID of the dialog in the resource file. Thus, the only changes for the radio button definition were the class name and the constructor.

How is the data transferred to and from the dialog controls? There are a number of ways, from manual to automatic to public data member access. In this sample, I will show a wide variety of ways.

Listing for File: RadioBtnsPP.h

```
#pragma once

/**********************************************************************/
/*                                                                    */
/*  RadioBtnsPP: Property Page to select which type of cursor is desired  */
/*                Use automatic DDX xfer method                       */
/*                                                                    */
/**********************************************************************/

class RadioBtnsPP : public CPropertyPage {
      DECLARE_DYNAMIC(RadioBtnsPP)
public:
 int which_btn_is_on;
 enum Order {Tree, Arrow}; // convenience enum to determine which button is on

              RadioBtnsPP();
      virtual ~RadioBtnsPP();
      enum { IDD = IDD_RADIO };

 afx_msg void OnBnClickedRadiobuttonTree();
 afx_msg void OnBnClickedRadiobuttonArrow();
 virtual BOOL OnApply();

protected:
 virtual void DoDataExchange(CDataExchange* pDX);      // DDX/DDV support
 DECLARE_MESSAGE_MAP()
};
```

To enable the Apply Now button, whenever a change is detected in any of the dialog controls, one must call

```
      SetModified (TRUE);
```

This enables the property sheet's Apply Now button. Thus, with radio buttons, add a member function to the Button Clicked property, as highlighted above.

Now to actually implement the Apply Now button, you need to respond to the OnApply message. That prototype is also highlighted above.

With this property page, the client is responsible for setting and getting the values in the public data members. This is also true of the CheckBoxPP page.

Listing for File: CheckBoxPP.h

```
#pragma once

/*************************************************************************/
/*                                                                       */
/*  CheckBoxPP: Property Page to determine what to display: names or cursor*/
/*              Use automatic DDX exchange method                        */
/*                                                                       */
/*************************************************************************/

class CheckBoxPP : public CPropertyPage {
       DECLARE_DYNAMIC(CheckBoxPP)
public:
 int  ck_show_name;        // show names when TRUE - accessed by parent
 int  ck_show_cursor;      // show cursor when TRUE - accessed by parent

 enum { IDD = IDD_CHECKBOX };

       CheckBoxPP();
       virtual ~CheckBoxPP();

 afx_msg void OnBnClickedCheckName();
 afx_msg void OnBnClickedCheckCursor();
 virtual BOOL OnApply();

protected:
       virtual void DoDataExchange(CDataExchange* pDX);      // DDX/DDV support
       DECLARE_MESSAGE_MAP()
};
```

The ListBoxLinesPP shows which line the first name will be shown in the main window. Our first problem now arises. In order to access the MainFrame's public members containing the strings to add and the current line number transfer buffer, **GetParent** was used. Now, however, the parent is the **CPropertySheet** class. One quick solution is to pass a pointer to the MainFrame object itself which can be saved in a protected member and used to access the numerous transfer fields required.

The other problem only surfaced during test runs. If a new line was selected and the OK button pressed, the new line selection was passed on back properly through the **OnOK** function. However, if after the selection was made a new page was activated and then OK pressed, the new line selection was not passed back; **OnOK** was not called. When a page looses the focus, the **OnKillActive** function is invoked; so I simply saved the current selection here as well.

The notification message that something has changed in the list control is the on selection change message.

Listing for File ListBoxLinesPP.h

```
#pragma once

class MainFrame;
```

```
/************************************************************************/
/*                                                                      */
/*  ListBoxLinesPP: Property page to select which line to display name on  */
/*                  Get a ptr to parent to access xfer information      */
/*                                                                      */
/************************************************************************/

class ListBoxLinesPP : public CPropertyPage {
 DECLARE_DYNAMIC(ListBoxLinesPP)

 MainFrame *ptrframe;

public:
              ListBoxLinesPP (MainFrame* ptrfrm);
 virtual      ~ListBoxLinesPP();
 virtual BOOL  OnInitDialog ();  // fill up list box

 afx_msg void OnLbnSelchangeListbox();
 virtual BOOL OnApply();

 enum { IDD = IDD_LISTBOX };

protected:
 afx_msg virtual void  OnOK ();  // trap ok button to send item index num
 afx_msg virtual BOOL  OnKillActive ();
 DECLARE_MESSAGE_MAP()
};
```

Finally, the NamesDlg was modified to a CPropertyPage. This dialog is passed a transfer buffer containing the first and last name strings. Here, the data transfer is done manually. Provision is made for a reset and clear operation as well.

Listing for File: TransferName.h

```
#pragma once

// transfer buffer for dialogs
const int MAX_NAME_LEN = 40;     // max length of first and last names allowed

struct  TRANSFER_NAMES {          // edit dialog transfer buffer structure
 char first_name[MAX_NAME_LEN]; // members must be in the same order as
 char last_name[MAX_NAME_LEN];  //  the CEdit controls are created
};
```

OnKillActive added for the same reason as before with the listbox. To avoid the **GetParent** problem, a pointer to the transfer buffer is passed to the constructor and saved in the inline constructor. The controls are Edits. To detect changes, respond to the changed property of the edit control, highlighted in boldface below.

Listing for File: NamesPP.h

```
#pragma once
#include "TransferNames.h"
```

```
/****************************************************************/
/*                                                              */
/*   NamesPP: Property Page entering first and last name        */
/*            Pass a pointer to the transfer buffer             */
/*            and in OnInitDialog copy from MainFrame xfer buffer */
/*            Using manual methods of data xfer                 */
/*                                                              */
/****************************************************************/

class NamesPP : public CPropertyPage {
        DECLARE_DYNAMIC(NamesPP)
public:
        enum { IDD = IDD_EDITDLG };

protected:
TRANSFER_NAMES original_names;   // saves original names before this edit
TRANSFER_NAMES *ptrparentbuf;    // points to parent's xfer buffer

public:
                NamesPP(TRANSFER_NAMES *ptrnam);
        virtual ~NamesPP();

afx_msg void    OnClear();    // blank both names
afx_msg void    OnReset();    // reset names back to originals
afx_msg void    OnOK ();      // get and save new name
afx_msg void    OnCancel ();  // pitch new name
afx_msg BOOL    OnKillActive (); // get new name here too
afx_msg void    OnEnChangeFirstname();
afx_msg void    OnEnChangeLastname();
virtual BOOL    OnApply();

protected:
 virtual BOOL   OnInitDialog (); // setup dialog controls
        DECLARE_MESSAGE_MAP()
};
```

The implementations are straightforward.

Listing for File: RadioBtns.cpp

```
...
IMPLEMENT_DYNAMIC(RadioBtnsPP, CPropertyPage)

RadioBtnsPP::RadioBtnsPP() : CPropertyPage(RadioBtnsPP::IDD),
                             which_btn_is_on(0) { }

RadioBtnsPP::~RadioBtnsPP() { }

void RadioBtnsPP::DoDataExchange(CDataExchange* pDX) {
 CPropertyPage::DoDataExchange(pDX);
 DDX_Radio (pDX, IDC_RADIOBUTTON_TREE, which_btn_is_on);
}

BEGIN_MESSAGE_MAP(RadioBtnsPP, CPropertyPage)
 ON_BN_CLICKED(IDC_RADIOBUTTON_TREE, &RadioBtnsPP::OnBnClickedRadiobuttonTree)
 ON_BN_CLICKED(IDC_RADIOBUTTON_ARROW,
                              &RadioBtnsPP::OnBnClickedRadiobuttonArrow)
END_MESSAGE_MAP()

void RadioBtnsPP::OnBnClickedRadiobuttonTree() {
 SetModified (TRUE);
}

void RadioBtnsPP::OnBnClickedRadiobuttonArrow() {
 SetModified (TRUE);
}

BOOL RadioBtnsPP::OnApply() {
 UpdateData (TRUE);
 return CPropertyPage::OnApply();
}
```

Listing for File: CheckBoxPP.cpp

```
IMPLEMENT_DYNAMIC(CheckBoxPP, CPropertyPage)

CheckBoxPP::CheckBoxPP() : CPropertyPage(CheckBoxPP::IDD),
                ck_show_name(0), ck_show_cursor(0) { }

CheckBoxPP::~CheckBoxPP() { }

void CheckBoxPP::DoDataExchange(CDataExchange* pDX) {
 CPropertyPage::DoDataExchange(pDX);
 DDX_Check (pDX, IDC_CHECK_NAME, ck_show_name);
 DDX_Check (pDX, IDC_CHECK_CURSOR, ck_show_cursor);
}

BEGIN_MESSAGE_MAP(CheckBoxPP, CPropertyPage)
 ON_BN_CLICKED(IDC_CHECK_NAME, &CheckBoxPP::OnBnClickedCheckName)
 ON_BN_CLICKED(IDC_CHECK_CURSOR, &CheckBoxPP::OnBnClickedCheckCursor)
END_MESSAGE_MAP()

void CheckBoxPP::OnBnClickedCheckName() {
 SetModified (TRUE);
}
```

```
void CheckBoxPP::OnBnClickedCheckCursor() {
 SetModified (TRUE);
}

BOOL CheckBoxPP::OnApply() {
 UpdateData (TRUE);
 return CPropertyPage::OnApply();
}
```

Listing for File: ListBoxPP.cpp

```
...
IMPLEMENT_DYNAMIC(ListBoxLinesPP, CPropertyPage)

ListBoxLinesPP::ListBoxLinesPP (MainFrame* ptrfrm)
                    : CPropertyPage(ListBoxLinesPP::IDD) {
 ptrframe = ptrfrm;
}


ListBoxLinesPP::~ListBoxLinesPP() { }

/*********************************************************************/
/*                                                                   */
/*   ListBoxLinesPP::OnInitDialog: fill up the list box              */
/*                                                                   */
/*********************************************************************/

BOOL  ListBoxLinesPP::OnInitDialog () {
 // obtain a pointer to the existing listbox
 CListBox *ptrlistbox = (CListBox*) (GetDlgItem (IDC_LISTBOX));

 // fill up list box from parent's line array
 for (int i=0; i<ptrframe->linetot; i++) {
  ptrlistbox->AddString (ptrframe->line[i]);  // insert lines into dlg
  if (i+3 == ptrframe->linenum) ptrlistbox->SetCurSel (i);
 }
 return TRUE;
}

BEGIN_MESSAGE_MAP(ListBoxLinesPP, CPropertyPage)
 ON_COMMAND(IDOK, OnOK)
 ON_LBN_SELCHANGE(IDC_LISTBOX, &ListBoxLinesPP::OnLbnSelchangeListbox)
END_MESSAGE_MAP()

/*********************************************************************/
/*                                                                   */
/*   ListBoxLinesPP::OnOK: notify parent of the selected index number */
/*                                                                   */
/*********************************************************************/

void   ListBoxLinesPP::OnOK () {
 // get a ptr to the listbox control itself
 CListBox *ptrlistbox = (CListBox*) (GetDlgItem (IDC_LISTBOX));
 // save the current user selection index
 ptrframe->linenumnew = ptrlistbox->GetCurSel ();
 CPropertyPage::OnOK (); // invoke base class to destroy
}
```

```
/*****************************************************************/
/*                                                               */
/*   ListBoxLinesPP::OnKillActive: notify parent of sel index number  */
/*                                                               */
/* Note: needed because OnOK is not called when OK is pressed if this page */
/*        is not the current visible page in the Sheet          */
/*                                                               */
/*****************************************************************/

BOOL  ListBoxLinesPP::OnKillActive () {
 // get a ptr to the listbox control itself
 CListBox *ptrlistbox = (CListBox*) (GetDlgItem (IDC_LISTBOX));

 // save the current user selection index
 ptrframe->linenumnew = ptrlistbox->GetCurSel ();

 return CPropertyPage::OnKillActive (); // invoke base class to destroy
}

void ListBoxLinesPP::OnLbnSelchangeListbox() {
 SetModified (TRUE);
}

BOOL ListBoxLinesPP::OnApply() {
 // get a ptr to the listbox control itself
 CListBox *ptrlistbox = (CListBox*) (GetDlgItem (IDC_LISTBOX));
 // save the current user selection index
 ptrframe->linenumnew = ptrlistbox->GetCurSel ();
 ptrframe->Invalidate ();
 return CPropertyPage::OnApply();
}
```

With controls, you have a choice. You can set up a data member for the control, here a **CListBox** or you can dynamically obtain a pointer to the control so that you can call its functions. Here, I chose to just obtain a pointer to the listbox when needed. In **OnInitDialog**, I obtained a pointer to the listbox and used the pointer to the MainFrame line strings to add them into the listbox.

Whenever a change in selection occurs, I store the index of the selection, which will become the new line number on which to display the first name back into the MainFrame variable.

Listing for File: NamesPP.cpp

```
...
IMPLEMENT_DYNAMIC(NamesPP, CPropertyPage)

NamesPP::NamesPP (TRANSFER_NAMES *ptrnam) : CPropertyPage(NamesPP::IDD) {
 ptrparentbuf = ptrnam;
}

NamesPP::~NamesPP() { }

BEGIN_MESSAGE_MAP(NamesPP, CPropertyPage)
 ON_BN_CLICKED(IDC_CLEARBUTTON, &NamesPP::OnClear)
 ON_BN_CLICKED(IDC_RESETBUTTON, &NamesPP::OnReset)
```

```
 ON_EN_CHANGE(IDC_FIRSTNAME, &NamesPP::OnEnChangeFirstname)
 ON_EN_CHANGE(IDC_LASTNAME, &NamesPP::OnEnChangeLastname)
END_MESSAGE_MAP()


/**********************************************************************/
/*                                                                    */
/*   NamesPP::OnInitDialog: loads xfer buffer,save area in case of restore */
/*                          and loads in init values for edit controls */
/*                                                                    */
/**********************************************************************/

BOOL       NamesPP::OnInitDialog () {
 // copy the original contents of the xfer buffer to dlg's save area
 memcpy (&original_names, ptrparentbuf, sizeof (TRANSFER_NAMES));

 // copy original contents into the dlg controls
 SetDlgItemText (IDC_FIRSTNAME, original_names.first_name);
 SetDlgItemText (IDC_LASTNAME,  original_names.last_name);
 return TRUE;
}


/**********************************************************************/
/*                                                                    */
/*   NamesPP::CmClear: remove contents of both fields, appears blank  */
/*                                                                    */
/**********************************************************************/

void NamesPP::OnClear() {
 // clear transfer buffer - set to nulls
 memset (ptrparentbuf, 0, sizeof (TRANSFER_NAMES));
 // clear dlg controls
 SetDlgItemText (IDC_FIRSTNAME, ptrparentbuf->first_name);
 SetDlgItemText (IDC_LASTNAME,  ptrparentbuf->last_name);
}


/**********************************************************************/
/*                                                                    */
/*   NamesPP::CmReset: reinsert the original values into the name fields */
/*                                                                    */
/**********************************************************************/

void NamesPP::OnReset() {
 // copy saved original values back into the transfer buffer
 memcpy (ptrparentbuf, &original_names, sizeof (TRANSFER_NAMES));
 // copy saved original values back into the edit controls boxes
 SetDlgItemText (IDC_FIRSTNAME, original_names.first_name);
 SetDlgItemText (IDC_LASTNAME,  original_names.last_name);
}


/**********************************************************************/
/*                                                                    */
/*   NamesPP::OnOk: retrieve new values                               */
/*                                                                    */
/**********************************************************************/

void NamesPP::OnOK () {
 // retrieve new values from edit controls and store in parent's xfer buffer
 GetDlgItemText (IDC_FIRSTNAME, ptrparentbuf->first_name, MAX_NAME_LEN);
```

```
 GetDlgItemText (IDC_LASTNAME,  ptrparentbuf->last_name, MAX_NAME_LEN);
 CPropertyPage::OnOK ();   // now continue the Ok process
}

/****************************************************************************/
/*                                                                        */
/* CNamesPP::OnKillActive: retrieve new values                            */
/*                                                                        */
/****************************************************************************/

BOOL NamesPP::OnKillActive () {
 // retrieve new values from edit controls and store in parent's xfer buffer
 GetDlgItemText (IDC_FIRSTNAME, ptrparentbuf->first_name, MAX_NAME_LEN);
 GetDlgItemText (IDC_LASTNAME,  ptrparentbuf->last_name, MAX_NAME_LEN);
 return CPropertyPage::OnKillActive ();   // now continue the Ok process
}

/****************************************************************************/
/*                                                                        */
/*  NamesPP::OnCancel: restore the original values into  transfer buffer  */
/*                                                                        */
/****************************************************************************/

void NamesPP::OnCancel () {
 // restore original values into the parent's transfer buffer
 memcpy (ptrparentbuf, &original_names, sizeof (TRANSFER_NAMES));
 CPropertyPage::OnCancel ();   // now continue the cancel process
}

void NamesPP::OnEnChangeFirstname () {
 SetModified (TRUE);
}

void NamesPP::OnEnChangeLastname () {
 SetModified (TRUE);
}

BOOL NamesPP::OnApply () {
 // retrieve new values from edit controls and store in parent's xfer buffer
 GetDlgItemText (IDC_FIRSTNAME, ptrparentbuf->first_name, MAX_NAME_LEN);
 GetDlgItemText (IDC_LASTNAME,  ptrparentbuf->last_name, MAX_NAME_LEN);
 GetParent()->Invalidate ();
 return CPropertyPage::OnApply ();
}
```

Launching the CPropertySheet

Next examine the implementation of the **CmPropertySheet** function in the MainFrame class that launches the action. First an automatic storage instance is allocated for each page and the transfer buffers filled by using the same coding that is removed from the corresponding dialog launchers. Then allocate one instance of the **CPropertySheet** class. Normally, the base class provides all the services required. The property sheet constructor is passed a string ID for the main title bar. Next, each page is added into the sheet using the **AddPage** function.

DoModal creates and executes the entire process, returning only when OK or Cancel buttons are pressed. Normally, one would respond only when IDOK is returned, then all the values must be recovered and implemented. However, in this case, the user may have pressed Apply Now. In this situation, he or she may then press Cancel, but the changes have already been applied. Hence, in all cases, act as if the values have been changed. However, you can so some testing of the new values versus the old, as I did below with a change in cursor.

```
void  MainFrame::CmPropertySheet () {
 RadioBtnsPP radio;
 radio.which_btn_is_on = which_cursor;// xfer current settings into dlg
 CheckBoxPP ckbox;
 ckbox.ck_show_name   = show_name;     // transfer current settings into dlg
 ckbox.ck_show_cursor = show_cursor;
 ListBoxLinesPP listbox (this);
 NamesPP edit(&xfer_edit_names);        // construct dialog
 memcpy (&xfer_edit_names, &real_names_db, sizeof (TRANSFER_NAMES));
 CPropertySheet tabdlg (IDS_TAB_TITLE);
 tabdlg.AddPage (&edit);
 tabdlg.AddPage (&listbox);
 tabdlg.AddPage (&radio);
 tabdlg.AddPage (&ckbox);

 tabdlg.DoModal (); // create & execute dlg
 if (which_cursor != radio.which_btn_is_on) {
  which_cursor = radio.which_btn_is_on;
  if (which_cursor == RadioBtnsPP::Tree) {  // install correct cursor
   hcursor =
         LoadCursor (AfxGetApp()->m_hInstance, MAKEINTRESOURCE (IDC_TREE));
   SetClassLong (m_hWnd, GCL_HCURSOR, (LONG) hcursor);
  }
  else {
   hcursor = AfxGetApp()->LoadStandardCursor (IDC_ARROW), // use arrow cur
   SetClassLong (m_hWnd, GCL_HCURSOR, (LONG) hcursor);
  }
 }
 show_name   = ckbox.ck_show_name;   // update our members for next time
 show_cursor = ckbox.ck_show_cursor;
 memcpy (&real_names_db, &xfer_edit_names, sizeof (TRANSFER_NAMES));
 if (linenumnew >= 0)              // if OK, set our new line number
  linenum = linenumnew + 3;        // save new line number
  Invalidate (); // force paint to display msg of new cursor
}
```

Listing for File: MainFrm.h

```
...
class MainFrame : public CFrameWnd {

/*****************************************************************************/
/*                                                                         */
/* Class Data Members                                                      */
/*                                                                         */
/*****************************************************************************/

public:
// transfer areas to/from dialogs - need to be public so they can be accessed
//                             from dialogs without using globals

 // accessed by location dlg directly
bool            track_on;      // when true, displays mouse coordinates

// accessed by edit names dlg directly
TRANSFER_NAMES  xfer_edit_names;  // edit names transfer buffer

// place to store current index of which radio btn is on - not accessed by dlg
int  which_cursor; // radio button xfer buffer = index of which btn is on

// place to store current checkbox statuses - not accessed by dlg
int  show_name;   // show names when TRUE - for checkboxes
int  show_cursor; // show cursor when TRUE

// members accessed by listbox dlg
char line[50][10];// lines for listbox
int  linetot;      // total lines in array that are used
int  linenumnew;   // set by CmOk
int  linenum;      // current line number to show names on

protected:
int             height;       // current client window height in pixels
int             width;        // current client window width in pixels

int             avg_caps_width;  // average capital letter width
int             avg_char_width;  // average character width
int             avg_char_height; // average character height

HCURSOR         hcursor;          // current cursor in use
HBRUSH          hbkgrndbrush;     // current background brush
LocateDlg       *ptrlocatedlg;    // ptr to the LocateDlg modeless dialog
TRANSFER_NAMES  real_names_db;    // real data base - first and last name

/*****************************************************************************/
/*                                                                         */
/* Class Functions:                                                        */
/*                                                                         */
/*****************************************************************************/

 public:
               MainFrame (const char* title); // constructor
               ~MainFrame () {}                 // destructor

 protected:
```

```
afx_msg void   OnPaint ();                        // paint the window - WM_PAINT
afx_msg int    OnCreate (LPCREATESTRUCT);         // set initial class members
afx_msg void   OnDestroy ();                      // delete inited class members
afx_msg void   OnClose ();                        // determines if app can quit yet
afx_msg void   OnSize (UINT, int, int);           // process window resize
afx_msg void   OnMouseMove (UINT, CPoint);        // track current position

afx_msg void   CmPropertySheet ();                // start tabbed dialog box
afx_msg void   CmLocationDlg ();                  // start cursor location dialog

public:
#ifdef _DEBUG
      virtual void AssertValid() const;
      virtual void Dump(CDumpContext& dc) const;
#endif
      DECLARE_MESSAGE_MAP()
};
```

Listing for File: MainFrm.cpp, Less CmPropertySheet Which Is Shown Previously

```
...
BEGIN_MESSAGE_MAP(MainFrame, CFrameWnd)
 ON_WM_SIZE ()
 ON_WM_PAINT ()
 ON_WM_CREATE ()
 ON_WM_CLOSE ()
 ON_WM_DESTROY ()
 ON_WM_MOUSEMOVE ()
 ON_COMMAND(CM_PROPERTYSHEET,CmPropertySheet)
 ON_COMMAND(CM_LOCATION_DLG, CmLocationDlg)
END_MESSAGE_MAP()


/*********************************************************************/
/*                                                                   */
/* MainFrame: initialize members and calls Create                    */
/*                                                                   */
/*********************************************************************/

MainFrame::MainFrame (const char* title)
                    : CFrameWnd () {
 DWORD style = WS_OVERLAPPEDWINDOW;               // set basic window styles
 style &= !(WS_MINIMIZEBOX | WS_MAXIMIZEBOX);     // remove max/min buttons
 style |= WS_SYSMENU | WS_THICKFRAME;

 CRect rect (10, 10, 600, 400);                   // set init pos and size

 LoadAccelTable ("MAINMENU"); // install keybd accelerators

 Create ( AfxRegisterWndClass (
          CS_VREDRAW | CS_HREDRAW,                // register window style UINT
          NULL,                                   // will load in our cursor next
          ::CreateSolidBrush (GetSysColor(COLOR_WINDOW)),
          AfxGetApp()->LoadIcon (IDI_TREE)),// set min icon
          title,             // window caption
          style,             // wndclass DWORD style
          rect,              // set initial window position
```

```
            0,                      // the parent window, here none
            "MAINMENU");            // assign the main menu

  ptrlocatedlg = NULL;    // set no TLocateDlg modeless cursor pos yet
  track_on = false;       // indicate mouse position tracking is not on yet

  // clear and set all transfer buffers

  memset (&real_names_db, 0, sizeof(TRANSFER_NAMES)); // initialize names

  which_cursor = RadioBtnsPP::Tree; // set our member to default cursor

  // load that cursor
  hcursor = LoadCursor (AfxGetApp()->m_hInstance, MAKEINTRESOURCE (IDC_TREE));
  SetClassLong (m_hWnd, GCL_HCURSOR, (LONG) hcursor);

  show_name    = FALSE;  // init check box xfer buf
  show_cursor  = TRUE;   // show cursor type but not names
  linenum      = 3;      // set default line for showing names on
}

/***************************************************************************/
/*                                                                         */
/* OnCreate: make toolbar and set up the window                            */
/*                                                                         */
/***************************************************************************/

int MainFrame::OnCreate(LPCREATESTRUCT lpCreateStruct) {
 if (CFrameWnd::OnCreate(lpCreateStruct) == -1)
  return -1;

 TEXTMETRIC  tm;

 // set the system font's characteristics in tm
 CClientDC *ptrdc = new CClientDC (this);  // acquire a DC
 ptrdc->GetTextMetrics (&tm);              // get the information
 delete ptrdc;                             // delete the dc

 // calculate average character parameters
 avg_char_width  = tm.tmAveCharWidth;
 avg_char_height = tm.tmHeight + tm.tmExternalLeading;
 avg_caps_width  = (tm.tmPitchAndFamily & 1 ? 3 : 2) * avg_char_width / 2;

 // the following illustrates how to change the background color AFTER
 // it has been set initially in the wndclass structure
 // you need to get the handle of the original brush so that it can be
 // deleted, if not, you will get a memory leak

 hbkgrndbrush = CreateSolidBrush (RGB (192, 192, 192)); // make backgnd brush

 // get old brush so we can delete it after installing new brush
 HBRUSH oldbrush = (HBRUSH) (GetClassLong (m_hWnd, GCL_HBRBACKGROUND));
 // install new brush
 SetClassLong (m_hWnd, GCL_HBRBACKGROUND, (LONG) hbkgrndbrush);
 DeleteObject (oldbrush); // failure to delete old brush = memory leak
      return 0;
 }
```

```
/**********************************************************************/
/*                                                                    */
/* OnDestroy:      delete inited items                                */
/*                                                                    */
/**********************************************************************/

void MainFrame::OnDestroy () {
 if (ptrlocatedlg) delete ptrlocatedlg;      // only delete it if it was newed
 CFrameWnd::OnDestroy ();
}


/**********************************************************************/
/*                                                                    */
/* OnSize: acquire the current dimensions of the client window        */
/*                                                                    */
/**********************************************************************/

void MainFrame::OnSize (UINT a, int b, int c) {
 CFrameWnd::OnSize (a, b, c);
 CRect rect;
 GetClientRect (&rect);              // get the size of the client window
 height = rect.Height();             // calc and save current height
 width  = rect.Width();              // calc and save current width

 char msg[10];
 int  i, j;

 // now dynamically adjust the number of possible lines upon which the names
 // can be displayed:

 // retrieve printf control string "Line %02d"
 LoadString (AfxGetApp()->m_hInstance, IDS_LINEMSG, msg, sizeof(msg));

 // insert line choices into the list box lines that will be loaded into box
 j = height / avg_char_height - 5;
 // -3 for the cursor msgs; -2 since 3 lines of names

 if (j<0) j=1;               // set at least line 3
 linetot = j;
 for (i=0; i<j; i++) wsprintf (line[i], msg, i+3);

 Invalidate ();              // force repainting of window
}


/**********************************************************************/
/*                                                                    */
/* OnMouseMove: display current mouse position                        */
/*                                                                    */
/**********************************************************************/

void MainFrame::OnMouseMove (UINT, CPoint pt) {
 // if tracking is on, force the modeless dialog to display new position
 if (track_on) ptrlocatedlg->ShowPos (pt);
}


/**********************************************************************/
/*                                                                    */
/* OnPaint: displays instructions and the current system color in use */
```

```
/*                                                                        */
/************************************************************************/

void MainFrame::OnPaint () {
 CPaintDC dc (this);
 CString msg;
 dc.SetBkMode (TRANSPARENT);

 if (show_cursor) {
  if (which_cursor == RadioBtnsPP::Tree) msg.LoadString (IDS_ISTREE);
  else msg.LoadString (IDS_ISARROW);
  dc.TextOut (avg_char_width, avg_char_height, msg);
 }
 if (show_name) {
  msg.LoadString (IDS_NAMEID);
  dc.TextOut (avg_char_width, avg_char_height*(linenum), msg);
  dc.TextOut (avg_char_width, avg_char_height*(linenum+1),
              real_names_db.first_name);
  dc.TextOut (avg_char_width, avg_char_height*(linenum+2),
              real_names_db.last_name);
 }
}

/************************************************************************/
/*                                                                        */
/* OnClose: determine if the app can be shut down                         */
/*                                                                        */
/************************************************************************/

void MainFrame::OnClose () {
 CString msgtitle;
 CString msgtext;
 msgtext.LoadString (IDS_MSG_QUIT);
 msgtitle.LoadString (IDS_MSG_QUERY);

 if (MessageBox (msgtext, msgtitle, MB_YESNO | MB_ICONQUESTION) == IDYES)
  CFrameWnd::OnClose ();
}

/************************************************************************/
/*                                                                        */
/* CmLocationDlg: cursor location modeless dialog activation              */
/*               No data xfer - ShowPos updates the dlg controls          */
/*                                                                        */
/************************************************************************/

void MainFrame::CmLocationDlg () {
 // note dialog already exists - simply Create a new instance and show it
 if (!track_on) {                      // avoid multiple instances of the dlg
  ptrlocatedlg = new LocateDlg (this);
  POINT p;
  GetCursorPos (&p);                    // retrieve current mouse position
  CPoint pt (p);                        // convert to CPoint
  ptrlocatedlg->ShowPos (pt);           // display new position
  ptrlocatedlg->ShowWindow (SW_SHOW);   // make dialog visible
  track_on = TRUE;                      // indicate tracking is active
 }
}
```

Using Sliders and Spin Controls

Slider (Track bar) and Spin (Up/Down) controls can sometime make the user interface easier for the person. In this case, the more frequently adjusted aspect of the display may well be on which line the first name appears. This is an ideal candidate for either of these controls. Figure 14.5 shows both in operation.

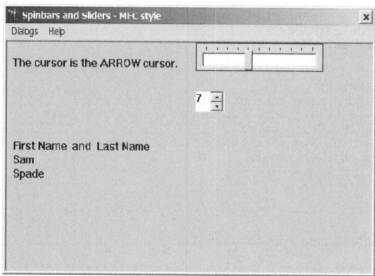

Figure 14.5 The Slider and Spin Controls

The slider or track bar is a smaller sized variation of the scroll bar giving clearer view of the position. The spin or Up/Down control (which can also be Left/Right control) allows for fast digital incrementing. Spin controls often have a corresponding edit control in which the numerical position is recorded or manually set by the user. This "buddy" edit window is coupled to the Up/Down arrows. Actually, the spin control appends itself onto the side of the edit control window. Anytime the spin buttons are pressed, the spin control converts the integer position into a string and displays it in the edit control.

Sliders send scroll messages and are identified with the TB_ prefix, Track bar and have numerically the same values as the corresponding SB_ scroll bar messages. Spin controls with buddy edit controls are accessed via the edit control's **CWnd** base class, **GetWindowText**.

In Pgm14b, a slider control appears at the top right of the main window area and can be used as an alternative method to set the line number on which the names are displayed. The spin and edit control appear just below the slider control and provide yet another method to set the display line number. The three independent methods of adjusting the display line number have to be coordinated with each other.

MFC Implementation of Sliders and Spin Control Buttons

To use any of the new controls, be sure that stdafx.h includes

```
#include <afxcmn.h>  // the common new controls
```

Sliders are implemented by the **CSliderCtrl** class; spin buttons by **CSpinButtonCtrl**. The edit control would be the normal **CEdit** class. Since these controls are going to be placed directly in our window and not in a dialog, they have to be constructed using the manual method instead of using the resource editor. Three control IDs are defined in the resource.h file:

```
#define IDC_SLIDER           213
#define IDC_SPINEDIT         214
#define IDC_SPINCTL          215
```

Next, the MainFrame class must define three members that are used to instantiate these controls:

```
CSliderCtrl    slider;  // slider control to adjust display
Cedit          editctl; // buddy edit box for the spin control
CSpinButtonCtrl spinctl; // up/down spin button
```

In the MainFrame's **OnCreate** function, after the base class has been constructed, instances of the three controls are created.

```
int       MainFrame::OnCreate (LPCREATESTRUCT lpCS) {
 int retcd = CFrameWnd::OnCreate (lpCS); // pass to base class
    ...
// construct the slider/trackbar control
CRect r (300,0,500,40);
slider.Create (TBS_HORZ | TBS_AUTOTICKS | TBS_BOTH |
               TBS_ENABLESELRANGE | WS_CHILD | WS_VISIBLE |
               WS_BORDER, r, this, IDC_SLIDER);
slider.SetRange (3, linetot + 2, TRUE); // force into range
slider.SetLineSize(1);      // set amt a click/arrow key reports
slider.SetPageSize(1);      // set amount one PgXX reports
slider.SetPos(3);           // set initial position
// create the edit control for the spin control's buddy window
CRect er (300,70,345,100);
editctl.Create (WS_CHILD | WS_VISIBLE, er, this, IDC_SPINEDIT);
// create the spin or up/down control
CRect sr (300,70,365,100);
spinctl.Create (UDS_ARROWKEYS | UDS_SETBUDDYINT |
                UDS_ALIGNRIGHT | WS_CHILD | WS_BORDER |
                WS_VISIBLE, sr, this, IDC_SPINCTL);
spinctl.SetBuddy (&editctl); // set edit ctrl as buddy window
spinctl.SetRange (3, linetot + 2); // set range of spin ctrl
spinctl.SetPos (3);                // set its initial position
return retcd;
}
```

Examine the **Create** for the slider. The first parameter is the window style for the control. Notice the new style options:

```
TBS_HORZ         - default horizontal orientation
TBS_VERT         - make slider vertical
TBS_AUTOTICKS    - create tick marks for each unit in the range
TBS_NOTICKS      - display no tick marks
TBS_BOTTOM       - place tick marks on bottom only
TBS_TOP          - place tick marks on top only
TBS_RIGHT        - place tick marks on right only
TBS_LEFT         - place tick marks on left only
TBS_BOTH         - place tick marks on both sides
TBS_ENABLESELRANGE - place triangles on each end point
```

Design Rule: Since the control is being manually constructed, you must add in the WS_CHILD, WS_VISIBLE, and WS_BORDER options or the control will not be visible.

The **CRect r** defines the initial placement of the slider as well as its dimensions. For all of these new controls, I have used absolute numbers so that you can quickly see their exact values and use. However, in most applications, you will position them proportionally to other items, such as the client area available.

Next, the initial range of slider motion is set using **SetRange**, giving the minimum and then maximum line numbers. The third parameter, when TRUE, forces a redrawing of the control with this new range, including the tick marks. Next, the **SetLineSize** and **SetPageSize** are used to set the integer number of scroll units to be reported for the scrolling events. I use a value of one for both in this example because the range is so small. Finally, the slider's thumb bar position is set to the initial position of line 3 by using **SetPos**. From now on, slider events send normal scrolling messages. Hence, **WM_HSCROLL** messages must be monitored.

To construct a spin control with its buddy edit window, the edit control is created and then the spin control. The spin control also has some new style identifiers including:

```
UDS_HORZ         - arrow buttons are left/right
                   note default is up/down
UDS_WRAP         - causes the position to wrap around the
                   limits - so an increment beyond max val
                   gives min val
UDS_ARROWKEYS    - allows the arrow keys to activate the
                   buttons
UDS_SETBUDDYINT  - sets the text in a buddy window on any
                   change
UDS_NOTHOUSANDS  - do not insert commas every three decimal
                   places
UDS_AUTOBUDDY    - automatically selects the previous window
                   as the buddy window - use with care
UDS_ALIGNRIGHT   - positions spin ctrl to the right of the
                   buddy
```

```
UDS_ALIGNLEFT     - positions spin ctrl to the left of the
                    buddy - note that spin ctrl size is forced
                    to fit the buddy window
```

Again you **must** add in the **WS_CHILD, WS_VISIBLE**, and **WS_BORDER** options or the control is not visible. Next, the buddy edit control window is attached as the spin control's buddy window by using the **SetBuddy** function which is passed the address of the base class **CWnd**. The range is set by **SetRange** providing the minimum and then the maximum values. Finally, the spin controls initial position is set with **SetPos**. Notice that the spin control subsequently sends the edit control a string version of its initial position, here line 3.

Now examine what steps are required when the user changes the main window's size, **OnSize**. The maximum number of lines is altered by the window's size. Thus, a new range of line number values must be installed using both the slider's and spin's **SetRange** functions. As a precaution, the current position is also reset.

```
void        MainFrame::OnSize (UINT a, int b, int c) {
  CFrameWnd::OnSize (a, b, c);
  CRect rect;
  GetClientRect (&rect);
  ...
  // set new slider and spin controls' range based on current
  // size and set their current position
  slider.SetRange (3, linetot + 2, TRUE);
  slider.SetPos (linenum);
  spinctl.SetRange (3, linetot + 2);
  spinctl.SetPos (linenum);
  Invalidate ();           // force repainting of window
}
```

In **OnPaint**, two messages are displayed to provide instructions for the user. **OnPaint** repaints the whole main window which then forces the two controls to repaint themselves, yielding screen flicker. But for a simple example, let's live with this.

```
void        MainFrame::OnPaint () {
  CPaintDC dc (this);
  CString msg;
  dc.SetBkMode (TRANSPARENT);
  // display heading for the slider and spin controls
  msg.LoadString (IDS_SLIDER);
  dc.TextOut (300, 45, msg);
  msg.LoadString (IDS_SPINEDIT);
  dc.TextOut (300, 102, msg);
  ...
}
```

Examine the small changes in the **CmPropertySheet** menu item function that launches the property sheet dialog. Since the user can change the line number from a property page, when the property sheet terminates, the current positions of the slider and spin controls must be updated:

```
void        MainFrame::CmPropertySheet () {
  ...
  tabdlg.DoModal();          // create & execute dlg
  which_cursor = radio.which_btn_is_on;  // update with check
  show_name   = ckbox.ck_show_name;
  show_cursor = ckbox.ck_show_cursor;
  memcpy (&real_names_db, &xfer_edit_names,
          sizeof (TRANSFER_NAMES));
  if (linenumnew >= 0) { // if OK, set our new line number
    linenum = linenumnew + 3; // save new line number
    slider.SetPos (linenum);  // update slider's position
    spinctl.SetPos (linenum); // update spin control's pos
  }
  ...
```

Now for the dynamic interactions with the controls. First let's see how the slider interacts. Whenever a slider motion occurs, whether by mouse or keyboard event, the slider sends its parent window a **WM_HSCROLL** message, using **TB_** identifiers that parallel and actually have the same numerical values as the corresponding **WM_HSCROLL** messages. The message map table has two new entries; one for the **WM_HSCROLL** slider messages and **EN_CHANGE** edit control messages. The edit control sends its message after it has altered the text in its small window. The message map appears.

```
BEGIN_MESSAGE_MAP(MainFrame, CFrameWnd)
  ON_WM_HSCROLL() // trap slider/track bar events
  // trap spin changes
  ON_EN_CHANGE (IDC_SPINEDIT, OnSpinChange)
  ...
END_MESSAGE_MAP()
```

The coding of the **OnHScroll** member function closely resembles a normal horizontal scroll bar event handler.

```
void MainFrame::OnHScroll (UINT type, UINT pos, CScrollBar*) {
  switch (type) {
  case TB_BOTTOM:        // slider to min value
    linenum = 3; break;
  case TB_LINEDOWN:      // right/down arrow
  case TB_PAGEDOWN:      // pgdn key or mouse click before slider
    linenum++; break;
  case TB_LINEUP:        // left/up arrow
  case TB_PAGEUP:        // pgup key or mouse click after slider
    linenum--; break;
  case TB_THUMBPOSITION: // slider moved using the mouse to pos
  case TB_THUMBTRACK:    // slider dragged using the mouse to pos
    linenum = pos; break;
  case TB_TOP:           // slider to max position
    linenum = linetot + 2; break;
```

```
};
// force into the current range
if (linenum <3) linenum = 3;
if (linenum > linetot + 2) linenum = linetot + 2;
// update all ctrls to new settings, both slider, spin and edit
slider.SetPos (linenum);
spinctl.SetPos (linenum);
Invalidate();       // repaint to display at the new line number
}
```

Notice that after assigning a proposed new line number, it is then forced back into range once more and the current position of both controls are updated. In the **OnSpinChange** function, the current text is retrieved using the **CWnd** member function **GetWindowText**, converted into an integer and forced back into range. Notice that only the slider's position is then reset. If we also attempted to reset the edit control, we would preclude the user entering a two digit number. Every time the user entered 1 for 13, we would reject it converting it back into a 3, the minimum number. While the display and slider are immediately reset and shown at line 3, the edit control still says 1, ready for the user to enter the second digit, 3, at which point all is adjusted to line 13.

```
void MainFrame::OnSpinChange () {
  CString msg;
  editctl.GetWindowText (msg); // get edit ctrl's new text
  linenum = atoi (msg);        // convert into line number
  // force into range
  if (linenum <3) linenum = 3;
  if (linenum > linetot + 2) linenum = linetot + 2;
  slider.SetPos (linenum);   // set corresponding slider position
  Invalidate();              // show name on new line number
}
```

Notice how easy it is to add sliders and spin controls. Their use enhances the user interface.

Owner-drawn Controls

Sometimes, one cannot get the behavior one needs from a stock control. Often, one can tweak it a bit by doing the control's drawing for it. As an example, suppose that we wish to create a stop light type of radio button. That is, the control will have three radio buttons, red, yellow, and green, yet they all apply to the same text item, such as "approaching credit limit," where red means one is at or over the limit, yellow means approaching the limit.

In this case, one needs to override the normal radio button drawing so that the inner circle is painted red, yellow, or green. Figure 14.6 shows the three radio buttons, with red currently selected.

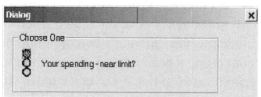

Figure 14.6 Owner-drawn Radio Buttons

To do this, we must derive our own button class from the MFC's **CButton** class, or in the MFC notation, make ours a subclass of **CButton**. To derive a class from an existing MFC class, use choose Project-Add Class menu item and pick MFC. Figure 14.7 shows how I did it.

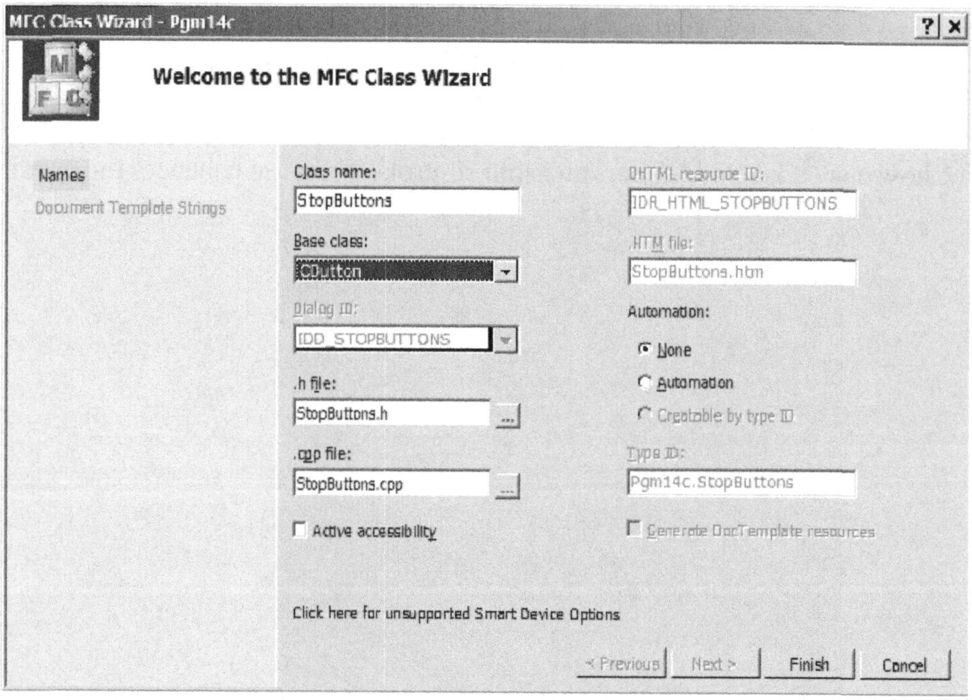

Figure 14.7 Using Class Wizard to Derive from CButton

The three buttons must work together as a group. I added a pointer to a **CBrush** object and a bool, checked as data members. When the control is created, its color must be set so that the correct brush can be dynamically allocated. The checked member keeps track of whether or not it is currently checked.

Listing for File: StopButtons.h—Pgm14c

```
...
class StopButtons : public CButton {
      DECLARE_DYNAMIC(StopButtons)

public:
              StopButtons();
      virtual ~StopButtons();
          void SetColor (int);
          bool GetChecked () const;
          void SetChecked (bool ck = false);

protected:
 CBrush *ptrbr;   // the colored brush to use
 bool    checked; // true if this one is checked

protected:
 virtual void DrawItem(LPDRAWITEMSTRUCT lpDrawItemStruct);
 virtual int  CompareItem(LPCOMPAREITEMSTRUCT lpCompareItemStruct);
 virtual void MeasureItem(LPMEASUREITEMSTRUCT lpMeasureItemStruct);
 DECLARE_MESSAGE_MAP()
};
```

Notice that there are three new functions to support facets of owner-drawn controls. Here we only need **DrawItem**. In our case, we can let the system determine the size and locations of the button, we just need to paint it our way. In SetColor, allocate a new brush of the appropriate color, based on the passed integer, 0 for red, 1 for yellow, and 2 for green. All of the coding is simple, except for the actual drawing in **DrawItem**.

Listing for File: StopButtons.cpp—Pgm14c

```
...
IMPLEMENT_DYNAMIC(StopButtons, CButton)

StopButtons::StopButtons() {
 ptrbr = NULL;
 checked = false;
}

StopButtons::~StopButtons() {
 if (ptrbr) delete ptrbr;
}

BEGIN_MESSAGE_MAP(StopButtons, CButton)
END_MESSAGE_MAP()
```

```
void StopButtons::SetColor (int i) {
 if (ptrbr) return;
 // make the colored brush
 if (i == 0) ptrbr = new CBrush (RGB(255,0,0));
 else if (i==1) ptrbr = new CBrush (RGB(255,255,0));
 else ptrbr = new CBrush (RGB(0,255,0));
}

bool StopButtons::GetChecked () const {
 return checked;
}

void StopButtons::SetChecked (bool ck) {
 checked = ck;
}

void StopButtons::DrawItem(LPDRAWITEMSTRUCT lpDrawItemStruct) {
 // get the dc given to us in the parameter structure
 CDC* pDC = CDC::FromHandle(lpDrawItemStruct->hDC);

 // get height, but not larger than 14 pixels
 int h = lpDrawItemStruct->rcItem.bottom - lpDrawItemStruct->rcItem.top;
 h = h>14 ? 14 : h;

 CRect r; // our drawing rectangle, based on where we are to draw image
 r.SetRect (lpDrawItemStruct->rcItem.left,lpDrawItemStruct->rcItem.top, h, h);
 CBrush *ptroldbr;

 // commented are possible drawing states, here I only want whether or
 // not the button is checked right now
     if (//(lpDrawItemStruct->itemState & ODS_SELECTED) != 0 ||
     //(lpDrawItemStruct->itemState & ODS_DEFAULT) != 0 ||
     //(lpDrawItemStruct->itemState & ODS_FOCUS) != 0 ||
     //(lpDrawItemStruct->itemState & ODS_CHECKED) != 0 ){
     checked)              {
 // draw with colored center circle
 ptroldbr =  (CBrush*) pDC->SelectStockObject (BLACK_BRUSH);
 pDC->Ellipse (&r);
 r.InflateRect (-1, -1);
 pDC->SelectStockObject (LTGRAY_BRUSH);
 pDC->Ellipse (&r);
 r.InflateRect (-2, -2);
 pDC->SelectObject (ptrbr);
 pDC->Ellipse (&r);
 pDC->SelectObject (ptroldbr);
 }
 else {
 // draw with grey center brush
 ptroldbr =  (CBrush*) pDC->SelectStockObject (BLACK_BRUSH);
 pDC->Ellipse (&r);
 r.InflateRect (-1, -1);
 pDC->SelectStockObject (LTGRAY_BRUSH);
 pDC->Ellipse (&r);
 r.InflateRect (-2, -2);
 pDC->SelectObject (ptroldbr);
 }

 // here, draw any focus rectangle needed when tabbing
```

```
 if ((lpDrawItemStruct->itemState & ODS_FOCUS) != 0 ) {
  r.InflateRect (3, 3);
  pDC->DrawFocusRect (&r);
 }
}

int StopButtons::CompareItem(LPCOMPAREITEMSTRUCT lpCompareItemStruct) {
 return 0;
}

void StopButtons::MeasureItem(LPMEASUREITEMSTRUCT lpMeasureItemStruct) {
 }
```

In DrawItem, we are given a pointer to the **DRAWITEMSTRUCTURE** structure. Its members are as follows.

UINT CtlType
: The type of control:
  ODT_BUTTON   Owner-drawn button
  ODT_COMBOBOX   Owner-drawn combo box
  ODT_LISTBOX   Owner-drawn list box
  ODT_MENU   Owner-drawn menu
  ODT_LISTVIEW   List view control
  ODT_STATIC   Owner-drawn static control
  ODT_TAB   Tab control

UINT CtlID
: The id of this child window (not used if this is a menu)

UINT itemID
: This is the menu item ID or the index of an item in a list box or combo box. If it is empty, the value is negative.

UINT itemAction
: This tells what drawing action is required and is one of three possibilities:
  ODA_DRAWENTIRE means draw whole control
  ODA_FOCUS means draw or remove the input focus rectangle (itemState tells which it is)
  ODA_SELECT means the selection state has changed. itemState tells whether it is selected or not.

UINT itemState
: This tells the visual state of the item after the current drawing action is done.
  ODS_GRAYED means the menu item is dimmed
  ODS_CHECKED means this item is checked
  ODS_DISABLED means draw as if item is disabled
  ODS_FOCUS means draw as if the item has the input focus.

ODS_SELECTED means this item is selected
ODS_COMBOBOXEDIT means to draw in the edit
    control of the combo box.
ODS_DEFAULT means draw the default item.

HWND hwndItem   This is the HMENU that contains this menu
                       item, if this is a menu item to be drawn

HDC hDC   **This is the HDC to use to do the drawing.**

RECT rcItem   This rectangle represents the boundaries of
                       the control.

DWORD itemData   This is the list box or combo box item index
                       or menu item index

The key fields needed are shown above in bold. We are given the DC on which to do the painting along with the rectangle the control occupies. **itemState** and **itemAction** defines what painting must be done this time. Thus, the first action is to turn the HDC into a CDC instance.

```
void StopButtons::DrawItem(LPDRAWITEMSTRUCT lpDrawItemStruct) {
 // get the dc given to us in the parameter structure
 CDC* pDC = CDC::FromHandle(lpDrawItemStruct->hDC);
```

Next, we only need fourteen pixels to draw the two circles representing a radio button. Hence, I force variable h to be the actual height, fourteen or less if the **rcItem** rectangle is too small. Using this h value, build our drawing rectangle, or square really, since we want circles.

```
 int h = lpDrawItemStruct->rcItem.bottom -
         lpDrawItemStruct->rcItem.top;
 h = h>14 ? 14 : h;

 CRect r;
  r.SetRect (lpDrawItemStruct->rcItem.left,
lpDrawItemStruct->rcItem.top, h, h);
 CBrush *ptroldbr;
```

Next, if the button is checked, use the special brush for the inner circle, if not, use the normal one. I am only going off the checked data member. However, I have commented out some other possibilities that one could check for and handle.

```
     if (//(lpDrawItemStruct->itemState & ODS_SELECTED) != 0 ||
     //(lpDrawItemStruct->itemState & ODS_DEFAULT) != 0 ||
     //(lpDrawItemStruct->itemState & ODS_FOCUS) != 0 ||
     //(lpDrawItemStruct->itemState & ODS_CHECKED) != 0 ){
     checked)        {
 // draw with colored center circle
 ptroldbr =  (CBrush*) pDC->SelectStockObject (BLACK_BRUSH);
 pDC->Ellipse (&r);
```

```
    r.InflateRect (-1, -1);
    pDC->SelectStockObject (LTGRAY_BRUSH);
    pDC->Ellipse (&r);
    r.InflateRect (-2, -2);
    pDC->SelectObject (ptrbr);
    pDC->Ellipse (&r);
    pDC->SelectObject (ptroldbr);
  }
 else {
    // draw with grey center brush
    ptroldbr =  (CBrush*) pDC->SelectStockObject (BLACK_BRUSH);
    pDC->Ellipse (&r);
    r.InflateRect (-1, -1);
    pDC->SelectStockObject (LTGRAY_BRUSH);
    pDC->Ellipse (&r);
    r.InflateRect (-2, -2);
    pDC->SelectObject (ptroldbr);
  }
```

Lastly, draw any focus rectangle that might be needed when the user is tabbing between dialog controls.

```
 if ((lpDrawItemStruct->itemState & ODS_FOCUS) != 0 ) {
   r.InflateRect (3, 3);
   pDC->DrawFocusRect (&r);
  }
}
```

Did you notice how easy this is using the **InflateRect** function?

Where the difficulties lie is in the dialog which creates instances of our new StopButtons class. First, let's examine the dialog resource file itself. Notice how I had to jam the three buttons on top of each other. Otherwise, they would not be sufficiently close to each other, giving the user the idea that they are three separate things, not one combined stop-go button. This is shown in Figure 14.8. Notice that just to the right of the three buttons is the static text containing the description for which the red-yellow-green control applies.

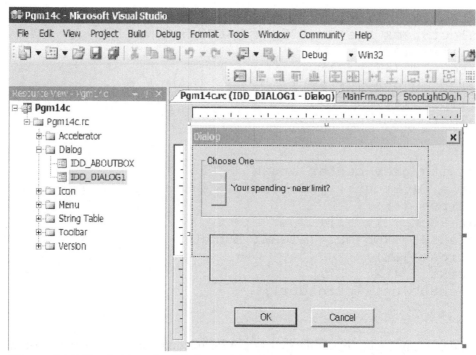

Figure 14.8 Designing the Dialog with Three Radio Buttons

Next, one must set the properties of each button to owner drawn. Specifically, in the properties window for each control, set Owner Draw to True and set no caption text. In the Control Events, add a function to respond to **BN_CLICKED**. In this function, we will toggle the checked state of the button.

Once owner-drawn is set, the radio buttons lose their normal behavior as a group and we must provide that functionality, since when red is checked or selected, yellow and green must be un-selected or un-checked.

All this means more work for the dialog class, which must now respond to a radio button press and coordinate between all three button's state, beyond maintaining which button is selected. In the listing below, ignore the RYGWindow and the couple of lines pertaining to the fancy method, we will discuss this alternative next.

Listing for File: StopLightDlg.h—Pgm14c

```
...
#include "RYGWindow.h"

class StopLightDlg : public CDialog {
     DECLARE_DYNAMIC(StopLightDlg)
public:
 StopButtons red, yellow, green; // crude method

 RYGWindow rygWindow;                 // fancy window version
```

```
int which_is_on;              // transfer buffer: crude method
int which_is_on2;             // transfer buffer: fancy method

enum { IDD = IDD_DIALOG1 };

      StopLightDlg(CWnd* pParent = NULL);   // standard constructor
  virtual ~StopLightDlg();

protected:
  virtual void DoDataExchange(CDataExchange* pDX);    // DDX/DDV support
  virtual BOOL OnInitDialog();

      // for the crude method: tracks which is on
      void MaintainRedYellowGreenChecks ();
 virtual void OnOK();
public:
 afx_msg void OnRedButtonClick();    // crude method: track which button
 afx_msg void OnYellowButtonClick();// is on
 afx_msg void OnGreenButtonClick();

 CButton tobereplaced; // fancy method - control to be overlaid by fancy
                       // window
 // handle tabbing to the fancy window buttons
 virtual BOOL PreTranslateMessage(MSG* pMsg);
DECLARE_MESSAGE_MAP()
};
```

In the implementation file, again, ignore the few lines that pertain to the fancy method. The transfer buffer into and out of the dialog is which_is_on, which defaults to the red light or 0 in the ctor. In the message map, respond to each button being clicked.

When subclassing an MFC control, after the dialog is created, then attempt to tie our StopButtons class to each of the radio buttons. I highlighted this coding below. If the subclassing works, then set the color of each control and call MaintainRedYellowGreenChecks to get all three coordinated together. It looks weird to have both red and yellow showing at the same time.

In OnOK, obtain which radio button instance is now checked and set its corresponding number in the transfer buffer, which_is_on.

Listing for File: StopLightsDlg.cpp—Pgm14c

```
IMPLEMENT_DYNAMIC(StopLightDlg, CDialog)

StopLightDlg::StopLightDlg(CWnd* pParent /*=NULL*/)
    : CDialog(StopLightDlg::IDD, pParent)
, which_is_on(0), which_is_on2 (0) { }

StopLightDlg::~StopLightDlg() { }

void StopLightDlg::DoDataExchange(CDataExchange* pDX) {
 CDialog::DoDataExchange(pDX);
 // fancy method: obtain the hidden control to be replaced by fancy window
 DDX_Control(pDX, IDC_BUTTONWINDOW, tobereplaced);
```

```
}

BEGIN_MESSAGE_MAP(StopLightDlg, CDialog)
 ON_BN_CLICKED(IDC_RADIO1, &StopLightDlg::OnRedButtonClick)
 ON_BN_CLICKED(IDC_RADIO2, &StopLightDlg::OnYellowButtonClick)
 ON_BN_CLICKED(IDC_RADIO3, &StopLightDlg::OnGreenButtonClick)
END_MESSAGE_MAP()


BOOL StopLightDlg::OnInitDialog() {
 CDialog::OnInitDialog();
 // crude method: subclass three radio buttons to our class
 if (!red.SubclassDlgItem(IDC_RADIO1, this) ||
     !yellow.SubclassDlgItem(IDC_RADIO2, this) ||
     !green.SubclassDlgItem(IDC_RADIO3, this)) {
  EndDialog(IDCANCEL);
  return FALSE;
 }
 // now set initial values for the crude method
 red.SetColor (0);
 yellow.SetColor (1);
 green.SetColor (2);
 MaintainRedYellowGreenChecks ();

 // fancy method: create the rygWindow and position it over the hidden
 // dummy button window
 CRect rect;
 tobereplaced.GetClientRect (&rect);
 tobereplaced.MapWindowPoints (this, &rect);
 // create a child view to occupy the client area of the frame
 if (!rygWindow.Create (NULL, NULL, AFX_WS_DEFAULT_VIEW | WS_TABSTOP,
  CRect(0, 0, 0, 0), this, AFX_IDW_PANE_FIRST, NULL)) {
  return -1;
 }
 rygWindow.SetWindowPos (0, rect.left, rect.top, rect.Width(), rect.Height (),
SWP_NOZORDER);
 // set its text and which button is on
 rygWindow.SetText ("Account approaching limit?");
 rygWindow.SetChecked (which_is_on2);

 return TRUE;
}

void StopLightDlg::OnOK() {
 UpdateData (true);

 which_is_on2 = rygWindow.GetChecked (); // fancy method: get which button

 // crude method: get which button is on
 if (red.GetChecked ()) {
  which_is_on = 0;
 }
 else if (yellow.GetChecked ()) {
  which_is_on = 1;
 }
 else {
  which_is_on = 2;
 }
```

```
  CDialog::OnOK();
}

// crude method: get which button was clicked and adjust all buttons
void StopLightDlg::OnRedButtonClick() {
 which_is_on = 0;
 MaintainRedYellowGreenChecks ();
}

void StopLightDlg::OnYellowButtonClick() {
 which_is_on = 1;
 MaintainRedYellowGreenChecks ();
}

void StopLightDlg::OnGreenButtonClick() {
 which_is_on = 2;
 MaintainRedYellowGreenChecks ();
}

void StopLightDlg::MaintainRedYellowGreenChecks () {
 if (which_is_on == 0) {
  red.SetChecked (true);
  yellow.SetChecked ();
  green.SetChecked ();
 }
 else if (which_is_on == 1) {
  red.SetChecked ();
  yellow.SetChecked (true);
  green.SetChecked ();
 }
 else if (which_is_on == 2) {
  red.SetChecked ();
  yellow.SetChecked ();
  green.SetChecked (true);
 }
 else
  return;
 red.Invalidate ();
 yellow.Invalidate ();
 green.Invalidate ();
}

// for fancy method, handle tabbing into that window
// want only tab key and only if green button above the
// fancy window was last tabbed to...
BOOL StopLightDlg::PreTranslateMessage(MSG* pMsg) {
 if (pMsg->message == WM_KEYDOWN && pMsg->wParam == VK_TAB &&
     green.GetState () & 0x0008) {
  // pass tab to fancy window
  rygWindow.SendMessage (WM_CHAR, VK_TAB, 42);
  // see if it still has the focus. If not, pass on to the
  // next dialog control
  if (rygWindow.StillHasFocus ())
   return TRUE;
 }
 return CDialog::PreTranslateMessage(pMsg);
}
```

In MaintainRedYellowGreenChecks, figure out which is on, set its checked member, and turn the other buttons off. If a change has occurred, call Invalidate on each to force a repainting of the three buttons.

Notice how much extra work we have made for the dialog class. Still it works. The application was a simple App Wizard generated single doc window with a main frame and child window. In the main frame, I added a call to the dialog and a simpleton display of the results.

```
void MainFrame::OnLaunchdlg() {
 StopLightDlg dlg (this);

 // fill transfer buffers
 dlg.which_is_on = 1;
 dlg.which_is_on2 = 2;

 // run the dialog
 dlg.DoModal ();

 // show selections
 const char* colormsgs[3] = {"Red", "Yellow", "Green"};
 CClientDC dc (this);
 CRect r(2, 90, 500, 170);
 dc.Rectangle (&r);
 CString msg = "First control has selected: ";
 msg += colormsgs[dlg.which_is_on];
 dc.TextOut (10, 100, msg);
 msg = "Second control has selected: ";
 msg += colormsgs[dlg.which_is_on2];
 dc.TextOut (10, 130, msg);
}
```

Figure 14.9 shows the results of a run.

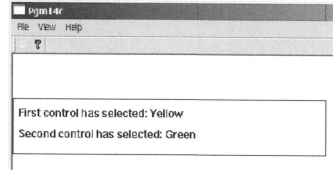

Figure 14.9 The Results of the Dialog Run

Writing Replacement Controls Based on CWnd

From the above example, you can see that subclassing a control is not always the best route to take. In this case, it was awkward for a user to create such a stoplight control in his dialog, plus he or she had to add an awful lot of basic behavior coding to their dialog class to manage the StopLight button instances.

An alternative it to write our own replacement **CWnd** based control that can more readily be used in a dialog. Essentially, our stop light control has three colored radio style buttons and one text area to their right. Our class must determine the precise location of each of these. OnSize is the proper place to do this, based upon whatever overall size the user has chosen for our control in the dialog template resource. Each button has an outer circle and an inner colored circle. We must track which is selected and which, if any, has a focus rectangle around it when the user is tabbing between dialog controls.

Since our three radio buttons are not really buttons or controls at all, but merely colored circles, we respond to left button down messages in our window. Simple hit testing can tell us if the click is within one of the outer three circles, meaning a selection of that "radio button."

Provision must be made for the dialog instance to transfer data into our control and out again, when OK is pressed. Only one member function is not obvious, StillHasFocus, which we will get to shortly.

I chose Project|Add Class and derived from **CWnd**.

Listing for File: RYGWindow.h—Pgm14c

```
...
class RYGWindow : public CWnd {
 DECLARE_DYNAMIC(RYGWindow)
public:
          RYGWindow();
 virtual ~RYGWindow();

 CString   text;          // text message to show right of buttons
 CPoint    textStart;     // coords of the text message
 // the three buttons, outer and inner colored circles
 CRect     outerRed;
 CRect     red;
 CRect     outerYellow;
 CRect     yellow;
 CRect     outerGreen;
 CRect     green;

 CRect     client;        // the client rect size
 CBrush    brushRed;
 CBrush    brushYellow;
 CBrush    brushGreen;
```

```
int        whichChecked; // transfer buffer, indicates which button is on
int        whichFocus;   // when tabbing, which button has the focus

protected:
 DECLARE_MESSAGE_MAP()
public:
 BOOL PreCreateWindow(CREATESTRUCT& cs);
 afx_msg void OnChar(UINT nChar, UINT nRepCnt, UINT nFlags);
 afx_msg int  OnCreate(LPCREATESTRUCT lpCreateStruct);
 afx_msg void OnLButtonDown(UINT nFlags, CPoint point);
 afx_msg void OnPaint();
 afx_msg void OnSize(UINT nType, int cx, int cy);
         void SetChecked (int which);
         int  GetChecked () const;
         bool StillHasFocus () const;
         void SetText (const char* txt);
};
```

The user may use the tab key to move from dialog control to control. However, our window "appears" to have three radio buttons. Hence, StillHasFocus returns true if the user and his tab key is still within our set of fake buttons.

In **PreCreateWindow**, register our class, specifying our background brush. The Get... and Set... functions are simple. StillHasFocus returns true if we are still tabbing within our three controls. A −1 indicates we have tabbed out of our control. In **OnCreate**, build our three colored brushed.

Listing for File: RYGWindow.cpp

```
...
IMPLEMENT_DYNAMIC (RYGWindow, CWnd)

RYGWindow::RYGWindow() {
 whichFocus = -1;    // say none has the focus
}

RYGWindow::~RYGWindow() { }

BOOL RYGWindow::PreCreateWindow(CREATESTRUCT& cs) {
 if (!CWnd::PreCreateWindow(cs))
  return FALSE;
 // register our the fancy window
 cs.lpszClass = AfxRegisterWndClass (
                CS_HREDRAW | CS_VREDRAW | CS_DBLCLKS,
                ::LoadCursor(NULL, IDC_ARROW),
                (HBRUSH) ::GetStockObject (LTGRAY_BRUSH),
                NULL);
 return TRUE;
}

BEGIN_MESSAGE_MAP(RYGWindow, CWnd)
 ON_WM_CHAR()
 ON_WM_CREATE()
 ON_WM_LBUTTONDOWN()
 ON_WM_PAINT()
```

```
 ON_WM_SIZE()
END_MESSAGE_MAP()

void RYGWindow::SetText (const char* txt) {
 text = txt;
}

void RYGWindow::SetChecked (int which) {
 if (which < 0 || which > 2) {
  MessageBox ("Requested radio button is out of range (0-2)", "Error", MB_OK);
  return;
 }
 whichChecked = which; // set the requested button as on
}

int RYGWindow::GetChecked () const {
 return whichChecked;  // return which button is on
}

void RYGWindow::OnChar(UINT nChar, UINT nRepCnt, UINT nFlags) {
 if (nChar == VK_TAB) { // tabbing through the buttons
  whichFocus++;          // increment to the next button
  if (whichFocus > 2)    // past the last one, so
   whichFocus = -1;      // indicate none and force a repaint
  Invalidate ();
 }
}

bool RYGWindow::StillHasFocus () const{
 return whichFocus != -1; // let dialog caller know we do or do not have focus
}

int RYGWindow::OnCreate(LPCREATESTRUCT lpCreateStruct) {
 if (CWnd::OnCreate(lpCreateStruct) == -1)
  return -1;
 // create our three colored brushes
 brushRed.CreateSolidBrush (RGB (255,0,0));
 brushYellow.CreateSolidBrush (RGB (255,255,0));
 brushGreen.CreateSolidBrush (RGB (0,255,0));
 return 0;
}

void RYGWindow::OnLButtonDown(UINT nFlags, CPoint point) {
 // sort out which button was clicked and set both
 // the integer indicator and force a repaint showing that one in
 // its color, while undoing the others colors
 if (red.PtInRect (point)) {
  whichChecked = 0;
  Invalidate ();
 }
 else if (yellow.PtInRect (point)) {
  whichChecked = 1;
  Invalidate ();
 }
 else if (green.PtInRect (point)) {
  whichChecked = 2;
  Invalidate ();
 }
```

```
}

// paint the buttons and any focus rectangle, along with the text
void RYGWindow::OnPaint() {
 CPaintDC dc(this);
 dc.SetBkMode (TRANSPARENT);
 GetClientRect (client);
 dc.SelectStockObject (LTGRAY_BRUSH);
 dc.Rectangle (client);  // erase our window
 // draw the three outer radio button circles
 dc.Ellipse (&outerRed);
 dc.Ellipse (&outerYellow);
 dc.Ellipse (&outerGreen);

 // for each button, if it is selected, insert the color brush
 // draw the center circle
 // if it has the focus, draw the focus rectangle
 if (whichChecked == 0) dc.SelectObject (brushRed);
 else dc.SelectObject (::GetStockObject (LTGRAY_BRUSH));
 dc.Ellipse (red);
 if (whichFocus == 0) dc.DrawFocusRect (outerRed);

 if (whichChecked == 1) dc.SelectObject (brushYellow);
 else dc.SelectObject (::GetStockObject (LTGRAY_BRUSH));
 dc.Ellipse (yellow);
 if (whichFocus == 1) dc.DrawFocusRect (outerYellow);

 if (whichChecked == 2) dc.SelectObject (brushGreen);
 else dc.SelectObject (::GetStockObject (LTGRAY_BRUSH));
 dc.Ellipse (green);
 if (whichFocus == 2) dc.DrawFocusRect (outerGreen);

 // show the text line
 dc.TextOut (textStart.x, textStart.y, text);
}

void RYGWindow::OnSize(UINT nType, int cx, int cy) {
 if (cx == 0) return;
 // layout the three radio buttons and text locations
 // each button has two parts: outer circle and inner circle
 // outer circle are 15 pixels in diameter or 45 total
 // place the three buttons centered vertically within the window's
 // height and 10 pixels from the left edge
 // place text 2 pixels above the start of the center button
 GetClientRect (client);
 int top = (client.Height () - 45)/2;
 outerRed.top = top;
 outerRed.bottom = outerRed.top + 15;
 outerYellow.top = outerRed.bottom;
 outerYellow.bottom = outerYellow.top + 15;
 outerGreen.top = outerYellow.bottom;
 outerGreen.bottom = outerGreen.top + 15;
 outerRed.left = outerYellow.left = outerGreen.left = 10;
 outerRed.right = outerYellow.right = outerGreen.right = outerRed.left + 15;

 textStart.x = outerYellow.right + 4;
 textStart.y = outerYellow.top - 2;
```

```
// inner colored circles are 4 pixels less in diameter
red = outerRed;
yellow = outerYellow;
green = outerGreen;
red.DeflateRect (2, 2);
yellow.DeflateRect (2, 2);
green.DeflateRect (2, 2);
}
```

In OnSize, when the size is not 0, we must determine the complete layout of our four components. Each outer circle is to be 15 pixels tall; each touches the other. Figure 14.10 shows how our control appears.

Figure 14.10 Fancy Control Appearance

We do not know in advance how tall the user has made our control, so I center the three radio buttons and text message within the height of the control. Obtain our size in **OnSize** and subtract 45 pixels from the height and divide by 2. The left edge is arbitrarily set to 10 pixels, because I thought that looked good. When **OnSize** is done, the rectangles for the three pairs of circles are filled in along with the point for the text message.

OnPaint then displays our window, using these rectangles to draw the circles. Draw all three outer circles. For each inner circle, either select in the light grey brush or the colored brush, if this one is selected or checked. Then, draw the inner circle. However, if this one has the tab focus, also draw a focus rectangle around it.

In **OnLButtonDown**, apply hit testing to see if the mouse position is within each of the three outer circles. Notice the use of the handy **CRect** function, **PtInRect**! If the mouse click is within one of these outer circles, set whichChecked to the appropriate one and Invalidate the window. Repainting causes the control to re-display itself with the right "radio button" activated and the others greyed.

All in all, pretty simple class to do, but what about the client, the dialog? And how does a user actually create our class in his resource template?

In the resource editor, the user installs a dummy push button whose dimensions are the size that he or she wishes our fancy window to occupy. Look back up at Figure 14.8 once more. Notice the funny looking large rectangle below the group box with the three overlapping radio buttons. This is the dummy button the client installs. Its properties must set Visible to false; it is never going to be seen by the user when the dialog runs. Rather, we are going to map our fancy window over the top of that button, using its dimensions as our window's dimensions.

In the dialog class, create a data member for our window and its transfer buffer. Also create an instance of the hidden button that will be overlain by our window.

```
RYGWindow rygWindow;        // fancy window version
int which_is_on2;           // transfer buffer: fancy method

CButton tobereplaced; // fancy method - control to be overlaid
                      // by fancy window

// handle tabbing to the fancy window buttons
virtual BOOL PreTranslateMessage(MSG* pMsg);
```
Additionally, we need to handle user tabbing between controls. Since our new class instance is not normally in the tabbing sequence, without our intervention, tabbing will skip over our window. The control just before ours in the tab sequence is the green button. Hence, we need to tie into the message processing loop and check for a tab keystroke. If one occurs, we need to see if the green button was the last one tabbed to and, if so, tab into our fancy window class. We make this hook by overriding **PreTranslateMessage**, whose prototype is above.

In **DoDataExchange**, we obtain a control to the button that is hidden and to be replaced by our fancy window.
```
void StopLightDlg::DoDataExchange(CDataExchange* pDX) {
 CDialog::DoDataExchange(pDX);
 // fancy method: obtain the hidden control to be replaced by fancy window
 DDX_Control(pDX, IDC_BUTTONWINDOW, tobereplaced);
}
```

In **OnInitDialog**, we obtain the dimensions of the hidden control and create our fancy control, using those dimensions, by calling **SetWindowPos**. Finally, set it's text and which button is initially to be on or selected.
```
 // fancy method: create the rygWindow and position it over the hidden
 // dummy button window
 CRect rect;
 tobereplaced.GetClientRect (&rect);
 tobereplaced.MapWindowPoints (this, &rect);
 // create a child view to occupy the client area of the frame
 if (!rygWindow.Create (NULL, NULL, AFX_WS_DEFAULT_VIEW | WS_TABSTOP,
  CRect(0, 0, 0, 0), this, AFX_IDW_PANE_FIRST, NULL)) {
  return -1;
 }
```

```
rygWindow.SetWindowPos (0, rect.left, rect.top, rect.Width(), rect.Height (),
                    SWP_NOZORDER);
// set its text and which button is on
rygWindow.SetText ("Account approaching limit?");
rygWindow.SetChecked (which_is_on2);
```

In OnOK, we retrieve the current user selection.

```
which_is_on2 = rygWindow.GetChecked ();
```

Finally, we handle user tabbing between controls. The 0x0008 value means it has the focus. Thus, this next tab key press means to tab into our fancy window to the red button. However, once the user has tabbed through the three buttons in our fancy window, we want tabbing to resume with the next dialog control, here the Ok button. Hence, if StillHasFocus returns false, we fall through and call the base class which then sends the tab message to the dialog class, which moves to the Ok button.

```
BOOL StopLightDlg::PreTranslateMessage(MSG* pMsg) {
 if (pMsg->message == WM_KEYDOWN && pMsg->wParam == VK_TAB &&
     green.GetState () & 0x0008) {
  // pass tab to fancy window
  rygWindow.SendMessage (WM_CHAR, VK_TAB, 42);
  // see if it still has the focus. If not, pass on to the
  // next dialog control
  if (rygWindow.StillHasFocus ())
   return TRUE;
 }
 return CDialog::PreTranslateMessage(pMsg);
}
```

Notice the vastly simpler coding on the part of the dialog class and in the resource file. Rolling our own controls can often be much easier on the user. In the next chapter, we will turn this window control into an ActiveX control.

Choose or Make a Folder, Progress Controls, Using the Recycle Bin, and Spawning Other Programs

Often an application needs to have the user select a folder or to request a new folder be made. Let's see how we can make a Choose Folder dialog class. We will need to parallel the Explorer's tree view of the user's My Computer, making heavy use of a tree control.

Progress controls are used when the application enters a time-consuming activity. It periodically updates a gauge by which the user can monitor the progress. When an application needs to delete a file, it can either go to the recycle bin or can be directly deleted. Finally, an application can spawn other applications, that is, launch another separate exe file. Pgm14d shows how this can be done.

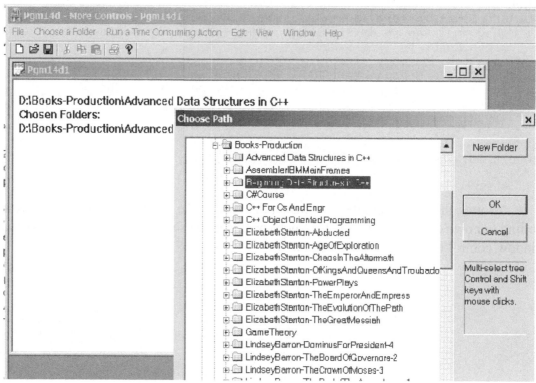

Figure 14.11 Pgm14d Choose Path Dialog

Figure 14.12 shows the progress control in operation.

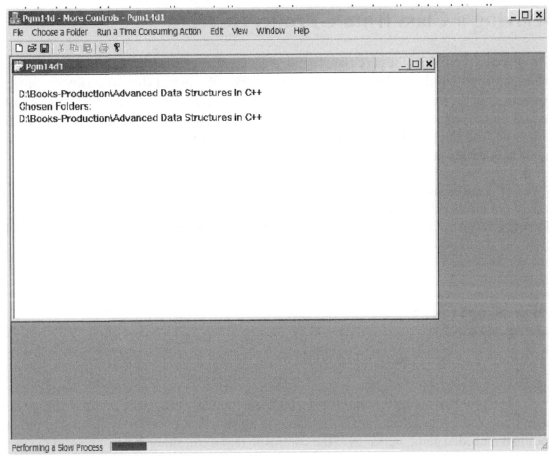

Figure 14.12 The Progress Control in Action

The wrapper classes are simple default doc-view classes, MDI style. The only changes are to the view class. Here I added members to store the current folder and the collections of so far chosen folders, along with two functions to respond to the menu choices to launch the two actions and their related functions.

```
long      avg_char_width;
long      avg_char_height;
CString   startFolder;
CPtrArray foldersChosen;

        void EmptyArray ();
        void Pump ();
afx_msg void OnChoose();
afx_msg void OnRun();
```

Let's examine the simpler control first, making a progress control.

Deriving a Class from CProgressCtrl

CProgressCtrl provides the base class for progress controls. However, let's put the progress control on the statusbar. The derived class is called ProgressBar. When you allocate an instance of it, provide the caption, here "Performing a Slow Process," the maximum range of travel (steps go from one to this maximum number, and the number of steps within this range. Each time one more step is completed, call the StepIt function to get the progress bar redrawn. The view class menu handler begins by creating an instance of the wait cursor, the hour glass.

```cpp
void Pgm14dView::OnRun() {
 CWaitCursor wc;
 long numSteps = 1000;
 ProgressBar bar (_T("Performing a Slow Process"), 80, numSteps);
 for (int i=0; i<numSteps; i++) {
  for (long j=0; j<100000; j++) {
   double jj = sqrt ((double) j);
  }
  bar.StepIt ();
  Pump ();
 }
}
```

The problem facing the application, which is suddenly in such an intensive processing mode that it must show a progress bar, is that there is no time left over for Windows to get around to sending the needed paint messages to the control so that it can show the progress on the screen! The is handled by either calling the **CWinAp::OnIdle** function or rolling your own message pumper, as I have done here. Calling Pump once is enough to get the progress bar's painting handled.

```cpp
void Pgm14dView::Pump () {
 MSG msg;
 while (::PeekMessage (&msg, NULL, 0, 0, PM_REMOVE)) {
  if (msg.message == WM_QUIT) return;
  if (!AfxGetApp()->PreTranslateMessage (&msg)) {
   ::TranslateMessage (&msg);
   ::DispatchMessage (&msg);
  }
 }
}
```

The ProgressBar Class

I adapted this class from a sample found on www.codeguru.com. Since the real underlying **CProgressCtrl** is going to be dynamically created, such creation may fail. Hence, I maintain an isValid member, which is set to true only if the real control is successfully created. With the progress control, some user text is displayed to the left of the gauge. Also, I need to store the dimensions of the gauge and its percentage of the total size available on the statusbar.

Listing for File: ProgressBar.h—Pgm14d

```
#pragma once

// ProgressBar window

class ProgressBar : public CProgressCtrl {
public:
 ProgressBar ();
 ProgressBar (LPCTSTR msg, int size=100, int mxVal=100,
            bool bsmooth=true);
 ~ProgressBar ();
 bool Create (LPCTSTR msg, int size=100, int mxValue=100,
            bool smooth=true);

protected:

bool          isValid;       // Successfully created?
int           percentSize;   // Percentage size of control
CString       message;       // Message to display
CRect         dimensions;    // size of the whole control

public:

bool IsValid () const { return isValid; }
void SetRange (int min, int max, int step = 1);
void SetText (const char* msg);
void SetSize (int size);
int  SetPos (int pos);
int  OffsetPos (int pos);
int  SetStep (int step);
int  StepIt ();
void Clear ();

protected:
 afx_msg BOOL OnEraseBkgnd(CDC* pDC);
 CStatusBar*  GetStatusBar ();
 void         Resize ();
DECLARE_MESSAGE_MAP()
};
```

Many of the functions are quite simple, providing the get/set interface for the many properties of the progress bar. Only a few functions need a discussion.

Listing for File: ProgressBar.cpp—Pgm14d

...

```cpp
BEGIN_MESSAGE_MAP(ProgressBar, CProgressCtrl)
 ON_WM_ERASEBKGND()
END_MESSAGE_MAP()

ProgressBar::ProgressBar () {
 isValid = false;
 dimensions.SetRect (0, 0, 0, 0);
}

ProgressBar::ProgressBar (const char* msg, int size, int mxValue,
                          bool smooth) {
 Create (msg, size, mxValue, smooth);
}

ProgressBar::~ProgressBar () {
 Clear ();
}

CStatusBar* ProgressBar::GetStatusBar () {
 CFrameWnd *ptrframe = (CFrameWnd*)AfxGetMainWnd();
 if (!ptrframe || !ptrframe->IsKindOf (RUNTIME_CLASS (CFrameWnd)))
  return 0;
 CStatusBar* ptrbar = (CStatusBar*) ptrframe->GetMessageBar ();
 if (!ptrbar || !ptrbar->IsKindOf (RUNTIME_CLASS (CStatusBar)))
  return NULL;
 return ptrbar;
}

// The actual CProgressCtrl will become a child of the status bar
// It will be positioned over the first pane
// Its dimensions will stretch across this pane
// The range will be from 0 upto maxValue, stepsize is 1
bool ProgressBar::Create (const char* msg, int size, int maxValue,
                          bool smooth /*=FALSE*/) {
 isValid = false;
 CStatusBar* ptrStatusBar = GetStatusBar ();
 if (!ptrStatusBar)
  return false;
 DWORD dwStyle = WS_CHILD | WS_VISIBLE;
#ifdef PBS_SMOOTH
 if (smooth) dwStyle |= PBS_SMOOTH;
#endif

 isValid = CProgressCtrl::Create (dwStyle, CRect(0,0,0,0), ptrStatusBar, 1) ?
                          true : false;
 if (!isValid)
  return false;

 // here it is constructed, so set its range and step
 SetRange (0, maxValue);
 SetStep (1);
 message = msg;
 percentSize = size;
 Resize (); // force control to resize to our new dimensions
 return true;
```

```
}

void ProgressBar::Clear () {
 // to avoid flicker by having the control being redrawn,
 // hide the window
 ModifyStyle (WS_VISIBLE, 0);

 // obtain the default IDLE_MESSAGE and display it on sbar
 CString msg;
 msg.LoadString (AFX_IDS_IDLEMESSAGE);
 CStatusBar* ptrStatusBar = GetStatusBar();
 if (ptrStatusBar)
  ptrStatusBar->SetWindowText (msg);
}

void ProgressBar::SetText (LPCTSTR msg) {
 message = msg;
 Resize ();
}

void ProgressBar::SetSize (int size) {
 percentSize = size;
 Resize();
}

void ProgressBar::SetRange (int min, int max, int step)       {
 if (!isValid) return;
 CProgressCtrl::SetRange (min, max);
 CProgressCtrl::SetStep (step);
}

int ProgressBar::SetPos (int position)       {
 ModifyStyle (0, WS_VISIBLE);
 return isValid ? CProgressCtrl::SetPos (position) : 0;
}

int ProgressBar::OffsetPos (int position) {
 ModifyStyle (0, WS_VISIBLE);
 return isValid ? CProgressCtrl::OffsetPos (position) : 0;
}

int ProgressBar::SetStep (int step) {
 ModifyStyle (0, WS_VISIBLE);
 return  isValid ? CProgressCtrl::SetStep (step) : 0;
}

int ProgressBar::StepIt ()       {
 ModifyStyle (0, WS_VISIBLE);
 return isValid ? CProgressCtrl::StepIt () : 0;
}

void ProgressBar::Resize () {
 CStatusBar* ptrStatusBar = GetStatusBar();
 if (!ptrStatusBar) return;
 if (::IsWindow (m_hWnd) && IsWindowVisible ()) {
  ptrStatusBar->SetWindowText (message);
  ptrStatusBar->UpdateWindow ();
 }
```

```
// get the length that the text takes up, using the current font that the
// statusbar is using
CClientDC dc (ptrStatusBar);
CFont* pOldFont = dc.SelectObject (ptrStatusBar->GetFont ());
CSize size = dc.GetTextExtent (message);
int marginSize = dc.GetTextExtent (_T(" ")).cx * 2; // margin of 2 chars
dc.SelectObject (pOldFont); // put old font back

// knowing the text size, figure the drawing rect for the progress bar
CRect r;
ptrStatusBar->GetItemRect (0, r);
r.left = size.cx + 2 * marginSize;
r.right = r.left + (r.right - r.left) * percentSize / 100;
if (r.right < r.left) r.right = r.left;

// leave a vertical margin of 10% between the top and bottom of the bar
int height = r.bottom - r.top;
r.bottom -= height / 10;
r.top    += height / 10;

// now resize the window and save our new dimensions
if (::IsWindow (m_hWnd) && (r != dimensions)) {
 MoveWindow (&r);
    dimensions = r;
 }
}

BOOL ProgressBar::OnEraseBkgnd (CDC* pDC) {
 Resize ();
 return CProgressCtrl::OnEraseBkgnd (pDC);
}
```

Let's first look at Create. First, a pointer to the statusbar is retrieved, which will become its parent window. The style will be child and visible; smooth is added if the platform can support it and the user requests smooth moving, the define **PBS_SMOOTH**. Then, the underlying control is created. The dimensions are zero because it will be later resized. Its id is 1.

```
bool ProgressBar::Create (const char* msg, int size, int maxValue,
                          bool smooth /*=FALSE*/) {
 isValid = false;
 CStatusBar* ptrStatusBar = GetStatusBar ();
 if (!ptrStatusBar)
  return false;
 DWORD dwStyle = WS_CHILD | WS_VISIBLE;
#ifdef PBS_SMOOTH
 if (smooth) dwStyle |= PBS_SMOOTH;
#endif

 isValid = CProgressCtrl::Create (dwStyle, CRect(0,0,0,0), ptrStatusBar, 1) ?
                          true : false;
 if (!isValid)
  return false;

// here it is constructed, so set its range and step
 SetRange (0, maxValue);
 SetStep (1);
 message = msg;
```

```
   percentSize = size;
   Resize (); // force control to resize to our new dimensions
   return true;
}
```

Once created as a point, it needs to be properly resized to fit the statusbar. After getting a pointer to the statusbar, if our window exists and is visible, the caption is shown using **SetWindowText**. Next, come the calculations. We must know how much of the statusbar's space is taken up by this caption text. To do that, we need the font in use on the statusbar so that we can call GetTextExtent of the message. I also added two characters worth of margin after the text and before the graphical control area.

```
void ProgressBar::Resize () {
 CStatusBar* ptrStatusBar = GetStatusBar();
 if (!ptrStatusBar) return;
 if (::IsWindow (m_hWnd) && IsWindowVisible ()) {
  ptrStatusBar->SetWindowText (message);
  ptrStatusBar->UpdateWindow ();
 }

 // get the length that the text takes up, using the current font that the
 // statusbar is using
 CClientDC dc (ptrStatusBar);
 CFont* pOldFont = dc.SelectObject (ptrStatusBar->GetFont ());
 CSize size = dc.GetTextExtent (message);
 int marginSize = dc.GetTextExtent (_T(" ")).cx * 2;   // margin of 2 chars
 dc.SelectObject (pOldFont); // put old font back
```

Knowing the text size, we can now determine the drawing rectangle for the progress bar. First, get the total area occupied by the statusbar. Then, remove the text by adding its size to the left point. Based on the percent size of the gauge, calculate the right side. As far as the top and bottom are concerned, reduce them by a small amount as well. If not, the progress bar will take all the height and look strange. 10% looks good.

```
 CRect r;
 ptrStatusBar->GetItemRect (0, r);
 r.left = size.cx + 2 * marginSize;
 r.right = r.left + (r.right - r.left) * percentSize / 100;
 if (r.right < r.left) r.right = r.left;

 // leave a vertical margin of 10% between the top and bottom of the bar
 int height = r.bottom - r.top;
 r.bottom -= height / 10;
 r.top    += height / 10;

 // now resize the window and save our new dimensions
 if (::IsWindow (m_hWnd) && (r != dimensions)) {
  MoveWindow (&r);
  dimensions = r;
 }
}
```

Progress bars on the statusbar work well in many applications. If the ability for the user to abort the lengthy process is required, then create a dialog that contains the progress control and an abort button.

Deleting Files, the Recycle Bin, and Spawn

Before tacking the more complex Choose Folder dialog, let's look at three simpler actions that sometimes must be handled by the application. The first is the deletion of files. The function DeleteFile actually deletes the file, bypassing the recycle bin. If you have a lot of files to delete, this method is drastically faster than copying them all into the recycle bin. Of course, un-deletion is then more difficult for the user. Let's see how simple deletion is done, then let's examine how to use the recycle bin. This coding is in the Utilities.cpp file. The header files needed are

```
#include <process.h>
#include <io.h>
```

After calling **DeleteFile**, the **GetLastError** returns the error code, should it fail. However, files with the read-only attribute are not deleted. Hence, if the error is not file or path not found, then check if the file attributes contain read-only. If so, change them to read-only and try the deletion again.

```
bool RemoveFile (const char *file, bool useRecycleBin) {
 if (!useRecycleBin) {
  if (!DeleteFile (file)) {
   DWORD d = GetLastError ();
   if (d == 2 || d == 3) return true; // file is not found or path not found
   DWORD s = GetFileAttributes (file);
   if (s != 0xffffffff && s | FILE_ATTRIBUTE_READONLY) {
    if (SetFileAttributes (file, FILE_ATTRIBUTE_NORMAL)) {
     if (DeleteFile (file)) return true;
    }
   }
   d = GetLastError ();
   if (d == 2 || d == 3) return true; // file is not found or path not found
   CString msg = "RemoveFile Error: ";
   msg += file;
   AfxMessageBox (msg, MB_OK);
   return false;
  }
  else return true;
 }
 else return MoveFileToTrash (file);
}
```

Using the recycle bin is more complex. Create an instance of the **SHFILEOPSTRUCT**, a shell file operation structure, and then fill it up. The starting point is to construct the list of files to be deleted, here one. The list is a number of filename strings, each with its own null terminator and the whole list ends with a second null terminator. In this sample, I am just deleting one file at a time. Then, fill up the structure.

Member **wFunc** is set to **FO_DELETE** for file deletion. The member fFlags ought to have **FOF_ALLOWUNDO** so that the user could undelete if needed. I also used **FOF_NOCONFIRMATION** so that annoying confirmation dialogs do not appear, **FOF_FILESONLY** and **FOF_SILENT**, so that it just goes ahead and does the delete.

Then pass the filled structure to the **SHFileOperation** function to get it carried out.

```
bool MoveFileToTrash (const char *f) {
 SHFILEOPSTRUCT sf;
 char *filelist;
 if(!f || !f[0]) return false;
 filelist = (char*) malloc(strlen(f)+2);
 strcpy_s (filelist, strlen(f)+2, f);
 filelist[strlen(f)+1] = 0; // adds the extra null terminator
 memset(&sf, 0, sizeof(sf));
 sf.hwnd = NULL;
 sf.wFunc = FO_DELETE;
 sf.pFrom = filelist;
 sf.pTo = NULL;
 sf.fFlags = FOF_NOCONFIRMATION | FOF_FILESONLY | FOF_ALLOWUNDO |FOF_SILENT;
 sf.fAnyOperationsAborted = 0;
 sf.hNameMappings = NULL;
 sf.lpszProgressTitle = "Progress";
 int rc = SHFileOperation(&sf);
 free(filelist);
 if (rc == 0) return true;
 else return false;
}
```

The _access Function

Another function, **_access**, can be used to determine if a file or folder exists.

```
    if ( _access (filename, 0) != -1)
        ; // the file exists
    else
        ;// file does not exist
```

Spawning Other Programs

Sometimes an application needs to startup another application. For example, suppose the main application has just completed a large amount of file operations and stored the results into a text file. While the application could open and show those results, it can be more convenient for the user if suddenly Notepad opens and displays the results, independently. Enter the Spawn function.

In this sample, Spawn will launch notepad, passing it the file to open. The DOS function is **_spawnlp**. First, you must construct the full filespec of the application to be launched. GetSystemDirectory returns the filespec of the computer's Windows installation folder. Do not count on it always being called C:\Windows\System32! Then append \Notepad.exe to it to form the complete filespec of the application to be launched. On some systems, Notepade is not in the System32 folder, but in the System subfolder. Hence, after forming up the full name, use the _access function to see if it is there. If not, remove the \System or \System32 from the system directory string and try again.

```
void Spawn (char *file) {
 char app[_MAX_PATH*2];
 GetSystemDirectory (app, sizeof (app));
 strcat_s (app, sizeof(app), "\\Notepad.exe");
 if (_access (app, 0) == -1) {
  GetSystemDirectory (app, sizeof (app));
  char *s = strstr (app, "\\SYSTEM");
  if (!s) return;
  strcpy_s (s, sizeof(app), "\\Notepad.exe");
  if (_access (app, 0) == -1) return;
 }
 _spawnlp (_P_NOWAITO, app, app, file, 0);
}
```

The **_spawnlp** function is passed the **_P_NOWAIT** flag, which says that the function is to return as soon as it gets the new application launched. Other options will force _spawn to not return until the other app is finished running. The second parameter is the file spec of the program being launched. This is then followed by a variable number of command line arguments. Always, argv[0] is the full filespec of the program being launched. Thus, you pass the same string twice. If the application expects a filename as a parameter in argv[1], pass it as the fourth parameter, here the file that Notepad is to open and display.

Choosing a Folder or Path Dialog

Look back at Figure 14.11 once more. The Choose Folder dialog is a complex one, in that the user can use multi-selection as well as create a new folder. With multi-selection, the user holds the shift or ctrl key while left clicking. The dialog must show the entire My Computer set of drives first, expanding them or collapsing them as the user clicks on them.

The main control is a **CTreeCtrl** inside the dialog. However, with the complexity involved, it makes sense to derive a multi-selection class from this basic tree control class, here called DirectoryTreeCtrl.

First, let's see how the main dialog is called from the view class, which defines the following to hold the results.

```
 CString    startFolder;
 CPtrArray  foldersChosen;

     void EmptyArray ();
```

Since I am using a **CPtrArray** to store the character strings, I provide EmptyArray to delete them upon dialog destruction. Launching the dialog is done as usual.

```
void Pgm14dView::OnChoose() {
 ChooseNewPathDlg dlg (&startFolder, &foldersChosen, true, this);
 if (dlg.DoModal () == IDOK) {
  Invalidate ();
 }
}
```

Then, in OnDraw, the array is displayed.

```
void Pgm14dView::OnDraw(CDC* pDC) {
 pDC->TextOut (avg_char_width, avg_char_height, startFolder);
 pDC->TextOut (avg_char_width, avg_char_height*2, "Chosen Folders:");
 for (int i=0; i<foldersChosen.GetSize(); i++) {
  CString* ptrs = (CString*) foldersChosen.GetAt (i);
  if (!ptrs) continue;
  pDC->TextOut (avg_char_width, avg_char_height*(i+3), *ptrs);
 }
}
```

Figure 14.13 shows the dialog template with the tree control.

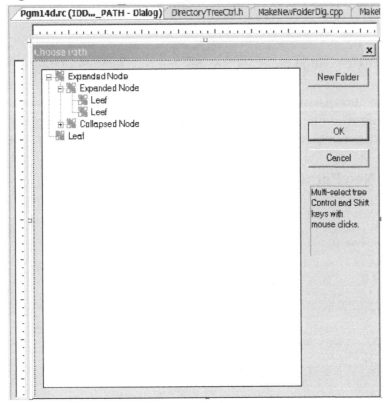

Figure 14.14 The Choose Path Dialog Template

The class definition is fairly simple. Member **m_tree** will hold our derived class instance. Member **ptrstartdir** holds the initial folder to be shown, if any. The member **ptra** holds the address of the client's return array to hold the chosen folders.

Listing for File: ChooseNewPathDlg.h

```
#pragma once
#include "DirectoryTreeCtrl.h"

class ChooseNewPathDlg : public CDialog {
public:
 ChooseNewPathDlg (CString *start, CPtrArray *ptrar, bool ismulti = false,
```

```
                              CWnd* pParent = NULL);    // standard constructor
enum { IDD = IDD_DIALOG_NEW_CHOOSE_PATH };

CStatic             m_static;
DirectoryTreeCtrl   m_tree;
bool                ismultiselect;
CString*            ptrstartdir;
CPtrArray*          ptra;

protected:
virtual void DoDataExchange(CDataExchange* pDX);
virtual void OnOK();
virtual BOOL OnInitDialog();
afx_msg void OnMakeNewFolder();

DECLARE_MESSAGE_MAP()
};
```

OnMakeNewFolder responds to the button press and creates and runs another dialog.

Most of the implementation is straightforward dialog coding. The ctor passes along the ismultiselect bool to the tree derived class. In **OnInitDialog**, if it is not multi-selection, then the static control's message is updated to say single selection. Only the **OnOK** function is involved.

Listing for File: ChooseNewPathDlg.cpp

```
ChooseNewPathDlg::ChooseNewPathDlg(CString *start, CPtrArray *ptrar,
                                    bool ismulti, CWnd* pParent)
       : CDialog(ChooseNewPathDlg::IDD, pParent) {
 ismultiselect = ismulti;
 ptra = ptrar;
 ptrstartdir = start;
 m_tree.SetMultiSelect (ismultiselect);
}

void ChooseNewPathDlg::DoDataExchange(CDataExchange* pDX) {
 CDialog::DoDataExchange(pDX);
 DDX_Control(pDX, IDC_STATIC_MULTI_INFO, m_static);
 DDX_Control(pDX, IDC_CHOOSE_NEW_PATH_TREE, m_tree);
}

BEGIN_MESSAGE_MAP(ChooseNewPathDlg, CDialog)
 ON_BN_CLICKED(IDC_MAKE_NEW_FOLDER, OnMakeNewFolder)
END_MESSAGE_MAP()

void ChooseNewPathDlg::OnOK() {
 if (ismultiselect) {
  HTREEITEM it = m_tree.GetFirstSelectedItem ();
  int which = 0;
  while (it) {
   CString *ptrs = new CString;
   *ptrs = m_tree.GetItemText (it);
   *ptrs = m_tree.GetFullPath (*ptrs, it);
   if (strlen (*ptrs) > 0) {
    which++;
    ptra->Add (ptrs);
```

```
    }
    else if (ptrs) delete ptrs;
    it = m_tree.GetNextSelectedItem (it);
   }
   if (!which) return;
  }
  else {
   CString *ptrs = new CString;
   *ptrs = m_tree.selectedPathString;
   if (strlen (*ptrs) == 0) {
    if (ptrs) delete ptrs;
    return;
   }
   ptra->Add (ptrs);
  }
  *ptrstartdir = m_tree.selectedPathString;
  CDialog::OnOK();
}

BOOL ChooseNewPathDlg::OnInitDialog() {
 CDialog::OnInitDialog();
 if (!ismultiselect) {
  m_static.SetWindowText ("Single Selection tree");
 }
 m_tree.Init();
 m_tree.SetSelPath (*ptrstartdir);
 return TRUE;
}

void ChooseNewPathDlg::OnMakeNewFolder() {
 m_tree.MakeNewDir ();
}
```

In **OnOK**, there are two possibilities, single selection or multi-selection. If it is multi-selection, then we must iterate through the various folders selected within the tree. GetFirstSelectedItem returns the **HTREEITEM** of that choice. A pair of member functions will retrieve that item's text string or folder chosen. However, we need the full filespec, not just the folder's name. The second function gives that to us, GetFullPath. Once retrieved, that string is then added to the caller's **CPtrArray**.

The GetNextSelectedItem function returns the next selection as an **HTREEITEM**. When it returns 0, there are no more selections.

```
void ChooseNewPathDlg::OnOK() {
 if (ismultiselect) {
  HTREEITEM it = m_tree.GetFirstSelectedItem ();
  int which = 0;
  while (it) {
   CString *ptrs = new CString;
   *ptrs = m_tree.GetItemText (it);
   *ptrs = m_tree.GetFullPath (*ptrs, it);
   if (strlen (*ptrs) > 0) {
    which++;
    ptra->Add (ptrs);
   }
   else if (ptrs) delete ptrs;
```

```
  it = m_tree.GetNextSelectedItem (it);
  }
 if (!which) return;
}
```

If it is single selection, the public data member, selectedPathString, contains the desired result. Copy that string into a new string and add it to the caller's array.

```
else {
 CString *ptrs = new CString;
 *ptrs = m_tree.selectedPathString;
 if (strlen (*ptrs) == 0) {
  if (ptrs) delete ptrs;
  return;
  }
 ptra->Add (ptrs);
 }
 *ptrstartdir = m_tree.selectedPathString;
 CDialog::OnOK();
}
```

Okay, that was the easy part. Now for the complex derived class. I am basing this sample on a sample that can be found on www.CodeGuru.com.

Several frequently used constants are defined first, including the size of the images to be displayed in the tree control. A set of integers will hold their zero-based index into the images bitmap. A **CStringArray** will hold the array of drive strings found on the computer. I'll show the complete coding and then go back and discuss it, function by function.

Listing for File: DirectoryTreeCtrl.h

```
...
#define IMAGE_SIZE               16
#define ALL_FILES                _T("*.*")
#define NONE                     _T("")
#define PATH_SEPERATOR           _T("\\")
#define INITIAL                  5
#define GROW                     7

#define DUMMY                    _T("AAAAA")
// a dummy value that will sort as the first item and will be deleted

class DirectoryTreeCtrl : public CTreeCtrl {
public:
 DirectoryTreeCtrl();

 //stores images of different items (drive, folder etc.,)
 int imageDrive;
 int imageCD;
 int imageFloppy;
 int imageNetwork;
 int imageClosedFolder;
 int imageOpenedFolder;
 int imageAllFiles;
```

```
CStringArray       driveStringsArray;
CImageList         imageList;
CString            driveString;
CString            selectedPathString;
UINT               folderItemMask;
TV_INSERTSTRUCT insertStruct;
HTREEITEM          hItemFirstSelection;
bool               isMultiSelect;

void SetMultiSelect (bool set);
void SplitFile (const char* path, char* drive, char* dir,
                char* file, char* ext, char* filename);
bool SplitPath (const char* path, char* drive,
                char* pathhigh, char* pathlow);
bool MakeDirectory (char *path);

virtual ~DirectoryTreeCtrl ();
void    DeleteDriveItem (CString driveName);
void    UpdateTree ();
void    SetFileFlag (bool fileFlag);
void    GetSelectedPath (CString& strPath);
void    Init ();
CString GetFullPath (CString strPath , HTREEITEM hItem);

//checks whether the item is directory or not
bool    IsDirectory (HTREEITEM hItem);

void    SetSubDirState (HTREEITEM i_hItem);

protected:
 afx_msg void OnItemExpanding (NMHDR* pNMHDR, LRESULT* pResult);
 afx_msg void OnLButtonDown (UINT nFlags, CPoint point);
 afx_msg void OnKeyDown (UINT nChar, UINT nRepCnt, UINT nFlags);

 HTREEITEM GetDriveItem (CString strPath);
 void      InsertDriveItem (CString strDriveString);
 bool      IsValidDir (HTREEITEM hItem);
 bool      IsDriveItem (HTREEITEM i_hItem);

 void DeleteAllItems (HTREEITEM hItem);//deletes all items of the given parent

 // fills the entire Directory structure of the given item
 bool FillItem (CString findCriteria, HTREEITEM hPresentItem);

 void InitDriveInfo ();
 // Reads all existing drives and Inserts with drive images

public:
 void       ClearSelection ();
 bool       SelectItems (HTREEITEM hItemFrom, HTREEITEM hItemTo);
 HTREEITEM  GetFirstSelectedItem ();
 HTREEITEM  GetNextSelectedItem (HTREEITEM hItem);
 HTREEITEM  GetPrevSelectedItem (HTREEITEM hItem);
 HTREEITEM  GetPrevItem (HTREEITEM hItem);
 HTREEITEM  GetNextItem (HTREEITEM hItem);
 void       MakeNewDir ();
 bool       SetSelPath (LPCTSTR strPath);
 HTREEITEM  SearchSiblingItem (HTREEITEM hItem, LPCTSTR strText);
```

```
DECLARE_MESSAGE_MAP()
};
```

Listing for File: DirectoryTreeCtrl.cpp

```
...
#include <io.h>
...
DirectoryTreeCtrl::DirectoryTreeCtrl() {
  folderItemMask = TVIF_HANDLE | TVIF_IMAGE | TVIF_SELECTEDIMAGE |
                   TVIF_STATE | TVIF_TEXT;
  isMultiSelect = false;
}

DirectoryTreeCtrl::~DirectoryTreeCtrl() { }

BEGIN_MESSAGE_MAP(DirectoryTreeCtrl, CTreeCtrl)
  ON_NOTIFY_REFLECT(TVN_ITEMEXPANDING, OnItemExpanding)
  ON_WM_LBUTTONDOWN()
END_MESSAGE_MAP()

void DirectoryTreeCtrl::Init() {
  HICON hIcon;
  imageList.Create (IMAGE_SIZE, IMAGE_SIZE, ILC_COLOR16, INITIAL, GROW);
  CWinApp* pApp = AfxGetApp();

  // load icons for drives
  hIcon = pApp-> LoadIcon (IDI_DRIVE);
  imageDrive = imageList.Add (hIcon);

  hIcon = pApp-> LoadIcon (IDI_NETWORK_DRIVE);
  imageNetwork = imageList.Add (hIcon);

  hIcon = pApp-> LoadIcon (IDI_FLOPPY_DRIVE);
  imageFloppy = imageList.Add (hIcon);

  hIcon = pApp-> LoadIcon (IDI_CD_DRIVE);
  imageCD = imageList.Add (hIcon);

  // load icons related to folders & files
  hIcon = pApp-> LoadIcon (IDI_CLOSE_FOLDER);
  imageClosedFolder = imageList.Add (hIcon);

  hIcon = pApp-> LoadIcon (IDI_OPEN_FOLDER);
  imageOpenedFolder = imageList.Add (hIcon);

  hIcon = pApp-> LoadIcon (IDI_DIREXPTYPE);
  imageAllFiles = imageList.Add (hIcon);

  InitDriveInfo ();
  Expand (GetRootItem (), TVE_EXPAND);
}

bool DirectoryTreeCtrl::FillItem (CString findCriteria,
                                  HTREEITEM hPresentItem) {
  HTREEITEM hTempItem;
  CString   strPath;
```

```
intptr_t   fileHandle;
intptr_t   tempHandle;
int nFind = findCriteria.Find (_T("*"));

// Retrieve path before *.ext (*.*, *.txt, etc.)
strPath = findCriteria.Mid (0, nFind);
CString strOrigiPath = strPath;
finddata_t data;
fileHandle = _tfindfirst ((LPCTSTR) findCriteria, &data);
if (fileHandle == -1) {
 CString msg = "Error: ";
 msg += findCriteria;
 MessageBox ("Cannot read drive", msg, MB_OK | MB_ICONSTOP);
 _findclose (fileHandle);
 return false;
}
do {
 // if the contents is a folder
 if (data.attrib & _A_SUBDIR) {
  //Ignore directory with dot "." and ".."
  if (!(_tcscmp (data.name, _T(".")) && _tcscmp (data.name, _T(".."))))
   continue;
  if (!_tcscmp (data.name, "RECYCLED"))
   continue;
  hTempItem = InsertItem (folderItemMask, data.name, imageClosedFolder,
     imageClosedFolder, 0, TVIS_EXPANDED | TVIS_EXPANDEDONCE | TVIS_SELECTED,
     0, hPresentItem, TVI_SORT);

  // Add a dummy item to SUB-DIR; this dummy item will be deleted
  // later when the item is expanded
  InsertItem (DUMMY, hTempItem);
 }
}
while (!(tempHandle = _tfindnext (fileHandle, &data)));
findclose (fileHandle);
return true;
}

void DirectoryTreeCtrl::OnItemExpanding (NMHDR* pNMHDR, LRESULT* pResult) {
 NM_TREEVIEW* pNMTreeView = (NM_TREEVIEW*) pNMHDR;
 CString findCriteria = GetItemText ((pNMTreeView->itemNew).hItem);

 UINT mask = GetItemState ((pNMTreeView->itemNew).hItem, TVIS_EXPANDEDONCE);
 if (!(mask & TVIS_EXPANDEDONCE)) { //the item is first time expanding
  if ((pNMTreeView->itemNew).hItem != GetRootItem ()) {
   findCriteria = GetFullPath (findCriteria, (pNMTreeView->itemNew).hItem);
   char x[_MAX_PATH];
   strcpy_s (x, sizeof(x), findCriteria);
   if (x[strlen(x)-1] != '\\')
    findCriteria += PATH_SEPERATOR;
   findCriteria += ALL_FILES;
   //get DUMMY child item
   HTREEITEM hItemTemp = GetChildItem ((pNMTreeView->itemNew).hItem);
   BeginWaitCursor ();
   bool retVal = FillItem (findCriteria, (pNMTreeView->itemNew).hItem);
   if (!retVal) {
    *pResult = 1; //return true to prevent item from expanding
    return;
```

```
  }
  //delete DUMMY item
  if (hItemTemp != NULL) DeleteItem (hItemTemp);
  EndWaitCursor ();
  }
 }
 if (IsDriveItem ((pNMTreeView->itemNew).hItem)) {
  *pResult = 0;
  return;
 }
 if (pNMTreeView->action == TVE_COLLAPSE)
  SetItemImage ((pNMTreeView->itemNew).hItem, imageClosedFolder,
               imageClosedFolder);
 if (pNMTreeView->action == TVE_EXPAND)
  SetItemImage ((pNMTreeView->itemNew).hItem, imageOpenedFolder,
               imageOpenedFolder);
 *pResult = 0;
}

CString DirectoryTreeCtrl::GetFullPath (CString strPath, HTREEITEM hItem) {
 CString   strParentText;
 HTREEITEM hParentItem;
 if (hItem == GetRootItem ())
  return strPath;
 hParentItem = GetParentItem (hItem);
 if (hParentItem == GetRootItem ())
  return strPath;
 strParentText = GetItemText (hParentItem);
 if (IsDriveItem (hParentItem))
  strPath = strParentText + strPath;
 else
  strPath = strParentText + PATH_SEPERATOR + strPath;
 strPath = GetFullPath (strPath, hParentItem);
 return strPath;
}

bool DirectoryTreeCtrl::IsDirectory (HTREEITEM hItem) {
 if (hItem == GetRootItem())
  return false;
 int image;
 GetItemImage (hItem, image, image);
 return image == imageAllFiles ? false : true;
}

void DirectoryTreeCtrl::SetSubDirState (HTREEITEM i_hItem) {
 HTREEITEM hChildItem = GetChildItem (i_hItem);
 int image;
 while (hChildItem != NULL) {
  if (IsDirectory (hChildItem)) {
   GetItemImage (hChildItem, image, image);
   if (image == imageOpenedFolder) { // folder is presently expanded
    // search for sub-sub directories states (expanded or collapsed)
    SetSubDirState (hChildItem);
   }
   else {
    DeleteAllItems (hChildItem);
    InsertItem (DUMMY, imageClosedFolder, imageClosedFolder, hChildItem);
    //set to never expanded
```

```
          SetItemState (hChildItem, 0, TVIS_EXPANDEDONCE);
      }
    }
    hChildItem = GetNextSiblingItem (hChildItem);
  }
}

void DirectoryTreeCtrl::DeleteAllItems (HTREEITEM hItem) {
 HTREEITEM hChildItem = GetChildItem (hItem);
 HTREEITEM hTempItem;
 while (hChildItem != NULL) {
  hTempItem = hChildItem;
  hChildItem = GetNextSiblingItem (hChildItem);
  DeleteItem (hTempItem);
 }
}

void DirectoryTreeCtrl::GetSelectedPath (CString & strPath) {
 strPath = selectedPathString;
}

HTREEITEM DirectoryTreeCtrl::GetDriveItem (CString strPath) {
 int pos = strPath.Find('\\');
 if (pos == -1)    return 0;
 HTREEITEM hDriveItem;
 HTREEITEM hRootItem;
 CString strDrive = strPath.Mid (0, pos + 1);
 hRootItem = GetRootItem ();
 hDriveItem = GetChildItem (hRootItem);
 while (hDriveItem) {
  if (!strDrive.CompareNoCase (GetItemText (hDriveItem))) {
   return hDriveItem;
  }
  hDriveItem = GetNextSiblingItem (hDriveItem);
 }
 return 0;
}

void DirectoryTreeCtrl::InsertDriveItem (CString strDriveString) {
 char temp[9];
 strcpy_s (temp, sizeof(temp), strDriveString);
 int type = ::GetDriveType (temp);
 HTREEITEM hRootItem = GetRootItem ();
 HTREEITEM hDriveItem;
 CString strTemp;

 switch (type) {
  case DRIVE_REMOVABLE:
   hDriveItem = InsertItem (folderItemMask, temp, imageFloppy, imageFloppy,
     0, TVIS_EXPANDED | TVIS_EXPANDEDONCE | TVIS_SELECTED, 0, hRootItem,
     TVI_SORT);
   break;

  case DRIVE_FIXED:
   hDriveItem = InsertItem (folderItemMask, temp, imageDrive, imageDrive,
     0, TVIS_EXPANDED | TVIS_EXPANDEDONCE | TVIS_SELECTED, 0, hRootItem,
     TVI_SORT);
   break;
```

```
 case DRIVE_REMOTE:
  hDriveItem = InsertItem (folderItemMask, temp, imageNetwork, imageNetwork,
     0, TVIS_EXPANDED | TVIS_EXPANDEDONCE | TVIS_SELECTED, 0, hRootItem,
     TVI_SORT);
  break;

 case DRIVE_CDROM:
  hDriveItem = InsertItem (folderItemMask, temp, imageCD, imageCD, 0,
     TVIS_EXPANDED | TVIS_EXPANDEDONCE | TVIS_SELECTED, 0, hRootItem,
     TVI_SORT);
  break;

 default:
  hDriveItem = InsertItem (folderItemMask, temp, imageDrive, imageDrive, 0,
     TVIS_EXPANDED | TVIS_EXPANDEDONCE | TVIS_SELECTED, 0, hRootItem,
     TVI_SORT);
  break;
 }
 InsertItem (DUMMY, hDriveItem);
 strTemp = temp;
 driveStringsArray.Add (strTemp);
}

void DirectoryTreeCtrl::InitDriveInfo () {
 int rootImage = imageList.Add (AfxGetApp()->LoadIcon (IDI_DIREXPTYPE));
 SetImageList (&imageList, TVSIL_NORMAL);  //attach image list to tree control
 HTREEITEM hRootItem = InsertItem ("My Computer", rootImage, rootImage);

 // drive string is a series of null term strings with extra null at very end
 char buf[MAX_PATH];
 ::GetLogicalDriveStrings (MAX_PATH, buf);
 TCHAR temp[20];
 int spot = 0, counter = 0;
 do   {
  // copy chars
  for (; buf[counter] != 0; temp[spot++] = buf[counter++]);
  temp[spot] = '\0'; // append null terminator
  InsertDriveItem (temp);
  spot = 0;  // reset spot for next string
  counter++; // continue with next string
 }
 while (buf[counter] != 0);
}

bool DirectoryTreeCtrl::IsDriveItem (HTREEITEM i_hItem) {
 if (GetRootItem() == i_hItem)
  return true;
 if (GetParentItem (i_hItem) != GetRootItem ())
  return false;
 else return true;
}

bool DirectoryTreeCtrl::IsValidDir (HTREEITEM hItem) {
 CString text = GetItemText (hItem);
 text = GetFullPath (text, hItem);
 text += "\\";
 text += ALL_FILES;
 finddata_t data;
```

```
intptr_t   handle;
handle = _tfindfirst ((LPCTSTR)text, &data);
if (handle == -1)
 return false;
else {
 _findclose (handle);
 return true;
 }
}

bool DirectoryTreeCtrl::SetSelPath (LPCTSTR strPath) {
 // Setting the Selection in the Tree
 char str[_MAX_PATH];
 char lstr[_MAX_PATH];
 strcpy_s (str, sizeof(str), strPath);
 if (str[strlen(str) -1] != '\\')
  strcat_s (str, sizeof(str), "\\");
 strcpy_s (lstr, sizeof(lstr), str);
 if (strlen (lstr) < 3)
  return false;
 lstr[3] = 0;
 HTREEITEM hParent = GetDriveItem (lstr);
 if (!hParent) return false;

 SelectItem (hParent); // select the last expanded item
 CString strText;
 strText = GetItemText (hParent);
 strText = GetFullPath (strText, hParent);
 selectedPathString = strText;
 hItemFirstSelection = hParent;
 HTREEITEM hChild;
 // str might be D:\Books\C++Course\
 // strText will be D:\
 // now get lstr to be just Books
 int len = (int) strlen (str);
 char* t;
 char* at = str + 3;
 char* end = str + strlen (str);
 while (at < end) {
  strcpy_s (lstr, sizeof(lstr), at);
  t = strchr (lstr, '\\');
  if (t) {
   *t = 0;
   at += t - lstr + 1;
  }
  else {
   at = end;
  }
  hChild = SearchSiblingItem (hParent, lstr);
  if (hChild) { // found it
   hParent = hChild;
   SelectItem (hParent); // select the last expanded item
   strText = GetItemText (hParent);
   strText = GetFullPath (strText, hParent);
   selectedPathString = strText;
   hItemFirstSelection = hParent;
  }
  else {
```

```
  SetRedraw (false);
  // the notification OnItemExpanded will not be called every time
  // after the call Expand. You must call Expand with
  // TVE_COLLAPSE | TVE_COLLAPSERESET to Reset the TVIS_EXPANDEDONCE Flag
  UINT uState = GetItemState (hParent, TVIS_EXPANDEDONCE);
  if (uState) {
   Expand (hParent, TVE_EXPAND);
   Expand (hParent, TVE_COLLAPSE | TVE_COLLAPSERESET);
   InsertItem ("", hParent);       // insert a blank child-item
   Expand (hParent, TVE_EXPAND); // now, expand send a notification
  }
  else
   Expand (hParent, TVE_EXPAND);
  hChild = SearchSiblingItem (hParent, lstr);
  if (hChild) { // found it
   hParent = hChild;
   SelectItem (hParent); // select the last expanded item
   strText = GetItemText (hParent);
   strText = GetFullPath (strText, hParent);
   selectedPathString = strText;
   hItemFirstSelection = hParent;
  }
  else {
   SetRedraw (true);
   break;
  }
  SetRedraw (true);
  }
 }
 return true;
}


HTREEITEM DirectoryTreeCtrl::SearchSiblingItem (HTREEITEM hItem,
                                                LPCTSTR strText) {
 HTREEITEM hFound = GetChildItem (hItem);
 CString strTemp;
 while (hFound)    {
  strTemp = GetItemText (hFound);
  if (strTemp.CompareNoCase (strText) == 0) return hFound;
  hFound = CTreeCtrl::GetNextItem (hFound, TVGN_NEXT);
 }
 return NULL;
}


// MultiSelectTreeCtrl message handlers

void DirectoryTreeCtrl::OnLButtonDown (UINT nFlags, CPoint point) {
 // Set focus to control if key strokes are needed.
 // Focus is not automatically given to control on lbuttondown
 UINT hitFlags; //TVHT_ONITEM|TVHT_ONITEMLABEL|TVHT_ONITEMSTATEICON;
 HTREEITEM hSelectedItem = HitTest (point, &hitFlags);
 CString strText;
 if (hSelectedItem)        {
  strText = GetItemText (hSelectedItem);
  strText = GetFullPath (strText, hSelectedItem);
  selectedPathString = strText;
 }
 if (!isMultiSelect) {
```

```
  CTreeCtrl::OnLButtonDown (nFlags, point);
  return;
}

// Control key is down
if (nFlags & MK_CONTROL) {
 HTREEITEM hItem = hSelectedItem;
 if (hItem) { // Toggle selection state
  UINT newSelState = GetItemState (hItem, TVIS_SELECTED) & TVIS_SELECTED ?
                     0 : TVIS_SELECTED;
  // Get old selected (focus) item and state
  HTREEITEM hItemOld = GetSelectedItem ();
  UINT oldSelState  = hItemOld ? GetItemState (hItemOld, TVIS_SELECTED) : 0;
  // Select new item
  if (GetSelectedItem () == hItem)
   SelectItem (0);  // to prevent edit
  CTreeCtrl::OnLButtonDown (nFlags, point);
  // Set proper selection (highlight) state for new item
  SetItemState (hItem, newSelState, TVIS_SELECTED);
  // Restore state of old selected item
  if (hItemOld && hItemOld != hItem)
   SetItemState (hItemOld, oldSelState, TVIS_SELECTED);
  hItemFirstSelection = 0;
  return;
 }
}
else if (nFlags & MK_SHIFT) {
 // Shift key is down
 HTREEITEM hItem = hSelectedItem; // HitTest (point, &flag);
 // Initialize the reference item if this is the first shift selection
 if (!hItemFirstSelection)
  hItemFirstSelection = GetSelectedItem ();
 // Select new item
 if (GetSelectedItem () == hItem)
  SelectItem (0);  // to prevent edit
 CTreeCtrl::OnLButtonDown (nFlags, point);
 if (hItemFirstSelection) {
  SelectItems (hItemFirstSelection, hItem);
  return;
 }
}
else {
// Normal - remove all selection and let the default handler do the rest
ClearSelection ();
 if (hSelectedItem) { // Toggle selection state
  UINT newSelState = GetItemState (hSelectedItem, TVIS_SELECTED) &
                                   TVIS_SELECTED ? 0 : TVIS_SELECTED;
  // Get old selected (focus) item and state
  HTREEITEM hItemOld = GetSelectedItem ();
  UINT oldSelState = hItemOld ? GetItemState (hItemOld, TVIS_SELECTED) : 0;
  // Select new item
  if (GetSelectedItem () == hSelectedItem)
   SelectItem (0); // to prevent edit
  CTreeCtrl::OnLButtonDown (nFlags, point);
  // Set proper selection (highlight) state for new item
  SetItemState (hSelectedItem, newSelState, TVIS_SELECTED);
  // Restore state of old selected item
  if (hItemOld && hItemOld != hSelectedItem)
```

```
                SetItemState (hItemOld, oldSelState, TVIS_SELECTED);
                        hItemFirstSelection = 0;
        return;
    }
  }
 CTreeCtrl::OnLButtonDown (nFlags, point);
}

void DirectoryTreeCtrl::OnKeyDown (UINT nChar, UINT nRepCnt, UINT nFlags) {
 if ((nChar==VK_UP || nChar==VK_DOWN) && GetKeyState (VK_SHIFT) & 0x8000) {
  // Initialize the reference item if this is the first shift selection
  if (!hItemFirstSelection) {
   hItemFirstSelection = GetSelectedItem ();
   ClearSelection ();
  }
  // Find which item is currently selected
  HTREEITEM hItemPrevSel = GetSelectedItem ();
  HTREEITEM hItemNext;
  if (nChar == VK_UP)
   hItemNext = GetPrevVisibleItem (hItemPrevSel);
  else
   hItemNext = GetNextVisibleItem (hItemPrevSel);
  if (hItemNext) {
   // Determine if we need to reselect previously selected item
   bool reselect = !(GetItemState (hItemNext, TVIS_SELECTED) & TVIS_SELECTED);
   // Select the next item - this will also deselect the previous item
   SelectItem (hItemNext);
   CString strText;
   if (hItemNext) {
    strText = GetItemText (hItemNext);
    strText = GetFullPath (strText, hItemNext);
    selectedPathString = strText;
   }
   // Reselect the previously selected item
   if (reselect && isMultiSelect)
    SetItemState (hItemPrevSel, TVIS_SELECTED, TVIS_SELECTED);
  }
  return;
 }
 else if (nChar >= VK_SPACE && isMultiSelect) {
  hItemFirstSelection = 0;
  ClearSelection ();
 }
 else if (nChar == VK_UP || nChar == VK_DOWN && !isMultiSelect) {
  CTreeCtrl::OnKeyDown (nChar, nRepCnt, nFlags);
  HTREEITEM hItemSel = GetSelectedItem ();
  CString strText;
  strText = GetItemText (hItemSel);
  strText = GetFullPath (strText, hItemSel);
  selectedPathString = strText;
 }
 else CTreeCtrl::OnKeyDown(nChar, nRepCnt, nFlags);
}

void DirectoryTreeCtrl::ClearSelection (){
 // This can be time consuming for very large trees
 // and is called every time the user does a normal selection
 // If performance is an issue, it may be better to maintain
```

```
// a list of selected items
 for (HTREEITEM hItem = GetRootItem (); hItem != NULL;
      hItem = GetNextItem (hItem))
   if (GetItemState (hItem, TVIS_SELECTED) & TVIS_SELECTED)
    SetItemState (hItem, 0, TVIS_SELECTED);
}

// SelectItems    - Selects items from hItemFrom to hItemTo. Does not
// - select child item if parent is collapsed. Removes
// - selection from all other items// hItemFrom - item to start selecting from
// hItemTo  - item to end selection at.
bool DirectoryTreeCtrl::SelectItems (HTREEITEM hItemFrom, HTREEITEM hItemTo) {
 HTREEITEM hItem = GetRootItem ();   // Clear selection upto the first item
 while (hItem && hItem != hItemFrom && hItem != hItemTo) {
  hItem = GetNextVisibleItem (hItem);
  SetItemState (hItem, 0, TVIS_SELECTED);
 }
 if (!hItem) return false;     // Item is not visible
 SelectItem (hItemTo);
 // Rearrange hItemFrom and hItemTo so that hItemFirst is at top
 if (hItem == hItemTo) {
  hItemTo = hItemFrom;
  hItemFrom = hItem;
 }
 // Go through remaining visible items
 bool select = true;
 while (hItem)      {
  // Select or remove selection depending on whether item
  // is still within the range.
  SetItemState (hItem, select ? TVIS_SELECTED : 0, TVIS_SELECTED);
  // Do we need to start removing items from selection
  if (hItem == hItemTo) select = false;
   hItem = GetNextVisibleItem (hItem);
  }
 return true;
}

HTREEITEM DirectoryTreeCtrl::GetFirstSelectedItem () {
 for (HTREEITEM hItem = GetRootItem (); hItem != NULL;
                                     hItem = GetNextItem (hItem))
  if (GetItemState (hItem, TVIS_SELECTED) & TVIS_SELECTED)
   return hItem;
 return NULL;
}

HTREEITEM DirectoryTreeCtrl::GetNextSelectedItem (HTREEITEM hItem) {
 for (hItem = GetNextItem (hItem); hItem != NULL; hItem = GetNextItem (hItem))
  if (GetItemState (hItem, TVIS_SELECTED) & TVIS_SELECTED)
   return hItem;
 return NULL;
}

HTREEITEM DirectoryTreeCtrl::GetPrevSelectedItem (HTREEITEM hItem){
 for (hItem = GetPrevItem (hItem); hItem != NULL; hItem = GetPrevItem (hItem))
  if (GetItemState (hItem, TVIS_SELECTED) & TVIS_SELECTED)
   return hItem;
 return NULL;
}
```

```
HTREEITEM DirectoryTreeCtrl::GetPrevItem (HTREEITEM hItem) {
 HTREEITEM hTreeItem;
 // Return a previous sibling item if it exists
 if (hTreeItem = GetPrevSiblingItem (hItem)) return hTreeItem;
 // No sibling, return the parent
 return GetParentItem (hItem);
}

HTREEITEM DirectoryTreeCtrl::GetNextItem (HTREEITEM hItem) {
 HTREEITEM hTreeItem;
 if (ItemHasChildren (hItem)) return GetChildItem (hItem);
 // return first child
 else {
  // return next sibling item
  // Go up the tree to find a parent's sibling if needed.
  while ((hTreeItem = GetNextSiblingItem (hItem)) == 0) {
   if ((hItem = GetParentItem (hItem)) == 0 ) return 0;
  }
 }
 return hTreeItem;
}

void DirectoryTreeCtrl::SetMultiSelect (bool set) {
 isMultiSelect = set;
}

void   DirectoryTreeCtrl::MakeNewDir () {
 if (strlen (selectedPathString) == 0) return;
 CString s = selectedPathString;
 s += "\\";
 MakeNewFolderDlg dlg (s, this);
 if (dlg.DoModal () == IDOK) {
  char ss[_MAX_PATH];
  strcpy_s (ss, sizeof(ss), s);
  if (MakeDirectory (ss)) {
   SetSelPath (s);
  }
 }
}

/**************************************************************************/
/*                                                                        */
/* MakeDirectory: make a directory by making all subdirs in this path     */
/*                                                                        */
/**************************************************************************/

bool DirectoryTreeCtrl::MakeDirectory (char *path) {
 if (strlen (path) == 0) return false;

 char drive[_MAX_DRIVE] = "";
 char dir [_MAX_PATH] = "";
 char file[_MAX_PATH] = "";
 char y[_MAX_PATH] = "";

 SplitPath (path, drive, dir, file);
 if (strlen (dir) <= 1) {
  if (strlen (file) > 0) {
   if (!CreateDirectory (path, NULL)) {
```

```
    DWORD x = GetLastError ();
    if ((x != ERROR_ALREADY_EXISTS)) {
     CString s2 = "Error: The desired folder cannot be created";
     CString s1 = "The path was: ";
     s1 += path;
     MessageBox (s1, s2, MB_OK);
     return false;
    }
   }
   return true;
  }
  return true;
 }
 strcpy_s (y, sizeof(y), drive);
 strcat_s (y, sizeof(y), dir);
 if (y[strlen (y)-1] == '\\') y[strlen (y)-1] = 0;
 if (MakeDirectory (y)) {
  if (!CreateDirectory (path, NULL)) {
   DWORD x = GetLastError ();
   if (x != ERROR_ALREADY_EXISTS) {
    CString s2 = "Error: The desired folder cannot be created";
    CString s1 = "The path was: ";
    s1 += path;
    MessageBox (s1, s2, MB_OK);
    return false;
   }
  }
  return true;
 }
 return false;
}


/******************************************************************/
/*                                                                */
/* SplitPath: takes path that does NOT have file info in it and removes */
/*            rightmost part - returns true if at the root        */
/* c:\path1\path2 yields  C:  \path1\  path2 and false            */
/* c:\            yields   C:  \ and true                         */
/*                                                                */
/******************************************************************/

bool DirectoryTreeCtrl::SplitPath (const char* path, char* drive,
                          char* pathhigh, char* pathlow) {
 char rest[_MAX_PATH];
 _splitpath_s (path, drive, _MAX_DRIVE, pathhigh, _MAX_PATH, pathlow, _MAX_PATH,
rest, _MAX_EXT);
 strcat_s (pathlow, _MAX_PATH, rest);
 if (pathlow[0] == 0 && strlen (pathhigh) < 2) return true;
 else return false;
}


/******************************************************************/
/*                                                                */
/* SplitFile: takes path that DOES have file info in it and removes */
/*            extension, file, path and drive part.               */
/* c:\path1\name.jpg yields  C:  \path1\  name .jpg name.jpg      */
/* c:\path1\name     yields  C:  \path1\  name 0 name             */
/*                                                                */
```

```
/* note: ext could be 256 bytes                                          */
/*                                                                       */
/*************************************************************************/

void DirectoryTreeCtrl::SplitFile (const char* path, char* drive, char* dir,
                           char* file, char* ext, char* filename) {
 _splitpath_s (path, drive, _MAX_DRIVE, dir, _MAX_PATH, file, _MAX_PATH, ext,
_MAX_EXT);
 strcpy_s (filename, sizeof(filename), file);
 strcat_s (filename, sizeof(filename), ext);
}
```

Well, there you have it. Do you need some explanations of what the coding does? Just teasing. Let's take it from the top, from the construction into the user clicking operations. The ctor sets up a mask that says which fields will be valid, the handle, the two images, the state, and the text to be shown. We only respond to two messages, the item expanding and the left button for user selections.

```
DirectoryTreeCtrl::DirectoryTreeCtrl() {
 folderItemMask = TVIF_HANDLE | TVIF_IMAGE | TVIF_SELECTEDIMAGE |
                  TVIF_STATE | TVIF_TEXT;
 isMultiSelect = false;
}


BEGIN_MESSAGE_MAP(DirectoryTreeCtrl, CTreeCtrl)
 ON_NOTIFY_REFLECT(TVN_ITEMEXPANDING, OnItemExpanding)
 ON_WM_LBUTTONDOWN()
END_MESSAGE_MAP()
```

In the Init function, the image bitmap is loaded and the various icons are loaded and added to the image list. Then the initial drive information is acquired and the initial folder expanded, by calling the tree function **Expand**.

```
void DirectoryTreeCtrl::Init() {
 HICON hIcon;
 imageList.Create(IMAGE_SIZE, IMAGE_SIZE, ILC_COLOR16, INITIAL, GROW);
 CWinApp* pApp = AfxGetApp();

 // load icons for drives
 hIcon = pApp->LoadIcon (IDI_DRIVE);
 imageDrive = imageList.Add (hIcon);
 ...
 InitDriveInfo ();
 Expand (GetRootItem (), TVE_EXPAND);
}
```

In InitDriveInfo, the top root is added, representing My Computer. Its image is added to the image list and the item added to the tree, this is the first item in the tree control. Next, obtain the list of available drives as a string. Again, this is a peculiar string, consisting of a series of null terminated strings. The very end has another null terminator to mark the end of the series of null strings.

```
void DirectoryTreeCtrl::InitDriveInfo () {
 int rootImage = imageList.Add (AfxGetApp()->LoadIcon (IDI_DIREXPTYPE));
 SetImageList (&imageList, TVSIL_NORMAL);  //attach image list to tree control
 HTREEITEM hRootItem = InsertItem ("My Computer", rootImage, rootImage);
```

```
// drive string is a series of null term strings with extra null at very end
```

So given the drive strings, we must split this series into individual strings and then add each drive to the tree in turn. I copy the characters of each string into a temp string, copying until a null terminator is found. Then the InsertDriveItem function is called to add this one. The process is repeated until the final extra null terminator is found.

```
char buf[MAX_PATH];
::GetLogicalDriveStrings (MAX_PATH, buf);
TCHAR temp[20];
int spot = 0, counter = 0;
do {
 // copy chars
 for (; buf[counter] != 0; temp[spot++] = buf[counter++]);
 temp[spot] = '\0'; // append null terminator
 InsertDriveItem (temp);
 spot = 0;  // reset spot for next string
 counter++; // continue with next string
}
while (buf[counter] != 0);
}
```

InsertDriveItem makes a local copy of the requested drive string, here called temp. **GetDriveType** returns what kind of drive it is, so that we can install the proper icon to represent it in the tree. The switch statement handles each possible type of drive, calling **InsertItem** with the proper image to be shown.

```
void DirectoryTreeCtrl::InsertDriveItem (CString strDriveString) {
 char temp[9];
 strcpy_s (temp, sizeof(temp), strDriveString);
 int type = ::GetDriveType (temp);
 HTREEITEM hRootItem = GetRootItem ();
 HTREEITEM hDriveItem;
 CString strTemp;

 switch (type) {
  case DRIVE_REMOVABLE:
   hDriveItem = InsertItem (folderItemMask, temp, imageFloppy, imageFloppy,
    0, TVIS_EXPANDED | TVIS_EXPANDEDONCE | TVIS_SELECTED, 0, hRootItem,
    TVI_SORT);
   break;

  case DRIVE_FIXED:
   hDriveItem = InsertItem (folderItemMask, temp, imageDrive, imageDrive,
    0, TVIS_EXPANDED | TVIS_EXPANDEDONCE | TVIS_SELECTED, 0, hRootItem,
    TVI_SORT);
   break;

  case DRIVE_REMOTE:
   hDriveItem = InsertItem (folderItemMask, temp, imageNetwork, imageNetwork,
    0, TVIS_EXPANDED | TVIS_EXPANDEDONCE | TVIS_SELECTED, 0, hRootItem,
    TVI_SORT);
   break;

  case DRIVE_CDROM:
   hDriveItem = InsertItem (folderItemMask, temp, imageCD, imageCD, 0,
    TVIS_EXPANDED | TVIS_EXPANDEDONCE | TVIS_SELECTED, 0, hRootItem,
```

```
     TVI_SORT);
   break;

  default:
   hDriveItem = InsertItem (folderItemMask, temp, imageDrive, imageDrive, 0,
     TVIS_EXPANDED | TVIS_EXPANDEDONCE | TVIS_SELECTED, 0, hRootItem,
     TVI_SORT);
   break;
 }
 InsertItem (DUMMY, hDriveItem);
 strTemp = temp;
 driveStringsArray.Add (strTemp);
}
```

At the very end, a dummy item is added as a place holder for us to use on expansion. It will be removed should this drive be expanded. Finally, this drive string is added to the driveStringsArray. Now the initial tree is visible.

The user then likely clicks on one of the icons to expand a node. OnItemExpanding is then called to handle it. **GetItemText** is called to obtain the string that we need to find to expand, here called findCriteria. **GetItemState** is also called to retrieve whether or not this node has been expanded once yet or not. If this is the first time this node has been expanded and is not the root, we have work to do.

```
void DirectoryTreeCtrl::OnItemExpanding (NMHDR* pNMHDR, LRESULT* pResult) {
 NM_TREEVIEW* pNMTreeView = (NM_TREEVIEW*) pNMHDR;
 CString findCriteria = GetItemText ((pNMTreeView->itemNew).hItem);

 UINT mask = GetItemState ((pNMTreeView->itemNew).hItem, TVIS_EXPANDEDONCE);
 if (!(mask & TVIS_EXPANDEDONCE)) { //the item is first time expanding
  if ((pNMTreeView->itemNew).hItem != GetRootItem ()) {
```

First, obtain the full path instead of the folder text only. GetFullPath is given the selected folder to expand and the current hitem. The findCriteria is replaced by the full path to it. How this is done we will examine shortly. If it does not end in a \, add a \ and then *.*. Then, set hItemTemp to this one and begin iterating through all subfolders beneath the one being expanded. This is done with the FillItem function, which we will examine shortly. Remember that we added a dummy item after each drive, so if this one is the dummy item, delete it.

If this is a request to expand the My Computer item, we've already added all those, the tree can automatically show those, so do nothing. The last action is to reset the icon to the open or closed image.

```
   findCriteria = GetFullPath (findCriteria, (pNMTreeView->itemNew).hItem);
   char x[_MAX_PATH];
   strcpy_s (x, sizeof(x), findCriteria);
   if (x[strlen(x)-1] != '\\')
    findCriteria += PATH_SEPERATOR;
   findCriteria += ALL_FILES;
   //get DUMMY child item
   HTREEITEM hItemTemp = GetChildItem ((pNMTreeView->itemNew).hItem);
   BeginWaitCursor ();
   bool retVal = FillItem (findCriteria, (pNMTreeView->itemNew).hItem);
   if (!retVal) {
    *pResult = 1; //return true to prevent item from expanding
```

```
   return;
  }
  //delete DUMMY item
  if (hItemTemp != NULL) DeleteItem (hItemTemp);
  EndWaitCursor ();
 }
}
if (IsDriveItem ((pNMTreeView->itemNew).hItem)) {
 *pResult = 0;
 return;
}
if (pNMTreeView->action == TVE_COLLAPSE)
 SetItemImage ((pNMTreeView->itemNew).hItem, imageClosedFolder,
               imageClosedFolder);
if (pNMTreeView->action == TVE_EXPAND)
 SetItemImage ((pNMTreeView->itemNew).hItem, imageOpenedFolder,
               imageOpenedFolder);
 *pResult = 0;
}
```

GetFullPath is a recursively called function. The objective is to build up the full path to the passed string, strPath, given the current hItem. If the hItem is the root, return what we have, we are done. If the parent is the root, we are also done, as this is My Computer. If not, retrieve the item's text, the folder name. If it is a drive item, concatenate the two. Otherwise, a \ must be inserted between the concatenated names. With this new piece of the path added, call GetFullPath once more to append the parent's info to the path.

```
CString DirectoryTreeCtrl::GetFullPath (CString strPath, HTREEITEM hItem) {
 CString    strParentText;
 HTREEITEM hParentItem;
 if (hItem == GetRootItem ())
  return strPath;
 hParentItem = GetParentItem (hItem);
 if (hParentItem == GetRootItem ())
  return strPath;
 strParentText = GetItemText (hParentItem);
 if (IsDriveItem (hParentItem))
  strPath = strParentText + strPath;
 else
  strPath = strParentText + PATH_SEPERATOR + strPath;
 strPath = GetFullPath (strPath, hParentItem);
 return strPath;
}
```

FillItem is given the present item and the findCriteria. We must now iterate through that directory looking for all subdirs and adding them to the tree. I am ignoring folders ., .., and recycled. If a folder is found, add it with a closed image and add the dummy item after it, which will be later removed.

```
bool DirectoryTreeCtrl::FillItem (CString findCriteria,
                                  HTREEITEM hPresentItem) {
 HTREEITEM hTempItem;
 CString    strPath;
 intptr_t  fileHandle;
 intptr_t  tempHandle;
 int nFind = findCriteria.Find (_T("*"));
```

```
// Retrieve path before *.ext (*.*, *.txt, etc.)
strPath = findCriteria.Mid (0, nFind);
CString strOrigiPath = strPath;
finddata_t data;
fileHandle = _tfindfirst ((LPCTSTR) findCriteria, &data);
if (fileHandle == -1) {
 CString msg = "Error: ";
 msg += findCriteria;
 MessageBox ("Cannot read drive", msg, MB_OK | MB_ICONSTOP);
 _findclose (fileHandle);
 return false;
}
do {
 // if the contents is a folder
 if (data.attrib & _A_SUBDIR) {
  //Ignore directory with dot "." and ".."
  if (!(_tcscmp (data.name, _T(".")) && _tcscmp (data.name, _T(".."))))
   continue;
  if (!_tcscmp (data.name, "RECYCLED"))
   continue;
  hTempItem = InsertItem (folderItemMask, data.name, imageClosedFolder,
     imageClosedFolder, 0, TVIS_EXPANDED | TVIS_EXPANDEDONCE | TVIS_SELECTED,
     0, hPresentItem, TVI_SORT);

  // Add a dummy item to SUB-DIR; this dummy item will be deleted
  // later when the item is expanded
  InsertItem (DUMMY, hTempItem);
 }
}
while (!(tempHandle = _tfindnext (fileHandle, &data)));
findclose (fileHandle);
return true;
}
```

Next, the user is likely to make a selection using a left mouse click. OnLButtonDown is then called. Here, we must switch between multi-select and single select, as well as handle the shift and ctrl keys being held down during clicking. Complicating the action are possible keystrokes the user may also be making. First, see if the click hits any item, **HitTest**. If something is hit, then obtain its full path and save it in the return string, selectedPathString. If this is a single selection, pass the message along to the tree control, since we are finished.

```
void DirectoryTreeCtrl::OnLButtonDown (UINT nFlags, CPoint point) {
 // Set focus to control if key strokes are needed.
 // Focus is not automatically given to control on lbuttondown
 UINT hitFlags; //TVHT_ONITEM|TVHT_ONITEMLABEL|TVHT_ONITEMSTATEICON;
 HTREEITEM hSelectedItem = HitTest (point, &hitFlags);
 CString strText;
 if (hSelectedItem)       {
  strText = GetItemText (hSelectedItem);
  strText = GetFullPath (strText, hSelectedItem);
  selectedPathString = strText;
 }
 if (!isMultiSelect) {
  CTreeCtrl::OnLButtonDown (nFlags, point);
  return;
 }
```

Here it is multi-select and we must pay attention to the control and shift keys. First, if the control key is down, toggle the current state of selection. That is, is it selected or unselected. However, be careful, one can also enter the edit mode to change text this way as well. This dialog is not allowing the user to rename folders. Next, let the base class handle the click. When it has finished, retrieve the new state for the item.

```
// Control key is down
if (nFlags & MK_CONTROL) {
 HTREEITEM hItem = hSelectedItem;
 if (hItem) { // Toggle selection state
  UINT newSelState = GetItemState (hItem, TVIS_SELECTED) & TVIS_SELECTED ?
                     0 : TVIS_SELECTED;
  // Get old selected (focus) item and state
  HTREEITEM hItemOld = GetSelectedItem ();
  UINT oldSelState  = hItemOld ? GetItemState (hItemOld, TVIS_SELECTED) : 0;
  // Select new item
  if (GetSelectedItem () == hItem)
   SelectItem (0);  // to prevent edit
  CTreeCtrl::OnLButtonDown (nFlags, point);
  // Set proper selection (highlight) state for new item
  SetItemState (hItem, newSelState, TVIS_SELECTED);
  // Restore state of old selected item
  if (hItemOld && hItemOld != hItem)
   SetItemState (hItemOld, oldSelState, TVIS_SELECTED);
  hItemFirstSelection = 0;
  return;
 }
}
```

With the shift key, the user could be selecting a group of folders. The key is whether or not this is the first selection or not. If it is not the first, then a block is being selected.

```
else if (nFlags & MK_SHIFT) {
 // Shift key is down
 HTREEITEM hItem = hSelectedItem; // HitTest (point, &flag);
 // Initialize the reference item if this is the first shift selection
 if (!hItemFirstSelection)
  hItemFirstSelection = GetSelectedItem ();
 // Select new item
 if (GetSelectedItem () == hItem)
  SelectItem (0);  // to prevent edit
 CTreeCtrl::OnLButtonDown (nFlags, point);
 if (hItemFirstSelection) {
  SelectItems (hItemFirstSelection, hItem);
  return;
 }
}
else {
 // Normal - remove all selection and let the default handler do the rest
 ClearSelection ();
 if (hSelectedItem) { // Toggle selection state
  UINT newSelState = GetItemState (hSelectedItem, TVIS_SELECTED) &
                     TVIS_SELECTED ? 0 : TVIS_SELECTED;
  // Get old selected (focus) item and state
  HTREEITEM hItemOld = GetSelectedItem ();
  UINT oldSelState = hItemOld ? GetItemState (hItemOld, TVIS_SELECTED) : 0;
  // Select new item
  if (GetSelectedItem () == hSelectedItem)
```

```
  SelectItem (0); // to prevent edit
 CTreeCtrl::OnLButtonDown (nFlags, point);
 // Set proper selection (highlight) state for new item
 SetItemState (hSelectedItem, newSelState, TVIS_SELECTED);
 // Restore state of old selected item
 if (hItemOld && hItemOld != hSelectedItem)
  SetItemState (hItemOld, oldSelState, TVIS_SELECTED);
                  hItemFirstSelection = 0;
  return;
  }
 }
 CTreeCtrl::OnLButtonDown (nFlags, point);
}
```

The keyboard interface also parallels this selection process, allowing the user to use the arrow keys to group select as well. The MakeNewFolder dialog is very simple as is the coding to actually make the directory. These are not shown here. See the complete programming sample for details.

Now let's turn our attention back onto the rygWindow control and see how we can better implement this control.

Chapter 15 ActiveX Controls

Microsoft defines an ActiveX control: "A Microsoft ActiveX control is essentially a simple OLE object that supports the IUnknown interface and . . . the control works well in the Internet environment, with the ultimate goal of delivering optimal quality of service to users. For example, because browser speed is one of the primary factors in users' perception of quality, this section aims to provide solutions that allow an HTML document or page to become visible as soon as possible and interactive very shortly thereafter, while allowing controls to retrieve large data blocks in the background."

Well, we certainly are going to need to define a bunch of terms before we can dive into writing an ActiveX control! First, **COM** or **Component Object Model**, is an older name for ActiveX, referring to the OLE (Object Linking and Embedding) technology and it now goes beyond simple document linking and embedding.

ActiveX is a technology that attempts to join Windows with the Internet. The coding is such that such components can be imbedded into web pages, browsers, and regular Windows applications, the latter, most often as fancy controls in dialogs. Any programming language that supports COM can create instances and use the ActiveX objects, without knowing or caring in what language the actual component was written. Sounds nice, doesn't it.

An **ActiveX component** is a server that provides one or more tables of function pointers through which other programs can then call to have the component perform useful operations for the caller. These function tables are called **interfaces** and are very similar to C++ v-tables or virtual function tables.

An **ActiveX control** in an ActiveX component that specifically works like a normal Windows control, such as a button. Microsoft lumps any ActiveX server into a control, but I like to think of controls as more restrictive in that they know how to interact with a window.

The terms: **ActiveX Object**, **COM Object**, **OLE Control**, and **OCX (OLE Control)** are all other names for ActiveX component or control.

An **ActiveX client** is any program that uses any ActiveX component.

An **ActiveX container** is a program that can accept and use any ActiveX control or document.

An **ActiveX server** is any program that provides one or more ActiveX objects for others to use.

An **ActiveX document** is any document that can be embedded or linked into another container. This is the original or traditional OLE functionality

Key Point: To a client program, an ActiveX object is nothing more that one or more tables of pointers to functions that the client can call!

All access and manipulation of the ActiveX object is done through these function calls. These tables of functions are called **Interfaces**. An **interface** is nothing more than a table(s) of function pointers, and an object can have as many tables of function pointers as desired. Interface names always begin with I, as in **IUnknown**.

Hence, the methods used to implement the controls are completely hidden from the client. You can completely re-write the entire control's coding, and as long as you do not change the interfaces, the client knows nothing about it. Objects do their thing and clients don't have to know anything about how they do it, terrific encapulation.

What about inheritance or class derivations? It's done differently, but it is still a vital aspect for code and component reuse. An ActiveX control can have another ActiveX control as one of its members, as in a derived and base class. It can handle the client's call directly and not call the embedded control (here, thought of as the base class), or it can call the embedded control's methods, or it can do some of its own instructions, then call the embedded class methods, and then continue with its own coding. These then simulate what we are used to seeing with Inheritance in C++. Further, this embedded object, the base class so to speak, doesn't have to be written in the same language, so you don't need the source code for it, nor do you need to call everyone of its methods, only those that you need.

Figure 15.1 shows these concepts.

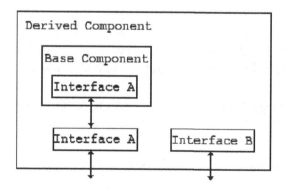

Figure 15.1 ActiveX Derived Component

Many of the functions return an **HRESULT**. If you also take up DirectX programming, **HRESULT** return codes are everywhere. What exactly is an **HRESULT**? It is a 32-bit return code that indicates the success or failure of the function. The first bit is on, if there is an error. However, the remaining bits are not zeros! The next fifteen bits are an indicator of the subsystem that generated the error, called a facility code by Microsoft. The remaining 16 bits contain the error code. (Note on a 32-bit system, an **HRESULT** is identical to an **SCODE**.) Since this value is never zero, even if the function completes successfully, you must test it using the provided macros: **SUCCEEDED** () and **FAILED** (). Also provided are some defined return values, such as **S_OK** and **E_FAIL** that you can use for your return values. While all ActiveX functions do not return an **HRESULT**, many do.

The next problem to be solved is one of identification. Just how does software identify one specific ActiveX component across the Internet and among a network of computers? Obviously, one cannot just call your component, say the Stoplight Control, for that may well collide with other components worldwide. Enter the **Universally Unique Identifier** or **UUID**. It is a 128-bit number formed in such a way as to be unique, well, mostly. When the system builds a UUID for you, it merges the date and time together with your unique computer's information, such as your network card's hardware address.

Microsoft calls the UUIDs by different names, depending upon their usage. **CLSID**s means a class unique identifier, **GUID**s for globally unique identifiers, and **IID**s for Interface ids. These are all just UUIDs. For the sample ActiveX control of this chapter, here is the id the compiler created for me:

```
uuid(C5BE9A1B-8C73-4B20-A32E-0E335969984F)
```

When you make a new ActiveX project, the wizard will build these for you automatically.

Let's look at the interfaces a bit. Every interface function table has the first three slots reserved for three very specific functions. These are known as the **IUnknown** interface function. This allows you to treat absolutely every ActiveX object the same way, you know they must have this interface and set of functions present. You could describe this in C++ terms as saying that the **IUnknown** is the base interface from which all others are derived.

What are the functions in this **IUnknown** interface? **AddRef** and **Release** are critical to the object's operation. When an instance of the ActiveX object is created, the **AddRef** function increments a reference count. Every time you acquire a different interface of that object, the count goes up by one. When you release that interface, the **Release** function decrements the count. When the count becomes zero, the object is no longer in use and it unloads itself from memory. Slick trick.

The final function is **QueryInterface**. You pass this function an IID and it lets you know if this object supports that interface. If so, it returns you a pointer to that interface so that you can begin to call those specific functions. There are a number of ways you can create an object, but often in a program it is by calling the **CoCreateInstance** function. Again, the application wizard handles this for you.

Putting this all together, we have the following rules:

1. All ActiveX controls must implement the **IUnknown** interface.

2. Microsoft defines a large number of other interfaces that you can implement or not as you see fit. Some of these are the **IMalloc** interface to allocate memory, the **IDispatch** interface to send messages, and the **IClassFactory** interface which knows how to create your object (**CoCreateInstance** uses it).

3. You are free to invent and add any number of your own interfaces.

Wait a minute here! If you are able to invent your own interfaces, how can any program know what to expect when using your ActiveX control? Enter the **type library**. The type library contains the data about the interfaces and objects in a machine-readable format. The application wizard builds your shell type library file for you and is part of the project. Its extension is **.idl**.

Okay, so that problem is solved, but there are more problems over the horizon. Suppose that the ActiveX control that your program needs is in a DLL, a dynamic link library. When you create your first instance, the DLL is loaded into memory of your client program and the function pointers point to the instructions there in your 2G address space. Fine.

But what if the control's server is in another exe file, a separate process running on the computer? Now, this will not work, the "real" address of the function is not in your process space and cannot be found! That is, you cannot pass pointers across process boundaries. Enter **proxies**. A **proxy** is a simple function that resides in the client's address space and it forwards calls over to another stub function in another process. In order to move data back and forth between the two functions residing in two different address spaces, **marshalling** is done. **Marshalling** is a technique that handles the transfer of data between two functions residing in two address spaces or processes. This is shown in Figure 15.2.

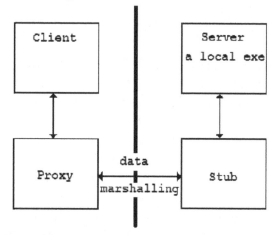

Figure 15.2 Proxy and Marshalling

ActiveX hides these details from us, the generated coding handles this for us. Whew. Well, nearly. Realize that you cannot pass things like an HDC, a device context, across to the other exe. It would have no meaning; the server cannot draw on it.

Ah, but what if the server is really a remote computer reached via the Internet or a computer on a network? Enter **RPC, Remote Procedure Calls**. Again, the data is marshalled and then sent via this technology over the network or internet to the server, who processes the request, that is, its function is called. Your interface is described using the **MIDL, Microsoft Interface Description Language**, which is used to communicate between network machines and/or the Internet.

The system registry is used to register the ActiveX control so that other applications can easily find and use it. Once more, the wizard handles this for us, when we create a new ActiveX project.

What about data types? Ah, here we are often forced to use **BSTR** and variants. A **BSTR** is a type of character string, where there is a two byte length of string preceding the actual null terminated series of characters. A **CString** can be converted into a **BSTR** by calling the **CString::AllocSysString** function.

A **VARIANT** is really a C union, the first field containing the type of data that follows. The first field is called **vt**, variant type. Table 15.1 shows some of the values it can have.

Table 15.1 Some of the VARIANT Types

Variant Type	Meaning
VT_EMPTY	No data present
VT_NULL	NULL value
VT_BSTR	A BSTR character string
VT_I2	A signed short int
VT_I4	A signed long int
VT_R4	A float – four byte version
VT_R8	A double – eight byte version
VT_BOOL	A bool
VT_CY	A currency variable
VT_DATE	A date
VT_DISPATCH	A pointer to an IDispatch function
VT_ERROR	An error code of type scode
VT_UNKNOWN	A pointer to an IUnknown function
VT_UI1	An unsigned character
VT_BYREF	Added to other types to indicate passing by reference

Creating ActiveX controls can be done with two tools: the MFC or the new ATL ActiveX or Advanced Template Library. The ATL requires that you know quite a lot about this subject, the MFC requires far less. Hence, I will be illustrating the MFC method.

Writing an ActiveX Control Using the MFC—Pgm15a—Stoplight Control

The objective is to convert the Stoplight control from chapter 14, the rygWindow into an ActiveX control and to put it into the resource toolbox so that it can easily be dragged into other program's dialogs.

Pgm15a will build the Stoplight control. Pgm15b will use the control in its dialog, similar to the way it was done in chapter 14. Figure 15.3 shows the control as inserted into Pgm15b's dialog.

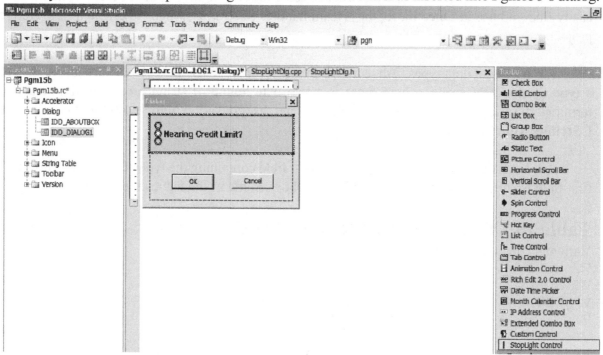

Figure 15.3 The Stoplight ActiveX Control Inserted into Pgm15b's Dialog

Notice at the bottom of the tools on the right panel is the StopLight Control with its red-yellow-green icon. Figure 15.4 shows the help message presented when the mouse floats over it.

Figure 15.4 Help Tip

Begin by choosing File|New Project and selecting MFC ActiveX Control. After entering the names of your classes, on the options page, the control is based on "none." Here, for example, you could base the control on a button behavior. You could take all the defaults, but it is fine to check Optimized Drawing, Flicker-free, and Available in Insert Object.

The wizard builds the necessary files for us. The key files are StopLightCtrl.h and cpp and StopLightPpg.h and cpp, representing the actual control class that does all of the main work and the property pages class that provides a mechanism to get and set properties of the control.

The wizard also created the .def and .idl files that provide its definition and type library information. The generated application class handles the details of the overall dll construction, which wraps the control.

Begin with the control class and add the needed data members and functions. I copied in much of the coding from the samples in chapter 14. Here is the definition file.

Listing for File: StopLightCtrl.h—Pgm15a

```
#pragma once

// StopLightCtrl.h : Declaration of the StopLightCtrl ActiveX Control class.

class StopLightCtrl : public COleControl {
 DECLARE_DYNCREATE(StopLightCtrl)

public:
 StopLightCtrl();

 CString caption;
 long    whichIsOn;

 CPoint   textStart;    // coords of the text message
 // the three buttons, outer and inner colored circles
 CRect    outerRed;
 CRect    red;
 CRect    outerYellow;
 CRect    yellow;
 CRect    outerGreen;
 CRect    green;

 CRect    client;       // the client rect size
 CBrush   brushRed;
 CBrush   brushYellow;
 CBrush   brushGreen;

 virtual void OnDraw(CDC* pdc, const CRect& rcBounds, const CRect& rcInvalid);
 virtual void DoPropExchange(CPropExchange* pPX);
 virtual void OnResetState();
 virtual DWORD GetControlFlags();

protected:
 ~StopLightCtrl();

 afx_msg void OnSize(UINT nType, int cx, int cy);
```

```
afx_msg void OnLButtonDown(UINT nFlags, CPoint point);
afx_msg int OnCreate(LPCREATESTRUCT lpCreateStruct);
void SetWhichIsOn(long which);
long GetWhichIsOn(void);
afx_msg void OnWhichIsOnChanged();
afx_msg void OnCaptionChanged();

DECLARE_OLECREATE_EX(StopLightCtrl)        // Class factory and guid
DECLARE_OLETYPELIB(StopLightCtrl)          // GetTypeInfo
DECLARE_PROPPAGEIDS(StopLightCtrl)         // Property page IDs
DECLARE_OLECTLTYPE(StopLightCtrl)          // Type name and misc status

DECLARE_MESSAGE_MAP()
DECLARE_DISPATCH_MAP()
DECLARE_EVENT_MAP()

// Dispatch and event IDs
public:
        enum {
        };
};
```

The control is painted in **OnDraw**, while the brushes are created in **OnCreate**. **OnSize** is where I size and position the three fake radio buttons and the label. **OnLButtonDown** handles the button selection process. I added a get and set function for the client to determine the settings of the buttons. When the property pages have a chance in the caption or which button is on, the two functions OnWhichIsChanged and OnCaptionChanged are called to update our two member variables. Look over the coding and then let's explore it in more detail.

Listing for File: StopLightCtrl.cpp—Pgm15a

```
// StopLightCtrl.cpp : Implementation of the StopLightCtrl ActiveX Control class.
#include "stdafx.h"
#include "Pgm15a.h"
#include "StopLightCtrl.h"
#include "StopLightPpg.h"

#ifdef _DEBUG
#define new DEBUG_NEW
#endif

IMPLEMENT_DYNCREATE(StopLightCtrl, COleControl)

// Message map
BEGIN_MESSAGE_MAP(StopLightCtrl, COleControl)
 ON_OLEVERB(AFX_IDS_VERB_PROPERTIES, OnProperties)
 ON_WM_SIZE()
 ON_WM_LBUTTONDOWN()
 ON_WM_CREATE()
END_MESSAGE_MAP()

// Dispatch map
BEGIN_DISPATCH_MAP(StopLightCtrl, COleControl)
 DISP_PROPERTY(StopLightCtrl, "Caption", caption, VT_BSTR)
 DISP_PROPERTY(StopLightCtrl, "Which Is On", whichIsOn, VT_I4)
```

```
DISP_FUNCTION(StopLightCtrl, "SetWhichIsOn", SetWhichIsOn, VT_EMPTY, VTS_I4)
DISP_FUNCTION(StopLightCtrl, "GetWhichIsOn", GetWhichIsOn, VT_I4, VTS_NONE)
DISP_PROPERTY_NOTIFY(StopLightCtrl, "Caption", caption, OnCaptionChanged,
                     VT_BSTR)
DISP_PROPERTY_NOTIFY(StopLightCtrl, "Which Is On", whichIsOn,
                     OnWhichIsOnChanged, VT_I4)
END_DISPATCH_MAP()

// Event map
BEGIN_EVENT_MAP(StopLightCtrl, COleControl)
END_EVENT_MAP()

// Property pages
// TODO: Add more property pages as needed.  Remember to increase the count!
BEGIN_PROPPAGEIDS(StopLightCtrl, 1)
 PROPPAGEID(StopLightPropPage::guid)
END_PROPPAGEIDS(StopLightCtrl)

// StopLightCtrl::DoPropExchange - Persistence support
void StopLightCtrl::DoPropExchange(CPropExchange* pPX) {
 ExchangeVersion(pPX, MAKELONG(_wVerMinor, _wVerMajor));
 COleControl::DoPropExchange(pPX);
 PX_String(pPX, _T("Caption"), caption);
 PX_Long (pPX, _T("Which Is On"), whichIsOn);
 // TODO: Call PX_ functions for each persistent custom property.
}

// Initialize class factory and guid
IMPLEMENT_OLECREATE_EX(StopLightCtrl, "StopLightCtrl.1",
 0xd0d3e66f, 0x6ef9, 0x48e7, 0x8a, 0xe4, 0xa0, 0x64, 0xa9, 0xe, 0x58, 0x5e)

// Type library ID and version
IMPLEMENT_OLETYPELIB(StopLightCtrl, _tlid, _wVerMajor, _wVerMinor)

// Interface IDs
const IID BASED_CODE IID_DPgm15a =
 { 0x9EAC2936, 0x662A, 0x49EE, { 0xA6, 0xBF, 0x4D, 0x31, 0xA0, 0xEA, 0x48, 0x29
} };
const IID BASED_CODE IID_DPgm15aEvents =
 { 0xF1950DF, 0xC4D1, 0x499F, { 0xA4, 0xE7, 0x9A, 0x78, 0xDD, 0x75, 0x8, 0x1E }
};

// Control type information
static const DWORD BASED_CODE _dwPgm15aOleMisc =
 OLEMISC_ACTIVATEWHENVISIBLE |
 OLEMISC_IGNOREACTIVATEWHENVISIBLE |
 OLEMISC_SETCLIENTSITEFIRST |
 OLEMISC_INSIDEOUT |
 OLEMISC_CANTLINKINSIDE |
 OLEMISC_RECOMPOSEONRESIZE;

IMPLEMENT_OLECTLTYPE(StopLightCtrl, IDS_PGM15A, _dwPgm15aOleMisc)

// StopLightCtrl::StopLightCtrlFactory::UpdateRegistry -
// Adds or removes system registry entries for StopLightCtrl
BOOL StopLightCtrl::StopLightCtrlFactory::UpdateRegistry(BOOL bRegister) {
 // TODO: Verify that your control follows apartment-model threading rules.
 // Refer to MFC TechNote 64 for more information.
```

```
// If your control does not conform to the apartment-model rules, then
// you must modify the code below, changing the 6th parameter from
// afxRegApartmentThreading to 0.
if (bRegister)
 return AfxOleRegisterControlClass(
  AfxGetInstanceHandle(),
  m_clsid,
  m_lpszProgID,
  IDS_PGM15A,
  IDB_PGM15A,
  afxRegApartmentThreading,
  _dwPgm15aOleMisc,
  _tlid,
  wVerMajor,
  wVerMinor);
 else
  return AfxOleUnregisterClass(m_clsid, m_lpszProgID);
}


// StopLightCtrl::StopLightCtrl - Constructor
StopLightCtrl::StopLightCtrl() {
 InitializeIIDs(&IID_DPgm15a, &IID_DPgm15aEvents);
 caption = "put your title here";
 whichIsOn = 0;
}


// StopLightCtrl::~StopLightCtrl - Destructor
StopLightCtrl::~StopLightCtrl() {
 // TODO: Cleanup your control's instance data here.
}


// StopLightCtrl::OnDraw - Drawing function
void StopLightCtrl::OnDraw (CDC* pdc, const CRect& rcBounds,
                            const CRect& rcInvalid) {
 if (!pdc)
  return;
 pdc->SetBkMode (TRANSPARENT);
 pdc->SelectStockObject (LTGRAY_BRUSH);
 pdc->Rectangle (rcBounds);  // erase our window
 // draw the three outer radio button circles
 pdc->Ellipse (&outerRed);
 pdc->Ellipse (&outerYellow);
 pdc->Ellipse (&outerGreen);

 // for each button, if it is selected, insert the color brush
 // draw the center circle
 // if it has the focus, draw the focus rectangle
 if (whichIsOn == 0) pdc->SelectObject (brushRed);
 else pdc->SelectObject (::GetStockObject (LTGRAY_BRUSH));
 pdc->Ellipse (red);

 if (whichIsOn == 1) pdc->SelectObject (brushYellow);
 else pdc->SelectObject (::GetStockObject (LTGRAY_BRUSH));
 pdc->Ellipse (yellow);

 if (whichIsOn == 2) pdc->SelectObject (brushGreen);
 else pdc->SelectObject (::GetStockObject (LTGRAY_BRUSH));
 pdc->Ellipse (green);
```

```
 // show the text line
 pdc->TextOut (textStart.x, textStart.y, caption);
}

void StopLightCtrl::OnWhichIsOnChanged() {
 Invalidate ();
 SetModifiedFlag ();
}

void StopLightCtrl::OnCaptionChanged() {
 Invalidate ();
 SetModifiedFlag ();
}

// StopLightCtrl::GetControlFlags -
// Flags to customize MFC's implementation of ActiveX controls.
DWORD StopLightCtrl::GetControlFlags() {
 DWORD dwFlags = COleControl::GetControlFlags();

 // The control can receive mouse notifications when inactive.
 // TODO: if you write handlers for WM_SETCURSOR and WM_MOUSEMOVE,
 //          avoid using the m_hWnd member variable without first
 //          checking that its value is non-NULL.
 dwFlags |= pointerInactive;
 return dwFlags;
}

// StopLightCtrl::OnResetState - Reset control to default state
void StopLightCtrl::OnResetState() {
 COleControl::OnResetState();  // Resets defaults found in DoPropExchange
 // TODO: Reset any other control state here.
}

// StopLightCtrl message handlers
void StopLightCtrl::OnSize(UINT nType, int cx, int cy) {
 COleControl::OnSize(nType, cx, cy);
 if (cx == 0) return;
 // layout the three radio buttons and text locations
 // each button has two parts: outer circle and inner circle
 // outer circle are 15 pixels in diameter or 45 total
 // place the three buttons centered vertically within the window's
 // height and 10 pixels from the left edge
 // place text 2 pixels above the start of the center button
 GetClientRect (client);
 int top = (client.Height () - 45)/2;
 outerRed.top = top;
 outerRed.bottom = outerRed.top + 15;
 outerYellow.top = outerRed.bottom;
 outerYellow.bottom = outerYellow.top + 15;
 outerGreen.top = outerYellow.bottom;
 outerGreen.bottom = outerGreen.top + 15;
 outerRed.left = outerYellow.left = outerGreen.left = 10;
 outerRed.right = outerYellow.right = outerGreen.right = outerRed.left + 15;

 textStart.x = outerYellow.right + 4;
 textStart.y = outerYellow.top - 2;

 // inner colored circles are 4 pixels less in diameter
```

```
 red = outerRed;
 yellow = outerYellow;
 green = outerGreen;
 red.DeflateRect (2, 2);
 yellow.DeflateRect (2, 2);
 green.DeflateRect (2, 2);
}

void StopLightCtrl::OnLButtonDown(UINT nFlags, CPoint point) {
 COleControl::OnLButtonDown(nFlags, point);
 // sort out which button was clicked and set both
 // the integer indicator and force a repaint showing that one in
 // its color, while undoing the others colors
 if (red.PtInRect (point)) {
  whichIsOn = 0;
  Invalidate ();
 }
 else if (yellow.PtInRect (point)) {
  whichIsOn = 1;
  Invalidate ();
 }
 else if (green.PtInRect (point)) {
  whichIsOn = 2;
  Invalidate ();
 }
}

int StopLightCtrl::OnCreate(LPCREATESTRUCT lpCreateStruct) {
 if (COleControl::OnCreate(lpCreateStruct) == -1)
  return -1;

 // create our three colored brushes
 brushRed.CreateSolidBrush (RGB (255,0,0));
 brushYellow.CreateSolidBrush (RGB (255,255,0));
 brushGreen.CreateSolidBrush (RGB (0,255,0));

 return 0;
}

void StopLightCtrl::SetWhichIsOn(long which) {
 if (which < 0 || which > 2)
  whichIsOn = 0;
 else
  whichIsOn = which;
 Invalidate ();
}

long StopLightCtrl::GetWhichIsOn (void) {
 return whichIsOn;
}
```

While the basic control coding is obvious, some sections are totally new and unfortunately require manual editing by you. Let's examine these, beginning with the Dispatch map.

```
// Dispatch map
BEGIN_DISPATCH_MAP(StopLightCtrl, COleControl)
 DISP_PROPERTY(StopLightCtrl, "Caption", caption, VT_BSTR)
 DISP_PROPERTY(StopLightCtrl, "Which Is On", whichIsOn, VT_I4)
```

```
DISP_FUNCTION(StopLightCtrl, "SetWhichIsOn", SetWhichIsOn, VT_EMPTY, VTS_I4)
DISP_FUNCTION(StopLightCtrl, "GetWhichIsOn", GetWhichIsOn, VT_I4, VTS_NONE)
DISP_PROPERTY_NOTIFY(StopLightCtrl, "Caption", caption, OnCaptionChanged,
                  VT_BSTR)
DISP_PROPERTY_NOTIFY(StopLightCtrl, "Which Is On", whichIsOn,
                  OnWhichIsOnChanged, VT_I4)
END_DISPATCH_MAP()
```

Here, you add a **DISP_PROPERTY** notice for each property of the control that is to be exposed to the world. The first parameter is the class, the second is a string name of the property, the third is the member variable, and the fourth is its data type in **VARIANT** notation. The caption is a **BSTR**, while whichIsOn is a long.

Next, add a **DISP_FUNCTION** macro for the two get/set functions. The fourth parameter is the return value's data type and the fifth is the parameter(s) data type(s). **VT_EMPTY** indicates a void return function. **VTS_I4** is a long, **VTS_NONE** indicates no parameters are passed.

Finally, add a **DISP_PROPERTY_NOTIFY** macro for each property. Thus, when the property page makes a change, the control will be notified so that it can update its members accordingly.

Next, we add **PX_nnn** macros to the property exchange function. Each type of data has its own PX_ macro. Here, **PX_String** handles character strings, while **PX_Long** handle a long.

```
// StopLightCtrl::DoPropExchange - Persistence support
void StopLightCtrl::DoPropExchange(CPropExchange* pPX) {
 ExchangeVersion(pPX, MAKELONG(_wVerMinor, _wVerMajor));
 COleControl::DoPropExchange(pPX);
 PX_String(pPX, _T("Caption"), caption);
 PX_Long (pPX, _T("Which Is On"), whichIsOn);
 // TODO: Call PX_ functions for each persistent custom property.
}
```

Some others are **PX_Short**, **PX_Float**, **PX_Double**, **PX_Bool**, and **PX_ULong**.

Next, notice that in **OnDraw**, we are given the DC on which to draw and the invalid rectangle, which represents our whole control, if this is a full repaint. I draw a rectangle around this while area to set off the control as a single visual element.

```
void StopLightCtrl::OnDraw (CDC* pdc, const CRect& rcBounds,
                          const CRect& rcInvalid) {
 if (!pdc)
  return;
 pdc->SetBkMode (TRANSPARENT);
 pdc->SelectStockObject (LTGRAY_BRUSH);
 pdc->Rectangle (rcBounds);
```

Essentially, that is all to the control class. Now let's look at the corresponding property page for the control. The first action is to open the resource file and edit the dialog property page, showing an edit control for each property that you wish to expose and allow users to modify. This is shown in Figure 15.5.

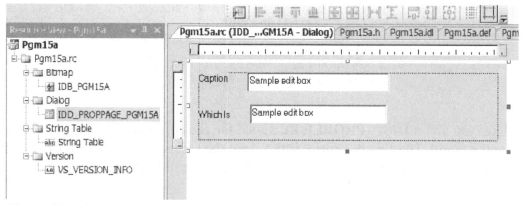

Figure 15.5 Creating the Property Page Dialog for the Control

Then, add data members for these in the property page class.

Listing for File: StopLightPpg.h—Pgm15a

```
#pragma once

// StopLightPpg.h : Declaration of the StopLightPropPage property page class.

class StopLightPropPage : public COlePropertyPage {
 DECLARE_DYNCREATE(StopLightPropPage)
 DECLARE_OLECREATE_EX(StopLightPropPage)

public:
 StopLightPropPage();
 CString   caption;
 long      whichIsOn;
 enum { IDD = IDD_PROPPAGE_PGM15A };

protected:
 virtual void DoDataExchange(CDataExchange* pDX);      // DDX/DDV support

 DECLARE_MESSAGE_MAP()
};
```
Coding the property page parallels that of a dialog.

Listing for File: StopLightPpg.cpp—Pgm15a

```
// StopLightPpg.cpp : Implementation of the StopLightPropPage property page

#include "stdafx.h"
#include "Pgm15a.h"
#include "StopLightPpg.h"

#ifdef _DEBUG
#define new DEBUG_NEW
#endif

IMPLEMENT_DYNCREATE(StopLightPropPage, COlePropertyPage)

// Message map
```

```
BEGIN_MESSAGE_MAP(StopLightPropPage, COlePropertyPage)
END_MESSAGE_MAP()

// Initialize class factory and guid
IMPLEMENT_OLECREATE_EX(StopLightPropPage, "StopLightPropPage.1",
 0xec55f717, 0xf301, 0x4e1e, 0xb0, 0x59, 0xb8, 0xab, 0xd6, 0xd1, 0xd2, 0x14)

// StopLightPropPage::StopLightPropPageFactory::UpdateRegistry -
// Adds or removes system registry entries for StopLightPropPage
BOOL StopLightPropPage::StopLightPropPageFactory::UpdateRegistry (
                        BOOL bRegister) {
 if (bRegister)
  return AfxOleRegisterPropertyPageClass(AfxGetInstanceHandle(),
                                  m_clsid, IDS_PGM15A_PPG);
 else
  return AfxOleUnregisterClass(m_clsid, NULL);
}

// StopLightPropPage::StopLightPropPage - Constructor
StopLightPropPage::StopLightPropPage() :
     COlePropertyPage(IDD, IDS_PGM15A_PPG_CAPTION) {
}

// StopLightPropPage::DoDataExchange - Moves data between page and properties
void StopLightPropPage::DoDataExchange(CDataExchange* pDX) {
 DDP_Text(pDX, IDC_EDIT_CAPTION, caption, _T("Caption"));
 DDX_Text(pDX, IDC_EDIT_CAPTION, caption);
 DDP_Text (pDX, IDC_EDIT_WHICHISON, whichIsOn, _T("Which Is On"));
 DDX_Text (pDX, IDC_EDIT_WHICHISON, whichIsOn);
 DDV_MinMaxInt (pDX, whichIsOn, 0, 2);
 DDP_PostProcessing(pDX);
}

// StopLightPropPage message handlers
```

The only new thing here is in the **DoDataExchange** function. A **DDP_** macro must precede each **DDX_** transfer macro. And the **DDP_PostProcessing** macro comes last. The **DDP_Text** macro specifies the resource ID number and the member name associated with it and the character string property name of the member.

Since this may be the first time that you've seen an ActiveX control project, here is the dll wrapper class, the app class. I made no changes in it from what the wizard generated for me.

Listing for File: Pgm15a.h
```
#pragma once

#if !defined( __AFXCTL_H__ )
#error "include 'afxctl.h' before including this file"
#endif

#include "resource.h"       // main symbols

class CPgm15aApp : public COleControlModule {
public:
     BOOL InitInstance();
     int ExitInstance();
```

```
};

extern const GUID CDECL _tlid;
extern const WORD _wVerMajor;
extern const WORD _wVerMinor;
```

Listing for File: Pgm15a.cpp

```cpp
#include "stdafx.h"
#include "Pgm15a.h"

#ifdef _DEBUG
#define new DEBUG_NEW
#endif

CPgm15aApp theApp;

const GUID CDECL BASED_CODE _tlid =
        { 0xC5BE9A1B, 0x8C73, 0x4B20, { 0xA3, 0x2E, 0xE, 0x33, 0x59, 0x69,
0x98, 0x4F } };
const WORD _wVerMajor = 1;
const WORD _wVerMinor = 0;

// CPgm15aApp::InitInstance - DLL initialization
BOOL CPgm15aApp::InitInstance() {
 BOOL bInit = COleControlModule::InitInstance();
 if (bInit)          {
  // TODO: Add your own module initialization code here.
 }
 return bInit;
}

// CPgm15aApp::ExitInstance - DLL termination
int CPgm15aApp::ExitInstance() {
 // TODO: Add your own module termination code here.
 return COleControlModule::ExitInstance();
}

// DllRegisterServer - Adds entries to the system registry
STDAPI DllRegisterServer(void) {
 AFX_MANAGE_STATE(_afxModuleAddrThis);
 if (!AfxOleRegisterTypeLib(AfxGetInstanceHandle(), _tlid))
  return ResultFromScode(SELFREG_E_TYPELIB);

 if (!COleObjectFactoryEx::UpdateRegistryAll(TRUE))
  return ResultFromScode(SELFREG_E_CLASS);

 return NOERROR;
}

// DllUnregisterServer - Removes entries from the system registry
STDAPI DllUnregisterServer(void) {
 AFX_MANAGE_STATE(_afxModuleAddrThis);

 if (!AfxOleUnregisterTypeLib(_tlid, _wVerMajor, _wVerMinor))
  return ResultFromScode(SELFREG_E_TYPELIB);

 if (!COleObjectFactoryEx::UpdateRegistryAll(FALSE))
  return ResultFromScode(SELFREG_E_CLASS);
```

```
    return NOERROR;
}
```

Here is the definition of our ocx file. I made no changes in it either.

Listing for File: Pgn15a.def

```
; Pgm15a.def : Declares the module parameters.

LIBRARY        "Pgm15a.OCX"

EXPORTS
       DllCanUnloadNow       PRIVATE
       DllGetClassObject     PRIVATE
       DllRegisterServer     PRIVATE
       DllUnregisterServer   PRIVATE
```

However, I did need to make some changes to the type lib file, the .idl file. Here is the file and the changes I made are in bold face.

Listing for File: Pgm15a.idl

```
// Pgm15a.idl : type library source for ActiveX Control project.

// This file will be processed by the MIDL compiler tool to
// produce the type library (Pgm15a.tlb) that will become a resource in
// Pgm15a.ocx.

#include <olectl.h>
#include <idispids.h>

[ uuid(C5BE9A1B-8C73-4B20-A32E-0E335969984F), version(1.0),
  helpfile("Pgm15a.hlp"),
  helpstring("Pgm15a ActiveX Control module"),
  control ]
library Pgm15aLib
{
       importlib(STDOLE_TLB);

       // Primary dispatch interface for StopLightCtrl

       [ uuid(9EAC2936-662A-49EE-A6BF-4D31A0EA4829),
         helpstring("Dispatch interface for StopLight Control")]
       dispinterface _DPgm15a
       {
               properties:
   [id(1)] BSTR caption;
   [id(2)] long whichIsOn;
               methods:
   [id(3)] void SetWhichIsOn (long which);
   [id(4)] long GetWhichIsOn(void);
       };

       // Event dispatch interface for StopLightCtrl

       [ uuid(0F1950DF-C4D1-499F-A4E7-9A78DD75081E),
         helpstring("Event interface for StopLight Control") ]
       dispinterface _DPgm15aEvents
```

```
{
        properties:
               //  Event interface has no properties

        methods:
};

//  Class information for StopLightCtrl

[ uuid(D0D3E66F-6EF9-48E7-8AE4-A064A90E585E),
  helpstring("StopLight Control"), control ]
coclass Pgm15a
{
        [default] dispinterface _DPgm15a;
        [default, source] dispinterface _DPgm15aEvents;
};

};
```

In the primary dispatch section, add the properties and methods you wish exposed for the users to call.

```
        properties:
[id(1)]  BSTR caption;
[id(2)]  long whichIsOn;
        methods:
[id(3)]  void SetWhichIsOn (long which);
[id(4)]  long GetWhichIsOn(void);
```

Use a different number for each property and method.

Finally, in the resource editor, edit the Version Information and perhaps create a fancy icon to represent your control.

When you build the project, Pgm15a.ocx is the final result. Next, you need to fully test it and get the bugs out. To do this, hit Start Debugging or Start without Debugging. Often Visual Studio needs to know what will be the testing container that will hold the control and call its methods and set its properties. Here is the dialog that comes up. Visual Studio provides a simple container for testing. I have chosen it as you can see in Figure 15.6.

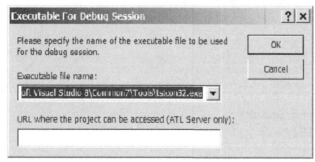

Figure 15.6 Picking the Test Container

When the Test Program comes up, choose Add New Control and find the StopLight control. Now you can use options to set the control's properties, resize it, click on the buttons and so on to watch it work. This is shown in Figure 15.7.

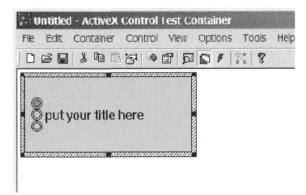

Figure 15.7 Testing the Control

With the control now working properly, the next step is to create a real tester program that uses our control in one of its dialogs.

Using the Stoplight Control—Pgm15b

Look back to Figure 15.3 to see how our control appears in the dialog template, as seen in the resource editor. Note, when you make the Pgm15b new project, you need to make sure that ActiveX controls is checked as one of the options before you generate the new classes and coding.

If you do not see the Stoplight control in your toolbox, click on Custom Control and put an instance of that onto your dialog template. Then, right click on it and choose Insert ActiveX Control. Scroll down and find the Stoplight control and select that one.

To get our control onto the toolbox, like a button, choose Tools, Choose Toolbox Items. Then click on the COM Components tab. Scroll down and **check** Stoplight Control. Click OK and the control is now in the toolbox so that you can drag it onto any dialog template.

Now if you right click on your instance of the Stoplight Control and choose properties, you can see our two, caption and whichIsOn. Thus, one could set their initial settings here in the resource editor, as well as in code when the dialog is launched.

If the control does not paint itself, right click on it and choose Edit Control, then it will become painted. Next, add a variable for the Stoplight control in the dialog class as usual. Notice that the wizard now adds a new pair of files to our solution, 11.h and 11.cpp, defining the ActiveX control's interface. In the dialog class, the data type is **C11** and it added a function, **OnFinalRelease** as well, highlighted in bold face.

Listing for File: StopLightDlg.h—Pgm15b

```
#include "11.h"

class StopLightDlg : public CDialog {
 DECLARE_DYNAMIC(StopLightDlg)

public:
 StopLightDlg(CWnd* pParent = NULL);    // standard constructor
 virtual ~StopLightDlg();
 enum { IDD = IDD_DIALOG1 };

 C11 m_rygControl;
 long whichIsOn;
 CString caption;

 void SetCaption (const char* cap);
 void SetWhichIsOn (long which);
 long GetWhichIsOn  () const;

 virtual void OnFinalRelease();
 virtual BOOL OnInitDialog();

protected:
 virtual void DoDataExchange(CDataExchange* pDX);     // DDX/DDV support

DECLARE_MESSAGE_MAP()
DECLARE_DISPATCH_MAP()
DECLARE_INTERFACE_MAP()
virtual void OnOK();
};
```

Let's see what was in that new class that was added. It is the **IDispatch** wrapper class, made from our type information. Notice that we do not ever modify this file, because the file can be remade by the compiler. If it does remake it, your changes will be lost.

Listing for file: 11.h—Pgm15b

```
#pragma once

// Machine generated IDispatch wrapper class(es) created by Microsoft Visual //
C++

// NOTE: Do not modify the contents of this file.  If this class is
// regenerated by
//  Microsoft Visual C++, your modifications will be overwritten.

/////////////////////////////////////////////////////////////////////////////
// C11 wrapper class

class C11 : public Cwnd {
protected:
 DECLARE_DYNCREATE(C11)
public:
 CLSID const& GetClsid() {
  static CLSID const clsid
```

```
   = { 0xD0D3E66F, 0x6EF9, 0x48E7, { 0x8A, 0xE4, 0xA0, 0x64, 0xA9, 0xE, 0x58,
0x5E } };
  return clsid;
}

virtual BOOL Create(LPCTSTR lpszClassName, LPCTSTR lpszWindowName,
                    DWORD dwStyle, const RECT& rect, CWnd* pParentWnd,
                    UINT nID, CCreateContext* pContext = NULL) {
 return CreateControl(GetClsid(), lpszWindowName, dwStyle, rect, pParentWnd,
                    nID);
}

BOOL Create(LPCTSTR lpszWindowName, DWORD dwStyle, const RECT& rect,
            CWnd* pParentWnd, UINT nID, CFile* pPersist = NULL,
            BOOL bStorage = FALSE, BSTR bstrLicKey = NULL) {
 return CreateControl(GetClsid(), lpszWindowName, dwStyle, rect, pParentWnd,
                    nID, pPersist, bStorage, bstrLicKey);
}

// Attributes
public:

// Operations
public:

// _DPgm15a

// Functions
//

void SetWhichIsOn(long which) {
 static BYTE parms[] = VTS_I4 ;
 InvokeHelper(0x3, DISPATCH_METHOD, VT_EMPTY, NULL, parms, which);
}

long GetWhichIsOn() {
 long result;
 InvokeHelper(0x4, DISPATCH_METHOD, VT_I4, (void*)&result, NULL);
 return result;
}

// Properties
//

CString Getcaption() {
 CString result;
 GetProperty(0x1, VT_BSTR, (void*)&result);
 return result;
}
void Setcaption(CString propVal) {
 SetProperty(0x1, VT_BSTR, propVal);
}

long GetwhichIsOn() {
 long result;
 GetProperty(0x2, VT_I4, (void*)&result);
 return result;
}
```

```
void SetwhichIsOn(long propVal) {
 SetProperty(0x2, VT_I4, propVal);
}
};
```

Listing for File: 11.cpp—Pgm15b

```
// Machine generated IDispatch wrapper class(es) created by Microsoft Visual
// C++

// NOTE: Do not modify the contents of this file.  If this class is
// regenerated by
//  Microsoft Visual C++, your modifications will be overwritten.

#include "stdafx.h"
#include "11.h"

/////////////////////////////////////////////////////////////////////////////
// C11

IMPLEMENT_DYNCREATE(C11, CWnd)

/////////////////////////////////////////////////////////////////////////////
// C11 properties

/////////////////////////////////////////////////////////////////////////////
// C11 operations
```

Our dialog class implementation has a few new things added to it. These are highlighted in bold face below.

Listing for File: StopLightDlg.cpp—Pgm15b

```
...
IMPLEMENT_DYNAMIC(StopLightDlg, CDialog)

StopLightDlg::StopLightDlg(CWnd* pParent /*=NULL*/)
                : CDialog(StopLightDlg::IDD, pParent) {
 EnableAutomation();
 caption = "";
 whichIsOn = -1;
}

StopLightDlg::~StopLightDlg() { }

void StopLightDlg::SetCaption (const char* cap) {
 caption = cap;
}

void StopLightDlg::SetWhichIsOn (long which) {
 whichIsOn = which;
}

long StopLightDlg::GetWhichIsOn  () const {
 return whichIsOn;
}
```

```
void StopLightDlg::OnFinalRelease() {
    CDialog::OnFinalRelease();
}

void StopLightDlg::DoDataExchange(CDataExchange* pDX) {
 CDialog::DoDataExchange(pDX);
 DDX_Control(pDX, IDC_11, m_rygControl);
}

BEGIN_MESSAGE_MAP(StopLightDlg, CDialog)
END_MESSAGE_MAP()

BEGIN_DISPATCH_MAP(StopLightDlg, CDialog)
END_DISPATCH_MAP()

// Note: we add support for IID_IStopLightDlg to support typesafe binding
//  from VBA.  This IID must match the GUID that is attached to the
//  dispinterface in the .IDL file.

// {F6F293C4-1102-49B9-BC8F-BFD0E2BFEB43}
static const IID IID_IStopLightDlg =
{ 0xF6F293C4, 0x1102, 0x49B9, { 0xBC, 0x8F, 0xBF, 0xD0, 0xE2, 0xBF, 0xEB, 0x43
} };

BEGIN_INTERFACE_MAP(StopLightDlg, CDialog)
 INTERFACE_PART(StopLightDlg, IID_IStopLightDlg, Dispatch)
END_INTERFACE_MAP()

BOOL StopLightDlg::OnInitDialog() {
 CDialog::OnInitDialog();
 if (!caption.IsEmpty()) {
  m_rygControl.Setcaption (caption);
 }
 if (whichIsOn != -1) {
  m_rygControl.SetWhichIsOn (whichIsOn);
 }
 return TRUE;
}

void StopLightDlg::OnOK() {
 whichIsOn = m_rygControl.GetWhichIsOn ();
 CDialog::OnOK();
}
```

We use the control just like any other control, using its member name to invoke SetCaption, SetWhichIsOn, and GetWhichIsOn. The wizard has inserted the IID of the StopLight control, added a OnFinalRelease function, a dispatch map, and an interface map, in which it has made the hookup to the control for us.

The MainFrame class creates and invokes the dialog as before. There is nothing new here.

```
void MainFrame::OnEditDialog() {
 StopLightDlg dlg;
 dlg.SetCaption ("Credit Limit Approaching?");
 dlg.SetWhichIsOn (2);
 dlg.DoModal ();
```

```
const char* colormsgs[3] = {"Red", "Yellow", "Green"};
CClientDC dc (this);
CRect r(2, 90, 500, 170);
dc.Rectangle (&r);
CString msg = "Control has selected: ";
msg += colormsgs[dlg.GetWhichIsOn()];
dc.TextOut (10, 100, msg);
}
```

What about the app class? There is a bit new here to initialize ActiveX.

```
BOOL Pgm15bApp::InitInstance() {
 // InitCommonControlsEx() is required on Windows XP if an application
 // manifest specifies use of ComCtl32.dll version 6 or later to enable
 // visual styles.  Otherwise, any window creation will fail.
 INITCOMMONCONTROLSEX InitCtrls;
 InitCtrls.dwSize = sizeof(InitCtrls);
 // Set this to include all the common control classes you want to use
 // in your application.
 InitCtrls.dwICC = ICC_WIN95_CLASSES;
 InitCommonControlsEx(&InitCtrls);

 CWinApp::InitInstance();

 // Initialize OLE libraries
 if (!AfxOleInit())       {
  AfxMessageBox(IDP_OLE_INIT_FAILED);
  return FALSE;
 }
 AfxEnableControlContainer();
 SetRegistryKey(_T("WindowsMFCII"));
 MainFrame* pFrame = new MainFrame;
```

Finally, what about the standard MFC includes, stfafx.h? There have been a lot of changes here, all automatically generated by the wizard.

```
#pragma once

#ifndef _SECURE_ATL
#define _SECURE_ATL 1
#endif

#ifndef VC_EXTRALEAN
#define VC_EXTRALEAN              // Exclude rarely-used stuff from Windows headers
#endif

// Modify the following defines if you have to target a platform prior to the //
ones specified below.
// Refer to MSDN for the latest info on corresponding values for different
// platforms.
#ifndef WINVER    // Allow use of features specific to Windows XP or later.
#define WINVER 0x0501
// Change this to the appropriate value to target other versions of Windows.
#endif

#ifndef _WIN32_WINNT// Allow use of features specific to Windows XP or later.

#define _WIN32_WINNT 0x0501
```

```
// Change this to the appropriate value to target other versions of Windows.
#endif

#ifndef _WIN32_WINDOWS
// Allow use of features specific to Windows 98 or later.
#define _WIN32_WINDOWS 0x0410
// Change this to the appropriate value to target Windows Me or later.
#endif

#ifndef _WIN32_IE  // Allow use of features specific to IE 6.0 or later.
#define _WIN32_IE 0x0600
// Change this to the appropriate value to target other versions of IE.
#endif

#define _ATL_CSTRING_EXPLICIT_CONSTRUCTORS
// some CString constructors will be explicit

// turns off MFC's hiding of some common and often safely ignored warning
// messages
#define _AFX_ALL_WARNINGS

#include <afxwin.h>         // MFC core and standard components
#include <afxext.h>         // MFC extensions
#include <afxdisp.h>        // MFC Automation classes

#ifndef _AFX_NO_OLE_SUPPORT
#include <afxdtctl.h>    // MFC support for Internet Explorer 4 Common Controls
#endif
#ifndef _AFX_NO_AFXCMN_SUPPORT
#include <afxcmn.h>       // MFC support for Windows Common Controls
#endif // _AFX_NO_AFXCMN_SUPPORT

#ifdef _UNICODE
#if defined _M_IX86
#pragma    comment(linker,"/manifestdependency:\"type='win32'
name='Microsoft.Windows.Common-Controls'    version='6.0.0.0'
processorArchitecture='x86' publicKeyToken='6595b64144ccf1df' language='*'\"")
#elif defined _M_IA64
#pragma    comment(linker,"/manifestdependency:\"type='win32'
name='Microsoft.Windows.Common-Controls'    version='6.0.0.0'
processorArchitecture='ia64' publicKeyToken='6595b64144ccf1df' language='*'\"")
#elif defined _M_X64
#pragma    comment(linker,"/manifestdependency:\"type='win32'
name='Microsoft.Windows.Common-Controls'    version='6.0.0.0'
processorArchitecture='amd64' publicKeyToken='6595b64144ccf1df' language='*'\"")
#else
#pragma    comment(linker,"/manifestdependency:\"type='win32'
name='Microsoft.Windows.Common-Controls'    version='6.0.0.0'
processorArchitecture='*' publicKeyToken='6595b64144ccf1df' language='*'\"")
#endif
#endif
```

I'm glad that I don't have to invent and code that bunch!

We've only scratched the surface of ActiveX controls. Make use of your online help to find out more about each of the different sections, functions, and identifiers in this sample. Then, see if you can make your own simple control.

Chapter 16 Writing DLLs

The Four Calling Conventions Used in Windows Programming

Before you can tackle writing your own dynamic link libraries, you must understand the four calling conventions that are used. Additionally, three others have now been dropped and are no longer supported.

A calling convention is a bargain between the caller and the function. Let's say that function Fun is passed two integers and returns an integer result, the larger of the two. The prototype would be:

```
int Fun (int number1, int number2);
```

It could crudely be implemented this way.

```
int Fun (int number1, int number2) {
 int big;
 big = number1 > number2 ? number1 : number2;
 return big;
}
```

The caller would invoke it this way.

```
 int n1, n2;
 int bigger = Fun (n1, n2);
```

All this has to be implemented by the compiler using assembler or machine instructions. Let's ignore multi-threading for now. Given the set of instructions, the layout in memory shown in Figure 16.1 illustrates that there are two key locations of which the computer executing the instructions must constantly keep track: the current instruction to execute and the top of the stack, where the automatic/local variables of the current function are located.

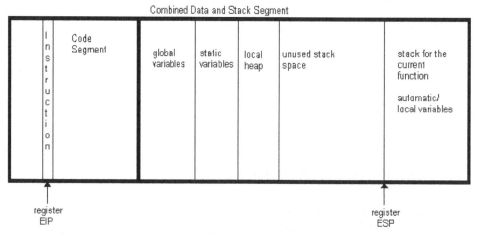

Figure 16.1 A Program with Registers EIP and ESP

The computer keeps track of the instruction to be executed with register EIP, the extended instruction pointer. It keeps track of the top of the stack with register ESP, extended stack pointer. If the computer knows this location, then it can find the current function's local or automatic storage variables at some offset from this location or address.

Now the caller invokes function Fun. At the first instruction within Fun, the two key registers EIP and ESP are updated as shown in Figure 16.2.

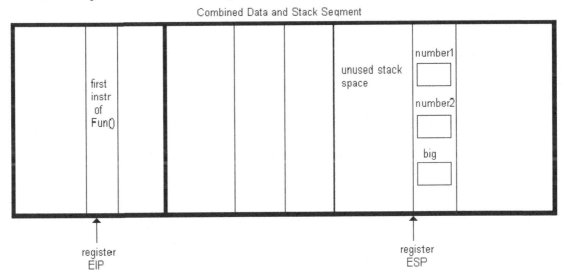

Figure 16.2 EIP and ESP at the First Instruction of Function Fun

A picture is worth a thousand words. Let's see this in operation. In the samples folder, find the folder for Pgm16Console and open that solution. Here is this dinky program discussed above. To keep the confusion down, I made the following project options changes:
C/C++ tab | General | set Debug Information Format to Program Database /Zi
C/C++ tab | Code Generation | set Basic Runtime Checks to Default
Linker tab | General | set Enable Incremental Linking to No

Place a break point on the line in main, where it calls function Fun. Choose Go Debug. When the break point triggers, use the Debug menu | Window | Registers to open the registers window and Debug |Window | Watch if you do not already have a Watch window opened. Finally, Debug | Window | Disassemble opens the disassembly window, showing the actual instructions. Now right click in the disassembly window and make sure that Show Address, Show Source Code, and show Code Bytes are checked.

You should see something that closely resembles Figure 16.3. In the figure, I have merged the registers window over the disassembly listing to save space. Notice it is about to call the function Fun. Notice the value in EIP is 00401014, which is where the yellow arrow is pointing in the code. Press F10, execute one instruction. Notice the new value in EIP and where it is at in the listing. It has just executed that first assembler instruction.

```
 Disassembly | Pgm16Console.cpp
Address: main(void)                ▼

   #include <iomanip>
   using namespace std;                          Registers
                                             EAX = 00359B50 EBX = 7FFDE000 ECX = 003564C8 EDX = 00000001
   int Fun (int n1, int n2);                 ESI = 0B02F9F4 EDI = 00000000 EIP = 00401014 ESP = 0012FF5C
                                             EBP = 0012FF68 EFL = 00000216
   int main () {
   00401000 55              push     ebp        0012FF64 = 0000002A
   00401001 8B EC           mov      ebp,esp
   00401003 83 EC 0C        sub      esp,0Ch
     int num1 = 10;
   00401006 C7 45 F4 0A 00 00 00 mov       dword ptr [num1],0Ah
     int num2 = 42;
   0040100D C7 45 FC 2A 00 00 00 mov       dword ptr [num2],2Ah

     int bigger = Fun (num1, num2);
 ▷ 00401014 8B 45 FC        mov      eax,dword ptr [num2]
   00401017 50              push     eax
   00401018 8B 4D F4        mov      ecx,dword ptr [num1]
   0040101B 51              push     ecx
   0040101C E8 1F 00 00 00  call     Fun (401040h)
   00401021 83 C4 08        add      esp,8
   00401024 89 45 F8        mov      dword ptr [bigger],eax

     cout << bigger;
   00401027 8B 55 F8        mov      edx,dword ptr [bigger]
   0040102A 52              push     edx
   0040102B 8B 0D 38 20 40 00 mov     ecx,dword ptr [__imp_std::cout (402038h)]
   00401031 FF 15 3C 20 40 00 call    dword ptr [__imp_std::basic_ostream<char,std::char_traits<char> >::operator<<

     return 0;
   00401037 33 C0           xor      eax,eax
   }
```

Figure 16.3 About to Call Function Fun — the Assembler Instructions to Do So

A mov instruction is moving data from memory location, num2 into the work register eax. The push instruction stores eax onto the stack. The call instruction invokes the function, transferring control to the first instruction in Fun. Experiment with F10 and see what is happening. Make sure that you hit F11 to step Into function Fun. F10 steps over the function, that is calling it and then regaining control once the function is done. Look what happens to the value in ESP when the call is done. Initially, it is pointing to 0012FF5C, or main's stack space. After the call, it is now pointing to Fun's stack space. By the time that you reach the code to find which number is larger, ESP has been changed to 0012FF44, Fun's stack space. Continue stepping through the program until Fun is done. Notice that it ends with a ret instruction, return to the caller.

Specifically, a push instruction of a 32-bit or four byte item decrements the ESP register by four and stores the four bytes onto the stack at that location. The pop of a 32-bit value retrieves the four bytes at the current ESP location and adds four to the ESP register. Also, using a mov or add instruction can alter the value in ESP, as add esp,8 would indicate.

When main calls Fun, it must pass the two parameters to Fun. It does this by pushing the two integers onto the stack.

```
mov  eax,dword ptr [num1]
push eax
```

When Fun returns big, since it is four bytes, it places the contents of big into register eax. Back in main, after the function returns to main, main then does

```
mov dword ptr [bigger],eax
```

which stores the answer back into variable bigger. The phrase dword ptr means a four byte size and you can think of the [] as meaning memory location of.

A calling convention is a protocol for passing parameters or arguments to a function, retrieving them, and the handling of the stack ESP during the call. There are three conventions in use in Microsoft coding.

```
__cdecl
__stdcall
thiscall
```

Yes, that is two _ characters preceding cdecl.

The __cdecl Convention

This convention is the default for C and C++ programs.

1. The arguments are passed from right to left, so that the left-most or first parameter appears first at the top of the stack.

2. It is the caller's responsibility to pop these arguments from the stack before issuing the return.

3.An _ underscore is prefixed to names.

Hence, in this convention, each function is slightly larger, as each time a function is called, it must generate code to remove the parameters from the stack.

Look again at your disassembly of Pgm16Console. Look at the call to Fun.

```
int bigger = Fun (num1, num2);
00401014 8B 45 FC            mov      eax,dword ptr [num2]
00401017 50                  push     eax
00401018 8B 4D F4            mov      ecx,dword ptr [num1]
0040101B 51                  push     ecx
0040101C E8 1F 00 00 00      call     Fun (401040h)
00401021 83 C4 08            add      esp,8
```

Notice that the second parameter, num2, is pushed first, then num1, the first parameter. Thus, as one looks down the stack, one sees first num1 and then num2, the parameters or arguments are in order. When the call executes, it pushes the ESP register onto the stack, here it places the value 00401021 onto the stack, the first instruction upon return from Fun. Upon return from the function, it adds 8 bytes to the ESP. This then places the top of the stack back over the two parameters which were pushed onto the stack just before the call to Fun.

Now look at the disassembly of the very start of Fun, before it gets to int big. You should see the following instructions.

```
int Fun (int n1, int n2) {
00401040 55                  push     ebp
00401041 8B EC               mov      ebp,esp
00401043 83 EC 08            sub      esp,8
```

It pushes onto the stack the current value of ebp, the extended base pointer, and replaces it with the current value of esp. Then, it sets esp to the start of the parameters.

Now look at the return portion of Fun.

```
00401065 8B E5               mov      esp,ebp
00401067 5D                  pop      ebp
00401068 C3                  ret
```

Notice that at the top of the stack, what is at the location specified by EBP is the previous value of ESP, that of function main. It is put into the ESP register, wiping out all of the parameters that were passed to Fun. Well, not wiped out really, it's just that the current location of the top of the stack is now pointing to main's variables, no longer Fun's variables. Then the return address is popped off the stack and the ret returns to main's next instruction. After it adds eight bytes to ESP, it is back to where it started.

Run the debugger and notice these effects. Particularly, note the ESP address before the first push as it is about to call Fun, then notice what it is after the return and addition of the eight bytes. It should be back to where it started.

Summarizing __cdecl, we have that the parameters are pushed onto the stack in reverse order and that the caller must adjust the ESP or stack pointer after the function returns to it to remove the parameters that it placed onto the stack before the call to the function.

This then allows a function to be passed a variable number of parameters, since only the caller knows precisely the number of parameters to be given to the function. This applies in particular to some of the standard functions, such as printf and scanf.

The __stdcall Convention

The __stdcall convention is used to call Win32 API functions. Often an alias is used, WINAPI or APIENTRY. In the file windef.h, Microsoft has the following define.
```
#define WINAPI __stdcall
```

The parameters or arguments are passed right to left, the same as the __cdecl. However, the function must pop its own parameters or arguments from the stack. In order for this to work, the function must know the precise number of bytes to remove from the stack. The compiler uses a "decorated name" for the function, appending an @ sign followed by the decimal number of bytes that the parameters or arguments occupy, as well as adding an _ before the name of the function. In the case of Fun, the compiled name of the function is: _Fun@8.

Again, open Pgm16Console. This time, change the calling convention property. Properties | C++ tab | Advanced tab | Calling Convention: change to __stdcall. Now rebuild the program. Note that main must remain __cdecl. All other functions called will use the __stdcall convention. Again set the break point on the call to Fun. Open the disassembly window and examine the code that was generated.
```
 int bigger = Fun (num1, num2);
00401014 8B 45 FC             mov             eax,dword ptr [num2]
00401017 50                   push            eax
00401018 8B 4D F4             mov             ecx,dword ptr [num1]
0040101B 51                   push            ecx
0040101C E8 1F 00 00 00       call            Fun (401040h)
00401021 89 45 F8             mov             dword ptr [bigger],eax
```

Notice that the arguments are pushed in reverse order as before and Fun is called. Absent is the add esp, 8 when the function returns. Now look at the code for Fun.

```
int Fun (int n1, int n2) {
00401040 55                      push          ebp
00401041 8B EC                   mov           ebp,esp
00401043 83 EC 08                sub           esp,8
 int big;
```

This is exactly the same. Now look at the return coding.

```
 return big;
00401062 8B 45 FC                mov           eax,dword ptr [big]
}
00401065 8B E5                   mov           esp,ebp
00401067 5D                      pop           ebp
00401068 C2 08 00                ret           8
```

After saving the return value in eax, it restores exp, pops ebp and issues a ret 8. The value of 8 is added to esp. Note that a simple ret always adds four bytes, the size of the return memory address. In __stdcall, it must also remove the 8 bytes of parameters or arguments that were passed. Thus, the ESP is back to where it was when control arrives back in the calling function.

The stack adjusting code is done once in the function. Hence, the overall code size of a program with many function calls to Fun is smaller, because this stack adjusting code is done once in the function. With __cdecl, that addition to ESP must be done in the callers after each function call, increasing the overall code size of the program.

Now when the compiler is building a project that includes all of the source files, if there is a mismatch between these, the compiler can handle it, forcing conventions where necessary.

What has this to do with DLL's? In a dll situation, the compiler cannot see the mismatches ahead of time and remedy them! There are two cases of mismatch.

First, say for example, the dll coding uses __cdecl and the main program that calls the dll's functions uses __stdcall for the calling convention. That is, the caller assumes a __stdcall convention is in use as it calls the dll function, which in turn assumes it is to use a __cdecl convention. Let's say Fun is now in the dll. What happens is that the ESP gets left 8 bytes too large with each function call. That is, our stack grows by 8 bytes per call to Fun. If many calls are made to Fun, eventually, stack size gets exceeded and the program crashes.

Second, let's have the dll coding use the __stdcall while the caller, main, uses __cdecl. In this case, the ESP ends up 8 bytes too short, effectively overlaying automatic or local variables of the caller function, main. This is called stack corruption, wild things can now occur, especially if one of the overlain variables of main is the number of elements in an array in main!

Stack Frames and Register EBP

In your beginning course in C++, I outlined the stack frame and its contents and use. Let's review this briefly. When main gets control from the startup code, on the stack will be the arguments to main, namely argc and argv. Also, as main is entered, it sets up space for its automatic or local variables on the stack. Thus, the stack frame for main consists of the following.

The return address for main's ret instruction
The parameters or arguments to main
The local variables defined in the main block of coding

When main enters a new block, such as the following, the stack frame, ESP, grows to create space for variable x.

```
if (z > 42) {
  int x = 0;
  ...
}
```

When the defining block is ended, the }, the stack frame shrinks by four bytes, removing x from the stack frame. In other words, as main goes along, it continually increases and decreases its stack pointer and frame.

However, when it gets to a function call, to Fun in this example, the ESP is frozen for main at this spot. A new stack frame is setup for Fun and control goes to Fun. Later on, if Fun calls another function, say sqrt, again ESP is frozen for Fun at that point and a new stack frame is built for sqrt. When sqrt returns back to Fun, Fun's stack frame becomes unfrozen and it can grow again as it enters other blocks which need space for new local variables.

Figure 16.4 shows this in operation. The caller, main, puts the parameters onto the stack. The call instruction pushes the return address onto the stack. Within the function Fun, register EBP, the base pointer, acts as an anchor to the start of the local variables portion of the stack frame.

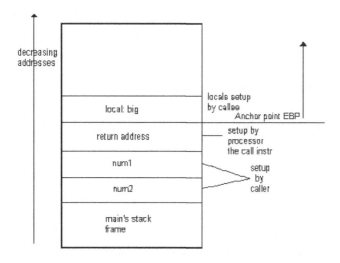

Figure 16.4 The Stack Frame for Function Fun

Notice then, that big is at location pointed to by ebp. The return address is at ebp + 4. Variable num1 is at ebp + 8, while num2 is at ebp + 12. If Fun had another int defined below big, it would be at ebp – 4, and so on. EBP is thus your stack frame pointer. Examine Figure 16.5 closely at the yellow point, where it is about to retrieve the value of num1 from the stack.

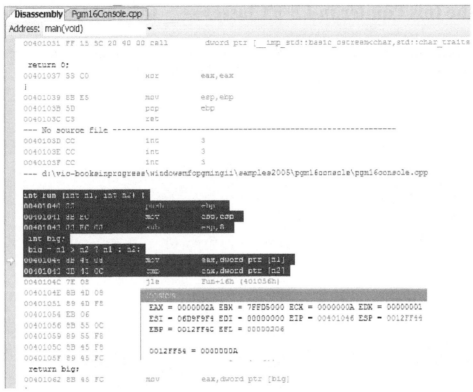

Figure 16.5 Accessing Argument num1 via EBP

I pasted the registers window over the listing. The code says it is going to do a mov into eax from dword ptr [n1], the first parameter, num1, whose value is 10 or A in hex. Per the figure 16.4, num1 or n1 as it is called in Fun ought to be 8 bytes from the address of the stack frame in EBP. EBP contains 0012ff4c. Adding 8 yields 0012ff54. In the registers window, it shows that is it going after, 0012ff54 and shows that it equals 0000000A, or 10.

Handling the this Pointer in C++ Classes— __thiscall Convention

We know that when a member function of a class is called, the compiler passes the address of the object as the first parameter. That is, consider the following situation.

```
class Fun {
protected:
 int x;
 int y;
public:
 Fun (int xx, int yy);
 int GetX () const;
};

Fun::Fun (int xx, int yy) : x(xx), y(yy) {}

int Fun::GetX () const {
 return x;
}
main:
Fun f (1, 2);
cout << f.GetX ();
```

We know that when it is compiled, the compiler effectively changes the GetX prototype to pass a first parameter of Fun* const this. Thus, we have the following compiled code.

```
Fun::Fun (Fun* const this, int xx, int yy) :
         this->x(10), this->y(yy) {}

int Fun::GetX (Fun* const this) const {
 return this->x;
}
```

This code is the second project in the Pgm16Console solution, called Pgm16ConsoleClass. Open it and set a beak point on the call to f.GetX(). Use Go Debug and then switch to the disassembly window. Now we see nearly the same type of coding.

```
 Fun f (1, 2);
00401046 6A 02              push        2
00401048 6A 01              push        1
0040104A 8D 4D F8           lea         ecx,[f]
0040104D E8 AE FF FF FF     call        Fun::Fun (401000h)
 int z = f.GetX ();
00401052 8D 4D F8           lea         ecx,[f]
00401055 E8 D6 FF FF FF     call        Fun::GetX (401030h)
0040105A 89 45 F4           mov         dword ptr [z],eax
```

What's different? In both cases, after pushing any parameters onto the stack, it does a lea ecx, [f]. LEA is load effective address, f is our instance of Fun. Thus it is pre-loading register ECX with the address of the instance object f! Here is the **this** parameter being passed.

Now let's look at the constructor function's code. Notice that it even uses this in the instructions to make what's going on clear. However, I call your attention to the return instruction. Once again, it is the callee's responsibility to remove its own parameters from the stack.

```
Fun::Fun (int xx, int yy) : x(xx), y(yy) {}
00401000 55                    push      ebp
00401001 8B EC                 mov       ebp,esp
00401003 51                    push      ecx
00401004 89 4D FC              mov       dword ptr [ebp-4],ecx
00401007 8B 45 FC              mov       eax,dword ptr [this]
0040100A 8B 4D 08              mov       ecx,dword ptr [xx]
0040100D 89 08                 mov       dword ptr [eax],ecx
0040100F 8B 55 FC              mov       edx,dword ptr [this]
00401012 8B 45 0C              mov       eax,dword ptr [yy]
00401015 89 42 04              mov       dword ptr [edx+4],eax
00401018 8B 45 FC              mov       eax,dword ptr [this]
0040101B 8B E5                 mov       esp,ebp
0040101D 5D                    pop       ebp
0040101E C2 08 00              ret       8
```

Summarizing the __thiscall convention, the arguments are passed from right to left as with the others, the address of the object, the this parameter, is passed in register ECX, and the callee is responsible for cleaning up the stack, that is the removal of its own parameters.

The __fastcall Convention

The __fastcall calling convention specifies that arguments to functions are to be passed in registers, when possible. The usual maximum number of parameters handled this way is two. If a function has more than two arguments, the remainder are passed from right to left on the stack as normal, but at least two are in registers for fast access.

The first two arguments which are up to a DWORD in size, that is, four bytes, are placed into registers ECX and EDX. Additional arguments or ones too large to fit are passed from right to left on the stack as usual.

Stack cleanup is the responsibility of the callee, who must remove the arguments from the stack.

Once again, the decorated name convention is used: an @ sign followed by the decimal number of bytes in the parameter list and with an _ prefix.

Obsolete Calling Conventions

Three other conventions once used and supported are no longer supported. These include: __pascal, __fortran, and __syscall. With the __pascal convention, parameters were passed from left to right, not right to left.

Basic DLL Theory

Instead of creating a monster sized exe application, loaded with features, many of which are seldom used by most users, the programmer can place many functions and classes inside of a dynamic link library or DLL. The DLL is only loaded into memory when its services are actually needed. This reduces the overall load time for the application exe, since it is now much smaller in total size. There are many benefits for using DLLs in larger applications.

A process begins with a running instance of a program, which begins as an exe on disk. It is loaded into some virtual memory address space and has access to 2G of memory on a WIN32 platform. On a 64-bit system, it can go even larger. A DLL is also on disk and consists of possibly global data, compiled functions, and perhaps even some resources, such as a dialog template or a string table. When it is needed, the DLL is loaded into memory and is mapped into the same virtual address space as the calling process, so you are still limited to 2G total space. Even if the DLL requests heap space, via new, the memory comes from the host process' address space. (No getting around that 2G limit.)

The DLL has functions that are then **exported** to the client program, the exe, which the client can then call. From the viewpoint of the client, it is **importing** those functions. When the DLL is loaded, Windows matches up the imports being requested with the exports from the DLL. It is critical that you understand how this matching is done, particularly with the calling conventions used.

The DLL contains a table of exported functions. The functions can be identified in two ways. You can specify the name of the function or by an integer ordinal number. That is, if a DLL has a function called Fun, the table can be setup like this.
Fun   its memory address
01   its memory address
where Fun is assumed to be associated with the ordinal number 01

When the client loads the DLL, it does not know the memory address of the function, which it needs in order to actually call the function. When the DLL is loaded, Windows searches the table to find the address of the function, matching on either the name of the function or on the ordinal number. In a more complex situation, a DLL could also be importing functions from some other DLL as well. Again, the loading process finds those addresses for the DLL as well.

Ordinal linkage, using a magic number, to specify the function is a thing of the past. Microsoft now recommends that we all use symbolic function names for linkage. How is this linkage setup? It is a several step operation.

1. In the DLL coding, one codes something like the following.
```
__declspec(dllexport) int Fun (int n1, int n2);
```

2. On the client side, one codes the followin.
```
__declspec(dllimport) int Fun (int n1, int n2);
```

However, and this is a big however, if you are using C++, the compiler generates a decorated name which other languages cannot use. These names include the class name, function name, and parameter types. These are listed in the .map file. Hence, since we greatly desire to just use the simple, plain function name, we need to alter these two declarations this way.

1-alternate. In the DLL
```
extern "C" __declspec(dllexport) int Fun (int n1, int n2);
```
2-alternate. In the client
```
extern "C" __declspec(dllimport) int Fun (int n1, int n2);
```

By default, the __cdecl convention is used. If you need __stdcall, then use that in your DLL export statement above.

3. In the client project settings, one must specify the DLL's import **.lib** file to the linker.

4. The client must actually call at least one of the DLL's functions.

These steps are called **implicit linking**, common to C++ programming. That is, the program starts up and it will need the DLL functions, so they are then loaded. When the DLL project is built, the output consists of two key files, the .dll file and the .lib file. The .lib file, containing no code, just the exported function definitions and addresses, is added to the project. The .lib file contains the name of the needed DLL, but not its path.

The opposite of this is **explicit linking**. In this style, the application loads the DLL only when it is actually needed at the point that it is needed. Call the **LoadLibrary** function, giving it the full filespec name of the DLL. It returns an **HINSTANCE** which is then passed to **GetProcAddress**, which converts a symbol into the address within the DLL to call. Assuming the DLL exports Fun above
```
extern "C" __declspec(dllexport) int Fun (int n1, int n2);
```
then the explicit linkage might go like this.
```
typedef int (FUN) (int, int);
HINSTANCE hInstance =
  ::LoadLibrary("D:\\WindowsMFCII\\Pgm16DLL\\Release\\Pgm16DLL");
FUN* Fun = (FUN*) ::GetProcAddress (hInstance, "Fun");
```

```
int ansr = Fun (n1, n2);
or
int ansr = (*Fun) (n1, n2);
```

DLL Loading

The main entry point in a DLL, ignoring the start up code, is called **DllMain**. It is called for the initial attachment and when the DLL is to be detached and unloaded from memory. Here is typical coding taken from the sample Pgm16DLL.

```
extern "C" int APIENTRY
DllMain(HINSTANCE hInstance, DWORD dwReason, LPVOID lpReserved) {
 UNREFERENCED_PARAMETER(lpReserved);
 if (dwReason == DLL_PROCESS_ATTACH) {
  TRACE0("Pgm16DLL.DLL Initializing!\n");
  // Extension DLL one-time initialization
  if (!AfxInitExtensionModule(Pgm16DLLDLL, hInstance))
   return 0;

  // Insert this DLL into the resource chain
  // NOTE: If this Extension DLL is being implicitly linked to by
  //  an MFC Regular DLL (such as an ActiveX Control)
  //  instead of an MFC application, then you will want to
  //  remove this line from DllMain and put it in a separate
  //  function exported from this Extension DLL.  The Regular DLL
  //  that uses this Extension DLL should then explicitly call that
  //  function to initialize this Extension DLL.  Otherwise,
  //  the CDynLinkLibrary object will not be attached to the
  //  Regular DLL's resource chain, and serious problems will
  //  result.

  new CDynLinkLibrary(Pgm16DLLDLL);

 }
 else if (dwReason == DLL_PROCESS_DETACH) {
  TRACE0("Pgm16DLL.DLL Terminating!\n");
  // Terminate the library before destructors are called
  AfxTermExtensionModule(Pgm16DLLDLL);
 }
 return 1;    // ok
}
```

Notice that it is allocating a new instance of a DLL. Fortunately, the wizard builds all this for you when you make a dll project. What is the searching order that Windows uses to find the mentioned DLL file?

1. It searches the folder containing the exe or project
2. It searches the current directory of the process
3. It searches the Windows system folder
4. It searches the folders in the Path environment variable

Wait a second. We often have two versions of our DLL, a debug version and a release version. They both cannot be in the same folder! The slick trick that is widely used is to rename the debug version by appending a d on the end of its name. Do the same to the lib file. Thus, if our DLL is called Pgm16DLL, then one would have the following four files.

Pgm16DLL.dll   release version
Pgm16DLL.lib
Pgm16DLLd.dll debug version
Pgm16DLLd.lib

In the project settings, one would code the two different names. In the settings for the debug version, use the ones with the d suffix. In release settings, use the ones without that suffix.

To automate this in the DLL project, copy the .def file and give the new filename the extra d letter, as in Pgm16DLLd.def. In that file, change the name of the result to
LIBRARY   "Pgm16DLLd"
In the project settings, Linker | General | output file, add the d:
$(OutDir)\$(ProjectName)d.dll
Linker | Input | Module Definition File:
.\Pgm16DLLd.def
When you build the project, the compiler will create the two needed files:

Pgm16DLLd.dll
Pgm16DLLd.lib

Copy them into your main project folder of the client program.

What changes are needed to the client project? In Project Properties, select the debug version and then Linker tab | Input | Additional Dependencies, add Pgm16DLLd.lib. Then switch to the release version and make the change to add Pgm16DLL.lib.

Note: in my sample dll programs, I set the Property General Tab | Character Set in use to Not Set. I did this for both the dll project and the client project.

Making MFC DLLs

Within the world of MFC programming, the Application Wizard allows you to build two kinds of DLLs that have the MFC class library support: **extension DLLs** and **regular DLLs**. The extension DLL supports a C++ interface, exporting whole classes which can link to the MFC library of classes and functions. As such, both the DLL and the client must be synchronized to the same MFC DLL libraries. Often extension DLLs are small. The sample one for this chapter is only 21K so it loads fast.

A regular DLL can be used by any other Win32 client, but big restriction is that a regular DLL can only export C-style functions, not classes, member functions, or overloaded functions. However, within a regular DLL, you can use classes and the MFC library as well. Further, the regular

DLLs can be either statically linked or dynamically linked to the MFC library and is thus totally self-contained, complete with its own **WinMain** function.

Usually, we want an extension MFC DLL. For your reference, the compiler defines that specify which are shown below.

Extension DLL and Dynamically Linked to a Shared MFC Library: **_AFXEXT, _AFXDLL**
Client exe is Dynamically Linked to a Shared MFC Library: **_AFXDLL**
Regular DLL that is Dynamically Linked to a Shared MFC Library: **_AFXDLL, _USRDLL**
Regular DLL that is Statically Linked: **_USRDLL**

When you export only whole classes from your extension DLL, the process is very easy. After the App Wizard has built the shell DLL application for you, insert your class, specifying the **AFX_EXT_CLASS** macro in the class definition. It is coded after the keyword class and before the class name.

```
class AFX_EXT_CLASS AcmePlot : public CView {
```

This change goes into the class header definition file of **both** the DLL project and the client project. The compiler generates different code depending upon whether the project is a DLL or a client. That is, it generates exports if it is a DLL and imports if it is a client project.

When the client program that is using an extension DLL needs to load some resource, it looks first in the client's resources, then the DLL's, and finally in the MFC's DLL's resources. If there are duplicates in both the client and DLL resources, the client's version wins.

If the DLL needs to load a resource, it looks first at the DLL's resources, then MFC's, and lastly the client's resources.

Pgm16DLL and Pgm16b Client Sample Program

Okay, enough background. Let's get down to business and write a substantial DLL and then use it. I chose to rework the sample program from chapter 5, the AcmePlot and AcmeView of sales data viewed together in a splitter window. I am going to put the entire AcmePlot class into the DLL.

This idea is that most of the time, applications will only need to view and edit the sales data. Only rarely will they desire to see the plot view, making it an ideal candidate to place into a DLL.

Begin by making a new project, only this time choose MFC DLL instead of an application. On the application settings property page, you have two choices for a regular DLL, which we don't want and one for the MFC extension DLL. Choose the extension DLL. The wizard then builds your complete shell.

Next, copy the AcmePlot .h and .cpp files into that folder and add them to the project. Modify the header to include the **_AFX_EXT_CLASS** macro between class and AcmePlot.

Next, make the project properties changes. I used Character Set: Not Set. Linker tab | Input | Module Definition File: .\Pgm16DLL.def. You can also set a different version for the debug dll as described earlier above, if you so choose. I did so in this sample so you can match my properties.

I made a slight modification to the AcmeDoc class from Pgm05b. I added a GetSalesArray function to return the address of the data array, paralleling the GetNumSales function. As an alternative, I also modified the various **UpdateAllView** calls of AcmeView to always pass the current number of elements in the array as the second parameter and the address of the array as the third parameter. In the **OnUpdate** function of AcmePlot, you can see both methods.

Do not hit build just yet. There are two major hurdles to overcome. First, the plot view needs to work with the sales data array and elements which are of class SalesData. These are not part of the AcmePlot definition, but belong really to the client. Second, in OnUpdate, the plot view must call two functions of AcmeDoc to obtain the array address and the number of elements. Again, this class is not to be part of the DLL, only AcmePlot.

What you must do is to copy those four files and place them into the DLL project folder and add them to the project, but do not insert the **_AFX_EXT_CLASS** macro into their headers, or else they will become part of the DLL too. When it compiles, it now knows what these classes and functions are and will link to those instances in the client coding.

Here is the simple .def file. You can make a duplicate of it adding a d to its name and to the name of the dll library for the debug version, if desired. I did so.

Listing for File: Pgm16DLL.def

```
; Pgm16DLL.def : Declares the module parameters for the DLL.

LIBRARY          "Pgm16DLL"

EXPORTS
    ; Explicit exports can go here
```

I am not going to reproduce the entire AcmePlot coding, because almost nothing is changed from chapter 5! Here is the start of the class definition, changes in bold face.

Listing for File: AcmePlot.h of Pgm16DLL

```
#pragma once
#include "acmedoc.h"
#include "SalesData.h"
```

```
/****************************************************************/
/*                                                              */
/* AcmePlot Class: Bar Graph of Sales                           */
/*                                                              */
/****************************************************************/
```

```
class AFX_EXT_CLASS AcmePlot : public CView {
```

```
DECLARE_DYNCREATE(AcmePlot)
```

Here is the slight revision for the **OnUpdate** function. Other than this, nothing changes in the cpp file from Pgm05b. You can see the two calls to the document class, which are not part of the DLL coding. I commented out the alternative method of retrieving the data via parameters passed to **OnUpdate**.

Listing for File: AcmePlot.cpp of Pgm16DLL

```
void AcmePlot::OnUpdate (CView* ptrv, LPARAM l, CObject* ptro) {
 num_sales = GetDocument()->GetNumSales ();
 ptrarray = GetDocument()->GetSalesArray ();
 CView::OnUpdate (ptrv, l, ptro);
// num_sales = (int) l;
// ptrarray = (SalesDataArray*) ptro;
}
```

After you compile and link the dll project into release and/or debug versions, make a new client project. Copy all of the Pgm05b files (h, cpp, and dat files) into the folder. Copy the AcmePlot.h file of the modified DLL version into the project folder and remove the AcmePlot.cpp file from the client folder, if it is there, and from the project source files, if it is there as well. Make sure that AcmePlot.h is part of the project though. In the project settings, Linker tab, Additional Dependencies, add Pgm16DLL.lib. Do this for both the release build configuration and the debug configuration, using the Pgm16DLLd.lib for the debug version, if so desired. Build the client project and run the sample program.

Viola. That is all there is to it. Pretty simple to do. Just remember that if you want to export classes, you must use the extension DLL type. If you only want to export C functions or data, then you could use a regular DLL.

Chapter 17 Multithreading

Multitasking is the concurrent execution of two or more tasks or programs. Only if the processor is a dual core or better can they execute simultaneously. Normally, Windows uses the computer's hardware clock to give each task a time slice in which to run. As long as the slices are small and none of the tasks is hogging the system resources, it appears that they are executing simultaneously. With dual core and quad core processors, the applications could be physically executing simultaneously.

Multithreading is the ability of a program to run multiple tasks within itself. The application splits itself into two or more separate pieces or threads or tasks that then run concurrently or possibly simultaneously if the CPU and the operating system supports it. A thread is basically a function that is executing. It can call many other functions as needed for it to do its job.

When a Windows application begins, it starts with one thread, WinMain, or main if it is a console app. While it is running, it can then create other threads to run concurrently. **CreateThread** constructs a separate thread. We see this in operation when Print Preview is activated, the preview is run in a separate thread from the main application, which is why one must be careful about storing character dimensions in such situations.

One common design problem is thread interaction. Thread A does one part of a calculation that is later needed by Thread B. One cannot assume that Thread A will complete its work before Thread B needs its result. Hence, some means of communication must be done, this is called using a semaphore, which means basically a system to signal messages between two terminals, as on old railroad lines.

Threads A and B define a semaphore signal between them. Thread A will post the all done flag or semaphore when it completes its task. When Thread B reaches that point in its code where it must have the result from Thread A, it then waits or stops execution until the semaphore signal is set by Thread A. Once the signal is received, Thread B can then continue its execution.

While this all sounds simple enough, another common problem designers face is called a deadlock, where two or more threads come to a standstill waiting on the semaphore to be signaled, which does not come. That is, A ends up waiting on B to finish, which is waiting on A to finish. Now nothing gets executed, both are in an infinite wait.

What would be a good use of multithreading in programming? The sample program for this chapter illustrates a very common and good use for using multiple threads. Here's the scenario. The main application must keep track of all the files in a folder. Perhaps it is making thumbnail images, perhaps it is cataloging them. The point is that the main application is working with the files in a specific folder. Now what happens in real time if a new file is added to that folder? Obviously, the main task needs to know that it now has a new file with which to deal.

A bad solution would be to periodically have the main task stop everything that it is doing and go see what is in that folder, detecting changes and additions. Once done, the main task can then handle any changes found and resume its normal work. We see this happening a lot with word processors and their timed backups. One is typing away and then the application suddenly halts everything while it makes the back up copy. Once done, then it resumes accepting keystrokes. (My word processor does this to me all the time, I find this very annoying indeed.)

Pardon my digression, back to the solution at hand. Instead of having the main application stop everything and go examine the folder, why not have the main task launch a worker thread, whose task is to monitor that folder in the background? The main task can then continue to do its main work without worrying about the folder's current status and contents. When the worker thread discovers something has changed within that folder, a new file appears or one is altered, it can then send a message to the main task, set a flag signal, or other things to let the main task know a change has occurred. At that point, the main task can then handle the new or changed file.

My image browser program does precisely this action. While it is off making thumbnails and allowing me to view jpgs, it has a worker thread running in the background looking for additions, deletions, and modifications to the files in the folder that I am currently viewing. When one of these events occurs, the main task makes new thumbnails and such.

This is what Pgm17a is all about, launching a worker thread to continuously monitor a folder for additions, deletions, and modifications to its files, notifying the main application of the changes.

The MFC has two types of threads: user-interface threads and worker threads. A user-interface thread handles user input and output as well as responding to messages and events signaled by the user. A worker thread commonly completes a task, such as a spreadsheet recalculation, checking for changes in a folder, doing a complex calculation—none of which requires any user interaction or input or guidance. The Win32 API does not distinguish between these two very different kind of threads, it just starts them. The MFC realizes that the user-interface thread must have a message processing loop in order to function, while the worker thread does not need its own message processing loop.

Always check your project settings for both Debug and Release builds to make sure that the C++ tab | Code Generation | Runtime Library is one of the Multithreaded choices. If not, the thread will not be able to run.

C Functions for Multithreading, a Quick Glance

The underlying function is CreateThread.
```
HANDLE WINAPI CreateThread (
    LPSECURITY_ATTRIBUTES lpThreadAttributes,
    SIZE_T dwStackSize, LPTHREAD_START_ROUTINE lpStartAddress,
    LPVOID lpParameter, DWORD dwCreationFlags, LPDWORD lpThreadId
);
```
Often the security attribute is 0. If the initial stack size is 0, the system provides an initial default and will grow the stack as needed during execution. The starting address is your thread function. The parameter is your means of exchanging data with the thread. The creation flags are usually 0, if you want the thread to begin immediately. If the flags are **CREATE_SUSPENDED**, then it does not start until you call **ResumeThread**. The thread id pointer receives the id of the created thread.

The prototype of the thread function is
```
DWORD WINAPI YourThread (void* parms);
```

Notice that these are using the __stddecl specification. Usually, C++ programmers desire __cdecl instead. Hence, include <process.h> and use the following function instead.
```
HANDLE _beginthread (your thread function, stacksize, parameter);
void __cdecl YourThread (void* parms);
```

The thread terminates itself by calling **ExitThread** passing the return code, 0 usually means it ended fine.

The MFC Multithreading Functions

The MFC provides two methods for launching C++ threads, one for worker threads, one for user interface threads. Let's examine the worker threads first, they are much simpler to code. The underlying class is **CWinThread**, though you do not need to derive from us usually. Instead, you call one of the two forms of the **AfxBeginThread** function, the one for worker threads looks like this.
```
CWinThread* AfxBeginThread (AFX_THREADPROC pfnThreadProc,
        LPVOID pParam, int nPriority = THREAD_PRIORITY_NORMAL,
        UINT nStackSize = 0, DWORD dwCreateFlags = 0,
        LPSECURITY_ATTRIBUTES lpSecurityAttrs = NULL
);
```
where your thread function prototype must be like this
```
UINT __cdecl MyThread ( LPVOID pParam );
```

If the security attributes is 0, the process inherits the same security attributes as the launching application. **AfxBeginThread** calls **CWinThread** and then **CreateThread**, returning the address of the thread, if successful.

The launcher of the thread can pass any kind of parameter information via the pParam parameter. Often, a pointer to a structure of numerous values is passed, as will be done in the sample program Pgm17a.

Usually the very next line of code will be to set the priority of the new thread. For example,
```
ptrthread->SetThreadPriority (THREAD_PRIORITY_LOWEST);
```

The thread priority can be one of the following identifiers or numbers.
```
THREAD_PRIORITY_ABOVE_NORMAL     1 Priority 1 point above the
                                   priority class.
THREAD_PRIORITY_BELOW_NORMAL    -1 Priority 1 point below the
                                   priority class.
THREAD_PRIORITY_HIGHEST          2 Priority 2 points above the
                                   priority class.
THREAD_PRIORITY_IDLE           -15
THREAD_PRIORITY_LOWEST          -2 Priority 2 points below the
                                   priority class.
THREAD_PRIORITY_NORMAL                   0   Normal   priority
THREAD_PRIORITY_TIME_CRITICAL 15
```
This parameter can also be -7, -6, -5, -4, -3, 3, 4, 5, or 6. Usually, a worker thread runs in the background and one uses lowest as the value.

The only way to stop a thread is to have the thread itself call **AfxEndThread**.
```
void AfxEndThread (return code, BOOL deleteThreadFromMemory);
```
Hence, if the launching process wishes to terminate the thread, some means of communication with the thread must be established, via the one parameter originally passed to the thread process.

Before we dive into too many more details, let's see the sample program that illustrates the worker thread, Pgm17a.

Pgm17a's Worker Thread Watches for Changes to Files in a Folder

The worker thread will watch for new .txt files appearing in the monitored folder, deletions, and updates of existing files. The thread can be started and stopped from toolbar buttons and menu items. The main view window displays all of the files in the folder, as shown in Figure 17-1

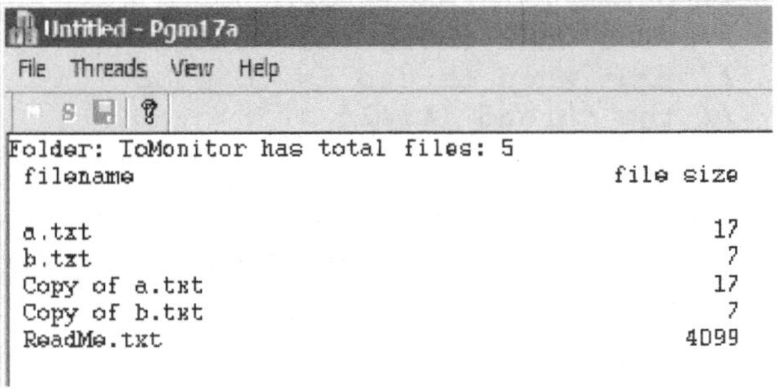

Figure 17-1 Monitoring a Folder for Changes

In this sample, I took a single document template, allowing the Application Wizard to build the app class, frame window class, document class, and view class. All but the view class are just what the wizard initially generated, less clean up of comments. All changes are in the view class.

First, we need to pass parameters to the thread. Specifically, the thread needs the folder to monitor. It must also have access to the launcher's bool variables that can tell it to abort and stop. When changes are found, the thread needs to have our HWND so that it can notify us of the change. I put these into a structure. Just below that is the prototype of the thread.

Listing for File: Pgm17aView.h

```
#pragma once

// structure to pass needed data to the thread
struct TxtThreadWatchParms {
 HWND hwnd;
 bool* ptrterminate;
 bool* ptrworking;
 char path[_MAX_PATH];
};

// thread prototype
UINT TxtFileChangedWatcherThread (LPVOID pParam);

class Pgm17aView : public CView {
protected:
 Pgm17aView();
 DECLARE_DYNCREATE(Pgm17aView)

 CPtrArray list;     // list of all files in the monitored folder
 CPtrArray newList;  // new list of all files now present

 int   avg_caps_width;   // average capital letter width
```

```
int    avg_char_width;    // average character width
int    avg_char_height;   // average character height

CString txtRootFolder;   // the folder being watched

public:

TxtThreadWatchParms watcherParms; // parms for the thread
bool                m_working;    // true when thread is active
bool                m_terminate;  // true when thread is to stop
CWinThread*         ptrthread;    // the thread itself

void CheckForChangesInMaintainedFolders (); // alternative method

void LoadList (CPtrArray& a);
void EmptyList (CPtrArray& a);
void CompareLists ();

Pgm17aDoc* GetDocument() const;
virtual void OnDraw(CDC* pDC);   // overridden to draw this view
virtual ~Pgm17aView();
#ifdef _DEBUG
virtual void AssertValid() const;
virtual void Dump(CDumpContext& dc) const;
#endif
public:
virtual void OnInitialUpdate();
afx_msg void OnDestroy();
afx_msg void OnStartThread();
afx_msg void OnStopThread();
afx_msg void OnUpdateStopThread(CCmdUI *pCmdUI);
afx_msg void OnUpdateStartThread(CCmdUI *pCmdUI);

// the message sent by the thread when changes are found
afx_msg LONG OnTxtThreadSawChanges (UINT wparam, LONG lparam);
DECLARE_MESSAGE_MAP()
};

#ifndef _DEBUG  // debug version in Pgm17aView.cpp
inline Pgm17aDoc* Pgm17aView::GetDocument() const
   { return reinterpret_cast<Pgm17aDoc*>(m_pDocument); }
#endif
```

The parameters structure will contain the address of our two bools, m_working and m_terminate. When the view needs to terminate the thread, it sets m_terminate to true and shortly after that, the thread will abort and remove itself from memory. This must be done, for instance, if the thread is running and the user closes the application down.

OnStartThread and OnStopThread respond to the menu items and toolbar buttons to launch and stop the thread. The command handlers disable or enable the menu items and buttons, depending upon whether or not the thread has been launched.

The view stores the data in a **CPtrArray** called list. Let's look at the view's coding down to the point where the thread gets involved. I will illustrate another method for finding the files in a folder.

Listing for File: Pgm17aView.cpp, Partial Listing

```
IMPLEMENT_DYNCREATE(Pgm17aView, CView)

BEGIN_MESSAGE_MAP(Pgm17aView, CView)
 ON_COMMAND(CM_START_THREAD, &Pgm17aView::OnStartThread)
 ON_COMMAND(CM_STOP_THREAD, &Pgm17aView::OnStopThread)
 ON_UPDATE_COMMAND_UI(CM_STOP_THREAD, &Pgm17aView::OnUpdateStopThread)
 ON_UPDATE_COMMAND_UI(CM_START_THREAD, &Pgm17aView::OnUpdateStartThread)
 ON_WM_DESTROY()
 ON_MESSAGE(WM_USER, &Pgm17aView::OnTxtThreadSawChanges)
END_MESSAGE_MAP()

Pgm17aView::Pgm17aView() {
 m_working = false;              // true when thread is active
 txtRootFolder = "ToMonitor";   // folder to watch
 LoadList (list);               // load all files in the watch folder
}

Pgm17aView::~Pgm17aView() {
 EmptyList (list);
 EmptyList (newList);
}

void Pgm17aView::OnInitialUpdate() {
 CView::OnInitialUpdate();
 // calculate average character parameters
 TEXTMETRIC  tm;
 CClientDC *ptrdc = new CClientDC (this);
 ptrdc->SelectStockObject(ANSI_FIXED_FONT);
 ptrdc->GetTextMetrics (&tm); // get the font information
 delete ptrdc;
 avg_char_width  = tm.tmAveCharWidth;
 avg_char_height = tm.tmHeight + tm.tmExternalLeading;
 avg_caps_width  = (tm.tmPitchAndFamily & 1 ? 3 : 2) * avg_char_width / 2;
}

// load all files in the folder being watched
// uses the WIN32_FIND_DATA method
void Pgm17aView::LoadList (CPtrArray& a) {
 CString path = txtRootFolder;
 path += "\\*.txt"; // append file types we are watching
 HANDLE hfile;
 WIN32_FIND_DATA* ptrData = new WIN32_FIND_DATA;
 if (!ptrData) {
  MessageBox ("Out of memory", "Error", MB_OK);
  return;
 }
 long ct = 0;
 if ((hfile=::FindFirstFile (path, ptrData)) == INVALID_HANDLE_VALUE) {
  return;
 }
```

```
 do {
  ct++;
  a.Add (ptrData); // add this file to the list
  ptrData = new WIN32_FIND_DATA;
  if (!ptrData) {
   MessageBox ("Out of memory", "Error", MB_OK);
   FindClose (hfile);
   return;
  }
 } while (FindNextFile(hfile, ptrData));
 FindClose (hfile);
}

void Pgm17aView::CompareLists () {
 // here one can compare newList to list to see the differences and handle
 // leave list with current files in the folder to be displayed onscreen
 EmptyList (list);
 WIN32_FIND_DATA* ptrData;
 for (int i=0; i<newList.GetSize(); i++) {
  ptrData = (WIN32_FIND_DATA*) newList.GetAt (i);
  list.Add (ptrData);
 }
 newList.RemoveAll ();
 Invalidate ();
}

void Pgm17aView::EmptyList (CPtrArray& a) {
 WIN32_FIND_DATA* ptrData;
 for (int i=0; i<a.GetSize(); i++) {
  ptrData = (WIN32_FIND_DATA*) a.GetAt (i);
  delete ptrData;
 }
 a.RemoveAll ();
}

void Pgm17aView::OnDraw(CDC* ptrdc) {
 ptrdc->SelectStockObject(ANSI_FIXED_FONT);
 char msg[200];
 int num = (int) list.GetSize ();
 sprintf_s (msg, sizeof(msg), "Folder: %s has total files: %d", txtRootFolder,
num);
 ptrdc->TextOut (avg_char_width, avg_char_height,
                 "filename                                   file size");
 ptrdc->TextOut (0, 0, msg);
 WIN32_FIND_DATA* ptrData;
 for (int i=0; i<list.GetSize(); i++) {
  ptrData = (WIN32_FIND_DATA*) list.GetAt (i);
  sprintf_s (msg, sizeof(msg), "%-40s %10ld", ptrData->cFileName,
             ptrData->nFileSizeLow);
  ptrdc->TextOut (avg_char_width, avg_char_height * (i+3), msg);
 }
}
```

I call your attention to the new coding in LoadList. An alternative method exists to find the data contained in a directory, using the **WIN32_FIND_DATA** structure, which has more information than previous methods. It's members are as follows. You can review the help system to find out more about it. The file attribute flags include **_ATTRIBUTE_DIRECTORY**, for example.

```
struct WIN32_FIND_DATA {
 DWORD     dwFileAttributes;
 FILETIME  ftCreationTime;
 FILETIME  ftLastAccessTime;
 FILETIME  ftLastWriteTime;
 DWORD     nFileSizeHigh;
 DWORD     nFileSizeLow;
 DWORD     dwReserved0;
 DWORD     dwReserved1;
 TCHAR     cFileName[MAX_PATH];
 TCHAR     cAlternateFileName[14];
};
```

The **FindFirstFile** function is passed the folder-file spec to search for and the address of the structure to fill up with the first matching directory entry.

```
void Pgm17aView::LoadList (CPtrArray& a) {
 CString path = txtRootFolder;
 path += "\\*.txt"; // append file types we are watching
 HANDLE hfile;
 WIN32_FIND_DATA* ptrData = new WIN32_FIND_DATA;
 if (!ptrData) {
  MessageBox ("Out of memory", "Error", MB_OK);
  return;
 }
 long ct = 0;
 if ((hfile=::FindFirstFile (path, ptrData)) == INVALID_HANDLE_VALUE) {
  return;
 }
 do {
  ct++;
  a.Add (ptrData); // add this file to the list
  ptrData = new WIN32_FIND_DATA;
  if (!ptrData) {
   MessageBox ("Out of memory", "Error", MB_OK);
   FindClose (hfile);
   return;
  }
 } while (FindNextFile(hfile, ptrData));
 FindClose (hfile);
```

FindNextFile continues the search for the next one that matches, while **FindClose** terminates the directory searching process. These functions work well with the newer versions of Windows, including Vista.

Launching and Coding of the Thread

When the user presses the S button or chooses the menu item to start the thread, OnStartThread is called. It makes sure that the thread is not already launched. If not, it fills up the parameter structure with the needed data and then calls **AfxBeginThread**, followed by **SetThreadPriority**.

Listing for File: Pgm17aView.cpp, Continued Listing

```cpp
// launch the thread to monitor changes in the folder being watched
void Pgm17aView::OnStartThread() {
 if (m_working) return;
 strcpy_s (watcherParms.path, sizeof(watcherParms.path), txtRootFolder);
 m_terminate = false;
 watcherParms.ptrterminate = &m_terminate;
 watcherParms.hwnd = GetSafeHwnd ();
 watcherParms.ptrworking = &m_working;
 m_working = true;
 ptrthread = AfxBeginThread (TxtFileChangedWatcherThread, &watcherParms);
 ptrthread->SetThreadPriority (THREAD_PRIORITY_LOWEST);
}

// stop the thread permanently
void Pgm17aView::OnStopThread() {
 m_terminate = true;
 ptrthread->SetThreadPriority (THREAD_PRIORITY_TIME_CRITICAL);
 ::WaitForSingleObject (ptrthread->m_hThread, INFINITE);
}

void Pgm17aView::OnUpdateStopThread(CCmdUI *pCmdUI) {
 pCmdUI->Enable (m_working);
}

void Pgm17aView::OnUpdateStartThread(CCmdUI *pCmdUI) {
 pCmdUI->Enable (!m_working);
}

// if app is closed while thread is active, stop thread
void Pgm17aView::OnDestroy() {
 if (m_working) OnStopThread ();
 CView::OnDestroy();
}
```

To stop the thread, either by menu item or by the view being destroyed, the bool m_terminate is set to true. Shortly, the thread will respond and terminate itself. However, the view coding cannot continue until the thread has done this. Thus, I reset the thread priority to the highest so that it gets all the processing time, **THREAD_PRIORITY_TIME_CRITICAL**. Now, the view must wait until the thread finishes.

This is done via waiting for a semaphore to be posted. **WaitForSingleObject** is called to do this. It is passed the thread pointer and the amount of time to wait before giving up. That value is normally in milliseconds. In this case, the view cannot continue until the thread does get done, so the key value **INFINITE** is used. Of course, if the thread ignores our request to terminate, the view will be waiting forever.

Now, let's examine the actual thread function itself. It introduces several new functions that are highly useful in this circumstance, detecting changes in the files in a folder. First, for convenience, I retrieved the values in the parameter structure and saved them in some local variables. The key lines are in bold face.

Listing for File: Pgm17aView.cpp, Continued Listing

```cpp
UINT TxtFileChangedWatcherThread (LPVOID pParam) {
TxtThreadWatchParms* ptrp = (TxtThreadWatchParms*) pParam;
HWND hwnd = ptrp->hwnd; // set window to notify
bool* ptrterminate = ptrp->ptrterminate;
bool* ptrworking = ptrp->ptrworking;
HANDLE dwChangeHandle = FindFirstChangeNotification (ptrp->path, true,
                FILE_NOTIFY_CHANGE_FILE_NAME | FILE_NOTIFY_CHANGE_DIR_NAME |
                FILE_NOTIFY_CHANGE_SIZE | FILE_NOTIFY_CHANGE_LAST_WRITE);
if (dwChangeHandle == INVALID_HANDLE_VALUE) {
 *ptrworking = false;
 // abort, something is very wrong - bad folder perhaps
 AfxEndThread (GetLastError(), TRUE);
}
// Change notification is set. Now wait on both notification
// handles and refresh accordingly.
DWORD rc;
while (!(*ptrterminate)) {
 // Wait for notification
 rc = WAIT_TIMEOUT;
 while (rc == WAIT_TIMEOUT) {
  rc = ::WaitForSingleObject (dwChangeHandle, 1000);
  if (*ptrterminate) {
   *ptrworking = false;
   ::FindCloseChangeNotification (dwChangeHandle);
   AfxEndThread (0, TRUE);
  }
 }
 if (rc == WAIT_OBJECT_0) {
  // A file was created, changed, or deleted in maintained folders
  ::PostMessage (hwnd, WM_USER, CM_TXT_THREAD_SAW_CHANGES, 0);
  if (FindNextChangeNotification (dwChangeHandle) == FALSE) {
   // again, something went wrong, so abort
   *ptrworking = false;
   ::FindCloseChangeNotification (dwChangeHandle);
   AfxEndThread (GetLastError(), true);
  }
 }
}
::FindCloseChangeNotification (dwChangeHandle);
*ptrworking = false;
return 0;
}
```

The **FindFirstChangeNotification** function builds a change notification handle and sets up initial change notification filter conditions. This wait on a notification handle is successful when a change that matches the filter conditions has occurred in the specified directory. However, it does not tell you what those changes actually were. Another function can be called to provide that information, if desired, the **ReadDirectoryChangesW** function.

```
HANDLE FindFirstChangeNotification (LPCTSTR lpPathName,
                    BOOL bWatchSubtree, DWORD dwNotifyFilter);
```

The lpPathName is a null-terminated string that specifies the path of the directory to watch, limited to MAX_PATH characters total, in ANSI. (The Unicode version handles a string 32,767 wide characters.)

The bWatchSubtree specifies whether the function will monitor the directory or the directory tree. If this parameter is TRUE, the function monitors the directory tree rooted at the specified directory; if it is FALSE, it monitors only the specified directory.

The dwNotifyFilter gives the conditions that satisfy a change notification wait. Possible values include the following.

FILE_NOTIFY_CHANGE_FILE_NAME	Any file name change in the watched directory or subtree causes a change notification wait operation to return. Changes include renaming, creating, or deleting a file name.
FILE_NOTIFY_CHANGE_DIR_NAME	Any directory-name change in the watched directory or subtree causes a change notification wait operation to return. Changes include creating or deleting a directory.
FILE_NOTIFY_CHANGE_ATTRIBUTES	Any attribute change in the watched directory or subtree causes a change notification wait operation to return.
FILE_NOTIFY_CHANGE_SIZE	Any file-size change in the watched directory or subtree causes a change notification wait operation to return. The operating system detects a change in file size only when the file is written to the disk. For operating systems that use extensive caching, detection occurs only when the cache is sufficiently flushed.
FILE_NOTIFY_CHANGE_LAST_WRITE	Any change to the last write-time of files in the watched directory or subtree causes a change notification wait operation to return. The operating system detects a change to the last write-time only when the file is written to the disk. For operating systems that use extensive caching, detection occurs only when the cache is sufficiently flushed.
FILE_NOTIFY_CHANGE_SECURITY	Any security-descriptor change in the watched directory or subtree causes a change notification wait operation to return.

If the function succeeds, it returns a handle to a find change notification object. If it fails, it returns **INVALID_HANDLE_VALUE**. In this case, you can call **GetLastError** to get the extended error information.

Once it returns successfully, the wait functions can monitor the specified directory or subtree by using the handle returned by the **FindFirstChangeNotification** function. Note that a wait is satisfied when one of the filter conditions occurs in the monitored directory.

When the wait is satisfied, you can respond to the condition and continue monitoring by calling **FindNextChangeNotification**. Be sure to call the **FindCloseChangeNotification** when done.

In this thread, if the call fails, then AfxEndThread is called to abort the thread. Now the main while loop is entered, waiting for changes to occur. Inside the loop, I wait for one second. Then, I check to see if terminate was requested. If the app is shutting down or the user wants the thread stopped, I do so, calling **FindCloseChangeNotification** and then **AfxEndThread**.

```
// Change notification is set. Now wait on both notification
// handles and refresh accordingly.
DWORD rc;
while (!(*ptrterminate)) {
 // Wait for notification
 rc = WAIT_TIMEOUT;
 while (rc == WAIT_TIMEOUT) {
  rc = ::WaitForSingleObject (dwChangeHandle, 1000);
  if (*ptrterminate) {
   *ptrworking = false;
   ::FindCloseChangeNotification (dwChangeHandle);
   AfxEndThread (0, TRUE);
  }
 }
```

Otherwise, I check the return code from the wait call. If it is **WAIT_OBJECT_0**, this is our indicator something has changed. This is the only object this thread waits upon. Since a change has occurred in the directory, the thread must notify the view of this. I chose to do this through posting a message to the view window. It is the user message, CM_TXT_THREAD_SAW_CHANGES, to which the view class can respond. Then, I call the continue function, **FindNextChangeNotification**.

```
 if (rc == WAIT_OBJECT_0) {
  // A file was created, changed, or deleted in maintained folders
  ::PostMessage (hwnd, WM_USER, CM_TXT_THREAD_SAW_CHANGES, 0);
  if (FindNextChangeNotification (dwChangeHandle) == FALSE) {
   // again, something went wrong, so abort
   *ptrworking = false;
   ::FindCloseChangeNotification (dwChangeHandle);
   AfxEndThread (GetLastError(), true);
  }
 }
}
::FindCloseChangeNotification (dwChangeHandle);
*ptrworking = false;
return 0;
```

}

Back in the view class, when that user message arrives, it is handled in OnTxtThreadSawChanges. This function then needs to retrieve a new listing of all files in the folder. Hence, I do not want the thread running while I update the view, so the function **SuspendThread** is called before I begin re-reading the directory in LoadList. Once the view is updated, then I call **ResumeThread** to get it going again. These two functions require no parameters.

Listing for File: Pgm17aView.cpp, Continued Listing

```
// message handler called when thread sees a change
// additional file, deleted file, or altered file
LONG Pgm17aView::OnTxtThreadSawChanges (UINT wparam, LONG lparam) {
 if (wparam != CM_TXT_THREAD_SAW_CHANGES) return 0;
 // suspend active thread while we handle changes
 if (m_working)
  ptrthread->SuspendThread ();

 // make a new list of files present
 LoadList (newList);
 CompareLists (); // compare lists for changes

 // resume thread monitoring
 if (m_working)
  ptrthread->ResumeThread ();
 return 0;
}

// an alternative function, showing thread suspension and resumption
void Pgm17aView::CheckForChangesInMaintainedFolders () {
 if (m_working)
  ptrthread->SuspendThread ();
 AfxMessageBox ("Spotted changes in csv folders or files", MB_OK);
 if (m_working)
  ptrthread->ResumeThread ();
}
```

I also show an alternative function. Sometimes the view itself may make changes to the files in the folder. In this case, the thread ought to be suspended while the view makes its changes or the thread will begin sending changed messages to the view. Again, use the simple **SuspendThread** and **ResumeThread** functions.

MFC User-Interface Threads

To create a user interface thread, call the second version of **AfxBeginThread** function.
```
CWinThread* AfxBeginThread (CRuntimeClass* pThreadClass,
                int nPriority = THREAD_PRIORITY_NORMAL,
                UINT nStackSize = 0, DWORD dwCreateFlags = 0,
                LPSECURITY_ATTRIBUTES lpSecurityAttrs = NULL );
```
Notice the key item is your runtime class that is being allocated.

A user-interface thread is normally handles user input and responds to user events, doing this independently of threads that are executing other portions of the application. The main application thread, that is your CWinApp-derived class, has started and is running. Now, you can launch a separate GUI thread, which will respond to various messages and thus needs its own message processing loop. Thus, you must derive your user-interface thread from **CWinThread**. Further, you must declare and implement this class, using the **DECLARE_DYNCREATE** and **IMPLEMENT_DYNCREATE** macros. Some inherited functions you must override, others are optional.

You must provide an override for **InitInstance** to dynamically allocate your runtime classes. If you need to delete items when terminating, you can override **ExitInstance** as well.

The call to **AfxBeginThread** creates a new instance of your class, initializes it with the information you pass, and calls **CWinThread::CreateThread** to start executing the thread. Obviously, a user-interface thread is much more complex to code than a worker thread.

MFC Synchronizations

Frequently, threads must synchronize with other events or actions or situations. For example, one thread wishes to update the data in an accounts database, while another thread wishes to read the data in the same database. Obviously, we cannot have both doing the same thing at the same time. The updating thread can lock out all other threads for the brief period when it is making changes and then all other threads can read it again.

Synchronization consists of a thread which needs some critical resource checks to see if it can obtain it. If not, the thread notifies the system what it needs and then goes to sleep. Later on, when the system determines that resource is available, the system wakes the thread up, giving that resource to the thread for its use. While waiting, the thread is **not** executing code while sleeping. Specifically, the waiting thread's execution is suspended.

The worst possible thing you can do in situations like this is along this line.
```
CreateThread. . . of low priority
```

```
. . .
while (critical resource is not available) {
 . . . kill time instructions
}
```

Putting in instructions to delay a bit of time causes the CPU to actually execute them, wasting CPU cycles. This creator thread that launched the thread is not in the wait state but is executing. Suppose that the created thread which will eventually release the critical resource is running at a lower priority than the creator thread. The CPU then gives all the CPU cycles to the creator thread, since it is running at a higher priority than the background thread of lower priority. Thus, the lower thread will never get the CPU long enough for it to finish its work and thus never release the critical resource that the creator thread is waiting upon so it can continue!

The MFC provides different classes to handle synchronization issues. They break down into synchronization objects and synchronization access objects. There are four different synchronization objects your threads can use, all are derived from the base class of **CSyncObject**. They include the following, Microsoft's Definitions.

CSemaphore: Semaphores are useful in controlling access to a shared resource, usually data, that can only support a limited number of users. The current count of the **CSemaphore** object is the number of additional users allowed. When the count reaches zero, all attempts to use the resource controlled by the **CSemaphore** object will be inserted into a system queue and wait until they either time out or the count rises above 0. The maximum number of users who can access the controlled resource at one time is specified during construction of the **CSemaphore** object.

CMutex: Mutexes, short for mutually exclusive, are useful when only one thread at a time can be allowed to modify data or some other controlled resource. For example, adding nodes to a linked list is a process that should only be allowed by one thread at a time. By using a **CMutex** object to control the linked list, only one thread at a time can gain access to the list. More than one application can use the resource, as contrasted with the **CCriticalSection**, which is for one application only.

CCriticalSection: Critical sections are useful when only one thread at a time can be allowed to modify data or some other controlled resource. For example, adding nodes to a linked list is a process that should only be allowed by one thread at a time. By using a **CCriticalSection** object to control the linked list, only one thread at a time can gain access to the list. Critical sections allow only one thread to access the shared data at a time and is the simplest to use.

CEvent: Events are useful when a thread needs to know when to perform its task. For example, a thread that copies data to a data archive would need to be notified when new data is available. By using a **CEvent** object to notify the copy thread when new data is available, the thread can perform its task as soon as possible. Events are used to signal that some operation has completed.

How do you choose which synchronization access class to use? Here are some guidelines. Does your application have to wait for something to happen before it can access the resource? If yes, the use **CEvent**. Can more than one thread within the same application access this resource at one time? If yes, then use **CSemaphore**. Can more than one application use this resource? If yes, then use **CMutex**. If no, then use **CCriticalSection**.

Once the synchronization object is setup, then the threads use either the **CMultiLock** or the **CSingleLock** to gain access to the resource, when it becomes available. Whether or not the thread have to wait on one thing or more than one can be the determining factor here.

Let's put this one into a role playing game situation, for some variety here. Suppose that you wish to simulate a village shop. At the shop, a player or customer can browse your merchandise and, if desired, visit your snack lunch counter. Your shop has a finite capacity of customers inside at one time.

What are the limits? First, only maxCustomers can be in the shop at one time. When some leave, new customers can enter. The total time that your shop is open is adjustable. Since customers arrive at random times, maxDelayBetweenCustomerCreation provides the range of such delay. The number of sales clerks you have to handle customer purchases is adjustable, stored in numberSalesClerks.

On the customer side, a customer will only wait so long to get inside the shop, a random value between one and maxWaitToGetIntoStore. Each customer spends a variable amount of time shopping, stored in maxTimeSpentShopping. When a customer is ready to make his or her purchases, they will wait up to maxTimeToWaitForSalesClerk.

Each customer has a one in two chance that they will get hungry and visit your snack bar. However, they will wait for a seat and service up to maxWaitTimeForLunch. Each will spend a variable amount of time eating, stored in maxTimeEatingLunch.

All of these parameters are adjustable in the form view. When the button Run Simulation is pressed, the current values in the edit controls are retrieved and the shop simulation is run. The results fill up the list box when done.

Figure 17.2 shows a sample run of Pgm17b.

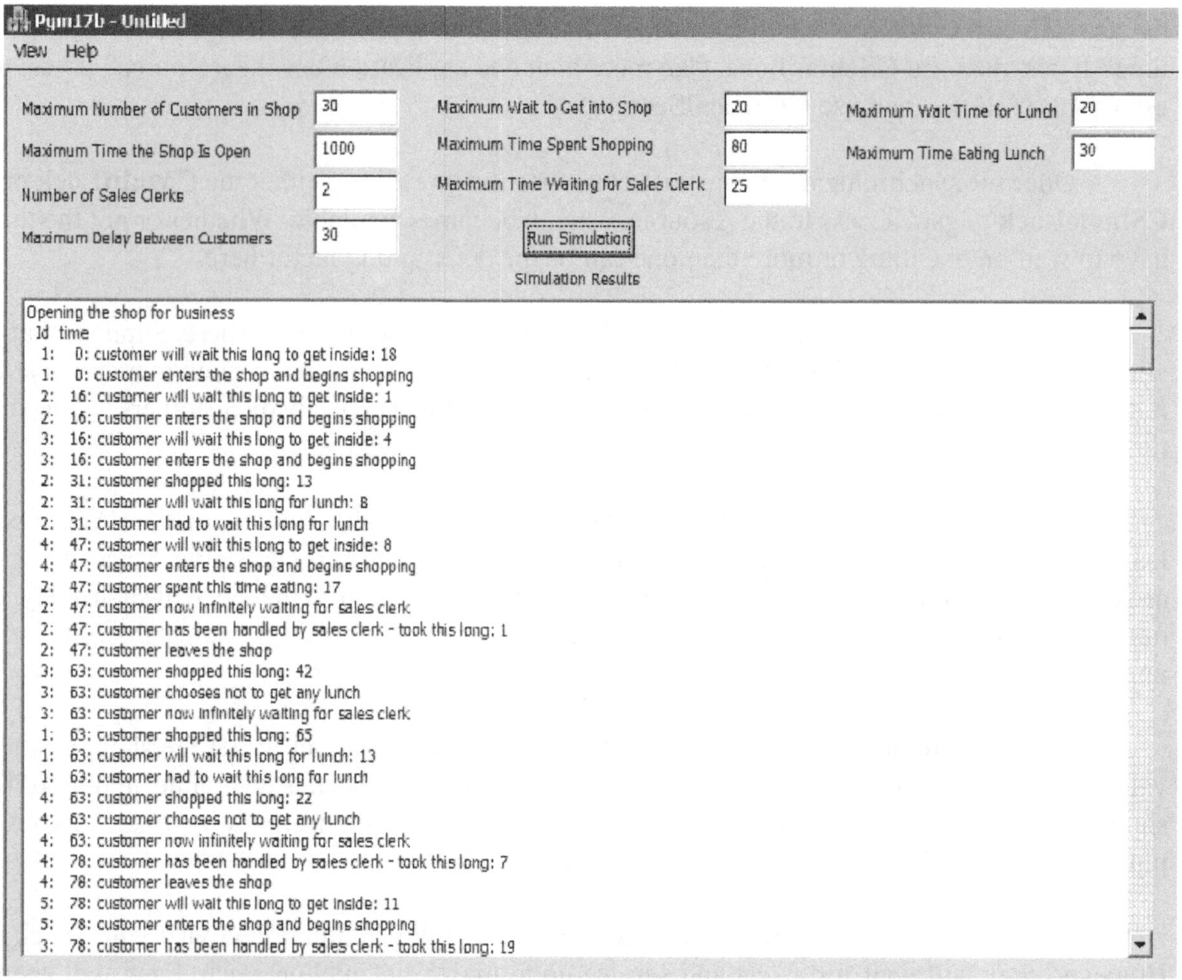

Figure 17.2 Shop Simulation with Many Threads

The document class owns the **CPtrArray** which holds all of the messages created by the form view and the many threads. Thus, this sample shows you how to handle multithreaded access to a restricted resource, since only one thread at a time can be adding a new message to the array.

```
class Pgm17bDoc : public CDocument {
protected:
 Pgm17bDoc();
 DECLARE_DYNCREATE(Pgm17bDoc)

public:
CPtrArray msgs;

 void EmptyMsgs ();
```

What are the needed synchronization instances? A static **CCriticalSection** instance controls everyone's access to the **CPtrArray** array. Another static **CMutex** instance is used to control access to the waitresses at the lunch counter. An ordinary C function is used to actually add the string messages to the array, AddMessage. To uses these items, we must include afxwin.h and afxmt.h.

Listing for Pgm17bForm.h

```
#pragma once
#include "afxwin.h"
#include "afxmt.h"

class Pgm17bForm : public CFormView {
 DECLARE_DYNCREATE(Pgm17bForm)

protected:
 Pgm17bForm();
 virtual ~Pgm17bForm();

public:
 enum { IDD = IDD_FORMVIEW };
#ifdef _DEBUG
 virtual void AssertValid() const;
#ifndef _WIN32_WCE
 virtual void Dump(CDumpContext& dc) const;
#endif
#endif

protected:
 virtual void DoDataExchange(CDataExchange* pDX);

 DECLARE_MESSAGE_MAP()
public:
 CListBox list;
 int maxCustomers;
 int openTime;
 int numberSalesClerks;
 int maxDelayBetweenCustomerCreation;
 int maxWaitToGetIntoStore;
 int maxTimeSpentShopping;
 int maxTimeToWaitForSalesClerk;
 int maxWaitTimeForLunch;
 int maxTimeEatingLunch;

static  CCriticalSection critSection;
static  CMutex           getLunch;

 afx_msg void OnRunSimulation();
};
```

```
void AddMessage (const char* m, CPtrArray* ptrarray,
                 CCriticalSection* ptrc);
```

CSemaphore instances handle the two resources what have a finite number of simultaneous users, namely the number of customers allowed into the shop at one time and the number of sales clerks. These do not have to be static.

What items will each customer thread need? First, it needs the customer maximum times and a unique shopper id number. Since I wish to also display the relative time for each customer event, the thread needs the starting time.

Each thread needs access to the four synchronization instances, highlighted in bold face below, along with a pointer to the array in which to store its messages.

Listing for Pgm17bForm.cpp—First Part

```
#include "stdafx.h"
#include "Pgm17b.h"
#include "Pgm17bForm.h"
#include "Random.h"
#include "Pgm17bDoc.h"

IMPLEMENT_DYNCREATE(Pgm17bForm, CFormView)

CCriticalSection Pgm17bForm::critSection;
CMutex           Pgm17bForm::getLunch;

// structure to pass needed data to the thread
struct CustomerParms {
  int                maxWaitToGetIntoStore;
  int                maxTimeSpentShopping;
  int                maxWaitTimeForLunch;
  int                maxTimeEatingLunch;
  int                maxTimeToWaitForSalesClerk;
  int                shopperId;
  DWORD              startTime;
  CSemaphore*        ptrGetIntoShop;
  CSemaphore*        ptrGetSalesClerk;
  CMutex*            ptrGetLunch;
  CPtrArray*         ptrarray;
  CCriticalSection*  ptrcrit;
};

// thread prototype
UINT CustomerThread (LPVOID pParam);

Pgm17bForm::Pgm17bForm() : CformView(Pgm17bForm::IDD),
```

```
  maxCustomers(30), openTime(1000),
  numberSalesClerks(2), maxDelayBetweenCustomerCreation(30),
  maxWaitToGetIntoStore(20), maxTimeSpentShopping(80),
  maxTimeToWaitForSalesClerk(25), maxWaitTimeForLunch(20),
  maxTimeEatingLunch(30) { }

Pgm17bForm::~Pgm17bForm() { }

void Pgm17bForm::DoDataExchange(CDataExchange* pDX) {
 CFormView::DoDataExchange(pDX);
 DDX_Control(pDX, IDC_LIST_RESULTS, list);
 DDX_Text(pDX, IDC_EDIT_MAXCUSTOMERS, maxCustomers);
 DDV_MinMaxInt (pDX, maxCustomers, 1, 50);
 DDX_Text(pDX, IDC_EDIT_MAXTIMEOPEN, openTime);
 DDV_MinMaxInt (pDX, openTime, 100, 10000);
 DDX_Text(pDX, IDC_EDIT_NUMCLERKS, numberSalesClerks);
 DDV_MinMaxInt (pDX, numberSalesClerks, 1, 5);
 DDX_Text(pDX, IDC_EDIT_MAX_DELAYTIME, maxDelayBetweenCustomerCreation);
 DDV_MinMaxInt (pDX, maxDelayBetweenCustomerCreation, 10, 1000);
 DDX_Text(pDX, IDC_EDIT_MAXWAITGETIN, maxWaitToGetIntoStore);
 DDV_MinMaxInt (pDX, maxWaitToGetIntoStore, 1, 100);
 DDX_Text(pDX, IDC_EDIT_MAXTIMESHOP, maxTimeSpentShopping);
 DDV_MinMaxInt (pDX, maxTimeSpentShopping, 10, 1000);
 DDX_Text(pDX, IDC_EDIT_MAXWAITFORCLERK, maxTimeToWaitForSalesClerk);
 DDV_MinMaxInt (pDX, maxTimeToWaitForSalesClerk, 10, 50);
 DDX_Text(pDX, IDC_EDIT_MAXWAITLUNCH, maxWaitTimeForLunch);
 DDV_MinMaxInt (pDX, maxWaitTimeForLunch, 10, 80);
 DDX_Text(pDX, IDC_EDIT_MAXEAT_TIME, maxTimeEatingLunch);
 DDV_MinMaxInt (pDX, maxTimeEatingLunch, 15, 100);
}

BEGIN_MESSAGE_MAP(Pgm17bForm, CFormView)
 ON_BN_CLICKED(IDC_BUTTON_RUN, &Pgm17bForm::OnRunSimulation)
END_MESSAGE_MAP()
```

The above coding handles the data transfer from the form view's edit controls. Nothing new in the above sequences. Now let's see what happens when the simulation is run. First, UpdateData is called to obtain the latest parameters from the form's controls. The listbox must be cleared of the previous simulation results and the array emptied of the prior messages.

Listing for Pgm17bForm.cpp—Second Part

```
void Pgm17bForm::OnRunSimulation() {
 CWaitCursor w;
 UpdateData (TRUE);    // get new parameters
 list.ResetContent (); // empty listbox

 Pgm17bDoc* pDoc = (Pgm17bDoc*) GetDocument();
 pDoc->EmptyMsgs ();    // empty array of messages
 CPtrArray* ptrarray = &pDoc->msgs;
```

Next, two semaphores are created, one holding the maximum number of customers allowed in the shop at one time and the number of sales clerks.

```
CSemaphore (LONG lInitialCount = 1, LONG lMaxCount = 1,
            LPCTSTR pstrName = NULL,
            LPSECURITY_ATTRIBUTES lpsaAttributes = NULL );
```

The lInitialCount contains the initial usage count for the semaphore and it must be greater than or equal to 0, and less than or equal to lMaxCount, which is the maximum usage count for the semaphore and must be greater than 0, obviously.

The pstrName is the name of the semaphore and must be supplied if you wish to use the semaphore across process boundaries. The lpsaAttributes are the security attributes for the semaphore object.

In this case, we do not want customers entering until we open for business, hence the initial count is 0. The sales clerk initial count is the same as the total number, indicating that they are all set to handle customer purchases.

When the store is ready to handle customers, ReleaseSemaphore is called, specifying how many of the maxCustomers can be allowed into the shop.

Time is tracked by tick counts. Relative time is calculated by subtracting the starting time from the current tick count.

```
// setup two semaphores
CSemaphore getIntoShop (0, maxCustomers);
CSemaphore getSalesClerk (numberSalesClerks, numberSalesClerks);

Random random;

DWORD closeTime;
int numberCustomers = 1;
int customer;

DWORD startTime = GetTickCount(); // store the starting time
closeTime = startTime + openTime; // calculate the closing time

AddMessage ("Opening the shop for business", ptrarray,
            &critSection);
AddMessage ("  Id  time", ptrarray, &critSection);

// clear semaphore so shoppers can enter the shop
ReleaseSemaphore (getIntoShop, maxCustomers, NULL);
```

The main processing loop launches new customer threads at random intervals until closing time occurs. However, some of these customers will have to wait in line to get into the shop, once the maximum capacity is reached.

Construction begins by allocating a new CustomerParms structure and filling it up with the data needed by each thread. Then, AfxBeginThread is called and the thread's priority is lowered.

```
// add new customers until closing time
while (GetTickCount() < closeTime) {
 // create the new thread's parameter instance
 CustomerParms* ptrparms = new CustomerParms;
 ptrparms->maxWaitToGetIntoStore = maxWaitToGetIntoStore;
 ptrparms->maxTimeSpentShopping = maxTimeSpentShopping;
 ptrparms->maxWaitTimeForLunch = maxWaitTimeForLunch;
 ptrparms->maxTimeEatingLunch = maxTimeEatingLunch;
 ptrparms->maxTimeToWaitForSalesClerk=maxTimeToWaitForSalesClerk;
 ptrparms->ptrGetIntoShop = &getIntoShop;
 ptrparms->ptrGetSalesClerk= &getSalesClerk;
 ptrparms->ptrGetLunch = &getLunch;
 ptrparms->ptrarray = ptrarray;
 ptrparms->ptrcrit = &critSection;
 ptrparms->shopperId = numberCustomers++;
 ptrparms->startTime = startTime;

 // create the new customer thread
 CWinThread* ptrthread = AfxBeginThread (CustomerThread,
                                         ptrparms);

 ptrthread->SetThreadPriority (THREAD_PRIORITY_LOWEST);

 // wait until another customer comes to the shop
 Sleep (random.GetRandom (maxDelayBetweenCustomerCreation));
}

// loop done, so it is time to close the shop
char msg[100];
wsprintf (msg,
"        %4lu: Wait for remaining shoppers to finish and leave",
        GetTickCount() - startTime);
AddMessage (msg, ptrarray, &critSection);
```

When closing time is reached, we must wait on all currently running threads to finish up. They finish up by releasing their lock count on the **CSemaphore** getIntoShop.

```
// wait for each running thread to terminate,
// based on semaphore getIntoShop
for (customer=1; customer <= maxCustomers; customer++) {
 WaitForSingleObject (getIntoShop, INFINITE);
 char m[100];
 wsprintf (m,
```

```
      "Ending countdown of customers that could still be in the store: %04d",
      customer);
  AddMessage (m, ptrarray, &critSection);
}
wsprintf (msg, "           %4lu: Shop has closed for the day",
          GetTickCount() - startTime);
AddMessage (msg, ptrarray, &critSection);
```

Finally, add all of the messages to the listbox.
```
for (long i=0; i<ptrarray->GetSize(); i++) {
  CString* ptrs = (CString*) ptrarray->GetAt (i);
  list.AddString (*ptrs);
  }
}
```

AddMessage shows how to control access to a restricted resource. Obviously, we cannot have many threads simultaneously attempting to add another string to the array. Only one thread at a time can get access to the array. In the implementation, you have two choices. You can use the MFC wrapper class **CSingleLock** or use the straight lower level function calls. In this case, the lower level calls are simpler.
```
void    AddMessage    (const    char*    m,    CPtrArray*    ptrarray,
CCriticalSection* ptrc) {
  CString* ptrs = new CString;
  *ptrs = m;
  // two choices to use the critical section
  // one is to lock and unlock directly
  // ptrc->Lock ();
  // ptrarray->Add (ptrs);
  // ptrc->Unlock ();
  // the other is to use CSingleLock
  CSingleLock singleLock (ptrc);
  singleLock.Lock(INFINITE);// attempt to lock the shared resource
  if (singleLock.IsLocked()) { // if the resource has been locked
    ptrarray->Add (ptrs);// use it - here add a string to the array
    singleLock.Unlock(); // and unlock it
  }
}
```

Okay, now comes the actual CustomerThread. I chose to also illustrate letting each thread have its own random number generator. Otherwise, one would need to add another resource to the critical section list. However, each must be given a unique seed or you will get nearly the same results for all shoppers, since the time difference between their launchings is so tiny.
```
UINT CustomerThread (LPVOID parm) {
  CustomerParms* ptrp = (CustomerParms*) parm;
  CPtrArray* ptrarray = ptrp->ptrarray;
  // seed the random number generator differently than other
```